Intimate Indigeneities

INTIMATE INDIGENEITIES

Race, Sex,
and History
in the
Small Spaces of
Andean Life

Andrew Canessa

DUKE UNIVERSITY PRESS
Durham & London 2012

© 2012 Duke University Press
All rights reserved

Printed in the United States of America on acid-free paper ∞
Designed by Jennifer Hill
Typeset in Arno Pro by Newgen

Library of Congress Cataloging-in-Publication Data
appear on the last printed page of this book.

To Teodosio Condori and Peter Dorward
Friends and yatiris both

CONTENTS

NARRATING NATIVE HISTORIES aims to foster a rethinking of the ethical, methodological, and conceptual frameworks within which we locate our work on Native histories and cultures. We seek to create a space for effective and ongoing conversations between North and South, Natives and non-Natives, and academics and activists throughout the Americas and the Pacific region. We are committed to complicating and transgressing the disciplinary and epistemological boundaries of established academic discourses on Native peoples.

This series encourages symmetrical, horizontal, collaborative, and autoethnographies; work that recognizes Native intellectuals, cultural interpreters, and alternative knowledge producers within broader academic and intellectual worlds; projects that decolonize the relationship between orality and textuality; narratives that productively work the tensions between the norms of Native cultures and the requirements for evidence in academic circles; and analyses that contribute to an understanding of Native peoples' relationships with nation-states, including histories of expropriation and exclusion as well as projects for autonomy and sovereignty.

How do native people in the Andes identify themselves? Do they see themselves as "indigenous" (that is, as of a distinct ethnicity) or as "indians" (as a subordinated and racialized group)? Do they identify primarily with a linguistic or ethnic group (as in "Aymara") or as members of a localized community? Most recent ethnographies of native identity have focused on politicized communities and indigenous organizations in order to answer this question. In *Intimate Indigeneities,* in contrast, Andrew Canessa demonstrates the value of returning to an ethnography of a rural community of Aymara speakers in Bolivia to produce an eloquent and textured account of how people see themselves. Canessa achieves this through an examination of historical memory, demonstrating how national events are remembered locally, and through close attention to how race is diffracted through gender differences and in relationships of rural dwellers with surrounding mestizo towns, as well as in the dynamics of schooling, resulting in a vivid depiction of a community whose members do not consider themselves to be "indigenous" or "indians," although those in the dominant society might place them in these categories.

Laura: what makes an anthropologist's ethnograph different from oral historians work? An attempt to stay outside of influence, more transparent about positionality, probably more thorough in secondary sources to triangulate info about what speakers are saying. Do we feel like Canessa more transparent ...

ACKNOWLEDGMENTS

This book is based on over two decades of work in Bolivia, and many people have helped me in myriad ways. I would first like to thank my friends in Wila Kjarka who received me, helped me, and supported me year after year since I first arrived in 1989. Remegio Patty and Agustina Alanoca lodged me and welcomed me into their family during my first stay in Wila Kjarka, a stay that lasted almost three years. On subsequent visits I became indebted to the family of Pastor Mendoza and Dominga Mamani as well as that of Maruja Alwiri and Eustaquio Mamani, who have become dear friends and taught me so much about life in Wila Kjarka. There is a long list of other people in Wila Kjarka to whom I owe a debt of gratitude, and I could not possibly list them all here, but among those are Teodosio Condori, friend and shaman with whom I have spent hours talking about his life and calling, and for whom I have a special affection and to whom this book is dedicated; Pastor Mendoza, who deserves a second mention in recognition of our close friendship and many hours of conversation as we herded together; Francisca Condori, who, like many Wila Kjarkeños, has led a difficult and tragic life, but has maintained a smile and sense of humor nevertheless; Pedro Choque, Wila

Kjarka's other yatiri, and his son Germán, a kind and intelligent man, to whom I became close when I first arrived in Wila Kjarka and who died in a flash flood in 1992; Beatriz Mendoza, Pastor's daughter, whom I have known since early childhood and is possessed with a fierce intelligence and equally fierce ambition, which most recently has taken her to São Paolo where she currently lives; Regina Oncollo, whose life seems destined to be filled with tragedy and despair but kindly shared her stories with me; and to Pastora Alegre, who recounted her life's ambitions and tribulations around her cooking fire. Others who deserve mention are Flora Alwiri, Arminda Chino, Celestino Chino, Edmundo Chino, Ignacio Chino, Toribio Chino, Victoria Chino, Zenobio Chino, Estanislao Choque, María Condori, Marcelo Kopa, Asunta Kuraka, Paulino Laruta, Adalid Mamani, Dominga Mamani, Juana Mamani, Justino Mamani, Erica Mendoza, Walter Mendoza, Marcelino Misme, Lucy Patty, Yola Patty, Manuel Qarani, Pedro Quispe, Raquel Quispe, José Sea, Eugenia Sea, and Ofelia Sea.

In Sorata, Johnny Resnikowsky and Roxana Jordán received me on many occasions in the wonderful house they had just built and allowed me to listen to their fabulous record collection, which stopped, as far as I could gather, in 1973. In my first years they provided me with a much-needed resting place where the music of The Band and the Doobie Brothers soothed my soul. Salomé and Natalio Arana have remained friends since the first day I arrived in Sorata, and to Salomé I owe a particular debt because it was she who first pointed the way to Wila Kjarka for me. It was, however, Diane Bellomy, who first suggested I visit Wila Kjarka on my way to Ambaná, and for this I am eternally grateful.

In Villa Esquivel, Fidel and Isabel Figueredo received me with the greatest warmth on several occasions, and I am also grateful to Juan Román and Pastor Mamani.

In La Paz, Wolfgang Schüler has for many years, along with his partner Julia Durango, offered me so much more than a place to stay. It was Wolfgang who first suggested I go to Bolivia as we were students of anthropology together in London. One of the quirkiest aspects of my time in Bolivia, and the result of a chance encounter on the train from Iquique, led me to the comfortable red couch of a house of Germans in Miraflores as my pied-à-terre in La Paz. Gudrun Birk and Eva Dietz and the other residents of the house in Calle Jamaica, Dorle Gutowski and Dagmar Adolph, taught me German and so much more and have become lifelong friends.

Much of the material in this book has benefited from the comments and criticisms that have been offered on the various occasions I have presented my work. I cannot thank all those people here, but I would like to mention those who have specifically commented, inspired, provoked, debated the content of the book over its long gestation and in its various forms, or otherwise helped in preparing the manuscript: I thank Denise Arnold, Bea Benito, Chetan Bhatt, Rebecca Bria, Pamela Calla, Olivia Harris, Aida Hernández, Jean Jackson, Sian Lazar, Tony Lucero, Lucinda Platt, Manuela Picq, Esther Lopez, Suzanne van Montfoort, Mike Roper, Sydney Silverstein, Alison Spedding, Kimberly Theidon, Peter Wade, Melanie Wright, and Elayne Zorn. Special thanks goes to Michelle Bigenho and Peter Dorward, who kindly read the complete manuscript and to whom I am greatly indebted for their many comments and suggestions. I also give thanks to the three anonymous reviewers from Duke University Press, whose comments greatly helped in sharpening the arguments presented in this book. I owe gratitude, too, to the staff at Duke University Press, to my editor Valerie Millholland and to Gisela Fosado for her patience above all. There were many people who were involved in the production of this book, but I want to especially mention Concepción McCracken, who was extraordinarily thorough in copyediting the final manuscript, going far beyond what I would expect from a copyeditor.

I would like to thank my children, Hannelore, Tarik, and Marisa, who grew up knowing their father would spend four weeks a year in Bolivia (although sometimes they accompanied me) but, these trips aside, I cannot claim to have spent weekends or evenings writing this book when I could have been with them. And I wouldn't have had it any other way. I do, however, thank them for the daily joy they give me and have done since the day each was born.

An earlier version of chapter 3 was previously published as "Forgetting the Revolution and Remembering the War: Memory and Violence in Highland Bolivia," in *History Workshop Journal* 67 (2009). Portions of chapter 5 appeared in "Fear and Loathing on the Kharisiri Trail: Alterity and Identity in the Andes," *Journal of the Royal Anthropological Institute* 6(4) (2000): 705–20. Some of the material for chapter 6 appeared in "Reproducing Racism: Schooling and Race in Highland Bolivia," in *Race Ethnicity and Education* 7(2) (2004): 185–204. An earlier version of chapter 8 appeared as "Sex and the Citizen: Barbies and Beauty Queens in the Age of Evo Morales," *Journal of Latin American Cultural Studies* 17(1) (2008): 41–64. Unless otherwise noted, all photographs are by the author. I am indebted to Vitaliano Huanca for transcribing many hours of interviews

and providing an initial translation into Spanish. Many of these translations were considerably worked subsequently and the responsibility for
the final translations from Aymara to English remains mine. All other
translations remain mine unless otherwise noted.

One evening in August 2011, an unusually cold August in Bolivia, I sat in the kitchen of my friend Maruja, as I have done so often over the past twenty years. Her mother-in-law, Francisca, with whom I have also had many long conversations, sat in the corner, and I opposite. Maruja cooked over a wood fire while engaging Francisca in rapid conversation, touching on scandal, gossip, and the hardness of life. We all punctuated Francisca's discourse with the lament, *tataaay*! But that was merely the appropriate response to the rise and fall of her speech; no one was really aggrieved. On this occasion her new daughter-in-law was there with Maruja's grandson. Everyone spoke in Aymara, an indigenous language of the Andes, and everyone—the anthropologist notwithstanding—was dressed in traditional indian fashion: large *pollera* skirts and long black braids. That is until Maruja's daughter, Yaquita, walked in wearing trousers, sporting a modern hairstyle. At one point Maruja's cell phone rang, and we took turns speaking to her husband, Eustaquio, who was away working in the lower valleys for several weeks. The heat of the fire and the presence of a happy baby warmed the atmosphere of what any casual observer would readily identify as an indigenous family in an indigenous village.

But what does it *mean* to be indigenous? And what does it mean to be indigenous in Bolivia, which has discriminated against indians in the past but recently elected an indigenous president? Above all, this book focuses on the question of what it means to be indigenous to indigenous people themselves, not only when they are running for office or marching in protest but especially when they are in the small spaces of their lives, when they are lamenting their lot, cooing with their babies, cooking in their kitchens, or talking to their husbands who are far away. These questions cannot be answered by asking someone "what does it mean to you to be indigenous?" Such a question is almost always a waste of time, not the least because there is no word for indigenous in Aymara. However, other insights and other answers may be gleaned by spending time with people as they work, cook, and talk and allow you to enter the warm, dark, intimate spaces of their kitchens and their lives. It is here that one can learn about how abstract concepts such as race, sex, and history are lived in reality and what it means to be indigenous. It is important, too, to recognize and understand the broader context of indigenous identity since the people of the village of Wila Kjarka, where Maruja's kitchen is situated, are most certainly not isolated from the political and economic currents of the nation.

In December 2005 Evo Morales became the first indigenous president to be elected in Bolivia—and indeed in Latin America in modern times—and he did so, moreover, with an unprecedented clear majority of the votes: a feat he repeated with an even greater majority in December 2009. It appeared to many observers then, as it does now, that for the first time since the Inkas' defeat, indigenous people are once again in power in the Andes. There can be no doubt that indigenous people and indigenous issues have become increasingly prominent in recent decades, as has been widely commented (e.g., Albó 1991; Wearne 1996). From Mexico to Chile indigenous people have been formally recognized in the constitutions of their countries (e.g., Colombia), have formed national governments (e.g., Ecuador), and have generally become much more visible in national politics.

The move toward greater recognition of indigenous people comes not only from activists themselves but from international agencies. Perhaps the most significant event has been the recognition of indigenous people by the International Labour Organization, whose Resolution 169 has for "global currency"

the first time given them a status in international law. The World Bank, too, in the 1990s "discovered" indigenous people and developed a series of projects aimed at "ethnodevelopment" targeted toward indigenous people. Countless NGOs, in turn, followed the World Bank by focusing their efforts on indigenous people's economic and political development. And in 2008 the United Nations published a Declaration on the Rights of Indigenous Peoples.

One of the key features of the efflorescence of indigenous sensibility is its global nature. When the Merana of Indonesia (Tsing 1993) or the San of Botswana (Lee 2001) argue for their rights to land or resources on the basis of their indigeneity, they do so because being indigenous has a global currency that NGOs and governments recognize (see also de la Cadena and Starn 2007).

In fact these processes exemplify well what Margaret Keck and Kathryn Sikking (1998) describe as the boomerang effect in relation to human rights discourses. In this case, however, groups of people all over the world learn the language of global indigeneity (often from local NGOs) and use it to lobby external agencies that, in turn, put pressure or exercise influence on national governments. In many countries, indigenous people are greatly marginalized politically; indeed, political marginality may be a key feature of indigeneity. One of the few ways people can influence political processes is through international agencies. In this way, concepts of indigeneity circulate and recirculate back to local groups that, in turn, may tailor their political language or even develop indigenous symbols and practices to better achieve their aims.

This may sound instrumental, but culture has never existed independent of political frameworks. In a recent work, Tony Lucero (2008) demonstrates how indigenous movements in Bolivia and Ecuador have had different trajectories because they operate in different political terrains. For those of us who are uneasy with the facile assumption that indigenous movements can be understood simply as political representations of indigenous people, Lucero's work provides an important antidote. He most certainly does not take an indigenous identity as somehow given, of having suffered a period of latency only to be awakened by indigenous politics, as if "'real' ethnic identities seemed simply to be awaiting the right conditions in order to emerge, almost geologically, through the cracks of shifting political formations" (2008: 15). In his careful examination of a wide range of groups he shows how history, region, class, and religion are critical elements in understanding how concerns come to be articulated

this lends itself to a new type of "intellectual history."

in terms of specifically indigenous identities. In some cases one might even say the indigenous movement has formed indigenous identity. This is not to say that indigenous people are cynically manipulated or shrewdly opportunistic but, rather, that a series of dialogues are taking place among a wide range of people, out of which an indigenous identity and movement can emerge. Lucero offers his readers a vision of pragmatic actors who are nevertheless embedded in historical social relations and who have a long history of being discriminated for their cultural practices. For Lucero, "indigenous movements in Ecuador and Bolivia are all genuine expressions of historical and political realities, yet they have been imagined and articulated in different ways" (2008: 111).

Changing political landscapes open up spaces for particular types of cultural expressions. In recent years I have been conducting fieldwork in the village of Khonkho on the Bolivian *altiplano* where people have used the excavation of a pre-Inka settlement to re-create traditions and revitalize political structures in order to push for greater control over their lives. All of this, of course, occurs in the context of Morales's victory and the growing legitimacy of indigenous symbols (Canessa 2007). Aside from the case of Tiwanaku, the nation's principal archaeological site, these activities, now widespread, would have been unimaginable only a few years ago, as would indeed have been Morales's victory as an indigenous president. The process by which indigeneity came to be so prominent in contemporary Bolivia is beyond the scope of this book (although, see Hylton and Thomson 2007; Lucero 2008), but it is important to remember that indigeneity is not an identity that is simply given; it did not lay dormant and suddenly emerge in the 1990s as a cultural and political force. Much of this has to do with the failure of class politics in the 1970s and 1980s and neoliberal reforms (Kohl and Farthing 2006) as well as the cultural turn globally.

Indigeneity is therefore highly contingent; indigenous identities are, moreover, thoroughly imbricated with gendered, racial, and linguistic identities and informed by a historical consciousness. In this book I explore these multiple identities of a community in the Bolivian highlands, through their own lived experiences and their own voices rather than the lens of globalized concepts and discourses. This perspective contrasts with those of others in Bolivia and elsewhere who read indigenous identity through its manifestations in public and political mobilizations. These are certainly important perspectives, but they deny a voice to those people who are unable or unwilling to articulate their identities in the public domain, whose identities and allegiances, moreover, are often taken for granted by indigenous politicians and scholars of indigenous movements alike. Such a perspective raises questions not only about indigenous politics but also about the very nature of indigenous identity.

In the community of Wila Kjarka, the majority of women and many men are monolingual Aymara speakers whose economic and ritual practices show considerable continuity with the past. Whereas there is some discussion about the indigenous identity of people who live in towns and cities and lead modern lives, most observers would readily and unambiguously describe the residents of Wila Kjarka as indigenous. The people of Wila Kjarka, however, do not. In fact, they positively reject the term. When speaking Aymara they describe themselves as people from Wila Kjarka (Wila Kjarkiri) or *jaqi*, a word that quite simply means *people*. In calling themselves *people* they share a feature of self-designation with many—perhaps the majority of—indigenous people in the Americas. But the jaqi are not just *people*; a better translation is perhaps *proper people* (cf. Pitarch 2010: 204). The jaqi are not the same as those who live in towns and cities and live very different lives from them; one can see that the people Wila Kjarkeños describe as jaqi are, broadly speaking, the same people whom other Bolivians or anthropologists might describe as indigenous or indian. These words are not, however, synonymous, and one of the central tasks of this book is to explore what *jaqi* means to the people of Wila Kjarka and how the term differs from *indigenous* or *indian*.

It is now so established as to be commonplace to note that the distinction between indians and nonindians is fluid, historically contingent, and arbitrary (see Larson and Harris 1995). Debates continue as to whether this distinction is best seen in class terms (e.g., Friedlander 1975) or more fundamentally in terms of cultural practices and beliefs (e.g., Allen 1988; Skar 1982), or indeed both simultaneously (Gose 1994 and van den Berghe and Primov 1997).[1] Between these positions lie those of many other scholars who note the shifting semantic field of the category indian in geographical and historical contexts (e.g., Abercrombie 1991 and Harris 1995, among others). What I offer here is an analysis of identity through the lives of people whose race, gender, ethnicity, and sexuality continue coming to the fore and then retreating; no single identity is constantly salient, and moreover each informs the other. Yet all are circumscribed by a particular historical, political, and economic position that can be glossed as *indigenous*. To take a particular example, the relationship of a married couple in Wila Kjarka exists in a context where being indian inflects the most intimate of spaces (I explore this example more fully in chapter 7). Terminology, as a consequence, is slippery and problematic.

INDIANS, INDIGENOUS, AYMARAS

The term *indian* is obviously one of European origin, and in its American usage denoted a simple power relationship between Europeans and a large number of diverse people whom they had the power to collectively assemble under a single term: Before 1492, there were no indians in the Americas. *Indianness* was not only created by the colonial state and society but perpetuated and re-created by its republican successors (Abercrombie 1992). This is not to say, however, that indians share completely these ideas of what it is to be an indian. They have little choice about the inequalities of power and the structures of underinvestment, urban bias, and exploitation that make them indians, but this does not mean that they understand this difference in the same way as the participants in hegemonic discourse would have it. On the one hand, the boundary between indians and nonindians is created through economic, political, and historical structures that construct indians as poor, backward, and culturally retarded; on the other hand, it is created through ritual practice, which constructs nonindians as amoral, alienated, and culturally bereft. The word Wila Kjarkeños use to designate whites is *q'ara*, which in other circumstances means "bare" or "peeled" (Gose 1994b: 21; Isbell 1978: 67); in other words, q'ara are stripped of their humanity.

 Over the past centuries, although the status of the indian and the way that identity has been understood have changed, the term has always denoted a difference in status and power and, moreover, nonindians have been the ones to decide who is and is not an indian. In this book, indian is used principally when talking from an etic—that is, external—perspective. One of the central issues of indian identity is that precisely because it denotes a historically marginalized and oppressed people, few actually want to be indian, even if they recognize such a status. It is—a few radical politicians notwithstanding—largely a designation offered by others and is rarely embraced by people not actively involved in indigenous politics.

To call someone an *indio* to their face in Bolivia today—and indeed, pretty much anywhere else in Latin America—is to insult them. Behind that term are centuries of images, discourses, and unequal power relations that are profoundly racist—a complex racism to be sure, one that changes over time and is not usually reducible to the simple concepts of blood and genetic inheritance with which northern readers are most familiar. A significant proportion of this book is given to describing this racism in its many forms to explore the ways people live with, resist, absorb, and even reproduce it.

The people of Wila Kjarka do not live in a binary world with white racists on one side and indian victims on the other, although at times it may appear to be so. One of the more invidious aspects of these centuries of racism is that it has become so pervasive that people have long stopped recognizing it is there—one of the consequences of five hundred years of colonialism. I am not simply suggesting that because of the long history of racial mixing in Latin America and the existence of multiple categories of racial differentiation, a stable white/indian racial binary does not exist. Nor am I arguing that somehow Bolivia is less racist than countries where the boundaries seem clear and ambiguous. Rather, the argument I am putting forward here is that precisely because there is no clear social binary, the categories white and indian are always relative: One can suffer racism for coming from a small town and consequently being tainted by the indianness of surrounding peasants and still visit a profound racism upon the people one lives with, even family members. One is more or less white; more or less indian.

This raises the question of why I use the word *indian* so regularly in the book over the more politically correct *indigenous*. *Indigenous* appears as a much more neutral descriptor and erases the power relations that are inescapable when talking about indians (cf. Weismantel 2001: xxiii). *Indigenous* can roll off the tongue without too much reflection, as the speaker will be sure that no one is likely to be offended. It is for this very reason that I use the word *indian*: it jars; it does—or should—make one think; and more than any other term, it refers to a long history of colonial oppression. I also write the word with a lower case "i." In the American context, *indian* is an ethnic, not national term and therefore I follow the usage of writing this word in lower case in the same way as other such categories (e.g., mestizo, black, mulatto) (see Wade 1997: 121).

Indígena, in contrast, has come to have a very inclusive reach. There are certainly some positive aspects to this term, not the least of which is the greater respect accorded indigenous people *qua* indigenous people, but it can obscure the long history of oppression of one people by another. An example of this historical and ecumenical indigeneity was offered to me by Gualberto Choque, an Aymara leader, in an interview in 2005: "And so the white people, the black people, and the Aymara people should be *modern ecumenical indigenism*

united. Once we are united we will come to an agreement. And we will call this 'indigenous.'"[2] Previously, during a public presentation, he declared, "We are all indigenous now," which echoes the twentieth-century voices of many who declared new *mestizo* nations across the Americas. This inclusive *mestizaje*, though lauding an indigenous past, was furiously assimilationist when it came to an indigenous present; indians were excluded from this new national imaginary until they became deracinated and adopted mestizo ways. The irony is that this modern ecumenical indigenism[3] will have the same effect of obscuring the historical injustices visited upon particular marginalized peoples. If we are all indigenous, then it becomes difficult to view these historical injustices clearly (Canessa 2006b).

Felipe Quispe

The radical Aymara leader Felipe Quispe was also in attendance at Gualberto Choque's presentation, and some days later I asked him about what Choque had said, if it was true that in Bolivia "we are all indigenous." He responded:

No, not in such clear terms, no. We are not all indios . . . some people are rich, others live in poverty, that is how we are; but it is well known that those of us who have this skin color work everywhere. We work in the mines, we work in the altiplano, we work on the hot earth in the valleys, scratching [a living] from the earth; it is we, we who feed those who live in the cities; it is we who sweep the streets. It is we who serve the *q'aras* [whites], bringing up their children; it is we who fetch their cooking water for them, wash their dirty clothes, take care of their children; we who are the soldiers in the barracks; our people, it is we who have stars [on our chests] . . . They are ministers and presidents; they are ambassadors. For us who work down here there is nothing: they do not allow us to take charge; they always keep us down, truly, they walk all over us. That is why I want to tell you that no, we are not all indians; they live in great comfort.[4]

Quispe did not immediately use the term I used in the question, *indígena*, and, indeed, the one Choque used, but immediately grasped the problem that such ecumenical indigenism implies; he corrected me and began using the term *indians*. Whereas being indigenous is a positive identification that can be widely embraced, Quispe is clearly aware that being an indian is to be one of the downtrodden: He explains the term indian in terms of race (mentioning skin color) as well as class (the occupations indians typically hold); thus, he offers a succinct analysis of indian oppression wherein racial identification serves to maintain a

Fausto Reinaga
Partido Indio de Bolivia

disadvantageous class position. In the rest of the interview he makes the long historical process of this oppression absolutely clear. So even though he named his party el Movimiento Indígena Pachakuti, he has a much longer historical engagement with the struggle of indians, rather than indigenous people of contemporary discourse, as he outlines in the book he wrote in prison, *Tupak Katari vive y vuelve—carajo* (Tupak Katari Lives and Will Return. Damn It!).[5]

Quispe is a passionate, even angry, politician, and although his political career has been eclipsed by Evo Morales, in the 1990s and 2000s he was the most inspiring and successful indigenous leader. He cites as his major inspiration the indigenous intellectual Fausto Reinaga, who for more than two decades was virtually the sole torch bearer for indian rights and founded el Partido Indio de Bolivia (the Bolivian Indian Party). For him, indio was an oppressive term that denoted the colonial relationship alluded to above. He quite simply loathed the term indígena (Canessa 2010; Reinaga 1969) and argued forcefully that it mischievously obscured the oppressive conditions under which indians have lived for centuries. He titled his major work *La Revolución India* (The Indian Revolution) and argued that "as indians they oppressed us and as indians we will liberate ourselves" (Reinaga 1969).

Felipe Quispe is the most obvious inheritor of Reinaga's mantle, although Evo Morales, too, cites him as his greatest political inspiration. I had seen Quispe speak publically on a number of occasions and had met him before, but when we spoke alone at dawn on a June morning in 2005, I was surprised to find how much I liked this firebrand of a politician whom so many of his detractors accuse of arrogance and racism. He seemed not to have slept that night and was wearing a thick jacket, which I guessed served as a bed for any rest he had taken. He had forgotten our appointment but nevertheless spoke to me for almost an hour. He was certainly tired that morning, but what came across clearly to me was that he was weary of the racism that he and his people have been facing since the arrival of the Spanish, leaving me with little doubt that his experience of being treated like an indio fuels his passion for politics.

The people of Wila Kjarka do not often use the term indio, but when they do they refer precisely to their status as members of the poor and oppressed classes. They don't want to be indios, but they are perfectly aware that they are; so when using the word indian, I do not intend to insult people but, rather, recognize their historical subaltern status, akin to Quispe's usage of the term in the interview above. It is especially important, in the context of the efflorescence of self-ascribed indigenous identity leading up to Evo Morales's election, to remember and recognize that whereas there are many urban people and intellectuals who embrace their newly found indigenous identity, there are still many people who are regarded as indios—even by those who proclaim an indigenous identity. This may seem paradoxical, or even perverse, but it is simply that being indigenous can mean little more than taking up a position against globalization, or embracing a particular kind of progressive politics, or even easily asserting a connection with national authenticity. One can do this from relatively comfortable circumstances, and I know several white middle-class leftist intellectuals who describe themselves as indigenous. I am not arguing that this is always so but, rather, that one can be comfortably indigenous; one can never be comfortably indian. Who would want to be an indio?

This raises and intriguing problem rarely considered: If one recognizes the right to maintain one's indian culture, is the converse also true? Does one have the right *not* to be an indian? And what does it mean to recognize this right? Some of these themes are explored in chapter 6.

METHODS AND METHODOLOGIES

Orin Starn (1991) in the 1990s offered an excoriating critique of ethnographies, especially Peruvian ones, which focused on communities while excluding broader political concerns, as if these did not matter. In his words, these anthropologists blinded themselves to the growing unrest and "missed the revolution" that was about to be unleashed in the form of the Maoist uprising known as *Sendero Luminoso* (Shining Path); and he was also highly critical of anthropologists' contributions to *Andeanism*— the view of Andean cultures through a romanticizing, if not essentializing, occidental lens. Although one might argue that Starn somewhat overstated his case, his criticisms have been important because they profoundly disrupted the assumptions many scholars had been making about the cultural and political isolation of indigenous communities.

An outstanding example of a response to Starn's criticisms is Michelle Bigenho's work, in particular her book *Sounding Indigenous* (2002). Bigenho explores music production in two indigenous communities, in the capital city of La Paz, in France, and, in later work, in Japan (2007, 2012). She explores the way indigenous authenticity is a variable currency: People, for example, demand a certain iconic indigenous Bolivianness in France, but one that is frustratingly ignorant of the variation in *has indigeniety ever been "from below"? → or "from within?"*

indigenous cultures within Bolivia, thus demonstrating how indigeneity as a cultural marker is often imposed from the outside as I explore further in chapter 6. Bigenho's (2002) multisited ethnography allows her to explore the way indigeneity in general and indigenous music specifically can mean different things in different contexts. The people of the community of Yura appear much more confident in their indigenous identity despite being much more integrated into the national economy and bureaucratic structures, whereas the people of the much less accessible community of Toropalca are nostalgic for their lost traditions and are concerned about becoming increasingly Spanish-speaking. Yureños are unconcerned about issues of cultural authenticity, even as they practice what outside observers may see as a much more authentic culture; Toropalqueños are ambivalent about their place in the world and have a sense of loss and declining authenticity. Such studies are invaluable in showing the variety of indigenous experiences and how indigeneity is often a power trope as marginal communities engage with state bureaucracies, local elites, and global culture.

Even as the chapters that follow offer, quite unapologetically, a study of a village community, this book is by no means blind to the broader contexts in which this community exists. This is not to say, however, that the book presents an image of a community isolated from the outside world, much less does it purport to offer an exposition of Andean culture. Quite the opposite: This book concerns itself mainly with how the members of an apparently isolated community are situated within wider regional, national, and international networks of power and cultural meanings. Rather than romanticizing the experiences of men and women in Wila Kjarka, I show their lives to be complex, conflictive, messy, and contradictory, rather like people's lives anywhere else in the world. I do not offer a view of village life under a microscope; I offer, rather, a view through a telescope of what the world looks like from the perspectives of people in a small village and how the world affects their lives.

One could quite easily paint a picture of the community of Wila Kjarka—high in the mountains, without a road—as an example of an isolated people leading a traditional life. They are, of course, not isolated. In fact, they have never been isolated. They have long enjoyed communication with the highlands and the lowlands and been thoroughly involved in empires European and Andean. The lack of roads, moreover, only represented isolation in the Andes in the second half of the twentieth century, when transportation in Bolivia shifted from mules to motorized

Even with the new roads, most people still travel by foot along these paths, many of them dating to pre-Columbian times.

transport. If anything, road building made Wila Kjarka more isolated, as it excluded them from the principal transportation network in a way that had not previously presented itself. Their late-twentieth-century isolation was only ever relative, however, and throughout this period Wila Kjarke-ños traveled, went to school, and listened to the radio.

The people of Wila Kjarka are not passive recipients of influences from beyond their community. In fact, not only do they contest some of these, they also generate their own meanings and understandings. Shane Greene has called this process one in which indigeneity is "customized" (2009). Often these understandings of, for example, race, religion, and gender, seem to connect seamlessly with those prevalent in the broader culture, but on closer inspection they are sometimes quite different. To put it simply: Wila Kjarkeños may identify themselves and others as different from dominant members of the nation and, in turn, the dominant members

of the nation may see the people of Wila Kjarka and others like them as distinct, but how each understands this distinction may be radically different. The constant and unresolved dialectic between metropolitan and rural, hispanic and indigenous, past and present, and so on, is the core substance of the book. So even if this work is almost entirely based on ethnography in a single site, its subject is infinitely broader.

GETTING THERE

James Clifford has criticized anthropological accounts for beginning with a "getting there" story in which the anthropologist climbs the mountain, paddles up the river, or arrives by boat to his isolated community and then disappears from the pages of the book. Readers who are particularly averse to "getting there" stories may wish to skip the next few pages but may also wish to consider the one or two methodological implications of conducting research in a particular village and the basis for the relationships I formed there. Moreover, although I am not absent from the subsequent pages, my presence is certainly light. Where my relationship with my interlocutor is relevant, I give that context but do not assume the reader to be interested in me much beyond that; this is, after all, an anthropological monograph not an autobiography.

In December 1989, after having spent a couple of months in La Paz sorting out paperwork and trying to learn Aymara, I was looking for a field site for my doctoral research project. I was utterly unprepared for this, and no one had told me how to go about it. I had previously spent two weeks getting lost in the province of Licoma, searching for a good location to undertake my studies. I had decided to find a community that was neither on the *altiplano*, the highland plain, nor in the deep valleys, the *yungas*. I left Licoma with a hand-drawn map, and a few days later I was absolutely and totally lost. Heading downhill with the idea that I would eventually get to a stream, and then a river, and then some habitable place, I eventually made it out, but I didn't see anyone for several days, much less find a community that welcomed me. The few people I did see that week regarded me with suspicion.

On my second reconnoitering trip I was a little more prepared and had a copy of a military map and a destination: Ambaná. I thought of spending two weeks on this trip. I started in the village of Sorata where Salomé Arana pointed me to Wila Kjarka, and off I went with an impossibly heavy backpack whose contents included a robust and reliable Nikon FE2

Wila Kjarka with Illampu in the background.

camera, three lenses, a shortwave radio, tent, cooking gear, food for two weeks, and several novels, including García Márquez's *One Hundred Years of Solitude*. I was clearly prepared to be alone for a while.

I arrived by nightfall in Wila Kjarka and asked to pitch my tent. That night I was visited by the curious, who told me that the following day they were playing soccer against the combined villages of Thikata and Villa Esquivel. They were one man short; would I play? I have never been much of a soccer player, but this was an offer I couldn't refuse.

The following day we walked over to the soccer field of Thikata, which, many years later, I realized was the main square of a pre-Columbian[6] settlement and which had a drop of about a thousand meters on three, almost four sides: The field was connected to the mountain by a narrow stretch of land. The perimeter of the field was guarded by small boys who would leap after the balls that crossed the boundary and usually caught them before they went too far down the mountain.

I saw myself as a curious mascot rather than a valuable player, but life is strange: As I was running toward the goal, the ball came my way, coincidentally hitting my boot and barreling into the goal. I had only once before in my life, when I was nine, scored a goal, and never again since that day. Our victory occasioned a celebration that night, and I contributed toward the beers, but the following day I was in no condition whatsoever to continue my journey, as every bone in my body was stiff and aching. Some of my soccer companions took me on a walk. As it happens, the three men—a year or two older than I—were Germán Choque, Zenobio Chino, and Pastor Mendoza, who were destined to become my friends. We didn't get very far as I was so exhausted, but they took me far enough to see my route to Ambaná.

They led me to the ruins of *Chullpa Patana* and pointed toward the distant mountains that were brooding under heavy clouds in a rather nefarious manner, which immediately reminded me of a scene from *Lord of the Rings* (even long before Peter Jackson's films) as the brave hobbits look toward Mordor. My companions appeared to be of the opinion that, even if there were not legions of orcs between me and my destination, it was certainly a perilous route. "In that village," I was told, "they will rob you and take everything you own. That one there, there they will throw stones at you; there, further on, they will steal your body fat; and there they will kill you." They were, needless to say, not very encouraging.

I had explained to them that I was keen to learn Aymara and I was looking for a place to do that; that evening someone suggested I stay in the empty storage area next to the teacher's house: In Wila Kjarka I would learn Aymara. I made arrangements to return and, when I did, Remegio Patty offered me the empty storeroom next to his house. For the next three years, I stayed there whenever I was in Wila Kjarka. To this day I have not set foot in Ambaná, my original destination, and have visited Wila Kjarka every year but two ever since.

Wila Kjarka was ideal: It was a community of two hundred and twenty people at just over 3,000 meters above sea level with a fabulous view of both the Illampu-Ancohuma massif and the Amazon basin. One might think it frivolous to consider the view, but, after all, I was going to spend quite some time there and would much rather gaze upon majestic snow-clad mountains and the Amazon basin than contemplate the perpetually darkened mountains that my companions indicated. It was also a few hours' walk from the road to La Paz and a couple of hours to the provincial capital of Sorata, which had a market and mail service once a week.

I did not know it then, but Wila Kjarka, more than many other villages in the area, is unusually cohesive with many young people and their children—many of the surrounding villages were and are on their way to becoming dominated by the very old. Wila Kjarka is fortunate in having land that goes from 2,300 meters above sea level to over 4,000, and this allows them to grow products across a wide ecological range.

Wila Kjarka thus became the site for my PhD research on cultural values, and since then my principal source of data on religion, gender, and identities. Spending so much time in one place has advantages and disadvantages. A disadvantage is that I don't get a very representative sample; an advantage is that I get to know a small community very well indeed, which has allowed me to learn things and ask questions that would be impossible in other contexts. It has also allowed me to see children grow up and adults grow old.

One of the people I have come to know well over the years is Teodosio Condori. Teodosio, I was told, was 100 years old when I first arrived in Wila Kjarka in 1989, and in 2011 I was told again he was 100 years old. There is certainly something quite ancient and timeless about Teodosio. Even in 1989 there was no member of the village who could remember Teodosio as anything other than an adult—that is, he was at least a generation older than anyone else. He was an adult during the Chaco War (1932–35) and already had children, so he was possibly born about 1915 but perhaps even before. I was drawn to Teodosio for a number of reasons: As the oldest member of the community he could tell me much about its history; and as the shaman, he was a font of knowledge about the ancestral spirits and healing; he also seemed to enjoy the long chats we had about topics that ranged from childbirth to offerings and was always keen to read my coca leaves.

In many ways this ancient monolingual shaman is quintessentially indigenous, and yet I learned that Teodosio doesn't quite fit the model of the pure-blooded indian immersed in the ways of the ancestors. To begin with, Teodosio Condori was not his original name. For much of his childhood and adult life he went by the name of Mendoza, the name given to him by his mother. His "natural" father was the overseer of the estate, a creole—that is, a white man—from the town of Ilabaya who, as was so common in those days, had sexual relations with a young indian woman who, in turn, at the age of fourteen, bore a son whom she called Teodosio. In other words, according to the conventional understanding of race mixing, Teodosio is a *mestizo*; he has much more European heritage than many—perhaps most—people self-identified or designated mestizo in the capital city of La Paz and elsewhere.

Teodosio is an expert in the ways of the ancestors, and his reputation reaches all the way to La Paz. The world of the chthonic spirits is contrasted with that of the Christian god whose son/sun is inimical to many of the rituals Teodosio performs (when I asked people about Jesus, many pointed to the sun in the sky). Yet Teodosio was not always so closely associated with autochthonous religion; as a child he attended the Lutheran missionary school at the bottom of the mountain and was a believing Christian. These Lutherans were, moreover, from the United States and evidently did not speak much Spanish. Teodosio has received more education in English than in Spanish, although today he speaks neither language.

Had Teodosio made different life choices or had different opportunities been open to him, he could today be a light-skinned Protestant mestizo with an English language education—a far cry from an indigenous Aymara shaman. In fact, in Bolivia's current ethnic and racial categorization, he would almost be at the opposite pole. The fact that he is not, and is unambiguously recognized as indigenous, even quintessentially so, illustrates the ways that indigenous identity is neither simple nor given. Teodosio also made some choices: He changed his name to the more indigenous "Condori" after the condor, which is a messenger of the gods, in the way that many people seeking to ascend the racial hierarchy change their names from indian ones to more Spanish-sounding ones.

The important point, however, is that Teodosio's unambiguous indigenous identity is not based on ancestry or "blood" but, rather, in a way of life that in some measure he has chosen for himself. The telling case of Teodosio Condori underlines the way ethnic and racial identity in Wila Kjarka is produced through the processes of living and cannot be taken for granted.

Rather, as Teodosio made a decision to change his name, I have had to make decisions about names of people and places. Wila Kjarka is not the real name of this community and the decision to give it a pseudonym is one that was particularly difficult. Wila Kjarkeños themselves would have liked a book to appear with the real name of the community and their own real names, but the nature of some of the material I recount here has the potential for causing people some very serious problems, so I have anonymized the name of the community, the names of other communities in the area, and the names of many of the people who appear in this book. I took the name from a real toponym on the territory of the community. *Wila Kjarka* means the red or bloody outcrop of rock, and indeed there are many red rocks around the community. Its neighbor was given the name *Jankho Kjarka,* which means "white outcrop of rock," which is also suitable to the kind of rock found there.

I am often asked how I was accepted into the community. The short answer is that insofar as I am "accepted" in Wila Kjarka at all, it is because of fictive kinship, labor, and commensality.

As is the case with many anthropologists in the Andes, I became godfather to a number of children. The relationship of *compadrazgo* is an important one for members of the community, for it is a way of extending their ties of obligation. People may choose a wealthy outsider as a *padrino* (godfather) whom they hope will give financial and political aid when needed, but this kind of godparent is often remote and not always accessible. There is therefore a risk to this sort of godfather. Often people balance these kinds of godparents with members from the village who will give practical daily assistance but will have few resources. Anthropologists combine both: They are wealthy and notionally powerful outsiders with considerable resources, but they can also be a source of free labor. In return my *compadres* would be obliged to defend me if there were ever conflict between me and others within the community. My compadrazgo ties give me important fictive kin links with the village and potential political support.

As mentioned above, my labor activities (which followed from my kinship ties) allowed me to perform tasks closely associated with a rural indigenous identity and certainly undermined the expectations of how wealthy outsiders behave. Similarly, eating with people around their hearths or sharing in communal meals called *wayq'asi* as well as sharing in community rituals gave me a position within the community. These factors, along with the fact that I return on an annual basis, make it so that people are now certainly familiar with my presence. I am not suggesting that anyone in Wila Kjarka has any illusions that I am not a wealthy white outsider, but my identity is at least ambiguous, and I am not easily assimilated into a clear indian/nonindian distinction. After all, labor, commensality, language, and ritual are the key distinguishing features that separate *jaqi* (indians) from *q'ara* (nonindians), but, as we shall see, they are by no means the only ones.

Gender is a theme that runs through this book and, at the risk of stating the obvious, my identity as a man has affected the kinds of data I collected, but it most certainly did not reduce my observations to an exclusively male perspective. In my first months and years of research I spoke mostly to young men who spoke at least some Spanish, but in subsequent years all my conversations have been in Aymara, and this has allowed me to have long discussions with women of all ages as well as men. I must confess, however, that I never achieved the fluency in Aymara I would have liked: Every year I learn a little more but seem to forget as well. I have also had the opportunity of developing friendships over many years with women, usually my *comadres*, who have spoken to me about a whole range of issues. For many years I was only able to travel to Bolivia in March/April, when most men are away harvesting rice, so whereas in the early years of my stays in Wila Kjarka my conversations were mostly in Spanish and with men, for some time now my conversations in Wila Kjarka have been exclusively in Aymara and usually with women (and older men who no longer engage in wage migration). My gender, although certainly a factor, does not impose an absolute limitation on the kind of data I have collected.

My racial identity has also affected my role as anthropologist. For all my efforts to minimize its effects, it is clearly a factor in my relationships with Wila Kjarkeños even if it is not always salient. My whiteness has been an advantage, however, in talking to people from the mestizo village of Villa Esquivel, whose members are keen to mark their ethnic and social difference from the Aymara peasants who surround them. My whiteness has also been an asset in the provincial capital of Sorata when talking to the few creoles left who, most likely, would not have made the

Remegio Patty in front of his house, carrying firewood, 1990.

disparaging comments about indians if they had not assumed we shared a racial identity.

My life in Wila Kjarka was not always pleasant or agreeable. Participant observation, that cornerstone of anthropological methods since Malinowski, is variably interpreted by anthropologists. Some difficult choices have to be made: to live alone and have privacy and independence but give up witnessing many of the intimacies of daily life. In a sense my decision was made for me; in offering me a place to stay, Remegio Patty invited me into his house, and I lived for several years in the storeroom next to the main family room, as would an elder son. In fact, when Remegio's son, Ricardo, grew up he occupied that room and I moved in with another *compadre*. This meant I could observe all the comings and goings as well as domestic conversations and quarrels. Since there was no door between the two rooms, I was also privy to nighttime noises as well.

In those days Remegio and Agustina slept in one bed with the youngest child; Remegio's mother, whom we simply called Awicha (grandmother), slept in the other bed with the next-youngest children; and everyone else slept on sheepskins on the floor. All went to bed at the same time: sheepskins were brought out, outer clothing removed, and then slowly people settled down to sleep. The smallest children may already have been asleep, and the others talked until, one by one, everyone was asleep. In more recent years the older children would try and finish their homework by the light of the kerosene lamp, but when I first went to Wila Kjarka the older children didn't go to school.

The idea that I would live with Remegio and Agustina and cook for myself would have struck them as nothing short of bizarre. Households have but one hearth, and this is, in fact, probably the clearest definition of a household unit: those that share a hearth. In the initial months, food was brought to me in the main room, and I sat and ate alone, as a guest, on one of the two beds the house possessed. I eventually ended up sharing my meals with the family in the small, smoky, and cramped kitchen with no window or chimney, so the smoke just wafts through the wicker roof. This is the only warm place in the house and a much more pleasant place to eat than the main room. Not only is it warm, it is also the most intimate part of the house, where the family sits close together literally and figuratively in a way that does not generally occur elsewhere. The kitchen is an informal and relaxed space, and there I often feel closest to people; people tell me things in their kitchens they don't anywhere else.

I was never expected to do field labor in Wila Kjarka, but my daily activities revolved around the family's, so I usually did go out with a hoe or iron rod for breaking earth and spent the day in the fields with the family and have continued this pattern in all subsequent visits. Sometimes before or shortly after breakfast I would visit people I wanted to talk to, but by midmorning almost everyone was out of their houses so, inasmuch as there wasn't anything to do in the village, I went out and learned about how to farm the way people do in Wila Kjarka. I would sometimes go for long walks, find a quiet place such as among the Inka ruins of Chullpa Patana above the village, and read or write, but on most days I accompanied Remegio, Agustina, and their children. In later years I more or less rotated between *compadres*. Not only did I learn how people farm but, next to kitchens, the fields where during work breaks we ate or chewed coca were the places I learned the most from people. At these moments people are relaxed and talk. This was not only an opportunity to ask questions but

Agustina Alanoca cooking.

also a time simply to listen to what people were saying about themselves: I gained many insights into life in Wila Kjarka by just listening to conversations. Very little of my investigations, especially in these early years, involved interviewing someone with a tape recorder in hand, but rather, it took participating in daily conversations, even if sometimes attempting to steer conversations into the direction in which I was most interested. Wila Kjarkeños, like most people around the world, are not used to being interviewed—that is, being asked a series of questions and being expected to answer them on one particular theme. This is a very unnatural way of conversing. The one exception is the shaman, Teodosio, who, as a specialist, was quite happy to answer my questions for hours on end. I did sometimes record conversations, but they were just that—recorded conversations, rather than interviews, in the sense that they usually wandered off the topic I most wanted to talk about, often onto something that turned out to be much more interesting. What people want to talk about is often far more compelling than what the anthropologist wants to talk about.

Working with people, however, involved a lot more than the kinds of conversations I was able to hear or participate in. Working in fields is one of the major distinctions between the jaqi of Wila Kjarka and the q'aras who live in Sorata and the cities. As a European, I was a q'ara par excellence, and it was made quite clear to me in my first days and weeks that I was expected to spend my time resting: "We are off to the fields. You will stay here and rest." Whenever I offered to help with anything, I was similarly told to rest. Q'aras, in the eyes of Wila Kjarkeños, spend a lot of time sitting or lying about, and they certainly don't do physical labor, so seeing me day after day in the fields caused a certain amount of comment. My blisters, somewhat to my chagrin, were treated with the greatest mirth, but it was commented again and again that I would work in the fields all day, and even many years after I last plowed a field with a team of oxen it was said that I was good at plowing. The latter is perhaps particularly significant since it is the signature productive activity of men. Most agricultural tasks are gendered, but plowing is one of the very few agricultural activities that women almost never do. My agricultural activity jarred with their conceptions of ethnicity and race, and my plowing in particular suggested a very jaqi type of masculinity.

In a rather similar fashion, the fact that I climbed up to Wila Kjarka carrying my own pack undermined their preconceptions about what q'aras do. For many years and until very recently (see the final chapter), people weighed my pack when I arrived and commented approvingly how heavy it was, and a few days later someone would tell me how much weight I carried up the mountain, or it would be a topic of conversation within my hearing. Wila Kjarkeños, men and women, regularly carry two, three, or four *arrobas* on their back (an arroba is about 12 kgs), so my two or three arrobas on a sophisticated Western backpack, which spreads the load evenly across my back, chest, and hips, is nothing to write home about. In fact, it feels a little like cheating: So many Wila Kjarkeños—much older, smaller, and less well fed than I—simply wrap up their load in an *awayu* cloth and tie it around their upper chest and trot off up the mountain.

What is significant about the fact that I carry my pack up the mountain is not just the weight but the fact that I do so at all. Wila Kjarkeños have quite simply never seen q'aras carrying anything other than a small backpack: Teachers, priests, engineers, agronomists, nurses, and everyone else gets their heavy loads carried for them. This is what q'aras have been doing with indians for five hundred years. Some years ago I worked as a very junior research assistant for a senior anthropologist in another part of Bolivia, and I witnessed a mestiza schoolteacher summon an old man to carry the anthropologist's backpack to the town. We each had our own backpacks, but my boss[7]—as she was then—was weary and did not want to carry hers any further. The teacher did not make a request but simply gave him the instruction, added some of her own goods to the load, and also told him to carry a basket of eggs, admonishing him that there would be hell to pay if he broke any. I felt rather sickened by this, not least because the monolingual Quechua-speaking man was quite elderly, and even more so because the anthropologist paid him only a couple of pesos for the two-hour walk. It struck me that everyone seemed to think that this kind of exchange was perfectly natural. Indians, after all, carry loads for q'aras.

In her discussion of race in the Andes, Mary Weismantel (2001) has demonstrated the myriad ways race adheres to substances and is articulated through them, but these substances are unlike the tropes of blood and genetics that are so familiar to Westerners. In a similar vein, Ben Orlove (1998) has shown how earth—the earth of roads, people's houses, pottery, and floors—serves to index racial difference between indians and mestizos. Race becomes inscribed, too, in short stature (due to malnutrition), tanned skin, and poor teeth, and the muscles that carry, feet that tread, and backs that bear loads. As Weismantel puts it, "race is indeed socially fabricated—and the construction site is the zone of interaction between our skin, flesh, bones, and the world around us" (2001: 188). The curiosity of a gringo carrying a load is similar to that experienced by David Roediger in Africa when Ghanaians cheerfully pointed out the incongruity of seeing a white man walk (Roediger 1994: 5, in Weismantel 2001: 188). It is a jarring image, one that seems to invite or even require comment because not only is it out of place but undermines what otherwise appears as an incontestable and axiomatic truth: indian bodies carry loads; white bodies do not. In Sorata and La Paz one regularly sees indian men, often quite elderly indian men, carry heavy loads onto and off trucks and across markets, and this is one of the least well-paid jobs anyone can do. It is not surprising then that one of the very first things any upwardly mobile person will do is ensure someone else carries the load.

In his celebrated film *La Nación Clandestina* writer-director Jorge Sanjinés illustrates the white/indian relationship in a scene in which indians have to carry a group of white people in their finery across a river, as indeed they used to do fifty years ago at the crossing near Villa Esquivel. Wila Kjarkeños even today remember with particular bitterness the way whites and mestizos crossed the river, even if they themselves were not compelled to do the carrying; it somehow encapsulates the brutal exploitation of indians before the National Revolution of 1952. This image and memory retains its power not only because it is such an obvious metaphor for exploitation more broadly, but surely because the indian doing the carrying is obliged to physically feel the white person's body on his shoulders. No distancing is possible in this kind of exploitation, and there is an unavoidable intimacy that immediately recalls the passage in Michael Taussig's book, *Shamanism, Colonialism, and the Wild Man,* where he writes about the intimacy of oppression: "We have to push the notion of hegemony into the lived space of realities in social relationships, in the give and take of social life, as in the sweaty, warm space between the arse of him who rides and the back of him who carries" (Taussig 1987: 288).

It is for this reason that this book explores those intimate social interactions to examine how identities are formed and articulated on a day-to-day level. It follows the insistence of postcolonial scholars such as Ann Stoler (after Albert Memmi 1965) that it is "in the banal and humble intimacies of the everyday" (2007: 36) that colonial relations of power produce both colonizer and colonized. Here my concern is much less for the colonizer who has disappeared in physical form from the lives of Wila Kjarkeños even as he haunts their most intimate spaces, but for the colonized who continue to live under the shadows of colonial discourses: people who continue to experience colonial oppression in warm, sweaty places where power continues to percolate.

Elizabeth Povinelli is another writer who has examined, after Foucault, the ways in which power relations are reproduced in the small spaces of life. She summarizes Foucault by saying that his aspiration was not "merely to know how power disciplined sexuality, sexual expression or sexual identity, but to understand how all of these were the means by which power in a robust sense—power over life and death, power to cripple and rot certain worlds while over-investing others with wealth and hope—is produced, reproduced, and distributed when we seem to be doing nothing more than kissing our lovers goodbye as we leave for the day" (2006: 10). In a similar vein, my interest in intimacies is not born of a simple curiosity for people's lives but out of a desire to understand how what appear to be large and remote power relations are reproduced and re-created in something as simple and innocent or as damning as a kiss.

Povinelli (2006) furthermore refers to "grammars of concatenation" to express the ways in which race, sex, and indigeneity are not only conceptually yoked together but how these can work—to put it in the terms of this book—to sexualize, indigenize, and feminize social institutions, histories of conquest, and stories of nationhood. Her intellectual project is to illustrate that sexuality should not be the province of those scholars interested in sexuality per se, and, as such, far from the concerns of more "serious" social scientists (see also Wade 2009); rather, it is precisely in intimate spaces where social identities, citizenship, and nationhood are produced. Indigenous identities are to be found in marches and banners, but they also emerge as sweat falls from the brow onto a wooden plow, through the smoke of my comadre's kitchen, in the doll strapped to a little girl's back, in the disputes between married couples—in short, indigenous identities form in the interstices of everyday life, in the intimate spaces where statecraft, history, and power seem miles away but where, in fact, they settle and emerge, sometimes unexpectedly.

FEARS AND DESIRES

In discussing identities—be they gendered, ethnic, national, or racial—I assume neither a bounded subject nor a fixed set of identities. That is to say, I make no assumption that the categories of man and woman, much less white and indian, are stable positions unambiguously occupied by bounded individuals. Gender and ethnicity are always relational terms, and as we shall see, particularly in chapter 7, people can be more or less indian, more or less female, or more or less Bolivian, depending on the context in which they find themselves.

In having unstable identities, people in Wila Kjarka are not unique, but they are unusual in being very clear that being, say, a man, or a jaqi, is not immutable. In this they are very similar to the Tzeltal of southern Mexico (Pitarch 2010) where "one is not born indigenous—it is not an inherited condition—one *becomes* indigenous, or at least this is the ideal goal" (p. 204; see also p. 90). This disturbs primordialist and essentialist assumptions about indigenous identities, since people can become jaqi or not in the course of their lifetimes.

This is not to say, however, that identities in Wila Kjarka are infinitely flexible, that people have wide choices about which identities to adopt; rather, people understand that identities have to be produced through action. For people in Wila Kjarka, who they are is in a constant state of process; that is, their identities are iterative, in the sense used by Henrietta Moore (2007). Moore draws on Judith Butler's (1993) notion of iterativity but moves away from her earlier idea of performance (1990) because, even though this was not Butler's intention, it seems to imply that people have a real choice in their identities, whereas, in fact, they are usually very heavily constrained. Moore, drawing on Butler's later work (1993), suggests that we think of gender identities (and to this we can add racial and ethnic ones) as iterative, as the products of a large number of small, often unconscious, acts. I find this idea of iteration particularly useful because it suggests much more clearly an interactive engagement with the social world; moreover, it captures well the sense of identities produced over time as a product of numerous small social interactions, rather than an exaggerated sense of agency that might be suggested by "performance." Each iteration reinforces or undermines a particular identity, but any single act is unlikely to have a major effect. Butler underlines this aspect of performativity in *Bodies That Matter*: "Performativity cannot be understood outside of a process of iterability, a regularized and constrained repetition of norms. And this repetition is not performed *by* a subject; this repetition is what enables a subject and constitutes the temporal condition for the subject. This iterability implies that 'performance' is not a singular 'act' or event, but a ritualized production, a ritual reiterated under and through constraint, under and through the force of prohibition and taboo, with the threat of ostracism and even death controlling and compelling the shape of the production, but not, I will insist, determining it fully in advance" (Butler 1993: 95).

In Wila Kjarka, there is a clear sense that bodies change over time; identity is produced through practice. In Mary Weismantel's words, "As it ingests, digests, and expels substances from the world around it, [the Andean body] provides its own identity drawn from worldly substances. Body and identity thus originate in the intimate physical relationship between persons and their social milieu" (2001: 192). These bodies are racialized in that social differences are inscribed into them. Even as they are essentialized, racial ideologies in the Andes differ from Euro-American ones in that race is clearly mutable; that is, iterative identities are produced through bodies and do not simply belong to the realm of the noncorporal social sphere.

In Wila Kjarka there are many ways to talk about racial difference—that is, to index social difference in terms of bodily substances or characteristics—but the one that carries the greatest ideological weight is body fat. Wila Kjarkeños hold, as do many other Andean people, that the food they eat and the labor they perform produce brown fat around their organs which white people simply do not possess. Their indianness inheres into that body fat, which is produced through a life of labor; in this way it is clearly essentialized even as people recognize that it is something that changes over time. This resonates with Pedro Pitarch's (2010) discussion of the relationship between indigenous souls and bodies in Mexico where "the body is thought of as belonging to the realm of the 'cultural,' or what human beings can and should morally do, and thus to be fabricated through human intervention, while the soul belongs to the realm of the 'sacred,' and comes to this world as something already given" (2010: 3). Unlike Tzeltal people, Wila Kjarkeños clearly do see their spiritual existence in collective terms, but what is important to underline is that neither holds the view that identity is ontologically rooted in the body. Perhaps this is simply noting that Europeans since the Enlightenment have seen social difference, such as race and gender, as being produced in bodies that can be measured, whose brains can be weighed, and more latterly, whose genes can be coded. We should not, then, be surprised when non-Europeans have very different conceptions of the body and how it produces identities.

This book offers many examples of how identities are produced iteratively through action, and there are many examples here of people having different beliefs and making different choices in how they lead their lives, and real choices can and are made. It is, however, important not to lose sight of the enormous inequalities of power that structure such agency and constrain choices. Wila Kjarkeños are born into a community on the margins, even now, of the national imaginary, with limited opportunities, where they are likely to experience profound and even brutal examples of racism and sexism. They are also born into a nation that promises inclusion and advancement but yet publicly ignores and actively excludes them. Many Wila Kjarkeños are simultaneously aware of the profound social injustices, and hold to the promise of a whitened and masculinized social advancement.

Wila Kjarkeños's desires for personal progress may become fetishized around skin color and dress because there are such close associations between power and (male) whiteness. For Slavoj Žižek (1989) ideology works in the realm of fantasy to make life tolerable, to cover the interstices of the symbolic order. Wila Kjarkeños share a set of coherent beliefs about personhood, gender, agency, and being human; but these are regularly contradicted by experiences that undermine these values. Some of these are generated by external forces (Canessa 1995), but others are generated from within the community and from within individuals.

As each individual comes to terms with his or her (changing) position, he or she produces and pursues desires that challenge and contest not only the beliefs widely held by others but his or her very own beliefs. There is a dynamism to this sense of self that makes the self appear unstable and fractured. From an anthropologist's point of view, this is made manifest in the contradictions and twists that one observes in what people say and do.

Žižek's work is important in placing fantasy and desire at the center of an understanding of hegemonic processes and the importance of fantasy in challenging and undermining as well as supporting those processes. For Žižek, desires and fantasies do not simply reside within the level of the individual but are profoundly social (see also Moore 2007). In the examples given here, fantasies of desire connect and even constitute wider social relations and processes.

Desire is always multidimensional, idiosyncratic, and personal, even as it is socially constructed. There can never be a straightforward prediction of the contours of desire. What must be absolutely clear is that even as desire is a "fuzzy" matrix (Whittier and Simon 2001), it is very hard to imagine any situation in Latin America where race (but also class, age, etc.) is *not* going to be a constitutive element in the construction of desire. David Murray's (1999) ethnography of Martinican men (those who expressed desire for women and those who expressed desire for men) would appear to confirm this point. Among Martinican men, he could find no consistent pattern of desire around race: Some desired white partners, and Murray links this to the influence of racial hypergamy and racial and sexual myths established in colonial plantation society; and some desire black partners, which Murray attributes to the influence of anticolonial narratives of liberation (1999: 168). What he found common to all Martinican men is the way race has a primary role in the construction of sexual desire: At its minimum it is the language through which other political desires and fantasies are expressed, but given Whittier and Simon's analysis, it appears more likely that fantasies of power are eroticized and those desires are satisfied through raced bodies. What is also worth noting about Murray's ethnography is that men—of whatever race or sexual orientation—have a common discourse of masculinity based on dominance through sexual activity: "Neither homosexual nor heterosexual men communicated narratives in which they made themselves into objects of desire. Neither did they acknowledge the possibility that desire could be constituted mutually. The emphasis on the sexual proclivities of the ideal partner enhanced the speaker's masculinity through the reduction of the partner to a sexual object of desire, a strategy that distances any possibility of experiencing the other's subjectivity" (Murray 1999: 169). And in some narratives, race plays a role in aiding the prevention of any subjective similarities between subjects. In Murray's ethnography the key element in constructing male desire for white or black, men or women, is the maintenance and assertion of hegemonic masculinity. In the words of Whittier and Simon, "There are many more reasons for desiring sex than there are ways of being sexual, the meaning of the desire being expressed cannot be fully understood by merely describing the behavior" (2001: 161).

People's physical desires and sexuality are therefore deeply embedded in racialized relations of power and difference—that is, in race. Sex and race in this context are consequently intimately linked to the point of being analytically inseparable. Some scholars, such as Verena Martínez Alier (1974), Donna Goldstein (2003), and Mary Weismantel (2001), have considered the way ideologies of sexuality and race are mutually reinforcing in Latin America, but it is perhaps surprising how few have attempted an integrated treatment of sex and race; fewer still have considered the role of desire in both configuring sexuality and racial identity. Peter Wade's recent work (2009) is a welcome exception, and he places desire at the very center of his analysis (see also Moore 2007; Murray 1999; Sangren 2004). He makes the important point that "desire/fear and power are intimately conjoined in their very production; so to say that sex is about one *rather than* or *as much as* the other does not really work" (2009: 36). It is, thus, an unsatisfactory shorthand to say that sex is about race or vice versa, or that they are both *about* power since they constitute each other.

This analytical position whereby power and sex are merely refractions of the same desire/fear helps explain one of the curious aspects of the nexus of race and sex—the fact that the despised racial other is often sexually desired; and indeed the ways in which sexual desire may not be exclusively configured around pleasure but other powerful emotional responses that may be quite negative. The obverse of desire is fear, and fearful fantasies play as much a role in constructing identities as desirous ones. In chapters 7 and 8, I discuss how fantasies of whiteness play a role in configuring ethnic and gender identities; as a consequence, race—that is, the embodiment of social difference—is a key element in the discussion of identity. In chapters 3 and 5, however, it is fantasies of fear that are shown to play a possibly more powerful role in developing racial identities. If Wila Kjarkeños desire whiteness, and whiteness appears as fetish of power, then they also fear its castrating potential: the *kharisiri* fat stealer who sucks out people's life force, their capacity for agency produced through a set of practices associated with an indigenous life. The profound terror people feel for the kharisiri is, in itself, constitutive of the difference between jaqi and nonjaqi, and in this sense physical fear is at least as much a somatization of race as skin color, which is highly variable among Wila Kjarkeños.

In a number of works (e.g., 2002, 2007), Neil Whitehead has stressed the importance of the role of the imagination in understanding terror. Terror is a violent act of the imagination or, perhaps more accurately, an act *for* the imagination. Whether the terror is produced by the *kanaimà* of Guyana, the kharisiri of the Andes, or the furtive agents against which the "War on Terror" is waged, the fear of violence plays a greater role in the cultural imaginary than the actual violence perpetrated. Although the terror may originate in a particular act of violence, its power is perpetuated and represented far more potently in the forms of fear that invade human bodies.

With respect to violence and terror, Whitehead has called for "a more explicit anthropology of experience and imagination in which individual meanings, emotive forces, and bodily practices, become central to the interpretation of violent acts" (2007: 233). What is offered in chapter 5 is such an anthropology of experience and imagination, which focuses on how people not only understand their bodily practices but how their bodies produce agency and how terror interrupts that agency. The terror the kharisiri invokes is much more than simply a product of the imagination: It is an essential part of the formation of the cultural imaginary that constitutes identity. It is not enough to assume that a given act (imagined or real) produces fear or terror; the very terror needs to be understood in culturally specific terms.

Fantasies of fear do not only play a role in the form of creatures with supernatural powers but also in the memories of real events. As we shall see in chapter 4, Wila Kjarkeños' accounts of acts of extreme violence fifty years ago are also a communal fantasy of revenge and retribution and an exaggerated sense of historical agency. Direct witnesses to the violence recount the incidents within a generic form, elevating it from a personal experience to a larger historical narrative. The extreme violence has a dramatic effect and consequently serves as a mnemonic device when the accounts are reproduced by people born long after the events. The final chapter of this book explores the ways in which fantasies of power and whiteness are played out on a national level as well as in the intimate lives of people.

Race, sex, and indigenous identity are big themes that play out in public stages: They are regulated, contested, and profoundly influential in people's lives. These identities configure—even if they don't fully determine—the ways individuals imagine their worlds and move through social spaces; they are also intensely personal. The title of this book alludes to the intimate space where race, sex, and indigeneity are experienced, imagined, and developed; it is in the small spaces of everyday life that these abstract concepts are made manifest and mold individuals.

Scale is therefore a clear organizing principle of this book; or, rather, the collapsing of scales is a central trope of the book. Intimate fantasies of sex, even as they break taboos, never exist in social and political vacuums; desires are similarly constructed in terms of what is beyond us. Not only is this not simply a community study, it also one where the subject of inquiry is the intimate spaces where people actually live, the better to explore the broader global questions of sex, race, and indigenous identity.

The structure of the book follows this schema: The first chapters establish the geographical and even temporal isolation of the community, as remote and "authentic" as any you are likely to find in the Andes; the later chapters expose this illusion as the focus pulls out to broader national and global issues even as they examine more closely the personal and the intimate. The deeper one delves into the intimate spaces of human lives, the greater the scale of the issues that are exposed; as such, this book intends to be more than a multisited study but, rather, a multiscalar study.

If one of the axes along which this book is organized is spatial, the other is temporal. There are two reasons for this: The first is that Wila Kjarkeños have a very intimate relationship with the past, a relationship that distinguishes them from q'aras, as we shall see in chapters 2 and 3; but beyond this, the very nature of an indigenous identity is a historical perspective. At its very core is the sense that present-day injustices are rooted in the injustices of the past, and the basis of this injustice is that "my people were here before your people." Indigeneity, be it in Botswana, Indonesia, or Bolivia, is about a sense of historical injustice, and so history and historical consciousness have a prominent role in this book. One of the key features of Aymara thought is that the past is not remote and inaccessible but, in contrast, visible and immanent. This idea is rooted in the very language: The word for past, *nayra,* is the same for eyes; and the word for future, *qhepha,* is the same for behind. The future is thus behind, unknowable and invisible, and the past is in front, visible through personal knowledge but also through communication with the ancestors. As we shall see, some Wila Kjarkeños claim to speak not only to their immediate ancestors but to the Inkas who, although in the past, are living in a different but ultimately accessible realm.

If space collapses in on itself as the global impacts on the very intimate, and the intimate is contoured by the global, so it is with time: The past irrupts into the present. This irruption can be pleasant and beneficial as is often the case with ancestors' interventions, or it can be an open wound of historical injustice that informs indigenous consciousness. Temporally or spatially, indigeneity for Wila Kjarkeños is a deeply intimate experience.

ONE

A Wila Kjarka Kaleidoscope

Clara, one of the very few creoles, that is, white people, left in Sorata, remembers the early decades of the twentieth century when Sorata, the cantonal capital, was a wealthy, bustling town: "There were beautiful houses and very fine people (*gente muy decente*). Now Sorata is worthless. We are left with the worst kind of people, peasants . . ." In that period, Sorata was divided into two groups: the creoles, some of whom were German speaking, and the *mestizos*, who were the small traders; social tension existed between these two groups of people, the former associated with the Liberal Party and the latter with the Republicans. "The liberals were the gentlemen, the *señores.*" In those days the creole elites feared the mestizos much more than the indians. During the revolution (as she referred to it) of 1920, "the republicans sacked the most beautiful stores of Sorata. The mestizos made a revolution against the whites." Another creole resident told me that her mother never forgot how the mestizos sacked her house and how she had to live with seeing people in the street wearing her clothes.

It was not simply that the creoles did not consider the indians a threat but, rather, they saw them as being on the same side. As Clara continued: "The *campesinos* were very respectful and always cried alongside the whites . . . They would address us as '*Mamaay, Tataay* . . . and not as *señor* or *señora*." This form of address, "mother" and "father," with the prolonged final vowel that indicates subservience, was hated by indians, who found it patronizing and humiliating but felt required to address creoles in this way. A number of older people in Wila Kjarka mentioned this to me specifically as one of the things they disliked most about this period. But for Clara these were simply terms of respect, and before the Agrarian Reform of 1953, the campesinos "knew their place" and "were very respectful. Now they are spoiled; now they do not respect people."

For Wila Kjarkeños, Sorata is a *q'ara* town par excellence, notwithstanding the fact that, as Clara ruefully notes, there are very few whites left. Sorata, with its residents and history, is the simplest manifestation of a worldview that sees the lives of people such as those in Wila Kjarka and similar communities as an age-long struggle between indians and whites.

It is tempting to read the history of Latin America as a struggle between white Europeans and native indians and to see the election of Evo Morales as the final chapter in that long history (e.g., Thomson and Hylton 2007). Even from the earliest decades, however, the picture has been much more complicated; the neat administrative and conceptual distinction between the Republic of Spaniards and Republic of Indians was immediately undermined by marriages and unions with indian women. The offspring, mestizos, were formally considered part of the Republic of Spaniards but were ineligible for a wide range of positions and posts.

Even this tripartite structure was almost immediately complicated by the recognition of various admixtures of white, indian, and African "blood" and the "society of castes" (Mörner 1967; Wade 2009: 87–88) expanded into structures of eight, sixteen, and even thirty-two racial categories with various ways of social and racial improvement through mixing. Nonwhites were *castas*, an unfavorable category. If one considers that Spaniards were themselves a mixture of Iberians, Goths, Romans, Moors, Jews, and Africans[1] with a fairly wide phenotypical range, it is easy to see the complications to a racial system where mestizos and *mulatos* were often much lighter skinned than "pure" Christian Spaniards.

Ethnic ascription was established according to a range of diagnostics such as trade, residence, marriage, language, and dress as well as phenotype. If these could not be sufficiently manipulated, the wealthy and powerful could resort to the courts and, as Lesley Rout points out, "Of course, nobody wanted to be considered *casta*, and requests for exemption were heard at court within the first three decades after Columbus's landing. Conquistadores like Pedro de Alvarado wanted their bastard heirs declared legitimate Spaniards, and they had enough of those magic persuaders—money and influence—to get their way. No one has ever explained how a royal declaration cleansed the blood of an innately vice-ridden *casta*, but this was only one example of a whole system that was riddled with logical inconsistencies" (1976: 127).

There was, however, substantial legal precedent for this as the Spanish Crown shored up its position vis-à-vis ethnic minorities and their descendants after the *Reconquista* of Iberia by restricting offices to those of pure Christian blood. However, the "Purity of Blood Laws," first codified in 1449, had to deal with the thorny problem of the fact that large proportions of the nobility had a history of intermarriage with Jews and Moors. This was neatly resolved by declaring that all nobles ipso facto possessed pure blood. An elegant solution, no doubt, but it did open up a number of challenges to the developing racial system in the New World as well as Spain, since the Spanish arrived with a racial system that was open to legal petition (Rout 1976; Twinam 1999).

Since the time of Pedro de Alvarado,[2] the question of who is white, mestizo, or indian has not been straightforward. For much of the colonial period, being indian was arguably a fiscal category (Harris 1995), wherein indians were required to offer their labor for the *mita* in the mines but were not liable for tax. In the Republican period—especially after the expansion of the haciendas in the nineteenth century—many indians were serfs on large estates and were not allowed to leave without the consent of the *hacendado*.

Throughout all these periods, people were able to undermine the system by a number of means, notably money, marriage, and migration. Several historians have shown how color, occupation, and wealth have affected racial ascription (e.g., McCaa 1984; Seed, 1988; Spalding, 1970). In a very influential work, Verena Martínez Alier (1974) showed how gender and sexuality were key elements in this system of racial hierarchies, as white male elites maintain their racial purity by controlling the sexuality of their women and their "legitimate" offspring. Within this hierarchy, however, lie the seeds of its own destruction. The population of white women in Latin American colonies was very small, and some poorer white men might marry the daughters of wealthier mestizos. The historical and contemporary situation is much more complex than this simple formulation might suggest, but there is no doubt that there are numerous examples of using marriage as a means of social ascent and in order to "whiten" (Wade 2009: 168–75).

To do justice to the historical and contemporary complexities of racial and social mobility is far beyond the scope of this book, but for our purposes here it is important to note that racial, ethnic, gender, and class categories are never straightforward. Sex and marriage serve to uphold racial hierarchies even as they can also undermine them. This leaves us with a highly complex situation in which race and ethnic identities are inherently unstable categories.

Billie Jean Isbell (1978) has suggested that one of ways of understanding Andean social structure is as if it were viewed through a kaleidoscope; more recently Laura Lewis (2003) has suggested that ethnicity and identity in Latin America are a "hall of mirrors," with an infinite number of reflections, as difference and identity constantly rebound on each other. I find this refractive view of race and ethnicity useful in understanding the world from the point of view of Wila Kjarkeños: A slight shift in the kaleidoscopic lens or a movement left or right in the hall of mirrors and a whole new set of configurations emerges. I can think of no better way to describe identities in the Andes and, in many ways, each chapter of this book can be understood as another turn in the kaleidoscope.

In the next two chapters we will look at how Wila Kjarka's identity has been configured historically, but here I want to look at the social geography of Wila Kjarka and surrounding communities, where people can be described as whites, mestizos, and indians in English; *criollos/vecinos, mistis,* and *campesinos/indios* in Spanish; or, alternatively *q'ara, misti,* and *jaqi* in Aymara—but these terms are very awkward translations of each other, as we shall see.

SORATA

The area around Wila Kjarka is economically and politically dominated by the provincial capital, Sorata, stunningly located at the foot of the great Illampu-Ancohuma massif.

Sorata (population 2,000) was one of many towns founded during the colonial period, but it is relatively unusual in that a considerable proportion of this colonial architecture has remained. Many of the area's hacendados maintained residences in the town, but it was in the beginning of the twentieth century that Sorata enjoyed its period of greatest wealth.

The market in Sorata.

Strategically situated on the walking route from the highlands to the Amazon jungle, it was ideally placed to profit from the rubber boom. Sorata's twentieth-century wealth was based on trade rather than agriculture, and its citizens were able to enjoy all the luxuries of the period—luxuries that were initially brought over the mountain by mule or oxcart and later by truck.

The first half of the twentieth century saw Sorata dominated by creoles, while a substantial number of mestizos periodically challenged the status quo. In those days everyone spoke Aymara: Indians did not speak Spanish and, since elite children were brought up by indian women and needed to speak Aymara to their servants, the creole elite as well as the mestizos were fluent speakers of Aymara.

Even before the 1952 Revolution, Sorata was beginning to change. The U.S. Government put a lot of pressure on the Bolivian authorities to curtail the commercial activities of the Sorata Germans, who were open Nazi sympathizers, as indeed were most of Bolivia's expatriate Germans. The exception, of course, was the substantial German Jewish community, which had its own school in La Paz as well as a German-language radio station (Spitzer 1998). By insisting that all imports be cleared at Customs in La Paz instead of Sorata, the town lost its role as an important entrepôt. There were still, however, many wealthy white families residing there after the Second World War, but many of the haciendas around Sorata were sacked during the 1952 Revolution and there was a major exodus of creoles. Over time the town came to be dominated by peasants from the surrounding area and their children.

Despite this and the fact that many merchants use Aymara to sell to indians, Spanish has remained the dominant language in Sorata; in fact, Aymara is spoken less now than it was fifty years ago, when everyone— creoles and indians alike—spoke the language. Contemporary residents, themselves children of peasants, are uncomfortable with the continuing immigration from the countryside. Some express concern that these campesinos are preventing the town from progressing and are particularly worried about the effect they have on their children: The presence of significant numbers of Aymara speakers in the classroom is believed to bring down educational standards generally. "They are simply not civilized," as one resident told me, and another: "They haven't learned citizenship." This is an exceptionally succinct expression of the ways indians simply are not considered—even today—as part of the nation. Citizenship has been defined since the dawn of the Republic as being Spanish-speaking and possessing European culture. The 1952 Revolution was revolutionary in that it offered the possibility of this liberal citizenship to indians, so long as they conformed to its tenets; it embraced rather than challenged the idea of Bolivia as a Spanish-speaking, culturally Western nation.

Wila Kjarkeños do not feel comfortable in Sorata; they don't feel that they belong, and they certainly do not trust the police and other officials. The difference between Wila Kjarkeños and Sorateños is that the latter live from trade; they buy and sell, but do not grow anything. They pay others to work their land if they have any, and they do not work with the people they hire. The traders use Aymara to talk to Wila Kjarkeños and other campesinos, but it is often in a sharp and impatient tone, which, even in commercial relationships that go back decades, conveys little amity, let alone affection.

Wila Kjarkeños mistrust the police, who since the "siege" of 2002, are confined to the town limits and do not venture into the rural communities—not that they ever showed much interest before.[3] It would be a rare event indeed for a Wila Kjarkeño to go to the police if he or she were in trouble. Nor do they have much faith in civil justice. As Zenobio told me, "The judges are not going to believe anyone like us; they will not listen to us [literally 'give us the word']. They will say: 'They are just jaqi.'"

*Natalio Arana in front of his store. Natalio and his wife, Salomé, speak
Aymara fluently, but their children do not.*

In decades past, indians were not allowed to traverse the main plaza;
now it is full of old and young people from the countryside. On one Saturday morning I found Clara sitting on a park bench and sat down beside
her. It was market day, so the plaza was full of people, sitting, walking,
and eating ice cream. As we both watched people pass, she began to tell
me what Sorata was like when she was young: "There were lots of people,
many families. Now no one is left." This may seem like something of an
odd thing to say when the plaza was absolutely full of people, but Clara
was not seeing people, she was seeing indians. In a similar vein, another
criolla of Sorata bemoaned to me once that there were only "five families"
who lived in the town. For these women, *gente*, that is, people, means *gente
decente*, which is a synonym for white.

And so there we sat in the middle of the square full of . . . well, people.
She was dressed in a housecoat and slippers, complaining because her
maid had locked her out. As she lamented the splendor of those days of
yore, before us passed two young girls dressed in fine *polleras* and shawls
and what looked to me like brand-new hats at a jaunty angle on their
heads. They passed with a spring in their step and laughing freely, the very
image of the social confidence among indigenous people who were about
to elect Evo Morales to the presidency. The contrast could not be greater:

Three men sitting on a park bench in Sorata. When they were boys,
indians were not allowed to sit on these benches.

a tired and defeated creole from the colonial past before bright and challenging youth of an indigenous present.

Clara's maid eventually arrived and paid no attention to the complaints of her mistress. She was sharp and impatient with Clara whom, she said, should never have gone to the plaza by herself. Off they went, with Clara shuffling behind her impatient servant, who marched toward the gates of the old house, keys in hand. This was in August 2005, four months before Evo Morales was elected with a clear majority of the votes, casting aside the traditional creole elite in the process. I watched them go and reflected on how they incarnated the new order of Bolivia.

VILLA ESQUIVEL AND SAN PEDRO

Downriver from Sorata are the villages of San Pedro and, across the river, Villa Esquivel. Many of these residents are quite fair skinned, and before the Bolivian Revolution there were very sharp distinctions between the mestizos of these communities and the indians of the surrounding communities.

Villa Esquivel is about eight hundred meters down the mountain from Wila Kjarka (i.e., it lies at approximately 2,200 meters above sea level) and, as such, enjoys a different climate: There are many more birds and the people of Villa Esquivel can grow tropical fruits that cannot be produced in Wila Kjarka. Today, few people live in Villa Esquivel; this mestizo village was much more populous in the past. There is little visible nowadays to mark the difference between this and other communities, other than the houses being larger and constructed around a central courtyard; kitchens are substantial structures, and carving on balconies is more ornate.

Fifty years ago the people of Villa Esquivel looked down upon the indians of Wila Kjarka, and many older people in Wila Kjarka today express considerable bitterness at the disdain they received in the past. They remember well how the mestizos would not sit with them, would not eat with them, and would not offer them maize beer in a glass—which is what they used—but in a *tutuma*—a gourd. They are also all very aware of how the Mamani family suffered at the hands of the Villa Esquiveleños. Mateo Mamani, although from Wila Kjarka, worked for a man in Villa Esquivel, Juan Botello. In those days the land in Villa Esquivel was very productive and a substantial amount of wheat was grown, but now, I was told, "the rains do not fall when they are supposed to and there is a drought." The mestizos did not work the land, however, and paid indians to do it for them.

I met Mateo's son, Pastor, at his uncle's funeral, shortly after arriving in Wila Kjarka. My first impression of Pastor Mamani was that he reminded me somewhat of Al Pacino, not only in physical appearance but in his edginess, so I privately nicknamed him "Al." My second impression of Pastor Mamani was more a realization: This man wanted to knock my head off my shoulders. Two things saved me from unpleasant decapitation: his inebriation (which meant that his swing was wildly off the mark) and the intervention of people such as the shaman, Teodosio, who persuaded him that I was not there to steal his uncle's lands. At that point I had not even actually met the monolingual Teodosio, nor knew that he was the shaman, but I had certainly noticed him: He was very old but strong and had exceptionally bright eyes. It turned out to be neither the first nor the last time that Teodosio intervened on my behalf, although I did not know it then. Pastor was upset at his uncle's death and, as I later learned, funerals are times of heightened emotion, times of maudlin sentiment, and occasionally times of quarrel. My relationship with Pastor moved from a cautious respect to one of open friendship, and so many years later as I walked through Villa Esquivel, my head still firmly on my shoulders, he was more than happy to stop his work and chat with me about times past.

Pastor Mamani harvesting wheat in Villa Esquivel.

As Pastor Mamani explained: "In those days the jaqi worked the fields. [The *mistis,* that is, mestizos] asked the jaqi and gave money to the people of Wila Kjarka. 'Come and work my field,' they would say and the jaqi worked the fields. In those days the mistis were very abusive and demanding (*munañanichitaynaxa mistinakaxa*). They said: 'You will have it all done completely.' In those days the jaqi did everything." When the war with Jankho Kjarka broke out, Mateo fled with his family—including the three-year-old Pastor—to Villa Esquivel, where he had been working as a sharecropper. The Revolution came, followed by the Agrarian Reform Act of 1953, and Juan Botello, like so many mistis, decided to leave the countryside, and in his case he moved to Sorata. Exceptionally, though, he gave all his land and legal title to Mateo Mamani, to the outrage of all his neighbors. Never had an indian owned land in Villa Esquivel. Evidently worse was that he paid for the education of Pastor and his brothers in Sorata.

After the Revolution things changed: "Some jaqi decided they would become mistis—there are some of those today; and there as some mistis who think of themselves as vecinos [literally 'neighbors,' but a standard euphemism for creoles]. But still there were those who called us indios. There is one, still today, who cannot write, who cannot even sign his name but he calls jaqi 'indios,'" Pastor said, laughing (suddenly reminding me more than ever of Al Pacino).

Nowadays jaqi express scorn for the pretensions of the people of Villa Esquivel. As one man put it to me one Saturday afternoon in the plaza in Sorata, "They are just the miserable descendants of the cast-off seed of Columbus."

Villa Esquivel is an important example of how ethnic and racial identity cannot simply be reduced to class because Villa Esquiveleños today are as poor as the Wila Kjarkeños, they are all fluent Aymara speakers, and all engage in almost exactly the same productive activities. They are not, however, indians. Villa Esquiveleños were very clear on that point. Speaking in Spanish, they called themselves *gente*—that is, people—in contradistinction to *campesinos*, which literally means *peasants* but here is obviously a substitute for *indian*, since they themselves are not any more or less peasants than the indians who surround them.

The difference is marked in a number of ways, one of which is that all the mistis of Villa Esquivel are fluent Spanish speakers, including the women, with the exception of Pastor Mamani's wife, who comes from a nearby Aymara community and never learned to speak Spanish. Fifty years ago, however, Aymara was the dominant language in Villa Esquivel, and many of my older informants told me that they learned Spanish as adults; yet they are much more fluent than anyone in Wila Kjarka. Eloy Figueredo told me that one of the important differences between them and people such as those from Wila Kjarka is that the latter were 100 percent monolingual and the Villa Esquiveleños spoke Spanish. What is certainly the case is that Villa Esquiveleños have Spanish surnames and Wila Kjarkeños (with the exception of the Mendozas) have indigenous ones. In those days, too, all or almost all the women wore polleras, which distinguished mistis from creoles, who wore dresses, and indians, who wore homespun (*bayeta*) tunics. With the Bolivian Revolution, indian women donned the dress of mistis and mistis took on the dress of creoles, so some of the women, such as Isabela, don't wear polleras, although as a child she did.

There are also important commonalities between the two communities. Villa Esquileños follow the custom of the first haircutting, the *rutucha*, and also make offerings to the house god, the *kunturmamani*. Despite looking down on Wila Kjarkeños, all of them appear to have visited Teodosio the shaman in Wila Kjarka on various occasions; and the mistis also have the custom of the communal meal, the *wayk'asi*.

As an illustration of how context affects racial ascription, Clara's sister, Eugenia, confessed to me over a *pisco* sour at the town fiesta while trying to trip me up in Aymara that she had thought I was one of those "mistis from downriver." Eugenia was making some money from the fiesta by selling pisco sours from the side door of her house. She had few customers, and we sat at a table that she had laid out with her son, who was one of the very first schoolteachers in Wila Kjarka. In those days after the Education Reform it was bilingual mestizos who were sought out as schoolteachers. He spoke fondly of the village, and I was able to tell him that yes, Teodosio, was still alive. For her part she teased me about the young Aymara maidens, *tawaqus*, clearly assuming that I was enjoying the race privilege of sexual access to indian women, a racist if historically accurate assumption that I came across again and again.

Eugenia confessed, with much humor, that she had seen me speaking Aymara in the plaza with a small rucksack on my back and wearing sandals made from recycled car tire treads, called *wiskhus*. Funny enough, the "mistis from downriver" would not be seen dead in wiskhus because someone might think they were indians. On that occasion I wasn't wearing wiskhus, and I rather wonder if she would have offered me a pisco sour if I had been. Footwear in the Andes is an important indicator of ethnic status (Orlove 1998; Urton 1998: 210; Van Vleet 2005; Weismantel 2001: 189), and residents of these villages who have moved in since the Agrarian Reform from surrounding indian villages make sure that they and their children are wearing boots or shoes, making a clear declaration that they are not to be considered indians. I recall one occasion when I attended the fiesta in San Pedro when I was greeted warmly by some mestizo friends who were proud to show me off as their white friend but were clearly pained at what I was wearing on my feet. On the one hand Isabela and Fidel saw me as one of them—a white person who spoke Aymara and was happy to live in the countryside—and some years past had hoped I would succumb to the charms of their redheaded daughter and marry her; on the other hand I was wearing these indian sandals. "Don Andrés, why do you wear such things on your feet?" Isabela asked me in evident distress. She and her family and friends, including the children, were all wearing spotlessly clean shoes and boots, and I suspect they carried them across from Villa Esquivel and only put them on just before entering San Pedro.

In navigating this ethnic kaleidoscope, context is all. Eugenia was not the only person to confuse my ethnic/racial identity. On one occasion the visiting priest to Wila Kjarka took me to be a peasant from the village (*campesino* [i.e., indian] *del lugar*). This, needless to say, caused great amusement among my companions and, witnessing their mirth, the priest defended himself with, "Well, if he is not a campesino what is he doing living here?" Phenotype is but one marker of ethnic identity and on this occasion, in the priest's eyes, location trumped any other diagnostic. On other occasions my surname caused confusion since Canasa is a very typical Aymara surname of the region and easily substitutable for Canessa. People in Wila Kjarka called me Anklisa Canasa (Anklisa being an Aymara phonologization of Andrés), and one could barely have had a more local name.

If people could so readily assume that I, a European, could be a mestizo or indian simply because of my physical context and the fact that I spoke Aymara, the converse is even more likely to be the case: When jaqi move to towns and cities and speak fluent Spanish they, in many cases, are no longer seen as jaqi.

Dominga, one of my *comadres*, is Pastuku's wife. Although I visit her often, she remains shy, if friendly, with me even though I spend a lot of time with her husband and, consequently, with her. On one occasion, as she stirred the toasting maize, she responded to my queries about mistis and jaqi: "No, we are not mistis; we are children of jaqi. Now, there are some people whom they say are mistis even though they are children of jaqi and came from this earth (*uraqin jupa wawax sarxaspha*). The son may go to another place and they say he is misti and he no longer comes to the village. And this is so with my sister who, if she were to arrive after many a long year, would say she is misti: She would arrive wearing trousers, or with a dress; she would surely be a misti (*mistisxamaphunispay uqham*)."

Dominga here is focusing on dress but, of course, it is not so much dress that makes someone misti or jaqi but what that dress stands for—an urban Spanish-speaking versus rural Aymara lifestyle. When I asked her why she wore a pollera, she replied, "Oh, I was brought up wearing a pollera, since I was very small. And so I will always wear a pollera; moreover, I don't know how to speak Spanish, and so with a pollera I will simply be, because I live in the countryside. Only in the cities do people wear dresses."

Dominga here clearly associates living in the countryside and being monolingual in Aymara as associated with wearing a pollera. There is something of an irony here because her mother did not grow up wearing a pollera, since, in those days, polleras were worn by mistis, not jaqi. Rural indians started wearing polleras only after the 1952 Revolution and until then, and for some time after, polleras were associated with the mistis of the valley, such as the residents of Villa Esquivel. There are, of course, many women in La Paz who wear polleras; it is the dress of market women and domestic servants. There are also many women who do not wear polleras and nevertheless consider themselves to be not only jaqi, but Aymara nationalists.

Dominga's comments illustrate the instability of these indices of identity over time and across space: In her mother's time wearing a pollera was an indicator of being a misti and bilingual, not jaqi monolingual; in La Paz today the pollera is widely worn by women born in the city and fluent in Spanish and is not simply an index of being indian. Significantly, for Dominga, the hundreds of thousands of La Paz and El Alto residents who identify as indigenous are not, in her eyes, jaqi—not even her sister.

My *compadre* Remegio, someone who was clearly concerned about the issues of the distinction between jaqi and q'ara, was less clear that jaqi can become misti but was more concerned with the way migrants reject their roots. "They don't even want to look at their own father, no, they are disgusted with him. 'Old man' they call him, and from afar they will even say he is not their father. They are disgusted and they disown him (*axtasxapxi desconosxapxiwa*). Yes, those are they who do not want to learn Aymara."

If my comadre Dominga is shy, my other comadre, Maruja, is the exact opposite. Maruja, as is the case with most women of her age, had only three years of (very bad) education—a fact that pains her—but there is no question that she is very intelligent, and I will never forget her insistent questions about the causes of the Iraq War. Perhaps it is her curiosity as much as anything else that ensures she always seems comfortable with me and confident in our discussions and debates. On one occasion I was probing her on the issues of racial identification and she lost no time in putting me straight, going further even than her sister-in-law, Dominga, in understanding the change of identity as one moves away from the Aymara-speaking rural world; for her, migration does not only mean becoming misti but even q'ara.

And so jaqi in the past may have gone to La Paz, their children may have gone. They may stay a very long time. They could come out of Caranavi and then make their homes in La Paz. [If you were to do that] you would no longer understand Aymara—those who are born in La Paz cannot speak Aymara—and then you would be called q'ara. The children of jaqi too can be called q'ara. Things can change a lot: You could have a lot of money and then jaqi will call you misti, you're really a misti, like the q'aras. My children's children could look like q'aras; jaqi would call them q'ara. That is the way it is.

Rather like Dominga, Maruja associates being q'ara with speaking Spanish and living an urban life, and perhaps the implicit difference between misti and q'ara here is money: Money is what makes you q'ara, and in the age-old Latin American formulation, "money whitens." It is interesting that Maruja didn't say that upwardly mobile people behave like q'aras, but that her grandchildren could *look* like q'aras.

To an extent, the converse is also true: If money whitens, poverty indianizes; but we must be careful not to overly determine ethnicity as a function of class. During a long conversation with Juana about the differences between mistis and jaqi, I raised the case of the people of Villa Esquivel who, despite working the fields, speaking Aymara, and being poor, were not jaqi. Juana reduced the difference between the Villa Esquiveleños and Wila Kjarkeños to something quite simple: "They are white people and we are brown people (*janquw jupanakas nanakas morenupta ukatay*). It is tempting to see this as a confirmation that all can be reduced to phenotype, but that would be an overly simple conclusion, although it does point to the role physical appearance has in someone's ethnic identity. The people of Villa Esquivel are, generally, fairer skinned than those of Wila Kjarka, but not all Villa Esquiveleños are lighter than all Wila Kjarkeños, many of whom, after all, are also descendants of Europeans. But Juana's comment does indicate that we must not forget that phenotype remains one of the diagnostics of identity, even if it is not the sole determinant or always the most salient.

OF STONES AND SAINTS

Religious practice is one of the key differences between Wila Kjarkeños and those they consider to be nonjaqi. It is, by now, almost five hundred years since the Spanish arrived with their horses, swords, and Bibles.

Religion was not just another European import along with rice, cows, and pigs; religion for the Spanish was explicitly a tool of conquest. Roman Catholicism supplied the ideological justification for the conquest and colonization of America and the subjugation of its people. The Conquistadores thus read out the *Requerimiento*, the Requirement, before going into battle. The Requerimiento was a response to a political crisis with its roots in the complaints of Dominican friars on Hispaniola who were heavily critical of the treatment of indians by the Spanish. The Requerimiento made clear the legitimacy of the Spanish Conquest of the New World and the role its new subjects would play in it. Here, below, is an excerpt of a long and tedious account of how the Pope came to be ruler over all the peoples on the earth and how he gave the New World to the King and Queen of Spain:

> One of these Pontiffs, who succeeded [St. Peter] in the dignity and seat which I have mentioned, as Lord of the world made donation of these isles and Terra Firma of the Ocean sea to the aforementioned King and Queen [of Castile and Leon] and to their successors in these kingdoms, with all that they hold, as is contained in certain writings which referred to the subject as previously mentioned, which you can see if you wish.
>
> So their Highnesses are kings and lords of these islands and land of Terra Firma by virtue of this donation: and since some islands, and indeed almost all those to whom this has been notified, have received and served their Highnesses, as lords and kings, in the way that subjects ought to do, with good will, without any resistance, immediately, without delay, when they were informed of the aforementioned facts, the religious men that their Highnesses sent in order to preach and teach our Holy Faith and all of these in their free and agreeable will, without recompense or condition, became Christian and remain so; and their Highnesses received them benignly and with joy and ordered that they be treated as their other subjects and vassals; and you are held and obliged to do the same.
>
> Wherefore, as best we can, we request and require that you consider what we have said, and that you take all the time that be necessary to understand and deliberate upon it, and that you acknowledge the Church as Queen and Superior of the whole world, and the High Pontiff called Pope, and in his name the King and Queen Doña Juana our lords, in his place, as superiors and Monarchs of these islands and this Terra Firma by virtue of said donation, and that you consent and give place that these religious fathers should declare and preach to you the aforementioned.

If you do so and that to which you are held and obliged, you will do well; and their Highnesses and we in their name, shall receive you with all love and charity, and shall leave you, your wives, and your children, and your lands, free without servitude, that you may do with them and with yourselves freely that which you like and think best, and they shall not compel you to turn Christians, unless you yourselves, when informed of the truth, should wish to be converted to our Holy Catholic Faith, as almost all the inhabitants of the rest of the islands have done. And, besides this, their Highnesses award you many privileges and exemptions and will grant you many benefits.

But, if you do not do this, and maliciously make delay, I certify to you that, with the help of God, we shall powerfully enter into your country, and shall make war against you in all ways and manners that we can, and shall subject you to the yoke and obedience of the Church and of their Highnesses; we shall take your persons and your wives and your children, and shall make slaves of them, and as such shall sell and dispose of them as their Highnesses may command; and we shall take your goods, and shall do you all the mischief and damage that we can, as we would to vassals who do not obey, and refuse to receive their lord, and resist and contradict him; and we protest that the deaths and damages which shall follow from this are your fault, and not that of their Highnesses, or ours, nor of these knights who come with us. (Zavala 1988: 215–17)

Any resistance, in other words, and the inhabitants of the New World would be subject to abject servitude and forced conversion. This was read out in Spanish (although there were some recorded attempts to translate it), often far from the ears of the uncomprehending indians—and sometimes even at sea—but it was clearly read out nevertheless, and there are even earlier versions of this 1513 Requerimiento.

The Spanish arrived in the New World having just completed what they termed the Reconquest of Iberia from Islam, and that momentum was simply and almost seamlessly carried into the Americas. The patron saint of Spain, who was known as Santiago Matamoros (Saint James Slayer of Moors) was renamed Santiago Mataindios (Saint James Slayer of Indians), and a statue of Santiago dressed as a conquistador stands in the church of Ilabaya today.

Although there were many groups, such as the Dominicans, who defended the treatment of indians, for much of the last five hundred years the Catholic Church has been an integral part of the colonial and repub-

Santiago as Conquistador.
Statue in the cantonal capital, Ilabaya.

lican bureaucracy, with the specific brief of caring for indians. As Michael Sallnow points out, the concomitant subordination of religion to politics ensured that "Catholicism in the Andes was to become first and foremost a mechanism of political and social control and only secondarily an ethical and spiritual teaching" (1987: 50). But this, of course, was a long time ago, and the fervor of the Conquest and later Extirpation of Idolatries gave way to a more tolerant Church, which learned to see indian customs as "superstitions" rather than "paganism," even as it maintained a privileged position in the colonial and republican states. Well into the twentieth century the Catholic Church opposed the education of indians on the grounds that it would corrupt them and allied itself with the landowning class, which held much of the population as serfs.

Today almost all Wila Kjarkeños unequivocally see themselves as believers of God and all are baptized. But what does this actually mean? In the past, and indeed today, priests would explicitly attempt to syncretize belief in the earth mother, *pachamama,* with the Virgin Mary. She is sometimes referred to as the Virgin pachamama, even though virginity is most certainly not a salient feature of the pachamama's identity; in fact, her virginity is antithetical to the ideas surrounding the pachamama, who is sexually opened every plowing season in August, a fact that accounts for why plowing is considered such a masculine task.

In more recent years the Catholic Church has embraced the idea of inculturation, which sees local practices, such as llama sacrifice, as "incultured" forms of the crucifixion (Orta 2004). When priests not only tolerate but give their imprimatur to such practices, they certainly lend legitimacy to them, but it is by no means clear that the people who participate and witness the ripping out of the beating heart of a llama have *any* sense at all of its parallels, apparently obvious to the priest, with more orthodox Christian beliefs.

I am not suggesting that we can imagine an orthodox Catholic faith on the one side and a pagan indian one on the other. As Thomas Abercrombie has so wonderfully detailed, much of contemporary indigenous religions borrows and has borrowed greatly from the Catholic tradition. One can, however, distinguish beliefs, practices, and rituals on the basis of the object to which they are offered. Wila Kjarkeños make a systematic distinction between Jesus and God in the sky, and everything else. Everything else may include saints and virgins, but they are understood as being in a different sphere to God and Jesus, if not actually antithetical to them. Shamans will conduct their rituals in darkness or, at least, in shade precisely because the sun/son of God is inimical to these rituals; the most powerful shaman is known as the *ch'amakani,* "he who controls the powers of darkness." Perhaps most important of all is the lack of any appreciation that God is a just god, much less a benevolent one.

On one of those very rare occasions that a priest came to Wila Kjarka, he gave a sermon (in Spanish) to the congregation. Leaving aside for a moment the fact that few understood what he was saying, it is worthy to note that on one occasion I witnessed he spoke at length of the *genuine* faith and religiosity of Wila Kjarkeños, and explicitly connected not only the pachamama to the Virgin Mary but the *achachilas,* the tutelary spirits of the earth and mountains, with God the Father. The Wila Kjarkeños I spoke to later most certainly did not grasp this association: God the Father lives in the sky/heaven (*alaxpacha*), and his primary role in human lives is to bring hail as punishment for not baptizing children. God the Father certainly exists in the eyes of Wila Kjarkeños, but he is neither a benign or munificent

Close-up of painting of Illampu on the altar of the church in Sorata.

god. The achachilas, on the other hand, are the ancestral spirits who not only bring rain but also wisdom and guidance. They live in the earth but especially in the high mountain peaks such as Illampu.

In the colonial church in Sorata is a painting of Illampu, right behind the altar and under a statue of Jesus. It has long been the practice to raise churches on top of temples and convert pagan shrines into Christian ones.

Mountain passes will often have *calvarios* in the form of a cross and a pile of stones at their base, where travelers offer libations to the *achachilas*. Even in recent times some of these have been converted into chapels. Wila Kjarka, as with every other indigenous community in the area, has its own calvario where people go, especially in the month of August, to make offerings to the chthonic spirits. In Wila Kjarka these offerings are most certainly not offered to God the Father in heaven, but it is not clear to whom those seated in the church in Sorata are offering their prayers. Nor are the motives of the Church in placing a painting of the mountain behind the altar clear; it seems very unlikely that this highly unusual act was not informed by the belief that this mountain was sacred to many of the local people.

It is not merely at the level of symbolism that Christian and non-Christian images can be juxtaposed in this way. Downriver from Sorata, the village of San Pedro provides a very good illustration of how the Church's rituals can be interwoven with indigenous rituals in a tight choreography but where the *object* of the ritual clearly diverges.

THE FIESTA OF SAN PEDRO

In the nearby village of San Pedro is a chapel with a figure in stone. This stone, depicting alternatively Saint Peter or Jesus Christ (depending on whom one asks), was found near the river and brought up to the village.

As the story goes, a long time ago the rock was found by the river. It had the form of a man killing a rattlesnake with his foot. They tried to take the rock to the village (or alternatively Sorata), but it became heavier and heavier. Then they tried to cut it down to a smaller size, but a piece flew off and broke a man's foot. The next day the stone mysteriously disappeared and was found again on a small plateau nearer the river. Once again, the villagers brought it up to the village only to have the same thing occur the following night. After this happened three times, the saint then appeared to a man in a dream and said his name was Pascual (cf. *Pascua,* that is, Easter) and that he didn't want to be moved. And so they built a church around the spot where the rock was first found.

This figure is said to have rid the valley of snakes and thus made it inhabitable. The elements of this myth are common to other parts of the Andes. Isbell (1978: 65) recounts a similar myth of a statue appearing in a place, placed in a church, and then reappearing at the site in which it was first found until a chapel was built. Sallnow (1987: 70) notes that the association with water—in this case a river—is characteristic of many of these shrines.

The fiesta of San Pedro is not held on the feast day of the eponymous Saint Peter (June 29) but on the Thursday after Easter—a very rare case of a movable feast for a village fiesta. The very name of the fiesta is a source of confusion. On the side of the church the plaques refer to La Fiesta de San Pedro, La Fiesta del Señor de San Pedro, La Fiesta del Señor de San Pedro de Pascua, and other combinations of these (The Feast of San Pedro, the Feast of Our Lord of San Pedro, the Feast of Our Lord of San Pedro of Easter). Most people, however, simply refer to it as the fiesta of San Pedro.

*Whereas mestizo sponsors contract expensive brass bands
from far away, they also contract local musicians.*

Brass band from the altiplano contracted by the fiesta sponsors.

The Rock of San Pedro. Any detail is obscured by the crucifix.

The Rock of San Pedro is processed by women before the saint/Jesus carried by men. It was impossible for me to get close enough to see any detail of the rock, but in this detail we see a similar juxtaposition to what we saw in the church in Sorata: the icon of chthonic power juxtaposed with the image of Jesus.

The fiesta attracts miners from the gold mines far to the east. On the eve of the fiesta they make their way with torches along the treacherous path that follows the river from Sorata to make offerings to the stone.[4] They become drunk, of course, as happens at every fiesta, and pour libations. They also offer coca and even gold dust as well as make a holocaust of a llama fetus (*sullu*). The following day the priest comes from Sorata to say mass and the stone is paraded by the sponsors (always miners). Meanwhile there is much dancing: *morenadas* depicting black slaves in the mines as well as the parrot dance with feathers from jungle birds. The dances and music index chthonic power. The power behind rocks and mountains is on the same plane as the jungle (*manqhapacha*), as all are deemed to be below the surface of the earth. The dead travel down to the jungle where, over time, they return as tutelary mountain spirits, or achachilas.

There is a tight juxtaposition of imagery and symbols here: Jesus for Wila Kjarkeños is explicitly associated with the sun, whereas the achachilas are associated with rain; the mestizos show their economic wealth by contracting expensive brass bands, whereas the indigenous people participate through explicitly autochthonous dance and music.

When I spoke to the priest a week later he was very clear that he was celebrating Easter four days late "as is the custom here." No one else seemed to think they were celebrating Easter. In fact, when I asked if this was an Easter celebration, my question was greeted with laughter. Did I not know that Easter was four days before?

At its most superficial, the fiesta is a Christian feast, and the priest even manages to convince himself that it is an Easter celebration. It is in the interest neither of the celebrants nor of the priest for the latter to be enlightened. The priest's attendance adds greater importance and legitimacy to the fiesta and the consecration of the stone. For the priest to abandon the fiesta would further alienate the peasants from the Church by reducing even more the contact they have with it, and so it is convenient for him to believe, as did so many priests when the fervor of the Extirpation died, that through the juxtaposition of practices and symbols the true message will eventually emerge.

The phenomenon of San Pedro is one of many examples of beliefs in the Andes in which humans or other beings are somehow petrified, their energy slowly radiating out (MacCormack 1991: 323; Sallnow 1987). It is also an example of how the cults around these rocks were co-opted by missionaries and the Extirpators of Idolatry into Christian shrines (Sallnow 1987); the shrines above them were destroyed and frequently Christian shrines built in their place. People continued to worship the *wak'a* and over time the saint or its image was attributed with the tellurian powers of the manqhapacha. San Pedro is but one example of this phenomenon, which occurs all over the Andes: "Andeans placed their own holy objects next to Christian images of saints. In this way, while seeming to revere a Christian image, Andeans could secretly pay homage to their huacas. Indeed, the very appearance of Spanish religious images invited such an approach. For their sheer naturalism, their lifelike glass eyes, their blushing complexions, and their wardrobes filled with jeweled clothing, invited Andeans to perceive in them the huacas and mallquis of Christians, whose very existence authorized the worship of their Andean counterparts" (MacCormack 1991: 180–81).

A supreme example of this is the cult of the Virgen de Copacabana. Copacabana is the site of a pilgrimage center dating back to before the Inca period and is on the shores of Lake Titicaca in the *altiplano* region. The Spanish converted this center into a focus for Christian pilgrimage by erecting a large cross on the hill and later a magnificent basilica on the site. Copacabana retains many of the elements of the pre-Christian religion to this day. On the path up to the top are the Stations of the Cross. As the pilgrims make their way up, they place a small stone on a pile as they would do for an *apachita*, a sacred mountain pass. At the very top is the large cross. But a few meters below are several small altars where the ritual practitioners, the *yatiris*, make burnt offerings to the *pachamama*. The Franciscans who administer the center take a relatively benign view of all the other practices around them, including the burnt offerings, largely I believe, as with the priest in San Pedro, because the consequences of disallowing such practices would mean the end of Copacabana as a site of pilgrimage for most of the devotees.

It would seem that the people of San Pedro and their neighbors, such as the people of Wila Kjarka, have succeeded in convincing at least their local priest of their religiosity. In conversation with me sometime later, it emerged, however, that his criteria for fellowship in the faith were remarkably basic: belief in God, Christian marriage, and baptism. He considered the comprehension of basic tenets of Catholic beliefs such as Transubstantiation, the Virgin Birth, and the Mystery of the Trinity to be quite beyond the indians, and therefore one could hardly have these as criteria for membership of the Catholic community. It is also perhaps worth noting that he did not mention Jesus. His stress on marriage and baptism not only to me but to Wila Kjarkeños on the one occasion he visited the community is quite significant. These are the two things Wila Kjarkeños require of the Church.

As far as Wila Kjarkeños are concerned, attendance at mass is an irrelevance, with the exception of the mass for the dead. They also think the notion that a priest should attend to a funeral ceremony quite bizarre. The distance from Sorata and the infrequency of the priest's visits allow Wila Kjarkeños to negotiate their own relationship with the Church to a large degree. With so little pressure from the Church, they are quite free to interpret Christian beliefs in a way that is meaningful to them without running the risk of being contradicted by the priest who does not, at any rate, speak Aymara.

The use of the cross in many rituals is not recognized as a referent to Jesus, at least not by Wila Kjarkeños. As Isbell (1978: 138) says of the people of Chuschi, it is a much broader symbol of general religious power that serves to remind participants of the sacredness and seriousness of the events under way. The place of the cross in religious belief is a good example of the appropriation of religious elements by indigenous Andeans. After the Conquest, and especially during the Extirpation of Idolatry, officers of the Holy Inquisition destroyed many of the visible icons and shrines of local religion. They were, however, unable to raze entire mountains, and in those cases they frequently built chapels on top of them, much in the manner of Copacabana. Mountain passes are, for many Andean people, an important focus of religious belief. These apachitas, as they are called, are mounds of stones offered to the achachilas and are often sites of simple offerings. Many of them have been marked with a cross, and the cross has become an emblem of the potency of the apachita. This process continues in modern times. One example is an apachita on the way to the altiplano, which was originally a pile of stones and stone altars, where offerings and sacrifices were given. Then a large cross was placed there, and finally, a chapel was built. The site continues to be the venue for offerings of alcohol and coca as well as small sacrifices.

The cross, then, is a symbol of power in a wider sense and its presence cannot be taken to mean that the site has a particularly Christian significance (Bastien 1978: 69; González 1986). This is further illustrated by the belief that large mountains, such as Illampu near Wila Kjarka, have crosses on their summits. Illampu is one of the principal named achachilas of northern Bolivia. On its summit there is reputed to be a solid-gold cross the height of a man and surrounded by orange and other fruit trees.[5] The polysemic property of the symbol of the cross, Joseph Bastien argues, can tokenly satisfy the conquering people with one meaning, while it can also refer to another meaning within the culture (1978: 60). This "polysemic property of the cross" may, however, be due more to the fortuitous juxtaposition of two separate symbols with different cultural referents than to a single symbol with the same referents for all involved. In fact, as Sallnow (1987: 175) has argued, it is generally the case that the Christian system is largely devoid of symbolism for Andean peoples; it is a system of emblems, arbitrarily signaling division and union, and equality and rank, but lacking intrinsic motivation.

Expanding on Stanley Tambiah's distinction between the indexical and symbolic component of ritual (1979: 154 passim) and following Sallnow (1987), we can see that this distinction illuminates the difference between Christianity and the autochthonous[6] religion of the animate landscape. "Both systems program ritual processes of differentiation and hierarchy. But whereas in the one these processes necessarily operate through cultural ideas of fertility and reproduction, in the other they operate for the most part independent of such understandings" (Sallnow 1987: 174). The duplex structure of ritual noted by Tambiah only holds true for Andean religion where the processes of natural and social reproduction are fused. Christian representation is devoid of symbolism in this sense and merely produces a series of indices of cultural difference, social status, civil power, and historical domination.

With an understanding of this singular rather than duplex nature of Christianity, the juxtaposition of religious elements from both Christianity and autochthonous religion does not then appear to constitute a syncretic synthesis because these elements do not have the same symbolic content. It is once again because of this singular nature of Christianity that it can be and is seen as historically contingent rather than constituting an indispensable element of religious and social life.

As we shall explore in greater detail in the next chapter, the arrival of God the Father with a light that blinded the *chullpa* ancestors and sent them underground is an act of power and domination, not of love or salvation. God is a political fact; not the route to redemption.

While accepting that God and Jesus preside over the cosmos in a broad sense, when it comes to daily life the forces of below—even those explicitly rejected by the Christian god—are of more practical help. There are no Christian rites for making rain, for averting frost, or for producing a good harvest, and it is in these agricultural rites that the pagan religion is most in force. There is no competition with the Christian deities because, contrary to the belief of the Spanish missionaries, indigenous spirits are not conceived of in the same sense as Christian ones. Wila Kjarkeños enter into an exchange relationship with the achachilas, pachamama, or *Tiu*, the mine deity, who possess the forces of production from the earth, rain, mines, and the like.

There is no elaborated transactional ethic in the relations people have with God: With God there is no exchange relationship at all. There exists only a relationship of negative reciprocity: God visits his wrath upon the people below for no apparent reason and the people have no way of appeasing him. The one general exception to this is the failure to baptize a child. This is the only occasion most of my informants could cite when God predictably, rather than capriciously, becomes angry. One informant, however, told me that the lack of a Christian wedding could likewise court disaster with God, and he expressed his concern at the fact that there were couples in Wila Kjarka who were not married and did not seem intent on ever doing so. Wila Kjarkeños, however, frequently do not baptize their children until their second or third birthday, and the lack of baptism is used as an ex post facto explanation for a calamity that has no other cause.

Despite the consistency of this belief among Wila Kjarkeños, no one could cite an occasion when the failure to baptize a child did, in fact, result in ecological calamity. This is all the more remarkable given the abundance of evidence of ecological disasters in Wila Kjarka such as erosion, droughts, crop pestilence, and floods. God's punishment is conceived by Wila Kjarkeños more as a continuous thing, the general and arbitrary source of sadness and pain, rather than a specific act of punishment. Víctor Ochoa, who worked in an altiplano community, quotes one of his informants, who renders the relationship between God and people quite simply: "God punishes the community and man. That is why we have the saying, *Diosaw k'apispacha* (God must be full of wrath), *ucatwa aqham llaquinac apayanistu* (this is why he visits these calamities upon us)" (1975: 10). This relationship with God is resonant of the view Wila Kjarkeños generally have of the outside world, one of arbitrary hostility. Catherine Allen describes the way the people of Sonqo in Peru see God as a "big Hacendado in the sky": "Imposed on a traumatised population after the Spanish Conquest, the Catholic God, modeled on the Hispanic *patrón*, epitomizes Hispanic domination. He has nothing to do with [native people], yet they live and die according to his beneficence" (Allen 1988: 52).

Allen provides us with an interesting insight, for we can begin to see why—if God is hostile to Wila Kjarkeños and given that they attribute their natural fertility so clearly to the pachamama, the earth goddess, and the attendant spirits of the tellurian realm—they would feel the need to have Christian baptisms and weddings. At root is the essential relation between Wila Kjarkeños and the world around them, which is drawn out in terms of cosmology in the following chapter. For all the elaboration of relationships with the chthonic world of the manqhapacha, Wila Kjarkeños realize and accept that the overarching presiding deity is the Christian one.

There are then two related reasons for the necessity of baptism and Christian marriage. It is my impression that these are regarded as a kind of insurance, a prophylaxis against a wrathful and jealous God. The second reason is that Wila Kjarkeños are very aware of the importance Christian baptism and marriage has in Bolivian society: It is a badge of civilization, the first step toward obtaining a Bolivian identity card and, like military service, an important step to becoming accepted by and included in that wider society. Moreover, as with the hacendado of old, Wila Kjarkeños depend on God to function well in the national society and, more important, they are dependent on his good will to cultivate *their* land. Wila Kjarkeños are analogously dependent on the Christian god, the power that be, for the freedom to cultivate their land and the land of their ancestors. As a result, the pachamama and achachilas are not sufficient to ensure the well-being and fertility of people and their crops. Wila Kjarkeños must harness the powers of the manqhapacha on the one hand, while at the same time ensuring that the wrathful eye of God is not cast upon them.

In the following two chapters we will look in greater depth at how the beings of the manqhapacha influence the lives of people on the surface of the earth. They do much more than simply act as presiding deities over the lives of jaqi, but rather, the very relationship people have with these beings is precisely what makes them jaqi in the first place.

TWO

Intimate Histories

As we saw in the previous chapter, Wila Kjarkeños are embedded in a set of social relationships that play out in a complex social geography. Their social relationships do not, however, simply extend across space but through time as well. The Andes is a profoundly historical place: Everywhere one travels there are churches, squares, houses, tombs, forts, and roads of the various people who have lived in the area over the centuries. The area around Wila Kjarka is no exception. For years I had speculated about the stone walls and ancient terracing I had seen, but in 2011 I visited Wila Kjarka with archaeologist Alejandra Korstanje, who confirmed (and corrected) many of my assumptions.[1]

The place where Wila Kjarkeños make their August offerings is clearly a pre-Columbian site with the indications of pre-Inka burials. In fact, through Alejandra's eyes I learned to see that the entire area is simply filled with burial sites, not to mention retaining walls to stop erosion (which still work), terracing, other stone walls, and roads. Within the village lands, approximately three hundred meters above the current nucleated settlement, lie the ruins of what Wila Kjarkeños call *Chullpa Patana*—a place where people find human remains and tell tales of the riches that one might find as well as the illnesses one might suffer when dealing with these ancient bones. Every now and again someone using a long metal pole to break the earth for planting hits something hollow. He might find a burial site and some ceramics, and a number of Wila Kjarkeños have their own pre-Columbian collections.

Higher up and just across the boundary with the village of Qhusim-ani is a more extensive site with terraces for crops and a *kancha,* an Inka square, oriented almost due east and facing Illampu squarely on. Nearby there is a large man-made platform, which, Alejandra informed me, is pre-Inka and was probably a site the Inkas used to impress upon local people their political and religious power. In Wila Kjarka itself lie the remains of pre-Columbian walls, and all is visible to the eye without any excavation or sophisticated investigation.

There can be no doubt that Wila Kjarka has been inhabited for hundreds if not thousands of years and that in the past this area was much more densely populated than today. For Wila Kjarkeños these people of the past, the *chullpas,* are their ancestors, not direct-line ancestors according to a genealogical model, but ancestors nevertheless.

If indigeneity means anything at all, it is a relationship between a contemporary people with others that predates the current hegemony, in this case, the arrival of the Spanish Conquistadors that turned Inkas, Collas, and the like into indians dominated by Europeans and their descendants. This may appear to be a somewhat oversimplified picture, but it is one that resonates strongly today.

It seems self-evident that the people of Wila Kjarka are descendants of those people who occupied the territory before Europeans arrived. One could offer an archaeological history of the Wila Kjarka area, starting with the civilization of Tiwanaku—which spanned the sixth to twelfth centuries—followed by Mollos, Collas, Inkas, Spaniards, and so on. One could then trace the continuities across time to make the case that Wila Kjarkeños are culturally as well as genealogically indigenous. There are, however, a number of problems with such an exercise, not least because historians such as Thomas Abercrombie (1999) and Sabine MacCormack (1991) have carefully documented the ways in which the culture of indigenous Andeans since the Conquest has developed through a process of contestation, absorption, and co-optation. There are various elements, especially in the area of religion, which have been imposed or imported but have nevertheless become deeply rooted in a non-European worldview.

Thomas Abercrombie, in his work, *Pathways of Memory and Power* (1998), uses extensive documentary and ethnographic resources to demonstrate that the cultural practices of Andean people have developed over time, absorbing many aspects of European culture and making them their own. His historiography undermines the distinction between indigenous and European practices. The people of Wila Kjarka today are certainly products of various historical processes, and to start to tease out indigenous and European influences would be a sterile exercise; indigenous authenticity is not to be found in "proving" historical continuities.

Judith Friedlander in her highly influential book, *Being Indian in Hueyapan: A Study of Forced Identity in Contemporary Mexico* (1975), which has recently been republished (2006), puts forward the contrasting argument that Mexican indigenous culture is essentially bankrupt:

> The Hueyapeños' indigenous culture is in ruins and has been for centuries. Nevertheless, the villagers are acutely aware of still being Indians, for they are continuously so designated by outsiders. Few pre-Spanish customs actually survive in Hueyapan today. What is more, most of those that do lost their prehispanic significance long ago and display only the merest traces of the past . . . Thus from the perspective of "culture," the villagers are virtually indistinguishable from non-Indian Mexicans. Where they do differ is in their social status within the larger society.
>
> I suggest that the Hueyapeños' so-called Indian identity relates far more precisely to their low socioeconomic position in the national stratification system than it does to their culture. Since early colonial times the villagers have served as a source of cheap labor for the upper classes. As they worked the colonizers' lands, their Indian blood was diluted and their culture dramatically altered . . . I hope to demonstrate that their Indian-ness is not a distinct cultural entity but, rather, a reflection of the culture of a highly stratified society. (Friedlander 1975: xv)

She notes that much of what constitutes indigenous culture today is nothing more than the castoffs of creole or mestizo cultures of previous generations. Being indian in Hueyapan is to suffer discrimination and poverty on the basis of an indian culture that is essentially illusory and only serves to index these poor Mexicans' marginal position (1975: 190–91).

Friedlander's arguments are important to consider because in recent years the debate as to who is indigenous has passed beyond the confines of the academic world. The International Labour Organization, the World Bank, and the United Nations—not to mention the countless NGOs that

follow these multilateral organizations in developing their policies—
define *indigenous* in terms of continuity with a pre-Conquest people. The
arguments that Friedlander has put forward for Hueyapeños are equally
applicable to almost any other indigenous group in the Americas and
raise some serious questions as to why multilateral agencies should be
directing their efforts toward one group of poor Latin Americans over another, simply on the basis of their putative indigeneity.

In a more recent intervention, Adam Kuper (2003) has raised a related
set of objections to the use of the concept *indigenous*. He makes the point,
quite rightly in my view, that *indigenous* is not sensu stricto an anthropological concept—that is, it is not a meaningful analytical category for
distinguishing one group of people from another in the same way as gender, class, and age. Anthropology is not equipped to make such distinctions, and as a profession we should certainly be wary of becoming mired
in arguing that, for example, Bushmen of the Kalahari are indigenous,
whereas their neighbors the Tswana are not or, in Latin American terms,
that the people of Wila Kjarka are indigenous but their neighbors in Villa
Esquivel are not. Nevertheless this is precisely what many anthropologists do, sometimes resurrecting quite essentialist categories they would
in other contexts be very uncomfortable wielding in order to defend the
land rights of a certain people.

In contemporary Bolivia there are many understandings of what it
means to be indigenous. Felipe Quispe, the most dominant indigenous
politician until Evo Morales's ascent, has often been accused of being racist by mestizo and creole commentators who see in much of what he says,
quite accurately, a challenge to their position within the country. So, for
example, when he proposed replacing the Department of Indigenous Affairs with a Department for Gringo Affairs, he was roundly criticized for
reducing social relations in Bolivia to stark categories of indians and nonindians and being racist toward white people. The sheer venom of the responses that this and other comments have elicited obscures the fact that
Quispe has much more of a sense of humor than many appreciate and
was merely pointing out the incongruity of a Department of Indigenous
Affairs when the fact that one is needed simply points out the marginal
position indigenous people have in the country. It is worth noting that
Evo Morales immediately abolished the department when coming into
office on the grounds that "all affairs in Bolivia are indigenous ones."

Quispe, nevertheless, does sometimes express a vision of Aymara identity in ways that resonate with nineteenth-century European ideas of race

and nation. He proposes an "Aymara nation" and an unbroken historical connection with the Tiwanaku civilization, offering an uncomplicated vision of historical continuity between the people of Tiwanaku almost two millennia ago and contemporary Aymara people. He proposes nothing less than the refounding of Qullasuyu, the name the Inkas gave for this part of their empire, more or less coterminous with highland Bolivia. This has been a powerful argument, because large numbers of people today identify as Aymara, whereas twenty years ago hardly anybody did. In conversation with me (in Aymara), Quispe offered a clear vision of historical injustice as well as an account of what "Aymara thought" might be, which was my question. I asked Quispe, "So today, at this moment in time, is there such a thing as an 'Aymara way of thinking'?" He responded:

> Well yes, as I just told you. There is such a thing as an Aymara way of thinking: govern this—our nation, our land. This land is ours from the greatest depths to the loftiest heights, right up there. This is what we have in our nation; we have a lot of wealth: we have gold, silver, petroleum, gas; we have agricultural products; we have lakes and rivers and we have mountains. This is a joy; this is a blessed nation. But all of these things are being sold; this is not good for us. And so, in other words, we want to recover our nation.
>
> From the day the Spanish came from their towns in Spain, truly from that day they humiliated us: they destroyed our people; they murdered our wise people; they murdered the Inkas; they destroyed our customs; they murdered us and exterminated us. Now we have nothing. Those who speak with strong voices, those who have resisted them, they quartered them: Tupak Katari, Tupak Amaru, Bartolina Sisa, Micaela Bastidas, and many other men and women who fought to free our people. But they brought with them a saying: I want everything for me alone. Only one person becomes wealthy, only one person exploits many people; that person becomes rich and governs. But that is not how it is in our culture: everything is for everyone and belongs to everyone; for the community, for those of us who live in a community or *ayllu*. In the ayllus we lived happily but now there are very few of those; under conditions of scarcity it was a help to everyone and we want to return to that. Let's talk about that, *ayni*. Ayni is when you help me when, for example, I am roofing my house. Someone may bring poles, another thatch; someone else will bring the food. A lot of help may appear and that is ayni. Another example is when someone is hosting a fiesta, there too we have this institution of

Remegio plowing his land. He only owns one of those cows. The other cow and the plow itself belong to someone else, for which he has borrowed, in an ayni *exchange.*

mutual help; but this help has to be returned, it will be returned; and in this, money makes no appearance. Money has no role; you cannot sell the labor of another person. The person who does *ayni* does it with all his heart, and in that you do not pay. Then there is *mink'a*: you have to ask for that but in mink'a you don't pay with money but, rather, with produce. Then there is *qamaña* [to live], where we live, with our children, with our elders, where the family lives. This is *qamäwi* [the way of life, literally, "the living"]. Finally I would like to refer to *waki*. In this one offers one's land to another who sows the seed. At harvest time the produce is divided in two. That is our culture, these are the four pillars of our culture, you could say.

Quispe here is not only offering a particular vision of historical injustice visited upon his people at the hands of the Spanish and their descendants but also a vision of Aymara culture which is about harmony, sharing, communal life, and the four pillars of mutual aid. It is not clear, however, how widely accepted this view of history is. The Inkas, with whom Quispe allies here and elsewhere, were, after all, the conquerors of Qullasuyu only a few decades before the arrival of the Spanish, and this is the reason that the Aymara-speaking lords supported the Spanish against the Inkas. Perhaps more interesting is the way Quispe presents a rather romantic view of Aymara culture: the four pillars, all of which are centered on communal living, mutual aid, and an economy that is not based on money.

A majority of the Bolivian population that was designated as indigenous in the 2001 census was urban (INE 2003), and it is difficult to see that these people would closely identify with the four pillars as outlined by Quispe. And those people who do live in rural communities, although many still use *ayni* and *mink'a* as well as *waki,* often have more complex views than Quispe suggests here. Many people choose to leave rural communities precisely to avoid the burdens of mutual aid: Ayni and mink'a can sometimes be ways of obscuring exploitative relationships; and *waki* can sometimes be translated as sharecropping, in which someone provides the seed and all work but only gets half the produce. Such practices have been widely discussed in the anthropological literature (e.g., Allen 1986; Gose 1994; Sallnow 1987), and I do not need to review them here, but the key point is the way Quispe offers a very idealized view of Aymara culture in order to provide a historical critique of Colonial exploitation and contemporary capitalism, which, any way you read it, leaves indians with few resources and on the economic margins.

Although one should be wary of these "strategic essentialisms," a concern for academic rigor should not blind us to historic injustices. Indeed, as I have argued elsewhere (2007), a claim to indigenous identity is at its root quite simply a claim to historical injustice; it is a claim to rights and resources on the basis of long-standing exclusion. This helps solve the methodological problem of how to explore indigenous consciousness among people who do not articulate an indigenous identity; the answer lies, surely, in looking at how they think of themselves as historical subjects.

What follows are two historical perspectives on the history of Wila Kjarka. The first is based on more or less standard Western historiography. I do this not necessarily to privilege such a historiography but, first, to give a context to Wila Kjarkeños' oral history, and second, because such a historical sketch, albeit brief, offers an account of why the people of Wila Kjarka came to be indians—that is, how they went from being relatively wealthy members of a Tiwanaku, Mollo, or Inka polity to being a poor and racialized minority in Bolivia. Moreover, and perhaps more important, this is the history on which indigenous leaders principally draw. This should not surprise us; indigenous leaders, as David Gow and Joanne Rappaport (2002) point out, are "bilingual" in the sense that they need to speak to two audiences: their own people and those who are in power. The stories they tell of the past and the way injustice is framed must be comprehensible to the state as well as to multilateral institutions such as the ILO. I am not convinced Evo Morales is bilingual in this way at all, but this is easily understood because his political background is that of a leader of a coca growers' union rather than an indigenous leader per se. What is perhaps more surprising is that Felipe Quispe's more radical position should owe so much to Western historical concepts. He produced ideas of nation, state, linear history, and a single national culture that resonate completely with a nineteenth-century idea of nationhood, not only in his interview with me but in speeches and interviews on Aymara radio and in the main square of Sorata. He also (as does Morales) adds another essentialism, which is that indigenous people are best placed to defend natural resources because of their particular affinity with them. If, as I suggest, an indigenous identity is rooted in historical consciousness, it is therefore worth looking at various historical perspectives to see how these may inform such a consciousness.

STONES, BONES, AND TOMES: A WESTERN HISTORY OF WILA KJARKA AND ITS ENVIRONS

Archaeological and other documentary evidence clearly indicates that the province of Larecaja, where Wila Kjarka is situated, was heavily populated when the Spanish arrived and had been so for at least five hundred years previously, when the area was part of the Mollo culture. In fact, everything tends to suggest that the area was more heavily populated than it is today. A few hundred meters up the mountain from Wila Kjarka are the clear remains of a village, possibly Mollo, with extant terraces and a plaza, which suggest that the site has been inhabited and cultivated for a thousand years at the very least, and quite possibly longer.

The known history of the Larecaja area goes back beyond the Inkas to the period of the Tiwanaku civilization, which reached its peak in the eighth and ninth centuries and was centered on the present-day village of Tiwanaku, thirty miles south of Lake Titicaca. Although Tiwanaku was an advanced agricultural settlement from approximately the first century onward, it was not until the fifth century that its influence began to expand beyond the immediate region of the southern shore of Lake Titicaca. At its height, its cultural and economic influence reached well into what is now Peru and Chile (Janusek 2008).

Recent archaeological work in the vicinity of Tiwanaku has revealed that its economy was founded on an extremely efficient agricultural system based on a series of canals and raised fields, which, in reconstruction, have been shown to produce seven times more potatoes per hectare than traditional methods. The water in the canals also acts as insulation against frost, which can occur at any time of the year on the altiplano (Kolata 1986).

There is some disagreement as to which language or languages were spoken by the inhabitants of Tiwanaku, and the issue is hotly debated. It seems almost certain that Aymara was one of the languages spoken, but there is compelling evidence, too, that Pukina[2] and Uru were spoken in the city as well as the environs. Not only was it multilingual, but within the city there is ample evidence that various ethnic groups lived and reproduced their local cultural styles (Janusek 2004). In short, there is overwhelming evidence that Tiwanaku was a cosmopolitan city (Janusek 2008: 157) where maybe even the elites spoke different languages.

In contemporary Bolivia, Tiwanaku is a focus of Aymara identity and nationalism, and in recent decades growing numbers of people have attended the winter solstice rites among the ruins. It was also the site of the "Tiwanaku Manifesto" in 1973, which attempted to give coherence to the indigenist *Katarismo* movement (Albó 1987: 396). In 1991, President Jaime Paz Zamora declared Tiwanaku the "diplomatic capital of Bolivia," and used the site as a setting for a number of political speeches and events. In 2006, President Evo Morales held his unconstitutional—but arguably much more legitimate in the eyes of the nation—inauguration there. The contemporary political view of Tiwanaku as an Aymara state inspires some indigenous activists to combat mestizo-creole hegemony and even seek to refound that state. The multicultural and multilingual nature of the enduring Tiwanaku civilization is ignored in favor of the single ethnic nation of nineteenth-century European nationalism.

The Mollo culture, centered in what is now the province of Larecaja, appears to have existed contemporaneously with Tiwanaku for several

centuries at a comparable, but somewhat less complex, level of development. The archaeological site of Iskanwaya, not far from Wila Kjarka, has
produced ample evidence of the sophistication of this ancient civilization, especially in the production of ceramics. The Mollo culture became
a more integral part of the Tiwanaku civilization in the latter's expansive
period between the eighth and eleventh centuries (otherwise known as
Tiwanaku V). Mollo pottery was influenced by Tiwanaku through the
ages, and during the period of Tiwanaku V much pottery in the Tiwanaku style and of Tiwanaku origin appears. Tiwanaku-style pottery has
been found dating several centuries after the fall of Tiwanaku proper in
the twelfth century. Current theory holds that the center of Tiwanaku collapsed due to a prolonged drought, which made its hydraulically based
agricultural system untenable. The population appears to have moved itself into the surrounding hills as well as to satellite cultures (Albarracín
Jordán and Mathews 1990; Janusek 2008; Kolata 1983).

To this day there are dozens of Mollo sites in the Wila Kjarka area, and
peasants are constantly coming across various types of ceramics, particularly ossuaries, in fields and other areas. In the valleys around Wila Kjarka
there are several Mollo forts surrounded by terraced fields, all within sight
of each other.

The demise of Mollo culture proper is difficult to date, but by the time
of the Inka expansion in the century preceding the Conquest there was
a coherent polity of Aymara-speaking kingdoms. The Colla "kingdom"
was one of the largest of these Aymara kingdoms and included the area
around what is present-day Wila Kjarka (Bouysse-Cassagne 1987: 211ff.).
It is unclear whether Mollo culture existed contemporaneously with or
was actually a part of the Colla kingdoms. These kingdoms were divided
into moieties, "each with its separate 'king,' and each controlling different territories. Linguistic and geographic evidence suggests that the Ur-
cusuyu [upper] division of any nation was primarily concentrated in the
mountaintop fortified centers to the west and southwest of Lake Titicaca,
with their colonies grouped along the Pacific coast, while the Umasuyu
[lower] division of any nation were in the eastern highlands and had most
of their colonies in the eastern associated valleys and montaña region"
(Klein 1992: 14).

These moieties, in turn, were composed of *ayllus*, kin groupings in
which each *ayllu* divided into an upper (*hanansaya*) half and a lower
(*urinsaya*) half. Ayllus also had colonists working and living in different
ecological zones. "Called *mitimaq*, these highland colonists were the vital

link binding the inter-regional and multi-ecological economy that was so crucial in maintaining the core highland populations" (Klein 1992: 17). To this day certain ayllus of the southern region of Norte de Potosí, such as the Macha, Laymi, and Quillaca, still maintain access to lowland areas for similar ends and in a similar manner.

The earliest record I could find for Wila Kjarka is a petition from 1618 dated August 19, 1618, in which "the principals and leaders of the *yungas ayllu* Huilajanco Carcas [i.e., Wila Kjarka and Jankho Kjarka]," of Hila-baya (Ilabaya), had cause to defend their land from the avaricious eye of a resident of La Paz and described their lands thus:

> These are lands for our natural sustenance, where we plant potatoes and ocas and other vegetables like *quinoa*, to support and maintain us, and . . . it is natural and right, since we plant maize to pay the rates and tributes; and in sterile years we make up a good bit of the rates with the *chuñu* [freeze-dried potatoes] we harvest from said lands.[3]

Access to land at higher as well as lower ecological levels has consequently long been critical to Wila Kjarkeños and their ability to hold on to lands across an altitude range—sometimes at considerable cost (as we shall see in the following chapter)—has allowed them to remain a relatively prosperous community.

The relationship of the people of this piedmont area and the highlands around Lake Titicaca appears to have been long and vital. The evidence of maize in Tiwanaku (Wright, Hastorf, and Lennstrom 2003) and Tiwanaku pottery and textiles in the valleys of Larecaja suggests a trading relationship between these two areas. Whether or not this relationship continued after the demise of Tiwanaku in the eleventh century is apparently difficult to ascertain, but it is very clear that the Inkas understood the importance of the valleys, the *yungas*, for the highland areas.

From the lowlands, maize (vital for making ritually important *k'usa*, maize beer) and fruit were exchanged for wool, meat, and various tubers. The yungas also produced a species of tuber that could not be grown in the highlands. Thus, the Inkas intensified the system of relations between colonies along a "vertical archipelago" to exploit the different ecological pistes (Murra 1980)—a relationship that existed since before Tiwanaku times. The Inkas sent colonists (*mitimaes*) to the yungas to ensure their control of the lowland areas. The colonists were also agents for political control, especially after the Aymara rebellions against Inka rule in the 1470s (Klein 1992: 19–20). The history of Larecaja is such that the ayllu organization collapsed and there was no longer the direct territorial link with the altiplano as before. It is not entirely the case, however, that "nowadays, the inhabitants of both zones, those who visit the markets and country fairs to exchange products, have lost even the memory of a kinship and common origin" (Saignes 1985: 96). As we shall see below, although Wila Kjarkeños are no longer part of a domain that includes areas of the highlands, they are very much aware of their cultural links with the peoples of the highlands and even their common origins.

This relationship appears to have been more pronounced in the first centuries of the Colonial period. Thierry Saignes quotes two people from the early Colonial period, in 1594 and 1647, who speak of the relationship with the highlanders. The first is a leader from the highlands and the second a valley dweller, both of whom respectively stress their relationship with the other region:

> It is true that the population of this province of Larecaja, since the time of the Inka, always was and has been with those said *mitimaes* indians because it is proven that there were no indians that one could describe as being native of this land and in the case that they in fact were, they could only have been few in number.
>
> We are mitimaes located here by the grandfathers and great-grandfathers of the last Inkas, generation after generation, and born and raised in those said valleys among those indigenous peoples of the yungas.[4] (Saignes 1985: 97)

Colonial Period

It took several years after the conquest of Peru for the Spanish to bring their attention to bear upon what they would call Alto (Upper) Peru, or Charkas. In 1538 Francisco Pizarro entered the highland area south of Lake Titicaca to pacify an attack of Inkas and Lupacas against the Collas, who had supported the Spanish during the conquest of Peru (Klein 1992: 34). It was this division between Aymara groups that enabled first the Inkas and then the Spanish to conquer the Aymara area.

Whatever the relationship with the people of the valleys during the Inka period, it is quite clear that those people who lived in what is now Wila Kjarka had a close association with the people of the highlands before the Spanish arrived and for many centuries previously. With the arrival of the Spanish this unity between highland and lowland was broken as the territory was divided into *corregimientos*—administrative units based on towns populated by Spanish landowners—and surrounded by *encomiendas* created from grants given by the Crown. It was common for the Crown to grant conquistadores the right to indian labor and the produce of their land (but not necessarily title to the land itself). This was known as the *encomienda* system, and the owners of these encomiendas were known as *encomenderos*. The *encomendero* was also required to pay for the religious education of the indians and otherwise acculturate the indians to Spanish norms (Klein 1992: 37).

The corregimiento of Larecaja with Sorata as its capital was founded in 1590. This administrative creation effected a bureaucratic separation between the Sorata area and the Omasuyos region with which it had been culturally and economically linked for centuries. The expropriation of lands had a more grievous effect on links between these areas because the ayllus no longer had lands in both ecological zones.

The indian communities that were not entirely co-opted into haciendas were legally recognized as independent indigenous communities. During the colonial period the Crown raised taxes from these independent communities headed by sometimes corrupt *curacas*, leaders, who would take their portion of the Crown's taxes and become wealthy. The Crown had an interest in keeping the independent communities viable, as they were a source of labor for the mine in Potosí (the *mita*). On some occasions, officials would come from La Paz or even the colonial capital, Lima (often referred to in the texts as the City of the Kings), to redress the grievances of indians whose lands had been stolen. These visits—or *visitas*, as they were known—were intended as a sort of survey to calculate the taxes due to the Crown and the supply of labor, the *mita*, to the mines of Potosí. It is interesting to note that the visitas of 1575 and 1583[5] reveal that native colonists from highland regions, the mitimaes, living in the Larecaja valleys outnumbered those designated as "natives" (*naturales*), that is, the original residents, by a factor of two to one.

As hacienda indians were exempt from the mita and the most burdensome taxes, it was thus one of the objects of these visitas to restore land to the communities that previously had their land illegally annexed by greedy landowners and thus ensure the continuance of the payment of taxes and the mita. These visitas then had a mitigating effect on the expropriation of independent communities' lands.

Titles to lands were, however, constantly ignored, and the Crown was forced to arrange for an extensive visita to the area by Don Gerónimo Luis de Cabrera in the years 1656–58.[6] The fact that a visita had to be repeated on various occasions indicates that the local Spaniards were progressively annexing the indians' lands to their own and largely ignoring the Crown's prerogatives. A visita by Don Gerónimo Luis de Cabrera in 1658, for example, had to be repeated as little as two years later because of the abuses that had occurred in the intervening time.

In his visita of 1660, Don Juan de Segura Danalo de Ayala, Canon of the Holy Cathedral Church of the city of La Paz and Titular Commissary of the Holy Office of the Inquisition, states that he has come to address this problem of land rights and to restore from the

> individual caciques and indians the fields, lands and estates which the General Don Geronimo Luis de Cabrera restored to their common good as much to Spaniards as to other mixtures and indians of different provinces taken this good which has been granted to the same *naturales* and *mitimaes* of said town [Ilabaya][7] thus making flee those present as well as those absent destituting them from their land grant something that must be remedied and solicited by all means according to His Majesty served by order in my keeping and of his women, children and relatives and that the Royal taxes and tributes may not lapse.[8] (Archivo de La Paz: ALP/ GLC I 1660 C.1–D.19)

This is a very clear and frank indication of the interest the Crown had in maintaining the viability of independent communities. With the overthrow of Spanish dominion in 1825, however, it was no longer in the interests of the new ruling classes to retain independent indigenous communities. In fact, as the government changed from one of Spanish officials to one of a landowning oligarchy, the attitude of the ruling elite toward indian lands changed accordingly. The indians had no one to mediate the disputes between themselves and rapacious neighboring landowners, for the latter were now the ruling class in Bolivia.

The Hacienda Period

Although independence and the foundation of a liberal republic brought indians formal recognition as citizens of the nation-state, political and judicial reality remained very far indeed from actually granting indians full citizenship rights. As Erick Langer (2009: 539) points out, during the nineteenth century the state used categories such as *indígena, indígena contribuyente,* or *indígena originario* (indigenous, contributory indigenous, originating indigenous)—all essentially fiscal categories—to designate indians; they were never referred to as citizens (a term reserved for creoles and mestizos (2009: 538). Rossana Barragán explains that the first Bolivian constitution makes a distinction between "Bolivians" and "citizens": "The requirement [of being a citizen] to read and write, to own property or have a minimal annual income, and of not being a servant, consequently divided the nation between Bolivians and citizens, and excluded the great majority of the population [from the latter category]" (1999: 23).

Nevertheless, in many cases indians maintained a relation with the state, insisting on paying tribute in order to continue the colonial contract (Platt 1982). When the state attempted to abrogate indians' rights, the latter appealed to maintain the colonial contract, not because they were conservative or because they were incapable of participating in a liberal state, but because the colonial documents they possessed were the only ones they could use in their defense (Baud 2009: 25). Even if the state denied indians a role in the nation—that is, refused them citizenship rights—for their part the indians continued to fight for a relationship with the state, even as the state continued to dispossess and marginalize indians throughout the nineteenth century (Langer 2009).

The worst part of this period was during the final decades of the nineteenth century. Corruption and despotism reached new heights under the administration of President Mariano Melgarejo (1864–71), who declared all indian communities extinct and sold off many of their lands to the highest bidder (Alexander 1982; Larson 2004: 216–19), although some were able to recoup their lands in 1871 (Langer 2009: 547). The combined effects of dispossession, dislocation of markets due to the Pacific War (1879–84), and a new racism that saw indians as biologically inferior (Demelas 1981; 1982) led to highland indians being pauperized and increasingly marginalized from a state in which they had hitherto played an active if subordinate role (Langer 2009; Platt 1993).

It is obviously difficult to know exactly what indians thought of these processes, but Platt (1993) suggests that they wished for a productive and dynamic relationship with the state. The uprisings of the last decades of the nineteenth century and the beginning of the twentieth have generally been interpreted as struggles for land, which rejected any role of the state in indians' lives. Even if the appropriation of land was a clear motive for these uprisings, they obscure the wish on the part of indigenous people to participate fully in the life of the nation. In the words of Marta Irurozqui, "The indigenous population did not limit itself to expressing its antagonism to the society which enveloped it, rather, through combining insurgency with other modes of public intervention such as petitions for Spanish language schooling, the right to address tribunals or participation in elections, they expressed a wish for an active, and not tutelary, role in the construction of the Bolivian nation state" (2000: 367).

The Federal War of 1899 offers us a good example. The conflict between liberals and conservatives produced an alliance between the liberals and the growing Aymara movement. Zárate "el temible" Willka, with the rank of colonel in the Bolivian army, took his Aymara troops to war, where they played an important role in the liberal victory. Although allied with the liberals in the war, the Aymaras clearly had goals that went rather further than those of the liberals. Willka expressed his vision quite clearly in the "Proclamation of Caracollo," in which he presented his ideas of a multiracial Bolivia, one where indians would be respected as citizens equal to whites (Condarco Morales 1983).

After that victory, Willka was almost immediately imprisoned for sedition. The massacre of soldiers by Aymara troops and their sentencing in the "Trial of Mohozo" threw the mestizo-creole nation into a profound debate over the position of indians in the country. Even though the liberals originally recognized Aymaras as autonomous allies, the Mohozo scandal and the anxiety about powerful indians acted to change the minds of the liberals who then agreed with the conservatives in the view that indians were savage beings incapable of any rational impulse or capacity for civilization. The role of indians in the Federal War was rewritten in terms of a war of the races (Irurozqui 2000: 107) in which an indian uprising was motivated by savagery and an irrational hatred of whites. The Bolivian creoles imagined themselves as forming part of a modern, white, and developed nation, but they were confronted, rather inconveniently, with the unpalatable fact that they formed but a small minority in the Bolivian nation-state: "The result was a rather ill defined national identity in which the construction of a homogeneous white nation became an ideal that was ever more difficult to realize given that the *mestizo* solution was equally unviable as this implied a cultural homogenization which would necessarily include *cholos,* who would not only endanger the social hierarchy and order which currently reigned, but the international respect to which the nation aspired" (Irurozqui 2000: 118).

Thus, the ruling classes neatly projected upon indians their own incapacities and inability to create a civilized and functioning society. All this rhetoric was accompanied by "scientific" evidence that indians were congenitally stupid, had smaller brains, were predisposed to indolence and treachery, and so on, and the ruling classes marshaled to "prove" that the indians were quite inimical to the development of a civilized society (Demelas 1981). The pernicious consequences of miscegenation are imaginatively described by the nineteenth-century historian Gabriel René Moreno: "The tendency of *mestizos* towards laziness, contentiousness, servility, intrigue, those seeds of scandal and 'caudillaje,' is notorious; to this we can add the stupidity and cowardice of the Inkaic indian all which combine to perpetuate the despotism of our society" (quoted in Demelas 1981: 62).

Not only was the subjugation of the indians desirable and even moral, but so was the theft of land, for only the white creoles could ever efficiently exploit the land. The total disregard for the indians' welfare or rights is illustrated by the actions of Liberal President General Ismael Montes (1903–9 and 1913–17). While touring the region around Lake Titicaca he came upon a surviving free community. Much impressed with the richness of the area that the community occupied, he promptly established his ownership of the land, ordered that all the members of the Aymara community be moved to La Paz, and forbade, under pain of death, any of them to return to their land. Indians from elsewhere were brought in to work the land for General Montes and it remained a large estate until the Agrarian Reform of 1953 (Alexander 1982: 52).

The prevailing attitudes of the day are neatly expressed by Saavedra: "As Le Bon says, if an inferior race is placed next to a superior one it must disappear, and if . . . we must exploit those Aymara and Quechua indians for our benefit or eliminate them because they constitute and obstacle to our progress, then let us do so frankly and energetically" (Saavedra 1955: 146). Bautista Saavedra was none other than the president of Bolivia in the 1920s. He was also a young lawyer who was the principal defense attorney in the famous Trial of Mohozo.

The area around Wila Kjarka was no exception to the story of dispossession that characterized the nineteenth century. According to the Lista de Contribuyentes (List of Contributors) of 1832, there were still by that date six independent communities (including Wila Kjarka) in the canton of Ilabaya and seventeen registered haciendas.[9] By the end of the nineteenth century there was only one independent community, much reduced in size.

TALKING TO THE INKAS AND OTHER INTIMACIES WITH THE PAST

Wila Kjarkeños' history as told to me does not begin with the Spanish or the Inkas or even the people of Tiwanaku (in fact, the latter are almost never mentioned in accounts), but rather, the dawn.

The Dawn

Broadly speaking, adult Wila Kjarkeños divide their history into three periods: *chullpa pacha, inka pacha,* and *patruna pacha,* and this basic historical framework is found all over the Andes. The earliest period mentioned by Wila Kjarkeños is the dawn of time, when the *chullpas* lived. People talk of chullpas all over the Andes, and Wila Kjarkeños share beliefs that chullpas lived in circular houses with the windows to the east. When the sun rose they were burned to a crisp.[10] When I asked Pedro Quispe, one of Wila Kjarka's oldest residents, to tell me who lived there long, long ago he began with the chullpas, whom he described as ancestors ("the grandfathers of the grandfathers, but they were few") who saw the dawn of the world. Pedro described the time of the chullpas as one in which the land was shared and there was enough for everyone.

The chullpas are clearly of the very distant past, but they are also, in an important way, in the present. Several middle-aged Wila Kjarkeños describe spirits such as the *pachamama* (earth mother) as being chullpas. Those chullpas who escaped the sun's rays hid in the earth, underground. The pachamama is the source of the earth's productivity, and she is feted with alcohol and animal sacrifices. To describe the pachamama as a chullpa is to acknowledge that the past has not simply disappeared but is also present, merely in a different place. There is also an important sense of kinship with the pachamama. The chullpas, the pachamama, and other spirits that sustain life are the spirits of the deceased ancestors of Wila Kjarkeños. It is this intimacy with the past and the spirits of the earth that is a clear element in older Wila Kjarkeños' sense of who they are as human beings.

The difference between older and middle-aged people's views on chullpas is that older people are able to give much more detail and present a rather more complex relationship between chullpas and other beings that live in the earth. Nevertheless, many adults were able to give accounts of the offering they make to the chullpas, such as a pig's trotter and maize beer. Chullpas are sometimes considered to be the cause of certain skin diseases and therefore need "feeding" to satisfy them. Teodosio, the shaman, gave this account of how to feed chullpas: "You need to give the chullpas a pig's fetus. Chullpas need to be paid on Tuesday or Friday: In one receptacle you need to offer them maize beer and in the other cooked quinua. You need to adorn the pig's fetus with alcohol and with incense. That is what you need to do."

Chullpas can sometimes be disturbed when, for example, a new road is dynamited. According to Teodosio, when they were opening the new road in Quruma the chullpas became extremely upset and stole the souls of some of the workers. They had to be placated with lots of alcohol and some gold.

Chullpas are described as being a very different kind of people: they lived in darkness (the night is their day), they did not know God, they were big and hairy, but they were still people. Francisca asserts that they were "people with big feet and heads." Older people in particular describe the chullpas as people, that is, they are jaqi—the word Wila Kjarkeños use to describe themselves and to distinguish themselves from mestizos and creoles. Herculiano (in his forties) describes them as "not people of this world; these others were not wanted by God and were non-believers. Those people of the past were of the underworld, they were called gentiles, we call them gentiles." But then he adds, "these jaqi are also our brethren, they are not really then different (*Ukax mä jaqi masisaskarikiw janiw ukaxa wasa jaqikikapunirakiti*)."

To some extent the chullpas exist(ed) in a sort of parallel world; not only was their world one of darkness but the wild animals of today were their domestic animals. Manuel, in his seventies, told me, "For them there is no longer life for them here. If they had beaten God, well where would we be now? Perhaps we would be suffering as they suffer. Their animals are now in the wild. The *wikhu* bird is their chicken. The skunk is their pig—you see, they have everything." A key element when discussing the chullpas is that they were once the predominant people and are now banished to the underworld; but they have not disappeared from the world altogether: They are of the past but equally exist in the present, albeit in a different spatial dimension. Manuel, for example, said that the chullpas still speak, that when you put the chullpa bones together they will still speak; they have words: " 'Qilla qilla,' they say. But what that means I do not know. 'Qilla qilla,' they say." Chullpas speak, but it is not in a language that is easily understood by contemporary people; yet they speak as living beings.

When talking about the chullpas, older women—and only older women—talked about how in those days animals and people could speak to each other and often intermarried. "Toads wore trousers and in those days people walked/lived with toads and foxes, too." "Young women went with snakes and gave birth to little snakes." "Foxes wore ties and seduced young women whose babies barked when they were born."[11]

Flora Alwiri.

Flora gives this account: "The foxes arrived with their ties, and when the young women wanted to stay with them [the foxes bit them] and they ran away saying 'The dawn is coming!' That is what they say it was like with the young women who went with lizards and foxes and skunks. That is how they say it was."

The time of the chullpas is clearly one in which different relations pertained between humans and animals and in which different social rules applied. One can discern, however, echoes of later ages when hacendados or their agents seduced indian girls (as was the case with Teodosio's mother). The fox's tie associates him with the nonindian world of creoles. Perhaps Juana here is expressing a historical sense of the exploitation of women even in the precolonial age.

Francisca and others also mentioned the treasures—pots of gold and silver—which the chullpas have and which people in Wila Kjarka will occasionally stir up when they are digging in their fields. The issue of treasure and wealth is also an important theme when discussing the Inkas who succeeded the chullpas on the surface of the land. Indians today are poor; it is almost their key defining feature in discussion with many Wila Kjarkeños. In the past, however, indians—that is, jaqi—were wealthy, and in this understanding lies the key to a very contemporary sense of social injustice: Indians are poor, and they are poor not because there is something in their condition as jaqi that makes them inherently poor but because great wealth was once violently taken away from them. The sun that killed the chullpas banished the survivors underground.[12] The sun also brought the Inkas, who included the sun as one of their central deities. For many Wila Kjarkeños the sun is equated with the Christian god, and this is a significant point because, according to them, it was not the Spanish who brought Christianity but the Inkas.

Inkas

This is how Pedro remembers the Inkas:

The Inka king was like that, up there on top of the mountain. Then we were children, we were like that small boy, and it is then that the Inka lived, although we did not see how he died. The Inkas stopped on top of that mountain . . . he was able to send big stones all over simply with the use of his whip . . . that is how he was . . . But in those times he didn't kill the Spaniards, they must have shot him . . . But when he was about to die, then he said, "there will be no more gold and silver," and so saying sent it all into the mountain with his whip. That is why the gold is in the mountain; that is why it is down there.

Pedro is here speaking as if he personally saw the Inka as a little boy, using the grammatical construction that denotes firsthand experience.[13] This is somewhat unusual, and Pedro is asserting an immediate connection with the Inkas. Pedro speaks with regret of the coming of the Spanish. He suggests that the Spanish may not have been bad, but "God made the Spanish fight with the Jews. That is why they were fighting, but if they hadn't killed the Inka king then things would have been different. He would have given us lots, he would have been alive . . . since he has been dead we do not know him. [The wealth] is lost and there is none." The poverty of Wila Kjarkeños today is understood in terms of the Spanish killing the Inka and forcing him to hide the wealth inside the mountains. For older people such as Teodosio the Inkas are present in the mountains and sometimes appear to him: They are dressed in finery and appear at the mouth of a cave. Teodosio says they speak directly to him. "If one is very fortunate and careful, one can make a deal with the Inka and he can give gold." This is dangerous because the Inka will ultimately take one's life in exchange for his wealth.

> The Inkas are living. You can go and look and shout and they will answer, saying "hello!" There is a door and a single house which can be seen from below. One day the Inka appeared to me.
>
> I saw her with a red dress and a brown hat and a shawl. It was raining and on top of the mountain called Ququr she was singing: "la la la" . . . Before I could ask where she was from she turned and disappeared. I was very close. "Why did you go there alone," I was told when I returned. "That is an enchanted place. It must have been a *yanqha* [female chthonic deity] that Inka lady. She could have killed you."

Teodosio insists, however, that his vision was not that of a yanqha, or of a water spirit or *sirinu*, but an Inka. That people can hear the Inka's voice is reported in other parts of the Andes (Arnold 2006: 180), but it is more common to hear that the Inka speak as the wind, especially in the windy month of August when the chthonic deities are most present; however, it is apparently rare for people to say they have actual waking conversations, and much more so for the Inka to be represented by a woman.

The Inka king was ultimately killed by the Spanish but, like the chullpas, did not disappear altogether, and some Wila Kjarkeños say that the Inkas simply entered the rocks (*Ukapi awist'askam q'arqaruw puritayna*). That is, rather like the chullpas going underground, the Inkas simply went to a different place, into rock or, as Pastuku told me, to Paititi:

> In the old days the Inka Atahuallpa used to go to Illampu on top of which is an old city . . . They say that from the capital of the Tiwanaku Empire they went with llamas to Illampu on the way to Paititi, which is in the jungle near Mapiri . . . I have seen it from afar but have not arrived there because one cannot . . . They say there is a big gold bell in the center of the plaza and four big jars of gold. They say that the jars are always full, but no one can reach this place because it is enchanted and protected by snakes.

The jungle is a place below/under/inside—that is, quintessentially chthonic. When the dead are remembered on All Saints', they are given foods of the jungle, for that is where they are considered to dwell, and they have become fond of these foods. It is also from the jungle that the ancestors bring rain, and, as we saw in the fiesta of San Pedro, people dance with jaguar skins and parrot feathers in the belief that these will be pleasing to the ancestors. Locating the Inkas in the jungle, then, is much more than a reference to the legend of the lost Inka redoubt in the jungle lowlands but a clear reference to the fact that the Inkas are ancestors and dwell, indeed, in the same place where all ancestors dwell.

THE SPANISH AND THE HACENDADOS

Wila Kjarkeños and others distinguish between jaqi people and q'ara, who are a different kind of people, living in cities and towns and don't have "proper" relationships with each other or with the spirits of the earth and mountains. The Inkas are unambiguously jaqi: "He was surely jaqi, that Inka king, he would have favored us" (*Jaqi kastatapaya uka inka riyixa, jaqi phawuratapaya*). It is also important to note that, for many older people, the Inka was a Christian. Christianity, many believed, came with the first dawn, which ushered in a Christian era. Herculiano, in his forties, however, demurs: "In those days they only worshipped the sun. It was not their custom to worship God the Father." Herculiano calls this period of the Spanish the time of the Yankees: "This time of the Yankees is the time when Christopher Columbus entered. Then they possessed the land of Bolivia, Qullasuyu . . . Then when the Spanish came, another people from another country entered the land of Bolivia. Then from that time appeared the Bible."

Pedro, as with other Wila Kjarkeños of his generation, however, does not associate Christianity with the arrival of the Spaniards:

> We know the Christians since the time of our ancestors. They were owners of these lands and they organized the fields in terms of *sayañas*. They distributed the land, and after then we had the land. We are continuing the path they left us, but [the q'aras] did not want us to learn to read. After the Agrarian Reform we learned how to read and they left with their laws. The Agrarian Reform gave us new laws: The *patrón* would say that if the indians knew how to write then they could contradict us; that is why they took away our lands . . . In those days the patrón was not afraid to whip us or insult us. "Stupid ass," he would call us. We had to plow the furrows without a single mistake. When we got behind in the fields we would be beaten with a whip. Now we work for ourselves, the places which belonged

to the hacienda are now ours. We eat from that earth (*nanakaya jichhaxa uraqi manq'asisipxkthxa*).

Pedro here, as with many others, associated the power of the Spaniards with literacy rather than a more powerful deity or superior technology. This is one theme that crosses all generations: the power of literacy, which can be used to dominate people and, as a consequence, to liberate them. In the words of Edmundo: "The Spanish came to abuse our people; they abused us and treated us as animals. Our ancestors did not speak or read Spanish, and that is why they treated our ancestors like animals."

This comment illustrates why language in itself is not necessarily salient in defining indigeneity, particularly since being an illiterate monolingual has historically meant an inability to defend one's land. The schools' movement in the first decades of the twentieth century was explicitly aimed at teaching Spanish in order to reclaim land stolen in previous decades. Today many parents (and teachers) are opposed to bilingual education because they fear that teaching children an indigenous language is designed to prevent them from acquiring the necessary linguistic skills (i.e., Spanish) to defend themselves and make economic and social progress. The inability to speak an indigenous language does not, therefore, have the same political and symbolic consequences as it might in other parts of the world where speaking an indigenous language is central to claiming an indigenous identity.

YOUTHS' VERSION OF HISTORY

The oldest Wila Kjarkeños and those more or less above the age of thirty shared a basic historical framework, although with some differences. All the people in this group noted that beings of the past were still accessible in the earth below, be they chullpas or Inkas. Younger Wila Kjarkeños had a very different historical consciousness. Most assured me that they knew absolutely nothing about Inkas and chullpas and told me to ask their grandparents. When pressed, they admitted they knew some very basic things about them, such as the Inka moving stones with his whip, but I found no one in this age group who could produce a historical sequence or express any kind of personal relationship with the past. They were generally reluctant to respond at all to my questions; they claimed simply not to know.

It may of course be that young people in Wila Kjarka—as perhaps it may be with young people elsewhere—are simply not yet interested in history, but it is also the case that this generation of young people has been exposed to much more schooling than the three years or less their parents received. Schooling, and the time spent on it, orients them away from activities related to the land and the spirits who animate it (Arnold 2006). The relationship lived with land and spirits simply becomes irrelevant. One of the clearest effects of schooling is that people look to "progress" through moving to the cities and speaking Spanish; in effect, upwardly mobile social progress implies a change of ethnic status. As part of this project I also asked young school-age people what their aspirations were. Without exception they all said they wanted to leave the village and live in a city or, at any rate, somewhere else. If younger people want to leave the village they may not be keen to emphasize profound ethnic differences between themselves and others. For the older generation who lived under the whip of the landowner, however, history provides a way of understanding the profound difference between indians and the whites and mestizos who dominated them. This history, too, rooted people in an intimate relationship with the land and its past inhabitants—that is, it gave them a clear sense of what we can call indigeneity, a sense of justice rooted in historical consciousness, even if they wouldn't use that word themselves. Younger people, however, have been brought up in a world where social progress is offered (if not always delivered), and they do not have the personal experiences of the violence and exclusion experienced by older generations.

What is significant about these accounts of the past is that, although there are some clear common elements, there is considerable diversity within this small population, some of it generalizable across generations and genders. I found no evidence of a continuous narrative relating contemporary political processes and institutions to Inka ones that are offered in the very detailed ethnohistorical work of scholars such as Arnold (2006), Abercrombie (1998), and Rappaport (1998). These works show an evolution in the relationship between particular indigenous groups and the Inka, colonial, and republican states. Implicit in the argument is that indigeneity is rooted in the continuous, albeit evolving, engagement and resistance with the state, where Inkaic models are consciously assimilated to contemporary ones. It is not always clear how generalizable these ethnographic examples are supposed to be nor, more important, is there a sense that there may be internal disagreement within the community in how they conceive of history and their relation to it. I suggest that, not only does historical consciousness vary considerably across the Andes but it varies within communities too, across generations and genders. Women, after all, have a different relationship with the (post) colonial state and the way it employs structures and imagery that render indians more feminine and indian women "more indian" (Canessa 2005; de la Cadena 1995) as well as more likely to have been subjected to the sexual predations of Conquistadores and their successors in power.

Wila Kjarkeños conflate two periods which are clearly demarcated in Western historiography: the Colonial and Republican periods up to the Revolution of 1952. The wars of independence are utterly irrelevant to Wila Kjarkeños because they did little more than transfer power from a European elite born in Spain to a European elite born in Bolivia (cf. Bigenho 2002: 24). Indeed, Wila Kjarkeños almost never mentioned the name of the Libertador, Simón Bolívar, when talking about their history, even though his picture is in the schools. This moment of independence, in contrast, looms large in history textbooks across the Americas; indeed it is *the* most important historical moment, for in it is rooted the American myth of decolonization. From the Boston Tea Party, in which American-born Europeans dressed as indians, to the balls held in Valparaiso, in which creoles dressed as Mapuche, white people identified with the natives of the soil in their struggle against the colonial oppressor. But neither on these or any other similar occasions across the continent did this indicate any solidarity with living indigenous people. These theatrical moments are nevertheless significant because they point to the moment when Europeans become "native," when they become "American" and take on the mantle of an attenuated autochthnonous identity that is, of being "of the land," which distinguished them from the colonizers. Bolivians, Mexicans, "Americans" fight against the Spanish and the British and free their countries from the yoke of colonial tyranny; invidious colonialism is replaced with benign republicanism in which all citizens are equal.

For indigenous Americans, however, there was little obvious difference between colonizers born in Europe and colonizers born in the Americas. Even as they were (often forcibly) offered citizenship in the new nations, they hardly enjoyed equal rights: Some citizens are, of course, more equal than others, and many people are not citizens at all, but this is an inconvenient fact often elided in history text books. In many cases they enjoyed more rights as subjects to the Crown, which, as we saw above, would, at least on some occasions, defend indian lands (and thus the Crown's source of tax revenue) from the predations of creoles. With "independence" and as creoles wrapped themselves in the virtues of enlightened republicanism and the unstoppable train of development and progress, indigenous Americans suffered an even more ferocious onslaught on their lands and persons than was visited upon them during the Conquest and the rest of the colonial period. It is not hard, then, to see why for so many people who identify as indigenous, the myth of decolonization is the cruelest joke, at best. For Wila Kjarkeños the celebration of the sixth of August—Bolivian Independence Day—is simply not for them, since they recognize it for the mestizo-creole myth that it is (see chapter 6).

For Wila Kjarkeños the true anticolonial moment, the point at which *patrunapacha*—the time of the patrones—becomes today is the midcentury, when indians finally rose up and wrenched power from the creole landowning elite. It is to this moment that we now turn.

THREE

The Jankho Kjarka War

The events that led to the inauguration of Evo Morales as president of Bolivia in January 2006 were widely heralded by journalists (foreign and national), academics, and the president himself as nothing less than a revolution, to be compared to the indigenous uprising of 1781, independence in 1825, and the Bolivian Revolution of 1952. I shall leave it to others to debate whether this is genuinely a revolution,[1] but I certainly agree with James Dunkerley that it is widely perceived as being one (2007: 25). Whether or not recent events hark back to the eighteenth-century revolt of Tupak Katari, the primary reference is undoubtedly 1952, when miners and peasants overthrew the government, nationalized the mines, and enacted a far-reaching agrarian reform. The election of Morales, hailed as the first indigenous president, can be seen as completing that mid-twentieth-century overthrow of white oligarchic rule and its unfinished business. It also raises questions about how that revolution is remembered.

The midcentury events loom large for politicians, journalists, and historians in their understanding of Bolivian history; as James Dunkerley has noted, they form a watershed where the "before" of monolingual indian peasants ruled by feudal oligarchs is contrasted with the "after" of a modern, increasingly mestizo, and much more urban nation. That the Revolution may not have the same significance for ordinary Bolivians is rarely considered. In this chapter I examine what Wila Kjarkeños remember—and forget—about the 1952 Bolivian Revolution, and how not only the fact but the very process of memory and amnesia is key to their understanding of who they are today.

1952 AND ALL THAT

According to a conventional chronology based on historical record, the Jankho Kjarka war, as Wila Kjarkeños call it (*kira*, cf. *guerra*, Sp.), began in 1951, when Wila Kjarka was destroyed and its inhabitants made refugees. In 1952, while the people of Wila Kjarka were still living dispersed in neighboring communities, the Bolivian Revolution broke out, causing the violent overthrow of the landowners. In 1953 the Agrarian Reform was declared, restricting large-scale landownership and returning land to the peasants who worked it. Wila Kjarkeños then returned and rebuilt their community.

Oral accounts of these events differ from the above, however, most notably on the position of the Bolivian Revolution, in the middle of the sequences of events. Here are the facts that most people agree on. Many years ago, when indians still lived as serfs, there was a war in the mountains of Larecaja between two Aymara-speaking hacienda communities, Wila Kjarka and Jankho Kjarka. These communities were owned by two hacendados related by marriage. The war centered around a disputed stretch of land called Salapata. Men in uniform walked up the mountain with guns to Wila Kjarka; crops were destroyed; houses were looted and burned; and livestock was stolen. People died. People fled. Wila Kjarka was destroyed. Its people hid in caves or dispersed among neighboring communities. Three years later the people of Wila Kjarka returned; they retook their lands as well as Salapata. The Agrarian Reform confirmed that Salapata belonged to Wila Kjarka and, moreover, it ultimately deprived the hacendados of title to any land in Wila Kjarka.

These are the bare facts of the event. But they are, in themselves, uninteresting (and the elision of the revolution in oral accounts unintelligible) because the ideological context that makes them comprehensible is missing—the "why" questions, the understanding of motives, and the politics of what was happening. As Alessandro Portelli notes, facts and representations do not exist independently of each other: "Representations work on facts and claim to *be* facts; facts are recognized and organized according to representations; facts and representations both converge on the subjectivity of human beings and are dressed in their language" (1997: 146). What happened is inseparable from why it happened and what meaning it has today, if only because if it had no meaning it would not be remembered.

These events occurred many years ago, but they underline the present in powerful ways, at least in Wila Kjarka. In recent years I have also been conducting fieldwork in Jankho Kjarka and other nearby communities. Jankho Kjarka is a smaller village of 119 people, according to the last census, which recorded Wila Kjarka as having 220 residents.[2] It is smaller not only in population but in the extent and productivity of land. Jankho Kjarka possesses no fields at higher altitude (ownership of Salapata would have given them such access) so its inhabitants can grow few potatoes, an important staple, and much of its lower land is heavily eroded. In the region, Wila Kjarka is considered to be cohesive and enjoy considerable solidarity— Jankho Kjarka much less so. Jankho Kjarka has suffered considerable soil erosion, and the population is in steady decline.

Until the "war," Jankho Kjarka and Wila Kjarka formed two halves or moieties of the same community. As is the common pattern in the Andes, the people from one moiety marry those of the other, and they also share a common cemetery. This continued to be the case long after the two villages had different owners. Since the "war," however, there is no sense that the two groups of people form part of the same community.

Beyond the barest of facts outlined above, people remember the "war" very differently. Wila Kjarkeños and Jankho Kjarkeños, perhaps unsurprisingly, have different views, but people from surrounding communities do as well; and there are also some differences between men and women. More significant, however, are the differences in what the violence means for the understanding of history and people's place in the present, and how they relate to the momentous events of the almost coeval revolution. These accounts do not easily separate into an "official" version and that of eyewitnesses, or even into those of victims and victors, eyewitnesses, and others. There are also profound differences in what is remembered and forgotten and who is doing the remembering and forgetting. I have been hearing about the "Jankho Kjarka war" from Wila Kjarkeños for over twenty years: It comes up in conversation here and there, recounted in great detail by young and old. In Jankho Kjarka most people claim never to have heard of it; insofar as they remember it at all, it is as a footnote in a larger historical event. For Wila Kjarkeños the footnote displaces that larger historical event.

This chapter explores the ways this violence is remembered and recounted, by eyewitnesses and through secondhand accounts, and how these memories incorporate or displace the major events happening at the same time, namely the Bolivian Revolution.

THE BOLIVIAN REVOLUTION OF 1952

Although the war between Jankho Kjarka and Wila Kjarka was not in itself about broader national political issues, the political background frames the way the violence is remembered. Bolivia's 1952 Revolution was one of the most far-reaching in Latin American history and, with the exception of the Cuban Revolution, the one with the most profound social consequences, especially in the area of land reform. The revolution overthrew the landowning oligarchy and ushered in a period of major social transformation: The Agrarian Reform of 1953 returned land to indigenous peasants; the Education Reform, also in 1953, initiated the construction of schools all over the countryside; and suffrage became universal. People of Wila Kjarka and Jankho Kjarka became, for the first time, full legal citizens of the nation, free to educate their children and move wherever they wished.[3] To understand the significance of the war for Wila Kjarkeños it is essential to grasp the social conditions prevalent at the time as well as the context of the Bolivian Revolution.

Since the debacle of the Chaco War against Paraguay (1932–35) a dissatisfaction had been growing in Bolivia against the ruling white oligarchy, and awareness was increasing of the plight of the majority of the Bolivian population, who were rural indians, many of whom were living in serf-like conditions on haciendas and had been slaughtered in the war. It was in the trenches of the war that indians and mestizos developed an awareness of their position as subjects in relation to the mining and landowning oligarchy (Bigenho 2002: 26). The reformist governments of Germán Busch (1936–39) and Gualberto Villarroel (1944–46) endeavored to give more rights to indians, including schooling and abolition of a much hated form of service known as *pongueaje*, whereby the indian (*pongo*) had to serve in the master's house without pay and under demeaning conditions. This detested word, pongo, comes from the Quechua and Aymara word for door, *punku*, and was given to this servant because he was habitually made to sleep in the doorway.

Many of the reforms were reversed, however, and Villarroel himself was killed and left hanging from a streetlamp opposite the presidential palace. By the end of the decade there was growing unrest, particularly in the areas around Cochabamba and the northern highland plain around Achacachi (in the neighboring province to Larecaja). In 1951 this unrest intensified when the Movimiento Nacionalista Revolucionario (MNR, Revolutionary Nationalist Movement) won the election but was prevented from taking office by a military junta that outgoing President Urriolagoitía installed. By April 1952 the country was in full-scale revolt, and by the end of the year the MNR was swept into power with Víctor Paz Estenssoro at its head.

The revolutionary government of 1952 eliminated the literacy requirements for voting, and in one stroke quintupled the voting population (Klein 1982: 232); the army was purged of 500 officers and its role dramatically reduced to the point that civilian militias effectively replaced it; and two-thirds of Bolivia's principal industry, mining, was nationalized (Klein 1982: 233). By the end of the year, the peasants were armed and mobilized to destroy records and seize land. The rural violence, which Herbert Klein likens to the movement known as the "Great Fear" of the French Revolution (Klein 1982: 234), was not evenly distributed throughout the county and was most concentrated in the Cochabamba valley and the rich agricultural lands of the altiplano around Lake Titicaca, where intense dispossession of indian lands had taken place at the end of the nineteenth century and in the early decades of the twentieth, in particular around Achacachi. These dispossessions occasioned a number of uprisings, mostly brutally repressed, which were held in people's memories decades later.[4]

Achacachi is approximately six hours' walk from Wila Kjarka, and the violence spilled into the area around Wila Kjarka. Indeed, some of the large Achacachi hacendados owned haciendas in the area. The old hacendado of Wila Kjarka, Eulogio Franco, was one of these and had a notorious reputation for his actions against peasants in his haciendas (Albó 1979: 26). Many haciendas, some of them literally within sight of Wila Kjarka, experienced serious violence, and peasant militias were a strong force in that area for several years after the revolution. In fact, when the revolutionary government sent officials to rein in the recalcitrant militias of Achacachi, they were famously killed and eaten; and the locals retain to this day the unenviable reputation of being cannibals.

This is merely one example of how the revolution was at best imperfectly controlled from the center. It was the widespread and spontaneous occupation of haciendas all over the country that forced the revolutionary government to announce the Agrarian Reform, which returned land to the peasants who worked it. For several months in 1952 and 1953 peasant militias moved across the countryside aiding their fellow peasants in the overthrow of hacendados, their wrath fueled by centuries of oppression and struggle. In community after community people violently ejected their landlords. With little choice but to accept the resulting land distribution, the government created a bureaucratic and legal process for recognizing the new occupiers of the land.

The Bolivian Revolution was one of the most successful and dramatic of the twentieth century in Latin America. Of all the major events during this period, the people of Wila Kjarka, including those who lived through those events, recall absolutely nothing; in fact, not a single person even mentioned the Revolution or, indeed, any of the national or local events that occurred in that year. What they do recount is the war with Jankho Kjarka in 1951 and their ultimate victory, not only over the people of Jankho Kjarka but over the *patrones*, who were overthrown neither by the revolution nor even directly by the Agrarian Reform—which immediately followed the revolution—but through the victorious efforts of Wila Kjarkeños in 1953. It is important to note that none of the Wila Kjarkeños interviewed mentioned any dates at all.

What I wish to explore here are the ways in which this historical moment is remembered and recounted and its conflation with a land war with the neighboring community. It seems that historical accounts have two related roles. The first is to make sense of the bloody conflict between two communities, which had, for centuries, been one. The second is to make the people of Wila Kjarka agents of the revolution because, just as the country was rising up against the hacendados, the people of Wila Kjarka were living as refugees in neighboring communities and were not in a good position to wage battle against anyone.

Before I explore oral historical accounts of the events, I would like to sketch out how the conflict appears in documentary accounts. This is not to say what "really" happened but rather to illustrate the contrast between accounts penned largely by the landowning class and their agents with those of people who experienced the conflict close at hand.

WILA KJARKA AND JANKHO KJARKA IN THE DOCUMENTARY RECORD

As we saw in the previous chapter, colonial records note the existence of the *ayllu* of Wila Kjarka and Jankho Kjarka. As was commonly the case, and often still is with contemporary ayllus, the lands were divided into an upper and lower moiety, Wila Kjarka and Jankho Kjarka, respectively. It can be surmised that the members of each moiety intermarried regularly, and it is also likely that they engaged in ritual battles called *tinkus*, still practiced across the Andes, which pit moieties against each other and of which the resulting spillage of blood serves as an offering to the local deities (Sallnow 1987: 136–46; Van Vleet 2009).

Blood is spilled during tinkus; indeed that is the point: The spilt blood of warriors is an offering to the tutelary spirits, and in some areas it is believed that the blood of the fallen continues to seep out of their graves and give strength to the earth (Allen 1988: 206; Sallnow 1987: 136–46). The dead are widely considered to be important sources of strength and fertility and particularly so if they have fallen in a tinku.[5] The key feature of tinkus is that they are between marriageable groups; the violence and death in tinkus[6] serve precisely to bind groups together rather than separate them. Indeed, that is widely considered to be their primary function and contrasts with the violence that occurred in the war that rent the two apart. Even in cases where it is deemed to be more about the "poetics of manhood" (Stobart 2006) than fertility, there is still no sense that an antagonism endures between the parties; they are finite in time and space.

This division was prefigured by the usurpation of the ayllu by landowners of the dominant class at the end of the nineteenth century, when it was converted into a hacienda and then split into two in 1897. This split was later to have disastrous consequences, as the land pertaining to each was apparently not clearly defined, but it is clear from contemporary accounts that people from each moiety—now different haciendas—continued to intermarry and continued being buried in the same cemetery, a particularly important marker of community identity as we shall see below (Connerton 1989).

The owner of the hacienda of Jankho Kjarka in the early twentieth century was Salomón Monterrey. He bought the neighboring hacienda of Wila Kjarka with his brother-in-law Eulogio Franco, who was one of the largest landowners in Omasuyos, the neighboring province, which comprises the rich agricultural land of the highland plain near Lake Titicaca.

Salomón Monterrey died some years after the purchase of Wila Kjarka in the Chaco War (1932–35). In 1937 Franco took over both haciendas (then valued at 60,000 pesos), and once again Wila Kjarka and Jankho Kjarka were effectively united. He furthermore produced a document dated 1929, showing the sale of the other half of the property to him while Mario, the eldest of the Monterrey children (and the only male), was absent in the United States. The sisters were either not aware of the situation or not willing or able to act until their elder brother's return. On Mario's return he contested this document, and apparently won, but it took him until 1944 to do so. The children of Monterrey—Mario, Aida, Adalid, and Olga—protested that Eulogio Franco "inspired by God knows what deviousness, got a judge from Achacachi, who is now dust in the cemetery, against all reason and justice, to arrive at a judgement against us; but superior justices rectified the sentence IN OUR FAVOR" (capitals in the original).[7]

At this point the Monterrey family accused the Franco family of instigating Wila Kjarkeños to steal land from Jankho Kjarka and persuaded the people of Jankho Kjarka that this was the case. Throughout the 1930s and '40s there were sporadic incidences of conflict and murder on both sides, with each hacendado claiming that the other had encouraged "his" peasants to attack the other hacienda. In these legal and other official documents, members of the Monterrey family present themselves as the victims, contesting the "disgusting intrigues and ambitions" of their uncle and their cousin's "despicable ambition to usurp the *hacienda* and leave [them] in the street" in a number of petitions to a variety of judicial officers. The indians living on the haciendas are barely mentioned and, when they are, they are not autonomous agents. The Monterrey family, for example, complains that their uncle's indians invaded their land, and in this they very much conform to the ideas of the time that indians belonged to the hacienda and were included in inventories of sale. As we shall see below, the idea that indians "belonged" to the hacendado was acknowledged by indians, too.

In 1953 with the passage of the Agrarian Reform, the people of Wila Kjarka had the right to claim the lands of the hacendado as theirs and claimed against Luís Mirmilan (Franco's son-in-law) rather than the Monterrey occupiers. The Agrarian Reform commission recognized the land as belonging to Mirmilan and his wife, including the disputed lands known as Salapata and Salapata Chico (twenty-four hectares) as well as one hundred hectares of pastureland. These lands were the particular bone of

contention between the two hacendados. Almost all the land was awarded
to the people of Wila Kjarka by the Agrarian Reform, but the Mirmilan
family, by dividing it among their children, kept title to some of the land
until as late as 1967.

This is the documented history of the dispute and the consequences
of the Agrarian Reform. There is neither mention of the sacking of Wila
Kjarka nor of the displacement of people to other communities. Most of the
documentation is about the dispute between landowners and, later (after
1953), concerns the Wila Kjarkeño claims against the patrones. In the documents relating to the conflict in the early 1950s we get some sense of what
the landowners thought as their words were recorded. Absent from these
accounts are the names of any indians, even those who were killed, much
less any indication of what they might have thought of the events reported.

REMEMBERING THE PATRONES

Not all Wila Kjarkeños are eager to talk about the past, and some have
little interest. Those who do, and even those who need a little prompting,
most often start with the *patrunapacha*, the time of the *patrones*. This is
the time against which the present is measured: The time of the patrones
was when people were abused, humiliated, and made to do menial ser-
vices; their overthrow enabled people to learn to read, defend their lands,
become independent, and have at least the potential for social mobility.
The overthrow of the patrones is critical in Wila Kjarkeños' understanding of who they are today, even as the great revolutionary moments of 1952
are not remembered at all. Whereas the 1952 Revolution is conventionally
understood as a major social revolution, for Wila Kjarkeños and others
the overthrow of the hacendados marks nothing less than the overthrow
of Spanish rule. Hacendados are sometimes referred to as *españoles* (Spaniards). Many older Wila Kjarkeños remember having to work as pongos.
This was one of the most hated aspects of the time of the patrones, as once
a year people had to walk to Achacachi, to the house of the patrón, and
work without recompense. People recall the extremely heavy loads they
had to carry to the hacendado's house and that when night fell they just
slept where they were and continued in the morning. Once there, among
other things, they had to weave, sweep, and look after the pigs, chickens,
ducks, and guinea pigs. It isn't, however, the hard work that people particularly remember, it's the whippings. Pongos, it seems, were constantly
being shouted at and regularly flogged.

In Wila Kjarka itself there was an overseer, a *mayordomo*, who was famous for his use of the whip. Francisca Condori recalls: "When something was not done right, he would threaten us with his whip. He used to hit us with it. Especially when we didn't weed very well, he would whip us. 'Who left those weeds?' he would ask, and then he would whip us. That's the way it was before."

People also remember the cowhide sandals they used to wear, which rubbed painfully between the big and second toes, and the fact that clothes were all made by hand—a marker of inferior indian status in the eyes of Wila Kjarkeños. María Choque remembers: "We didn't know the time; we didn't have watches. Nor did we have soap. We used to keep our urine and that is how we washed our heads. We also washed our clothes with urine. We used our urine as soap. That is how we got rid of our dirt."

In Wila Kjarka people say they had to work from eight o'clock in the morning until after sunset. If someone was slow he or she would be beaten and sworn at, as Marcelino Misme remembers: "'Ass, brute, filthy, lazy,' that is what he would say as he whipped us. That's the way it was; that is how we suffered: we suffered like donkeys; we didn't know anything. We all spoke (only) Aymara. We were like beasts; we couldn't even read our own names. But now we can read; now there are doctors and lawyers. That is why now the people have risen up; but in the early times they just did what they wanted to us."

In first- and secondhand accounts of the hacienda period, people talk of the whippings meted out by the hacendado and his mayordomo, and in contrast to Barry Lyons's (2006) example from Ecuador, no one in Wila Kjarka thought the whippings had any moral purpose or value at all. Whips are symbols of authority, and community leaders carry whips as a badge of their office. These whips are not used on people, however; instead, they evoke, not the whippings of the patrón, but the whips the Inka king used to move stones and thus create massive walls and buildings. Whipping is a key element of stories of the *patrunapacha*, but it is also the case that if there is one thing people mention about the Inkas, it is the king's power to move stones with his whip. The illegitimate authority of the patrón is contrasted with the legitimate authority of the Inka king who favored indians (jaqi). The tales of whippings and the words that accompanied them (*indio borrego*—indian brute—most often recalled) furthermore serve to contrast the status of people in the time of the patrones, treated quite literally like beasts, with a much better life now.

Francisca Condori.

Marcelino is also typical in seeing his people's oppression as rooted in their inability to speak and read Spanish, and one direct consequence of the departure of the patrones, in the eyes of many Wila Kjarkeños, was the reform that brought schooling to Wila Kjarka and other communities. In fact, the patrón class, along with the Catholic Church, had actively resisted education for indians until that point. The importance of education in defining the new era cannot be underestimated: Some people even refer to the contemporary period as *iskwilapacha,* the time of schooling (cf. Sp. *escuela,* school). One of the key features of the arrival of the Spanish was their use of books and literacy in oppressing indians. With the overthrow of the Spanish, indians symbolically took back the authority of the whip and mastered the technology of reading in order to defend themselves and their land.

For many people, control over the land and over their lives is very closely linked to the overthrow of the hacendados and the ability to defend themselves through written documents. It is not simply that the events of the early 1950s occasioned great social change: Wila Kjarkeños and others see it as *the* anticolonial moment. For Wila Kjarkeños, when asked, the Spanish left Bolivia after the Jankho Kjarka war. It was this and the Agrarian Reform that followed which finally expelled them from the country. In this context the apparent erasure of the Bolivian Revolution is even more striking and begs the question what people do remember and recount about the events of 1951–53.

THE WAR

The oldest survivor of the period is Teodosio Condori, who offered this account of the Jankho Kjarka War: "The patrones of Jankho Kjarka told us that the *aynoqa* fields of Salapata were theirs. They told us that we could not grow our crops there. We did, and the day we planted they started with their guns. They took some people prisoner and killed them. Then there was help. They came from above: from Quqanita, Murumanita, Chuqupata, T'ula T'ula; that is how they came. Six hundred people came, and in all three hundred died. Women died, men died."

Teodosio was probably in his late thirties or early forties when the events he reports happened, yet he clearly exaggerates the numbers of people involved; three hundred people is more than the combined population of Jankho Kjarka and Wila Kjarka in 1951, and although other accounts mention a large number of dead people, none reported hundreds of people dying. It cannot, therefore, be assumed that eyewitness accounts are any more accurate at this level of detail than secondhand accounts.

In his groundbreaking study of the anthropology of violence, David Riches distinguishes between performers, victims, and witnesses, a schema Pamela Stewart and Andrew Strathern have called the triangle of violence (Riches 1986; Stewart and Strathern 2002). In the recollection of violence, however, the triangle can become confused: the victims can be transformed into performers, and direct witnesses may change their accounts over time, blurring the distinction between first- and secondhand reports. Although the direct witnesses of the violence may speak with the greatest authority, it would be a mistake to assume that secondary witnesses do not affect the recollections of those who witnessed events firsthand. Witnessing can become, over time, a communal event as the acts of violence become part of the cultural imaginary. Memory then, as Maurice Halbwachs (1968) pointed out, is very much a social act; the ways in which firsthand accounts approximate secondhand ones are partly due to the fact that personal memories are really only intelligible in relation to collective structures of representation.

People's recollections do differ, however, not only on the number of dead but in other areas of recollection, too. Women—either from personal memory or from what they have heard—tell of homes being destroyed, everything of value being sacked, and the rest being burned. Some women even recall taking doors off their hinges. In the words of Francisca Condori: "They took everything from our houses. Each one of us had some things of value: they took all of these things; we were just left with a blanket each. They destroyed us, and then we had to start from nothing."

Other women mentioned the blankets, the pots, and the pans that were taken, whereas none of the men I spoke to mentioned such contents of the house. Women were also more likely to mention the sheep stolen. Women are concerned with herding and rearing of sheep as well as the houses. Consequently, they identify different elements of the sacking in their accounts. Men in contrast were more likely to say that all the houses were burned down and there was nothing left.

One incident, however, is recalled by all Wila Kjarkeños, witnesses, and others: the cannibalism of some of their number. Contemporaries say they could smell the odor of burnt flesh wafting up the mountain; and this olfactory memory is the most common and consistent in the accounts. Most people say three men were roasted and eaten; some say only one.

Others again say that of nine men captured, three were set free and then shot in the back, three were buried alive, and three were eaten. Pastora Alegre gave me this more or less typical account: "They say [the people of Jankho Kjarka] killed many people, the women. They say that they had the ovens warming up and killed someone with a bullet and roasted him in the oven; they say they ate him, the person . . . They ate people, they say that they cut the legs and arms off and threw [the pieces] into the oven. They then roasted them like suckling pigs in the oven. They killed many people." Adalid Mamani, who was fourteen when I spoke to him about these events, gave the following account: "They took two people prisoner from here. Then they collected firewood from the other side and heated the oven. They put the people in the oven as if they were suckling pigs; they put them in with their clothes and everything. And then they ate them." There are various versions to this account, some people say that a woman was caught as she was collecting firewood and that they used her firewood to heat the oven. In other accounts the victims were placed in the oven alive and "once they were dead, they ate them." There is no single authoritative account, but everyone in Wila Kjarka mentions the ovens, the roasting, and the cannibalism.

It is not, however, only Wila Kjarkeños who recall these events; people from neighboring communities do as well. Santiago Flores from Choquepata (in sight of both Wila Kjarka and Jankho Kjarka) was told the story by his mother.

FLORES: My mother told me like this, she said: Jankho Kjarka made war; she said there was war in these parts. My mother told me that the bullet reached them and they fell, and the people of Jankho Kjarka felled [the Wila Kjarkeños]. Those from Jankho Kjarka killed many from Wila Kjarka, they say, and [the Wila Kjarkeños] shooting from above couldn't hit their targets, from up there it was difficult to shoot straight; the bullets didn't touch the people. Yes, after that they got them, they brought those from Wila Kjarka down, and they butchered them and cooked them.

CANESSA: Did they burn them in an oven?

FLORES: Not in an oven but in a [large earthenware pot used for making maize beer]. They brought them this way and that way . . . and mounted their heads. One of them was Josesito; his daughter still lives. They made him carry [the others];

they made him by kicking him; but the poor man didn't have much strength. That is it: they say that happened; that is how it was told to me.

It is impossible, of course, to ascertain exactly what happened here, not least because, perhaps unsurprisingly, the people of Jankho Kjarka deny such an event occurred. Indeed, most of the people of Jankho Kjarka claim to have no memory of any of these events, although people from other villages do confirm many of the details I had heard and often provided extremely detailed accounts of their own. In Jankho Kjarka there was an exceptional unwillingness to talk about the past at all, and at one point several young men escorted me from the village for talking to older people.

This had never happened to me before: I have long been accustomed to arriving at the villages near to Wila Kjarka and talking freely and easily with people, and I had once assisted in building a house in Jankho Kjarka. On the occasion when I was asking about the past, however, some people were clearly concerned about my presence. I was, however, able to return after formally asking permission from the village leader (whose manner rapidly changed and who immediately asked me to be godfather to his son), and I found some people willing to talk to me.

The people I spoke to, the few remaining eyewitnesses in Jankho Kjarka, talk of the events as being entirely enacted by other people, soldiers brought by the hacendado; moreover, they present themselves as being among the principal sufferers. Looking around Jankho Kjarka today, it is not difficult to see why they might see themselves as the victims: The many empty houses give it a sense of being abandoned; there are, moreover, few young people in Jankho Kjarka and, in sharp contrast to Wila Kjarka, very few children. Since the construction of the new road in 2006, which reached Wila Kjarka in 2007, and the consequent displacement of the path, Jankho Kjarka does not now have even the foot traffic of people walking from Choquepata to Wila Kjarka, Thikata, Qhusimani, and other villages. As Kimberly Theidon has pointed out, there is an important economic aspect to what is remembered, as well as the cultural and political ones that are more often cited (Theidon 2004).

In Jankho Kjarka one of those who spoke to me was Paulino Laruta, who speaks about the origin of the conflict in terms of the loan of a pongo to the hacendado of Wila Kjarka by his sister, Maclovia. This unnamed pongo was beaten severely by Franco with a metal pipe used to

Paulino Laruta.

blow on the cooking fire (*phusaña*). In Paulino's account, the crime was not the beating but the fact that the pongo did not belong to Franco. In another context he clearly states that "we were the hacendado's indians" (*jaqipäpxatathwa*).

> She lent her brother a pongo. We had to work as pongos for the patrones . . . He beat the pongo in his house, with a phusaña he beat him, and he shouted a lot. But the police were nearby and the soldiers were ready. They heard the cries and said, "Bloody hell, what's happening?" They climbed up a ladder and entered the house and . . . rescued the pongo . . . He shouted, "This is not my patrón!" Maclovia said, "I lent my brother this pongo; I lent my brother money to buy Wila Kjarka; he told me he would give me half of the produce, but he has not given me half the produce."

From Paulino's perspective it was this incident of illegitimately beating the pongo against the background of Franco not sharing the produce of Wila Kjarka that caused the conflict. The police and the soldiers—he does not explain how they happened to be there—immediately occupied Wila Kjarka. Paulino, like many others from Jankho Kjarka, suggests no role for the people of Jankho Kjarka in the conflict.

The partial exception here is María Condori, also from Jankho Kjarka, who frames her account in terms of the manipulation of the hacendados in which both people, from Wila Kjarka and Jankho Kjarka, were ultimately the victims:

> Yes, we lived in those times. We walked/lived to cry: we slept in the road; we slept among the rocks, in bushes; we slept by the rivers; we had to tie up the animals by the rivers and could not move them because we were always being watched. *Qhaxx!* From above they shot at us with rifles. We were in the lower part and those from above could see us when we moved . . .
>
> There were dead on both sides; those from above also had victims. Here, too. That is how it was in those times. The sergeants went up there and broke everything. They sacked the place because they were mad . . . Then there was no one left in the community higher up. The houses were without roofs. They all escaped . . .
>
> We had to have guards all the time. We couldn't walk out in the open . . . That is how we walked (lived): to cry. It was difficult to live in this time of violence but it was the patrones who made us fight . . .
>
> Then one by one they returned to the village above. They built their houses again, and in a couple of years the village was full again. They multiplied. Now we live well together.

María stresses the general pain and misery of those times and notes that there were people killed on both sides. When she began telling me about the three people from Wila Kjarka who were killed, people whom she knew and could name, tears flowed down her face. She would not tell me how the three people died, saying she could not remember, but the event clearly continued to distress her more than fifty years after the event. María finishes her account by stressing that Wila Kjarka recovered quickly, and that there is now no animosity between the communities. For María this is a painful story with victims on both sides, with none of the triumphalism of the Wila Kjarka accounts.

What *really* happened is perhaps not the point and, in any case, impossible to ascertain. What is of greater interest is the way the accounts are highly structured, particularly around the figure three.[8] Three people in three

Maria Condori.

events. Teodosio earlier spoke of three hundred men and six hundred men. The number three structures mythic stories but also structures relations with the dead: there are three days of remembrance; the dead are remembered for three years; a pact with spirits lasts for three years; and so on. The number three (and its multiples) indexes relations with the dead and with chthonic spirits. Structuring in threes is a means of underlining the truth and the broader meaning of the events. Even for people who witnessed the events with their own eyes, what happened in 1951 and afterward assumes mythic proportions: It is, after all, the moment of a great *pachakuti*, a revolution in time rather like the ones that brought the world into light, saw the arrival of the Inkas and then the Spanish, and saw their overthrow.

The memory of the cannibalism events and their retelling, consequently, needs to be considered in terms beyond those who seek to determine if they really happened. Eyewitnesses as well as others describe

Teodosio Condori.

the cannibalism, but younger people, who heard of the events only secondhand, describe this incident in the greatest detail; the roasting and
consumption of human flesh may even be the only particular event they
can recount of the Jankho Kjarka war. The memory of the violence has a
number of functions, one of which is to construct the Other as scarcely
human, thus justifying the division.

There are similarities here with the violence meted out in highland
Peru in the war with Sendero Luminoso during the 1980s and '90s. In the
many examples of people being executed by hooded figures who were
from the same or nearby communities, the perpetrators are described
as being barely human or not human at all. The political and ideological
dimension of Peru's war are, however, absent in the case of Wila Kjarka
and Jankho Kjarka; and although each community had to deal with the
violence of their immediate neighbors, they were spared the situation

Pedro Mamani.

described by Kimberly Theidon (2004) of knowingly living amid their rapists and assailants and the murderers of their kin.

It is certainly possible that the events described really did occur in some form or other. There have been occasional reports of cannibalism in the area. Manuel Qarani from Qhusimani recalls an incident in the nearby community of Waychu: He told me that a few years ago the people of Waychu were continually bothered by people who came from beyond the mountains, stole their sheep, and raided their houses. The people of Waychu captured one of the rustlers and ate him. They were not bothered by rustling again. The key issue is not whether the act of cannibalism actually occurred but, rather, that it is mentioned in accounts as a way of dealing with one's enemies.

Accounts of cannibalism are infrequent in the area—they are extreme events—whereas incidents of being buried alive are regularly reported.

*The Jankho Kjarka cemetery. The trees of Wila Kjarka can
just about be seen in the distance.*

No one who was alive at the time told me where these incidents occurred, other than vaguely "in Jankho Kjarka," but it is interesting to compare accounts from witnesses and participants with those that have been handed down. Several younger people told me that the killings happened on or near the spot where the Jankho Kjarka cemetery now exists, and that at the time of the war, both communities shared a cemetery. The burial of living people is oxymoronic and perverts the normal process of burying dead people. Live burial is, in fact, a well-known form of communal justice in the area. In Bolivia the state is weak, particularly in small communities with little or no road access and where police presence is rare or nonexistent. The community has to police itself, normally through fines or expulsion, but in extreme cases even through extrajudicial execution, such as burial alive.[9]

When people are buried in the cemetery they are remembered for three years, after which they become ancestral mountain deities, achachilas (the largest of which is the snow-capped mountain of Illampu). Burying people alive is more than simply unpleasant: It disrupts the normal communication of people and spirits—the living and the dead—and the conversion of humans into achachilas. As Paul Connerton has noted, cemeteries are important sites where communities are imagined and re-created (Connerton 1989). The splitting of the historical ayllu into two separate communities was one consequence of the Jankho Kjarka war, and the stories of burying alive serve to mark the unsuitability of the people of Jankho Kjarka as partners in the exchanges with the achachilas. In the eyes of Wila Kjarkeños it is not coincidence that, after the war, Jankho Kjarka suffered population loss and erosion and is now a much smaller and poorer community than Wila Kjarka; rather, it is a direct consequence of losing a relationship with the ancestors.

The violence recounted is certainly extreme and sadistic. Cannibalism is a way of not only devouring one's enemies but also of incorporating them (Conklin 2001). It has been suggested that when cannibalism occurs in this area, certain key organs are consumed, such as brains or testicles,[10] as the perpetrators consume their victim's physical, mental, and spiritual strength. As such, there is clearly a powerful symbolic element to the act, but from the view of the victims—that is, people from Wila Kjarka—the symbolism lies in the extreme antisocial violence: This is not the violence of the tinku, with its generalized benefit of fertilizing the earth or serving as a sacrifice to the achachilas; the dead are not consumed by the earth but by their enemies, and thus they are no longer part of the sacrificial cycle between ancestors and people. Cannibalism is consequently the structural opposite of tinku sacrifice; it serves to render the parties inappropriate as tinku partners.

It is clear that the accounts of the Jankho Kjarka war are constructed around powerful mythic themes: relations with the dead, the end of Spanish rule, schism, and genesis. To describe these accounts as mythical is not to suggest that they are somehow false: Myths are not necessarily false in relation to the "facts" nor in the broader ideological truth they index. A myth "is a story that becomes significant as it amplifies the meaning of an individual event (factual or not) into a symbolic and narrative formalization of a culture's shared self-representations" (Portelli 1997: 153). Myths in this sense are powerful social memories in that they are not about individual recollections pure and simple (if such a thing were possible) but are structured around shared meanings, in this case of the significance of particular acts of violence, the consequences of the war, and what it means for people today. It is not surprising then that individual accounts conform to a mythic structure.

These accounts furthermore function as what Steve Stern (2004) calls an "emblematic memory": Cannibalism marks the extreme antisocial violence of the event as well as dramatically asserting the "otherness" of the people of Jankho Kjarka. In Stern's formulation, emblematic memories are not simply homogenized collective memories but also have a hegemonic aspect to them; accounts and personal memories become patterned around this key event. As people make sense of the past in terms of the present, and vice versa, even eyewitness accounts become patterned in particular ways. In Holocaust memories, for example, it has been noted that from the late 1960s, personal accounts followed certain genre patterns—such as descriptions of the extreme sadistic violence of the ss officers—largely absent from earlier accounts (Finkelstein 2000) by, for example, Bettelheim, Levi, and Spellman. As personal memories of the Holocaust gave way to a collective history "owned" by very large numbers of people, personal accounts conformed to the import of this larger history and became generic, to the point that in Roberto Benigni's 1997 film, *La Vita è Bella*, the various stock scenes of Holocaust accounts serve as a backdrop to a film that is profoundly ahistorical.

In his account of the 1944 massacre at Civitella in Val di Chiana, Portelli (1997) examines how recollections of the massacre change over time and particular themes become prominent that were muted or even absent from the earliest accounts: the Catholic Austrians' participation in Mass; the "good Germans" returning to ask for forgiveness. These are important to the citizens of Civitella because they follow the contours of a broader Christian narrative and allow continued antipathy toward the partisans—peasants who inhabited villages beyond the town walls—who killed the German soldiers and thus provoked the retaliatory massacre.

In a similar way the events surrounding the Jankho Kjarka war are beyond simple personal recollection when the events in question are part of public culture and the memories become definitive in themselves. In this case, reiterating the extreme violence perpetrated by the people of Jankho Kjarka justifies the loss of community, which splitting with them entailed. This is not an easy thing for Wila Kjarkeños to do, since the people of Jankho Kjarka and Wila Kjarka had constituted the same community for centuries. It seems likely that focusing on the accounts of cannibalism is a way of distancing oneself from the people of Jankho Kjarka, a distancing that has lasted until the present day. Not everyone who was alive at the time, however, says they remember the Jankho Kjarka war. Domitilia, who had just married a man from Jankho Kjarka before the war broke out and was living with him in her parents' house at the time, claims to have no memory of the event whatsoever.

What is striking in this case is that Jankho Kjarka and Wila Kjarka had such a strong common history cemented by generations of intermarriage. It is possible that the atrocities perpetrated were not in fact done by the people of Jankho Kjarka but others (the soldiers) brought in by the hacendado to pursue his land claims. The memory of cannibalism attributed to the people of Jankho Kjarka in any case serves to underline the relational distance that may have been a response to the violence rather than its immediate cause. Many Wila Kjarkeños (as do the people from Jankho Kjarka) readily admit that both sides were manipulated by the hacendados.

This leads me to an important aspect of how the Jankho Kjarka war is remembered in Wila Kjarka. More than simply being a subsequent moral justification for the act of breaking the community, the Jankho Kjarka war, as recalled in Wila Kjarka, is intimately tied to the struggle against the patrones.

THE WAR AND THE PATRONES

One way of understanding such testimonies is as memories of past events, but as Portelli's (1981b) work has shown, the act of remembering is itself an event, one in the present. What is being remembered and recounted is framed by the present and by what has meaning in the present. The Jankho Kjarka war continues to be remembered and recounted, not only because it accounts for and justifies the split with Jankho Kjarka but also because it is how people in Wila Kjarka narrate the overthrow of hacienda rule and the creation of their autonomy.

The events of the Jankho Kjarka war are not conceptualized within a Western calendrical system. No one in Wila Kjarka could tell me the year of the Jankho Kjarka war, although a mestizo from a neighboring village told me it was in 1951, the year before the Bolivian Revolution. Wila Kjarkeños frame the events in terms of *patrunapacha*, the time of the patrón, and the Jankho Kjarka war is important in personal and collective memory because it provides the narrative for the end of the rule of the hacendado. According to Teodosio:

> One of the things the aggressors did was destroy the Virgin, the patron saint of Wila Kjarka. That saint [Virgin] is not a true one: It is made of wood. They came from up there with much shouting, and they came out of the church. They took everything out of the church and threw everything against the rocks. Then they put everything into the caves where the skunks live. The arms were made of nothing but wood and put together with wire. This saint was thrown all broken into the river. Nothing at all happened. If it were truly sacred, something would have happened to the village. Nothing at all happened.

I was told that this Virgin was brought by the hacendado, and that it was false, not really an icon of chthonic power, not made of stone: If it had been, then a major calamity would have befallen the village, as Teodosio suggests. The sacking of the church and the destruction of the Virgin was indeed traumatic, but in Teodosio's account it also illustrates the illusion of hacendado power. With this realization, the people of Wila Kjarka were able to resist and, ultimately victorious, take back not only the lands of Wila Kjarka but the disputed lands as well; not for the hacendado but for themselves, as the rightful owners of the land. In Teodosio's account the enemy is the hacendado of Jankho Kjarka, who acts through his soldiers, and the people of Jankho Kjarka, who ate human flesh.

What neither Teodosio nor anyone else in the village mentioned is that less than a year after the violence in Wila Kjarka, the country erupted in a major revolution, which saw many communities wresting lands from the hacendados. Residents of many surrounding villages where Wila Kjarkeños had lived as refugees talk of how destitute and miserable they were and how they returned to rebuild their homes and their lives after the Agrarian Reform. Manuel Qarani from Qhusimani recalls Wila Kjarkeños' miserable plight: "They worked others' fields; everywhere they worked others' fields. They helped in the potato harvest; they suffered. They were thrown out [of their community] and they found refuge high above among the *chhijmu* grass, where we graze the mules. One night they arrived there and they ate the grass."

People from other villages, who act rather like a Greek chorus, could tell me in great detail about the sacking, murder, and cannibalism, but failed to mention any heroic return of the Wila Kjarkeños to their village. In fact Manuel tells a far different tale: "Before they returned, once, Martín [Chino]'s father said help would come. And saying this he sent his sister [to Wila Kjarka]. But she never returned. She fell in a trap and they surely captured her . . . Another Chino also died [by being captured] . . . They were living miserably then, in Thikata."

Similarly, residents of other villages spoke in some detail about the peasant militias that were very active in the area, but no one in Wila Kjarka did, or of any other revolt, uprising, or violence in any other community. When recounting the events of the Jankho Kjarka war, Wila Kjarkeños in contrast almost always tell of their victory over their neighbors and patrón, as if they were the sole agents. For example, in one account from Pedro Quispe, who was an eyewitness: "We fought with arms. There were dead on both sides. After a lot of fighting [the *patrones*] began to harvest, but by the end they didn't take anything—we don't even give them a fistful of food; now we just work for ourselves."

The fighting and death instigated by the patrones ends with them receiving no crops from the people at all: a double victory. In a similar vein, Benedicto told me of how Wila Kjarkeños returned from exile and torched the *mayordomo*'s (overseer's) house, which, because of its thatched roof, caught flame quickly, and all jeered as he left in fear, never to return. One of the key features of accounts of the sacking of Wila Kjarka is the burning of all the houses; not one roof was left untouched, I was frequently told. The burning of the principal hacienda building is one of those stock narrative details of the Revolution. It is possible, of course, that the mayordomo's house was repaired, but, since there were no peasants to oversee, it is difficult to see why anyone would have bothered.

Pedro was one of the very few to mention the political context of the events. He is the only one to date the events two years before the Agrarian Reform and say: "Víctor Paz and Hernán Siles signed our liberty; they were the political leaders (*mandatarios*); they defeated the patrones as far as the lands are concerned." Everyone else put the people of Wila Kjarka as the agents of resistance and, ultimately, defeat of the patrones; and even Pedro Quispe on other occasions ascribed agency to the Wila Kjarkeños rather than the reform government. A very good example of this sense of agency is given by Marcelino Misme: "Many people died, sixteen or twenty: They died from our side and theirs . . . There they cornered us with their guns. I got mine and grabbed it like this, but it was no use against all of theirs, and the bullets passed through me here and here [indicating various parts of his body]. It was not my destiny [to die], and I threw myself down there, and after, I recovered. All the houses were completely sacked; none of them had roofs."

Marcelino is riddled with bullets but defends himself valiantly with his gun (although he is not clear how he came to possess one, and this is before the peasant militias were armed). The important element of his account is not his victimhood but his agency and his valiant resistance to live and fight another day. This sense of agency is common to many other accounts of these events; for example, Pedro Quispe recounts how the Wila Kjarkeños had assembled "a battalion, a company to attack Jankho Kjarka. We could have done to them what they did to us, but we just took our lands back and after that no one interfered with us." In Marcelino's account, he describes the violence and says that it was a three-year war with equal casualties on both sides. In passing, he mentions that the three-year war stopped with the ascension of Víctor Paz Estenssoro, who settled matters in the favor of Wila Kjarkeños, but this is secondary to the victory of Wila Kjarkeños over the people of Jankho Kjarka in his and other accounts. Marcelino said that Paz Estenssoro was sent by the Americans to throw out the patrones, removing even further any sense that there was a national revolution of peasants taking up arms across the country and installing a new president.

People in other villages do not recall a three-year war but a period of three years in which Wila Kjarkeños were impotent refugees. They remember far more casualties on the Wila Kjarka side than on that of Jankho Kjarka. Wila Kjarkeños are not unusual in eliding or displacing the Revolution and Agrarian Reform in personal memory, as Alison Spedding (2003) has shown for the *yungas* area and Into Goudsmit for Norte de Potosí (2006). This forgetting is not because the memory is too painful but because it disrupts the narrative that Wila Kjarkeños tell about

themselves today. In her account of Greek Macedonia, Anastasia Karakasidou (1997) gives a detailed account of how Turkish and Bulgarian pasts
are erased because, like Wila Kjarka's histories, these stories contradict
the more important narrative of national unity.[11] The national genre of
Greek history and its accompanying ideology of the homogeneity of
Greece leave little narrative space for memories and accounts that contradict it. In a comparable way, the overriding narrative of the vanquished
patrones, which for Wila Kjarkeños is nothing less than the overthrow of
Spanish rule after centuries of colonization, displaces accounts of misery
and defeat during this great historical moment.[12]

In his oft-quoted paper, "The Time of my Life," Alessandro Portelli
(1981a) tells the story of how the death of Luigi Trastulli is remembered in
the Italian town of Terni.[13] Many people remembered the death of Luigi
Trastulli in a demonstration in 1949, but half of Portelli's informants, including eyewitnesses, dated his death in 1953, when there was major street
fighting after the sacking of steelworkers. This apparent confusion, despite the fact that many of the informants daily went past a monument to
Trastulli with the correct date of his death, is attributed by Portelli to the
collective shame of not responding to the valiant man's death. The events
are collapsed in order for some workers to "affirm that they retaliated."

A similar interpretation can be offered for Wila Kjarka. It seems likely,
or at least possible, that when neighboring haciendas were erupting in
violence, the people of Wila Kjarka were refugees and in no position to
fight. In this case there is not so much a collapsing of two events but the
displacement of one by the other. Rather than seeing the violence between Jankho Kjarka and Wila Kjarka within a broader context of revolution, the latter is erased or at the very least given very little significance.
Wila Kjarkeños, in defeating the people of Jankho Kjarka, also, ultimately,
defeated the hacendados who had instigated the battle in the first place.
The Revolution of official history is elided and the true agents of major
historical change become the Wila Kjarkeños, who remember overthrow-
ing the hacendado and regaining their lands in one go.

Many scholars have noted the importance of forgetting in personal
narratives; forgetting is an essential part of the process of remembering
(e.g., Theidon 2006; Tonkin 1992; Zur 1998). Janet Carsten suggests that
knowledge and information that is not passed on through memory "have
a kind of negative significance in that they allow other images of shared
identity in the present and future to come to the fore" (1995: 318). For
Wila Kjarkeños to forget many aspects of the revolution enables them to

imagine a present and future in which they are agents of history, not its victims; and how they understand themselves today as a people and community is very much rooted in the accounts of violence and victory in the past.

The Jankho Kjarka war, as it is referred to in Wila Kjarka, is not simply an event but a memory to be recalled. The violence within the community and indeed between families cannot be simply forgotten because the result is in daily view: the two cemeteries, the eroding fields, and the ever-decreasing size of Jankho Kjarka. The extreme violence of cannibalism, which is a key feature of accounts, serves to justify the split by demonizing the people of Jankho Kjarka, but its recounting has another purpose: It frames the events in terms of the victory of Wila Kjarka over not only the people of Jankho Kjarka but also the hacendado. Victims become victors, and the true villains, the hacendados, are ultimately defeated. That the violence is remembered and recounted in generic ways serves to offer a foundational myth for the new liberated community.

As twenty-first-century Wila Kjarkeños contemplate their present and future in the days of the latest Bolivian Revolution, they do so through the lens of history: For them the events of the mid-twentieth century are indeed a major point of reference, but it is not a history that will be easily recognized by historians and politicians. For Wila Kjarkeños their historical consciousness profoundly informs the distinction between jaqi and q'ara, which so inflects their everyday lives. It is tempting to see these terms as simply mapping on to the conventional categories of indian (or indigenous) and nonindian, but to do so would be to try to understand Wila Kjarkeño identity in outside terms. A clear element here is being a member of a community, the kind of community many outsiders readily identify as being indigenous. But how does one become a member of the community?

FOUR

From Fetuses to Mountain Ancestors

Encarnación lived on the other side of the plaza, but I really got to know her when she fell off a ladder and ripped open her cheek. By that time I had become known for my first-aid kit, and Encarnación came to see me, her teeth visible though her cheek, and asked me to sew it up for her. I was impressed by the calm with which she made this proposition and wondered about the pain she must have been enduring. I must confess that I declined to sew up her cheek, but cleaned and dressed the wound and suggested she go to Choquepata or Sorata and have it sutured professionally.

I did not know it then, but Encarnación was pregnant, and as her belly grew, her scar healed. One night she went into labor. I was aware of some of what was going on: Teodosio had been called. I did not hear cries of pain across the plaza, but this did not surprise me as I had already learned that Encarnación could endure pain stoically. My comadre, Agustina, told me that things were not going well; there were problems. "Will the baby be all right?" I asked stupidly. I got absolutely no response from Agustina. It was, at any rate, a stupid question because one does not refer to *babies* in childbirth but *sullus* (fetuses), and of course, the concern was primarily about Encarnación. In the developed West, women now very rarely die in childbirth, and the death of a child is seen as a tragedy; in Wila Kjarka both are relatively frequent, although infant mortality is much higher. The primary concern is more for the mother, a productive and full member of the community, than for the fetus.[1]

Encarnación died that night. As far as I can gather, she hemorrhaged. I was led to understand that she gave birth, but the baby subsequently died. No one could or would tell me how. Encarnación was given a full community burial, but people simply did not respond to my questions about the baby, who seemed not to have been buried—at least, not in the cemetery, which showed only one new grave.

This episode in the early months of my fieldwork impressed on me how little I knew about anything that happened in Wila Kjarka. I did not even know what questions to ask. But I did know that this sad incident raised questions about the status of fetuses and babies in Wila Kjarka, as well as how a mother's health is valued over that of her fetus. It also raised questions about how one becomes a fully fledged member of a community, and how this is recognized and marked, especially at death.

At its simplest, one might suppose that just being born into the community to parents of the community would confer membership, and that a birth would be a highly celebrated event. In fact, birth is a largely private event, not marked by the community, unlike any other socially significant event in one's life. In contrast to other parts of the Bolivian Andes (e.g., Abercrombie 1986; Arnold 1989), there are no descent groups in Wila Kjarka, so birth does not even confer membership to such a group. That is, there is no notion of descent in the sense of belonging to a lineage understood in genealogical terms. This is not to say, however, that there is no communal sense of identity with the ancestors; in fact, quite the contrary is true: The ancestral spirits, the achachilas, give legitimacy to the human use of their land. Nevertheless, even though people are related to the achachilas, it would not be correct to say that people understand themselves to be directly descended from them.

In Wila Kjarka, as appears to be the case in many Austronesian societies (Bloch 1992), personhood is a process that arguably is only completed on the death of an adult, an event that is of far greater social significance than a birth. Personhood, including its gendered aspects, is not understood to be rooted in substance but in practice, how one acts upon the world and the kinds of human and extrahuman relationships one has: The process of being jaqi, being a gendered person, and being a human being are, unsurprisingly, tightly intertwined. To understand what it means to be jaqi, we need to understand how one becomes human.

In Western discourse one is simply born human, and there are many parts of the Western world where people extend the recognition of human nature to the fetus and embryo. Wherever one positions oneself on this debate, the point at which one is human is clearly defined: at birth, at conception, or when the fetus is viable outside the womb. The Western debates are about the point, the moment that defines human from non-human. Such clear-cut definitions are quite alien to Wila Kjarkeños, who have a much more fluid understanding of ontology.

Wila Kjarkeños use the word *sarnaqaña* to talk about their way of life, and it literally means *walking*. Life is a movement along a path, *thaki* (see also Arnold 2006), and one translation of *custom* is *sarnaqawi*, or one's walking. What makes people different from each other is the way they move through their lives, what they do, and where they are going. People follow different paths, and according to which path one follows one may become jaqi or, indeed, q'ara, and the path begins with how one comes into the world.

The ability to produce children is important to adults and is one of many manifestations of their ability to engage productively with the world and produce from it. At all levels, production is underwritten by the spirits. Fields will not produce if the relevant spirit is not feted, nor will animals reproduce if the right rituals are not performed, and human procreation is similarly assisted by the spirits. There are numerous spirits that have various manifestations, genders, and names. They are not, however, different entities, for they are part of the same tellurian matrix (Sallnow 1987: 126). The major manifestations are the (female) earth spirit; the *pachamama*; the (male) mountain spirits, the *achachilas*; and the house spirit, the *kunturmamani*. It is the kunturmamani that is most closely associated with the birth of humans as he presides over household production. People are explicit about these spirits being profoundly connected, and on more than one occasion people have explained the kunturmamani to me by saying he is the "pachamama" of the house. The kunturmamani "cares for us" (*uywapxituxa*), where *uywaña* is a word for caring but also for "bringing up," as in caring for a child.

The kunturmamani and, by extension the other tellurian beings, are ultimately responsible for the fertility of the married couple and the arrival of the fetus into the world. The act of conceiving and giving birth does not, however, produce a person; whereas birth is an important indication that a woman and a man have achieved personhood to the extent that they can productively maintain a household and reproduce, for the child, birth merely produces the raw material out of which a person may be created.

CONCEPTION

Both conceptions and births are reckoned in terms of fiestas. Early on in my fieldwork I was impressed that a midwife (*uswiri*) could so confidently predict that Yula's baby would come on the feast of the Holy Name. The baby was, in fact, born a week and a half later, so I was surprised to hear people not only profess ignorance of the birth date but talk of the birth as having occurred on the feast of the Holy Name. The significance of this is not that people in Wila Kjarka have difficulty with the calendar but that a birth event should occur at a time when the community assembles and fetes one or other aspect of the tellurian spirit world.

Conception too, is said to occur during fiestas. To comprehend the importance of fiestas in birth, one must appreciate the difference a fiesta makes to the life of villagers. For most of the year, the people of Wila Kjarka live and work in their household units, occasionally exchanging labor with close kin and fictive kin. At these times there is little social contact between villagers; there is, for example, no generalized visiting, even among kin. The exception would be when children visit an elderly grandparent to take them food or when a sister or mother visits early in the morning. In these cases, close kin sit in the doorway or just outside it. Nor do people stop to chat on the way to and from the fields. People do talk during work breaks, but that is within the family unit and compadres who are helping each other. Young men often play soccer an hour before sunset, but there is very little of what one might describe as generalized sociality.

The contrast between the profane time of day-to-day existence and the sacred time of fiestas is quite striking: During fiestas, all agricultural work ceases or is handed over to adolescents and children; in some of the larger fiestas, the adults of the community eat and drink together for several days. It is a time of heightened sensitivity: People cry, laugh, shout, fight, and flirt with great intensity.

It is during fiestas that the community is most engaged with the powers of the tellurian spirits who bring rain, enable the earth to produce crops, confer wisdom and agency on people, and also accord humans the ability to produce children. Communication is generally achieved through making offerings directly to the underworld spirits in the form of alcohol, coca, cigarettes, and sacrificed animals, but also through households sharing food, alcohol, and conviviality. The consumption of alcohol on such occasions, as Thierry Saignes points out, generally for the Andes, "contributes in uniting men with themselves as well as with spirits, gods or the dead (its use annuls the division between sacred and profane spheres)" (1989: 104).[2] The sharing of coca leaves also has a similar effect as Catherine Allen has carefully documented for a community in Peru (1988: 137).

An important feature of fiestas is the strong sense of community solidarity that is expressed, and people went to great pains to point out to me how everyone in the village was in attendance (even if this was sometimes not the case). In Wila Kjarka there is a running tension between household interests and community interests—a conflict that is never ultimately resolved (cf. Albó 1975). Indeed, it is also the case that many tensions surface during fiestas, assisted no doubt by alcohol. As people are sleep deprived and drunk, these tensions surface, often violently, but they are also quickly resolved, and this may have a cathartic effect in preventing disputes and rivalries from smoldering indefinitely.

More positively, fiestas are occasions when the whole community acts as one household sharing food, drink, and coca together as well as dancing, which has an explicitly procreative aspect. Dancing is said to sexually stimulate the earth goddess, the pachamama, and thus increases her munificence of procreative powers. It is thus through fiestas and the sharing of food, alcohol, and coca with each other and the spirits that the community and its identity is created and affirmed.

There are two broad reasons why conceptions are believed to occur during fiestas. First, because this is the time when the enabling power of the spirits is most immanent, and second, because this is when people are more relaxed, less inhibited, and consequently more amorous. Several people from Wila Kjarka told me that sexual intercourse between couples occurred with much greater frequency during fiestas than in the periods between them.[3] A sharp contrast is made between the sex acts of adolescents, which occasionally occur when they are herding (cf. Millones and Pratt 1989: 35), and the sex acts of adults, which occur within a stable relationship and in the domesticated space of the household. Adolescent sex is considered "wild" because the adolescents are unmarried and is performed beyond the community boundaries. As such, they invite neither sanction, condemnation, or interest on the part of adults (de la Cadena

1997: 141; Harris 1980; Isbell 1976: 59; Millones and Pratt 1989: 38–40). These acts are not so much immoral as valueless, since they occur in a place far from the community between people who are socially immature. Luis Millones and Mary Louise Pratt suggest that adolescents adopt the role of violating the sexual mores of the community, whereas married people reinforce it. I am not sure this is an accurate interpretation of attitudes toward adolescent sex—at least, not for Wila Kjarka. In my view, it is not so much that adolescents break rules, it is that there are simply very few rules for them to break. Sex between adolescents beyond the confines of the community simply does not matter: Nobody cares. Once these acts occur within the community, they become much more significant, and the clear assumption is that the couple will form a stable union. The movement from sex in the high mountains to sex within the community characteristically occurs during fiesta time when young couples traditionally choose to elope or, rather, formalize their union.

Young couples may very well have initiated a sexual relationship long before, and this relationship may indeed be known if not acknowledged by both sets of parents; but the first stage in a marriage is when a young man takes a young woman to his parents' house, where they spend the night. If a young woman or girl were to become pregnant before this event it would be very difficult to persuade the potential father to support her, but once the relationship is made public in this way he would be considered responsible for the maintenance of any offspring.

Conception occurs with the union of semen and menstrual blood (*jatha wilampi juntasiya*). As a result, some Wila Kjarkeños stated that conception is easiest during menstruation—a belief shared by people in the Aymara-speaking communities of Qaqachaka (Arnold 1989: 202; Arnold and Yapita 1996). Menstruation is known as *wila phaxsi*, the monthly blood, but the clear reference to monthly intervals notwithstanding, many women from Wila Kjarka do not menstruate regularly due to long periods of lactation, frequent pregnancies, and poor nutrition.

Despite the fact that the man and woman contribute to the creation of the fetus, there is no sense that semen and blood contribute to certain parts, such as blood and bones (cf. Bloch 1992), or that in conception there is a sense of bloodlines and semen lines intermingling (cf. Arnold 1989), as indeed we might suspect, given that there is no meaningful sense of "lineage" in Wila Kjarka. Without such corporate units, or matrilateral and patrilateral kin recognized in a distinguishable way, ideas surrounding conception quite simply reflect the belief that men and women create children together.

Blood and semen combine to create a growing formless bloody mass (*wila muruqu*) until the fourth month of gestation, when the fetus begins to move. At this point, the fetus has hair and bones and is known as a fetus (*sullu*). People say that if a pregnancy aborts before the fetus begins to move in the belly, what comes out is blood and tissue of no determinate shape; after this, it looks like a fetus.

Throughout the pregnancy the couple will make regular offerings to the condor-falcon (*kunturmamani*), who is the principal household god. This is especially important should the woman become sick during pregnancy. Offerings made to the kunturmamani will ensure that her spirit (*ajayu*) returns and the pregnancy proceeds to its full course.

During pregnancy, the woman will continue her chores, but they will gradually diminish, particularly the heavy ones, as the pregnancy develops. A pregnant mother has access to specialists in case there are any problems during her pregnancy: the *yatiri* (shaman) and the uswiri, one of the many women in the community who has experience with childbirth. The yatiri deals with problems of a more spiritual nature, those matters that involve the ajayu. The uswiri massages the abdomen and predicts the date of the birth. This date is the date of the fiesta during which the uswiri believes the child will be born. She will also make sure the fetus is positioned properly by performing *thalthapiña*—having the mother lie on an *awayu* (carrying cloth) and maneuvering the awayu by the ends.

BIRTH

A birth is very much a private, household affair, and not much attention is accorded it by villagers beyond those directly involved. A birth generally takes place at home, where the mother-to-be is attended by her husband. In Wila Kjarka, it is the man's duty to make sure his wife is comfortable, warm, and well fed. She will birth squatting or standing with her knees bent, supported by her husband or whoever is attending (cf. Bradby 1998: 51; Platt 2002). The man's role is also to fill the room with smoke, as this is thought to assist the birth and specifically move the contractions on (cf. Platt 2002: 139). The mother is given lamb broth as well as other rich and fortifying foods during labor and for several days after the birth. When a birth is difficult, the yatiri, Teodosio, is sometimes called. He told me he cuts his nails and spreads lard on his arms in order to help him get the baby out. Sometimes, he said, he has to put his arms in up to his elbows, but then it comes out easily.[4]

The focus here is unambiguously on maternal, not fetal, health. Tristan Platt and his colleagues (2002) have suggested that recent developments in reproductive health policy have moved the focus away from maternal health to fetal health at the expense of women. This is consistent with the position of the Catholic Church, which prioritizes fetal health over maternal health, even if the woman should die as a result. I concur with Platt and his colleagues, who observe that the death of an infant is an occasion for sadness and tears but "does not even remotely have the traumatic significance of the death of a mother" (Platt 2002: 130). For Platt a parturient woman is engaged in nothing less than a battle for life, an inversion of the male role on the battlefield (2002: 132).

What is most certainly the case is that motherhood in Wila Kjarka is understood very differently from that of the self-sacrificing mother that is referenced in school celebrations and national discourses, much less the *mater dolorosa* of orthodox Catholicism. In a culture where reproduction is not valued particularly highly and women are admired more for their productive capacities than their reproductive ones, women are neither defined in terms of the children they produce nor even are they principally defined as mothers. Women are much more likely to be ashamed than proud of the number of children to which they have given birth. Birth is most certainly not a singular experience that defines a woman as an adult or fully contributing member of society (although it certainly plays a role); rather, it is a dangerous and potentially traumatic event that must be overcome.

Whether women in Wila Kjarka think of themselves as warriors or not, they are certainly aware that they have a very good chance of not surviving childbirth, since they will know many women who have died giving birth. Most births, happily, do not end in this way, and once the baby is born the attendant cuts the umbilical cord and waits for the placenta to emerge. The cut has to be measured from the umbilicus: two fingers for a female child and three fingers for a male child, so that his penis will grow. This is a very rare example of an instance when Wila Kjarkeños explicitly recognize that gender is rooted in physical differences, because gender—as with personhood generally—is usually spoken of in terms of processes and activities. It is obvious that, even though they treat small children as genderless, parents know that they will grow into male and female; that the outer expression of gender is ultimately attributable to the genitals they have a birth; or rather, that genitals signal gender, even if they do not necessarily determine it. Moreover, Teodosio's account of what must be done to ensure that males and females grow properly suggests that physical sex does not develop "naturally" but, rather, it must be assisted by the agency of the knife.

In this, people in Wila Kjarka are similar to those cultures that practice genital cutting in order to ensure the "proper" development of a child's genitalia, be they to remove the foreskin of the penis to make it protrude more, or removing the clitoris "in case it grows large like a penis" (Talle 1993). In these cases, people understand the physical body to develop into male and female with the assistance of human intervention. Even in Wila Kjarka, as in other Andean communities, where people do not see genitals as the root explanation of gender, it is interesting to note that genital development is dependent, at least partly, on human intervention; and consequently, human culture plays a role in determining someone's sex. Even at this stage of development, one's identity as male or female as well as one's identity as jaqi or q'ara is part of a social process; it is not simply "given."

After the umbilical cord is cut, attention is given to the placenta. Teodosio comments: "The hot placenta has fat, and with a large needle I take that fat out and, with the blood of the placenta, I cover [the baby] completely.[5] The fat must be white, opaque, and that is why it must be taken out with a needle. It is with that fat that the child is spread." Covering the child with this fat protects it from bad airs and malign spirits.

Children are very vulnerable to illness because their ajayu spirit is not considered to be well settled in the body. They are consequently prone to ajayu flight, which causes illness, and, if it is not quickly returned, will result in death. This vulnerability to soul flight, which can be occasioned by something as simple as fright, is evidence of their tenuous tenancy of the land of people on the surface of the earth.

As the child enters the world of humans, the physical link with the spirits below must be cut. The placenta, part of the world of spirits, must be carefully returned. After the birth, the placenta is taken at night to a place in the stream where the stream spirits, the *sirinus*, dwell, and there it is washed (*sirintaña*). Then it is returned to the home, where it is buried in a corner of the house of the kunturmamani, the house spirit.

The baby and placenta come into the world together, and the umbilical cord is what links the child to the world from which it came. It is not surprising then that the umbilical cord is a very powerful offering to the

achachilas and is an excellent substitute for human fat. Having had its umbilical cord cut (a task usually left to the child's father), the child can now
grow up to be a (gendered) human being, but the placenta returns to the
world of the spirits, which is associated with the underground and with
darkness. Daubing the child with fat from the placenta offers it protection
in its new world, and it can also be seen as a form of blessing on the part
of the kunturmamani.

Once the child is born it is cleaned and swaddled, but it is not fed until
at least twenty-four hours after birth; in some areas, I was told, the baby is
not fed for three days. The reason given is that this makes the baby hardy,
but it may also be the case that a very weak baby will die quickly and thus
not tax the resources of the family. Babies are tightly swaddled, and around
the swaddling clothes is tied a wide woven belt called a *wak'a*. The wak'a is
usually woven by the mother, and its purpose is to protect the child from
evil spirits and to keep the soul, the ajayu, bound within the body. There
is also the belief that if the child is not tightly bound it will be deformed.[6]

If a child dies shortly after birth and before it has been formally named
(see below), he or she is not buried in the cemetery, but at some distance
from the village in a place called Kimurpata. As Domitilia told me, "Those
without name are buried down by the waters where there are many
rocks; down there by the river they are buried. Six I have buried there, six
(*Wawaxa k'irt'añaya, allitattawayxchispaxaya*)."

At this stage of its existence the baby is totally unsocialized and in a
sense nonhuman, for it has neither speech nor even a name. An unnamed
baby is considered still to be a fetus (sullu), and it is for this reason that
data on neonatal deaths are so difficult to obtain. It is impossible to know
if one is recording infanticide or neonatal deaths, and after some time,
mothers tend not to consider neonatal deaths as births at all. On several
occasions when talking to women about the number of babies they had
had, they omitted births of babies who had died in the first weeks or even
months of life and of which I happened to be aware. It is during the period before the naming ceremony that infanticide, when it does occur,
is most likely to take place. Infanticide during this period is considered
something like a late abortion. Nancy Scheper-Hughes has put forward
a similar interpretation for mothers in Brazil who cease to care for their
babies because they, for one reason or another, do not think they are
worth making the effort (1992: 432–33). Unwanted pregnancies in Wila
Kjarka are usually dealt with by recourse to herbal abortifacients or,
exceptionally, by a visit to the pharmacist in the nearest market town. In

the words of a friend, "When you have too many children, you must cure yourself (*qullasiñawa*). You must take some medicine, and you just need to expel the fetus (*jaqsuyañaspaya*) . . . You drink, and then it comes out." This is not a pronatalist community, and people are very aware of the cost to the household of too many children as well as the burden of children who will not be productive.

Contraception is not easily available in Wila Kjarka. Coitus interruptus is not widely practiced, and many couples complain of the difficulties of abstention: "It is too easy to make a mistake (*pantjasiñjamapuniwa*)." Indeed, given that sexual activity increases during fiestas, when people are very often drunk, it is easy to see why contraception, by whatever method, is not deemed to be very successful in Wila Kjarka. Although people clearly desire fewer children and often spoke to me about methods of contraception, it is not generally openly discussed. Arminda Chinu told me that people don't talk about it for fear of being criticized: "Some speak badly, others will scold and criticize; that is why people remain silent."[7] According to the health worker in Choquepata, only two women in Wila Kjarka are availing themselves of free contraception. In the health worker's view, this is because women are ignorant, because their husbands want to have children, or because they themselves want to have children. Many women in Wila Kjarka, however, are wary of the substandard medication that is often given in the health post in Choquepata. This is one woman's experience:

> I went for one year, and for one year I did not bleed; but then I became pregnant. It didn't work: I had the injections in vain; and now I have my daughter . . . She is eight months old now. I went. You cannot make a mistake; you cannot go too early or too late. You must go on the right day. I went, but the attendant wasn't there. I had to go the next day and then she gave me the injection, but it didn't work. They say that you cannot make any mistake.

This experience, if it is generalized, may account for the poor uptake of contraception in Wila Kjarka. Other methods are either unavailable, considered unsafe (such as the coil), or too expensive. In practice, then, few options are open to women in Wila Kjarka to limit their pregnancies. Some people despair at the strain of bringing up children in very limited circumstances. One woman clearly had enough: "I am in great sorrow. I wish [my children] would all die; I wish they would die I say. They make me very angry; they make each other angry. I only have boys and they are always fighting."[8] Such despair is extreme, but many people share the sense of frustration and the desire to have fewer children. It is very rare for people to speak of the joys of having children.

People do, therefore, attempt to limit their family size through abstention or abortion. These are always difficult decisions, but sometimes difficult decisions have to be made after the birth of a baby. People in Wila Kjarka are poor and some are very poor, to the point that caring for a sick or severely handicapped infant puts an unbearable strain on the family's resources. Data on infanticide are difficult to obtain but, as far as I can gather, infanticide occurs when the baby has a physical defect or if it appears quite sick. Some babies are simply left to die, but I have also been told that some babies are simply left out on a cold night and other friends suggested that they are smothered. People are naturally uncomfortable about this topic and, unsurprisingly, some people not only deny that infanticide occurs in Wila Kjarka, they also say that neonates are buried in the cemetery rather than Kimurpata.

One morning as we sat around her cooking fire shelling beans together, my comadre Maruja told me that a long, long time ago, people used to throw newborns—some dead, some alive—off Kimurpata: "I have never been to Kimurpata; I don't even know where it is!" However, a little later in the conversation, when I asked again where Kimurpata was, I received the following directions: "Follow the path past the Wila Kjarka cemetery and beyond the turn to the Jankho Kjarka cemetery. Don't go down the path toward Sorata, just keep going to the cliff. It is right above [the place called] *Siku sikuri*. That is Kimurpata. But I have never been there."

Kimurpata is above the big river, *Jach'a Jawira*, at a place where the waters thunder down over large boulders through a narrow canyon. This is a place of water spirits, *sirinus*, par excellence, and there is a homology between taking neonates to the river and the practice of washing the placenta at the stream where the water gushes out. Both places are like the fetus and placenta themselves: wet and emanating from the realm of the achachilas and other spirits of the manqhapacha. By tossing the bodies of babies over Kimurpata it would seem people are simply returning them whence they came.

Teodosio told me why it was important to bury the unnamed babies in Kimurpata: "[If we buried them in the cemetery] it would be a sin. The lightning from above with bolts would come and thus that lightning would make our (jaqi) bones tremble and so enter our bodies. And so, then, all this would come to pass."[9]

The view of the river with Kimurpata on the left above the escarpment called Siku sikuri, so named because the formation looks like panpipes (sikuri). The river flows fast to the land below, where the dead dwell.

Lightning is quintessentially a message from the achachilas, and indeed being hit by lightning is one of the diagnostics of having been chosen to be a yatiri. In the case of burying an unnamed baby in the cemetery, the lightning is clearly punishment from the gods, and there is an interesting parallel here with the punishment from the Christian god who brings hail on those communities that do not baptize their babies. But why would the achachilas visit such violence upon jaqi? The achachilas get angry when the normal exchanges between humans and ancestors are interrupted or blocked. In this case it appears that unnamed babies (i.e., fetuses) simply do not belong to the realm of humans and must be returned directly to the achachilas and the wet and dark world below (which is why they are buried down by the river, deep in a gorge). To bury them in the earth is to imply a relationship with achachilas that simply does not exist and, among other things, would delay their reincorporation into the world of the ancestors.

Tristan Platt, basing his writing on the Quechua-speaking Macha some distance to the south of Wila Kjarka, presents these relationships much more clearly. He argues that the fetus is animated by the souls of pagan ancestors and that every birth is a reenactment of the mythohistorical event when chullpas were defeated by the sun and humans became Christian (2002: 128). According to this argument, fetuses are chullpas, and some support is given to this argument by the fact that the sun/son of God is inimical to newborns. The care of infants in this regard goes beyond a concern that they may overheat or burn, but rather that the sun's rays are positively harmful even in small doses. Whether each birth is in some manner a reenactment of the arrival of the sun and destruction of the chullpas is a different matter; and I could find no data in Wila Kjarka that resonate with such an intriguing argument.

What is clear, however, is that fetuses do not have the status in Wila Kjarka as Christian souls, which, according to the Roman Catholic Church since 1871, fetuses have from the point of conception. Of course, the Church could not have come to this position before the late nineteenth century, since medical technology only confirmed the union of egg and sperm and its role in procreation in 1854. Although Lazzaro Spallazani (1729–99) observed the fertilization of frog egg and sperm, it wasn't until the nineteenth century, with the work of George Newport (1854) and William Harvey, that the process became better understood and the implications for human conception fully accepted. Before this time the Catholic Church considered the point of ensoulment or animation to occur when the fetus begins to move, when "quickening" occurs (between 14 and 18 weeks of gestation), although there was some debate as to whether male fetuses were ensouled before female ones. In turn, it took until well into the twentieth century for the idea to be widely accepted, even in conservative Catholic communities, that aborting fetuses in the early stages of pregnancy was murder. It is therefore not the least bit surprising that this recent development in Catholic theology has not been fully embraced in indigenous communities in Bolivia when priests are still struggling to persuade people that the purpose of baptism is other than avoiding hail. On one occasion I was talking to a Spanish priest who had spent over twenty years in Bolivia, learning Quechua and administering to a wide-flung parish. He bemoaned the fact that, after more than twenty years, he still hadn't persuaded local people that baptism is about joining the community of loving Christians and has nothing to do with averting the wrath of God in the form of hail. "Twenty years?" I responded, "Isn't it more like five hundred?"

The general weakness of the Catholic Church's ability to impose orthodoxy on indigenous people notwithstanding, there is a reticence in Wila Kjarka in talking about abortion (*sullsuña*), more so among men. One Saturday morning I met up with three friends from Wila Kjarka in the market of Sorata and invited them to a pizza. Sorata has a plethora of pizzerias. Some years ago, there was a very good Italian restaurant, and its Italian owner trained his staff. When he closed his restaurant, many of his waiters opened pizzerias in the main square and, by keeping overheads low, they all seemed to survive. The plaza of Sorata, with its restaurants, cyber cafés, and shops selling cell phones, seems a world away from Wila Kjarka. Over a large ham-and-black-olives pizza we talked about the changes taking place in Wila Kjarka and we also talked about family size. For my three companions, whom I have known since the day I arrived in Wila Kjarka, having smaller families is as much a sign of progress as the new road, chemical fertilizer, and owning a cell phone.

These men agreed that contraception was damaging to a woman's health, abortion in particular. "You have to take care of yourself," said Zenobio. "You can sleep together or not, it is up to you. Make love or not."[10] Perhaps because we were in the shadow of the church or simply in the center of Sorata negotiating stringy mozzarella, they were all keen to demonstrate to me that they were not party to the dubious customs of which I may have heard. Yet they showed detailed familiarity with the practice of abortion, even if all these incidents occurred "in the past" or somewhere else. Typical was the story of incest in, perhaps inevitably, Jankho Kjarka, where the girl buried the baby alive and the father/grandfather was expelled from the community. In Wila Kjarka men distance themselves from these accounts even more than do women, although in general people are much more relaxed in talking about their lives and practices than they are in Sorata. For example, as we shared our pizza, my friends were keen to impress upon me that they did not follow "pagan" rituals, even though I have participated in many of these with them in Wila Kjarka. People are clearly aware that such practices are taboo, especially in the mestizo world of pizzerias and cyber cafés.

What I found no evidence of in Wila Kjarka is that men sought to control their wives' fertility or prevented them from planning their families; men were certainly interested in having a relatively small number of children. In this, men and women generally concur: The ideal family size is four healthy children. If it is true that women asked me about contraception more often than men, it is also true that men showed a keen interest. I gave many demonstrations on condom use on the handle of a hoe to men, and this was most certainly not my initiative. Condoms, however, have to be bought or obtained from the health post in Choquepata, where people have a profound mistrust of the health workers. In other Aymara-speaking communities, anal sex (*chinajat ikasiña*) is apparently used as a form of contraception, as reported to me by a resident of the altiplano, but I found no evidence that it was widely practiced in Wila Kjarka, where it seems not to be considered a normal sexual practice.

Nor did I find any suggestion that men thought that contraception would lead to promiscuity on the part of their wives, or even that a large number of children was a sign of virility. The kind of sexual jealousy that is iconic of machismo in much of Latin America, including indigenous Latin America, appears largely absent in Wila Kjarka. I am not saying that no one is ever jealous but, rather, that it is not something about which men or women are particularly anxious.

NAMING

Despite the widespread anxiety surrounding family size and births, many babies are, of course, born in Wila Kjarka. The newborn's status as fetus clearly indicates that birth in itself does not produce persons, even if it does provide some of the raw materials: Personhood is something that is ritually conferred on a being by the community and the world of the spirits. The first ritual of life is the naming ceremony, known as *sutiyaña*, which takes place a couple of weeks after the birth. Sutiyaña is a fairly minor affair and, unlike all other ceremonies marking a change of status, it is attended only by immediate family members and, sometimes, the catechist appointed by a priest, who baptizes the child. This is the only form of Christian baptism that takes place in Wila Kjarka until the priest's visit, which occurs on average once every two to three years. On these occasions, the priest performs the baptism once again, but it is a very different affair. The priest's baptism is done in the school, where he baptizes twenty or more children in a row. The importance of this baptism for parents is that the office of the priest makes the relationship they have with the godparents (*padrinos*) much more formal and, consequently, implies a stronger bond.

For the sutiyaña, salt and water are mixed into a paste and then daubed on the baby's mouth and head. Salt is considered to be a quintessentially human attribute, and anointing the infant with salt is the first step of incorporation into human society.[11] The fact that the child is daubed on the mouth is consistent with the belief that speech is a fundamentally human characteristic.[12] Teodosio told me that he anoints the child twice, once for each of the two "souls," the kuraji and ajayu; both are particularly vulnerable in a newborn. The distinction among kuraji, ajayu, and chuyma was never clearly explained to me, but all three animate the body of a human: kuraji (Sp. *coraje*) may linger after death as a ghost and is the least elaborated of the three; ajayu is the soul that wanders and must be reattached to the body to prevent death and after death to prevent the ajayu from wandering angrily in search of its body; chuyma is sometimes translated as "heart," as it is believed to be rooted in vital organs.

Body fat, which the paste of salt and water is said to resemble, is believed to be a source of essential life force (chuyma), and the diminution or loss of it entails illness or death. This is how Teodosio told me he cured a child from ajayu loss:

> With the Rosary I call it. Before this, I perform llawi with everything. I call it from these four places here. I pay and after paying I say: "Ajayu, do not tarry in returning." With the child's clothes or some other item I make the soul return. It comes like a shadow—not a person—just like a shadow. And then I bring it, and with that shadow I envelop the baby; and with a blessing to the left I tie up the baby well. I can also see the chuyma through reading coca leaves. That is how I cure the baby.

Fat (lik'i) is a common offering to the autochthonous spirits as a substitute for human sacrifice (Bastien 1978; Sallnow 1987). Here, however, the offering of the "fat" is reversed. By being anointed with salt, the child enters human society, and this creates a debt: The debt can be delayed by offerings such as the sacrifice of live animals or animal fat, but in the end the human body and its life force must return whence it came. Immediately at birth the child is greased with the fat of the placenta, a week later she or he is daubed with salt in a "fatty" paste on its mouth. Both of these acts are to protect the child and mark its entrance into the human world, but the difference is that the salt is a different kind of fat to that of the placenta; it is fat that is a product of human agency. It also marks ambivalence about the relationship with the earth spirits: The earth spirits are known not to like salt, and the shaman will often desist from eating salt before communing with the achachilas. The salt distinguishes the human world from the chthonic world, even as the chthonic world is the source of human agency.

Now we can make more sense of why birth and conception are always reckoned with respect to fiestas when there is no shortage of empirical evidence to contradict this (at least in the case of birth). Considering births and conceptions as occurring during fiestas—that is, sacred time, when there is an intensity of human energy and an irruption of chthonic energy (Allen 1988)—is a recognition that fertility and human life are dependent on the supernatural world. It is not only that during fiestas people are closest to and in greatest communication with the spirit world but also that during fiesta time the tellurian beings are most satisfied. Fiestas are explicitly seen as times when one "pays" the spirits. In return for this payment the spirits of the mountains and earth bring rain, ensure the fertility of the crops and the well-being of people, and, as we have seen, ensure human fertility as well.

Immediately after the anointing with salt, the child is usually baptized by the local catechist. After establishing its relationship with the earth spirits, the child is anointed in a ritual that makes him or her a Christian (*kristyanu*). Baptism is important to the child for, apart from having a relationship with the earth spirits, he or she must also live in a world where other forces may dominate. In a Christian age, not to be a Christian leaves one vulnerable to the powers of a hostile God who will destroy crops with hail if a child is not baptized. The sutiyaña ceremony introduces the child not only to its family but also to the spirit world and its relationships with the various presiding deities: a reciprocal relationship with the tellurian spirits and a relationship with the Christian celestial spirit marked by negative reciprocity. The Christian god rarely intervenes in the life of humans except to wreak his vengeance, thus the common saying that "God only punishes." Possession of a baptismal certificate is, furthermore, the easiest way of obtaining a Bolivian identity card and, in practice, the only way open to indians. This baptism is not officially recognized by the Church, and the priest must perform an official baptism himself at a later date, either in the cantonal capital for a substantial fee or for a much smaller fee when he makes his biannual visit.

Both aspects of this ritual indicate that the acquisition of identity, and indeed personhood, is contingent on the sanction of society. A person from Wila Kjarka is defined by his or her insertion into the group—the primary kinship group and the extended network of fictive kin—and the reciprocal ties he or she has with this network and with the community in which he or she lives (cf. Albó 1985: 8; Spedding 1989: 292). This process of inclusion begins with the first naming, but it is not until the first hair-cutting, the *rutucha*, that the child is ritually introduced into the commu-nity. Somewhat ironically, despite being accorded a name in the sutiyaña, it is not until this second ceremony that the child is actually addressed by his or her name. Until this time the child is referred to by the generic "wawa" which means "baby."

RUTUCHA

The rutucha exists all over the Andes (Allen 1988; Bastien 1978; Carter and Mamani 1982) and marks the entry of a child into the world as a so-cial person. Rutucha in Wila Kjarka is frequently referred to as muruña, which means haircutting but also refers to the cutting off of a bull's horns; a hornless bull is known as muru. Muruña in both cases refers to the cut-ting off of the "wild" part of bulls or children, that is, the domestication of the subject (Harris 1982: 64).

The rutucha takes place when the child is approximately a year and a half old and has already begun to speak. Unlike the naming ceremony, the rutucha involves the wider community. The ceremony begins with a liba-tion to the spirit of the house, the kunturmamani. *Kunturmamani* comes from a combination of two words, *kuntur* (condor) and *mamani* (falcon), birds associated with the tellurian forces, especially when they act as mes-sengers. The *pärinu* and *märina* (godfather and godmother) start cut-ting the child's matted locks and put money for the child in an *inkuña*, a woven cloth used for offerings made from llama wool. This process is repeated by all the adults present, albeit with considerably less money. If there is any hair left after all have had their turn, the godparents finish the cut. The locks of hair are then put in the rafters of the house. Then, all those present join in thanks to the pachamama and the kunturmamani and proceed with communal drinking and eating. The drinking is also ac-companied by coca chewing, with the mother of the child passing around sugar and sweets wrapped in coca leaves. This is one of the rare occasions when women chew coca, and the sweet element differentiates this type of chewing from that usually done by men, which, instead, is done with a reactive agent based on ash (*yuhta*).[13]

The haircutting ceremony is the ritual that formally introduces the child into the community, whereas the sutiyaña marks the inclusion of

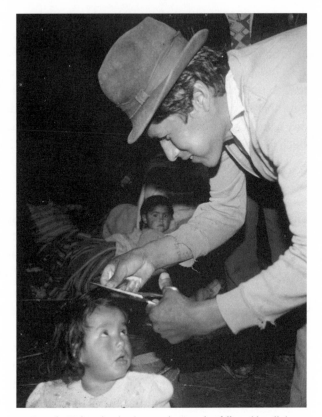

Rutucha Valerio has her hair cut by Pastuku, followed by all the adults present. Note the bank note in his hand, which he will put, along with the hair, in the inkuña.

the child into the kinship unit. It also marks the transition from infancy (*wawa*) to becoming a boy or girl (*yuqalla* and *imilla*, respectively). After this point, the child's death may be officially mourned and commemorated during *Todos Santos*, or the Feast of the Dead, where favorite food may be placed at his or her grave, as is the case with deceased adults. Even so, it is rare for a child to be mourned in this way, and it is almost exclusively adults who are remembered during *Todos Santos*.

The first haircutting also marks the beginning of the age of responsibility, and from this age forward the child is said to begin with household chores. In practice, however, a couple of years pass before the child begins to make a significant contribution to the household. The point, though, is that the child is deemed capable of productive labor—to act upon the world productively—an ability that is deemed to come ultimately from the mountain spirits. Related to this is the importance of labor in creating and defining human beings. A person is not someone who simply is but someone who does; that is, personhood is processual. A gendered person, similarly, is someone who performs the tasks appropriate to a particular gender and only secondarily a person of a particular physical sex. Thus, a child does not become a social person until she or he is capable of performing certain tasks. This ability is accorded by the community and the earth spirits, who first publicly recognize the child at the rutucha ceremony. The child moves from a semiwild state—with dirty, matted locks—in which he or she is not even referred to by name, to becoming a human being, recognized and anointed by the community and capable of productive action. The rutucha can thus be seen as the "spiritual" birth of the child as opposed to the biological birth much in the same way as baptism in Christianity acts as a spiritual birth for the child. Maurice Bloch and Stephen Guggenheim's (1981) observation that such "second birth" rituals imply that biological birth is insufficient to create a "proper" human being holds equally well for the rutucha. It is clear that a baby born without any ritual is considered something less than a person in any sense.

CREATING PERSONS: MEN AND WOMEN

I implied above that the rutucha is the ceremony that created a socially recognized human being, but, in fact, it would be more correct to see the rutucha as just one of the first rungs on the ladder to personhood. The process of life is one of progressive integration into the life of the community, as one comes ever closer to the world of the spirits (cf. Pitarch 2010). In other rituals through life, such as marriage and the assumption of community offices, people approximate more and more the state of the mountain ancestors. With maturity one becomes more and more integrated into the community, until some years after death one loses identity and becomes part of the generalized earth matrix of the chthonic spirits. Out of this generalized force comes human life and agency.

Although one might consider personhood to be only fully achieved at death, it is marriage that confers on an individual the status of person on a social and practical level. Marriage is the union of a man and a woman, and it is this union that completes the person. There is a strong sense, in Wila Kjarka as in other parts of the Andes,[14] that without a marriage partner an individual is seriously deficient and will have great difficulties in reaching the world of the dead. Marriage in Wila Kjarka is frequently referred to as *jaqichasiña*, which means quite literally "the making of a person." To be an unmarried adult is highly anomalous, and if such a person were to die, I was told, they should be buried with a chicken or rooster (depending on their sex) in order to go to the other world complete; but there were no unmarried adults in Wila Kjarka.

Being prematurely widowed is more than a personal tragedy, and the community becomes very much involved in matching up widows and widowers. A good example is that of the case of Edmundo Chino and Flora Alwiri. Edmundo Chino had been a widower for almost four years since his wife died after suffering from "an illness of the uterus," leaving him with two young daughters. When Flora Alwiri's husband, Alfredo, died from having his fat stolen by a kharisiri (see the next chapter), Flora was already a grandmother and nine years older than Edmundo; everyone clearly thought they would make an ideal couple. Despite the considerable encouragement from all quarters, Flora and Edmundo showed no signs of coming together. Something had to be done. And so it was that, during the funeral of Mateo Mamani in Villa Esquivel, Flora and Edmundo were bundled into a house, which was then locked behind them by Armando, Edmundo's brother, and not opened until the following morning. The wake continued outside and occasionally people made suggestions, doubtless helpful ones, as to how Edmundo and Flora should be spending their time. Little was said when the door was opened the following morning, but from that day on Edmundo and Flora have lived together.

Edmundo and Flora, however, tell it slightly differently. Edmundo says that they got drunk together at fiestas and talked to each other (*umawiñanakan parltawayapta umasiña*), whereas Flora says Armando "grabbed us together" (*apthapayapxitu*).[15]

Flora and Edmundo's second experience of marriage is somewhat unusual, but their accounts are quite typical in their laconic style and brevity and the absence of any discourse on romance or affect. I asked many people over many years how they came to meet their partner, and whatever the age or sex, no one ever gave a romantic account of meeting their spouse. Despite considerable prompting at times, people just said that they met and then got together. A typical response was "He came to me and asked me if I wanted to be with him. And so we were together." Older women say that their husbands asked their parents or even that their parents forced them to marry. Juana, for example, told me that her husband's mother arranged her marriage: "That's how it was back then. They got us together whether we wanted to or not."[16] Men say rather similar things:

"She is from here, so I knew her already. I asked her [to marry me]; she said yes" or "I was out herding and as I was going along we talked. Later, talking, we got together [literally we tied ourselves together]; we had children [literally, we met children]. That's how it was."[17]

The single exception is the account given to me by Pastor Mamani, who was born in Wila Kjarka but has lived in the mestizo village of Villa Esquivel since he was three years old, so he is perhaps influenced by more metropolitan discourses of "falling in love."

CANESSA: So how did you meet your wife [who is from up the mountain in Thikata (opposite Wila Kjarka)]?
MAMANI: We just talked.
CANESSA: So what did you talk about?
MAMANI: Getting to know each other we developed a friendship (Sp. *amistad*).
CANESSA: What did you say to her?
MAMANI: I told her "I love you." [laughter] That was it; then we lived well together. We just lived well together. We never fought.

Flora gives a fuller account of how she came to know her first husband, but it is certainly not a story of romance and love:

My sister was already married here so, as an unmarried girl, I came to help her. That is how they knew me. But I didn't know my husband; without talking we came together. I did not know my husband. One afternoon when I was here with my sister, they all arrived and I asked myself, "Why are all these people here?" My sister said: "We will live here, marry this young man." And then my mother-in-law told me: "We will be here together, and we will not make you suffer. Your sister is here so you will have her for company." And then my sister began to cry: "I am alone here!" So I thought to myself that they would not allow me to suffer here, and I am just alone [in Waychu] taking care of the goats, so many goats. So they hid me; and my father and mother looked for me in vain. Eventually they went to ask my parents [for my hand in marriage], and my father was strongly opposed, and they did not pay any attention to him. After a long time had passed, my father came and forgave me. I did not go to him because I was scared he might beat me, and this is how I got married. Nowadays young men and women talk, but I did not know him and he did not know me. I cried for those days because in the emptiness and darkness we knew each other and he took me away.[18]

In the wonderfully detailed autobiography of Sofía Vázquez edited by Hans and Judith-María Buechler (1996), Sofía is uncharacteristically terse when she recounts how she met the father of her child. A young man was looking for a room to rent: "I rented him a room across the patio where people store meat now. One year later Rocío was born" (1996: 198). It is thus not surprising that Andean ethnographies have little to say about love and romance, even when focused on courtship and marriage (e.g., Valderrama and Escalante 1998).[19]

The one apparent exception is the work of Luis Millones and Mary Pratt (1989). However, despite the title of *El Amor Brujo* (The Bewitching Love), there is very little in the book about love and romance; it is much more about courtship and marriage. They, for example, give wonderfully detailed accounts of how young men will indicate their sexual interest in a woman by stealing an item of clothing and waiting for her interested response in the form of stone throwing or coming to retrieve the item, each indicating a desire for sex (1989: 36). The stories of theft, stone throwing, and sex resonate strongly with what I was told about adolescents in Wila Kjarka,[20] where theft and violence (the young girl may indicate her interest in sex by beating the pretender with her herding stick or anything else she may have at hand) are key elements in accounts. The young girl indicates her interest in having sex with the young man through her acts of violence. The suitor may provoke the act of violence by starting the stone throwing, but there is no suggestion that the sex act itself is violent or that the girl is violently taken; she is the principal agent of violence. What men and women in Wila Kjarka do not talk about, nor, apparently, Millones and Pratts's informants, is any emotional or romantic content to the encounter.

Unlike in other parts of the Andes (e.g., Van Vleet 2008) apart from some older folk, people do not generally talk of brides being captured, literally or figuratively. It is the role of the girl's parents to beat the young man for taking away their daughter, but, although the blows may be hard enough, there is no anger behind them.

One important difference between marriage in Wila Kjarka and other parts of the Andes is that almost all marriages are contracted within the community. In a survey I conducted in 1992, of almost all the extant marriages in Wila Kjarka (i.e., where both partners were still living), 83 percent of those marriages were between two Wila Kjarkeños. This number rises to 93 percent if we include the neighboring villages of Thikata and Jankho Kjarka. Older people, many of whom were widowed when the

survey was taken, were much more likely to have been married to someone from beyond their natal village, and it appears that this very strong
rate of endogamy is a post-hacienda phenomenon. At any rate, most
young women in Wila Kjarka today do not face the prospect of living in a
distant community when they marry. The advantage for a young woman
in marrying within the community is that, not only does she stay in a familiar place, but her father and brothers can be relied upon to protect her
if her husband is seen to be excessively abusive.

Finding a husband or wife appears to be based on pragmatism rather
than on affect. Krista Van Vleet in her study of the people of Sullk'ata
notes that "most couples would not admit that they felt affection for their
partner before marriage. Most Sullk'atas do not say they married because
they 'fell in love' " (2008: 141). Van Vleet rightly points out that companionate marriage is a relatively recent phenomenon in Western culture, but
"falling in love" most certainly is not. In the European Middle Ages, the
bardic and literary genre of Courtly Love is a testament to a highly developed sense of sexual passion and romance, even if not associated with
marriage; and, of course, the Psalms and the Songs of Solomon in the
Bible point to similar sensibilities for the ancient Hebrews. Love poetry
and songs long predate companionate marriage. One can also look at the
many examples of erotic love in Asian literature and legend, and the work
of Jacques Lizot on the Yanomami of Venezuela (1991) shows that some
lowland groups at least talk of love and passion.

I am not saying that people in Wila Kjarka do not love each other or
that they do not have amorous passion but, rather, that there is no sense
that this is normal or expected or even desired within or without marriage,
nor is it apparently spoken about. Although Wila Kjarkeños tell many stories, and some of these are about marriage, none of these is about love or
romance; they tend to be about condors taking and marrying young girls
rather than about marriage between two humans.

People do talk about sexual attraction, although not directly linked to
love, and here, as in so many other cultures, food offers the language for
talking about sex. To ask for food, to offer food, and to take it, are the
modes through which people seduce each other and are the source of
much ribald humor. Young people also throw stones at each other when
out herding. Any herder soon learns to be an excellent shot in order to
protect the sheep from predators, so the girls are as adept at hitting their
suitors in the head as are the boys. What is also absent in any discourse
about meeting a partner is kissing. I can honestly say that I have never

seen two Wila Kjarkeños kiss, on the lips or on the cheek, be they a couple, siblings, relatives, or parent and child; nor have I ever heard of anyone kissing either. I cannot, of course, be sure of the fact that they never kiss, but it certainly does not happen in public, or even in front of intimates, nor do people talk about it. I have, however, seen people kiss lambs on many occasions, just not humans. At any rate, this is not a culture where sexuality and affection are publicly expressed, but it is not the case that people are necessarily prudish or place a high value on sexual "virtue."

Despite almost five hundred years of Catholic evangelization, virginity is not valued among the people of Wila Kjarka. Everyone has sex before they get married and often wait until they have several children to formalize their union. There is no sense at all that men desire virgins in particular or that girls are keen to preserve their virginity. Parents are not concerned about their daughters losing their virginity, although they are concerned that they may become pregnant before being in a stable union. The concern of parents and youth alike is not so much about any physical purity, which is such a dominant trope within orthodox Catholicism—in fact, I would say that people have no sense at all of "physical purity"—but rather, the ability to create a family and household in the correct way. After marriage a couple is considered to possess the agency to produce children, run their own household, and take up those communal offices and responsibilities. For Denise Arnold (2006: 129), it is the marriage ceremony that functions as the spiritual birth of the person in Andean indigenous cultures, but perhaps it is more accurate to see the life cycle as a series of births and transformations, and it is only at death that one becomes "truly" social. That is to say, being jaqi is a continual process, a series of becomings without a clear beginning or end.

In the preceding discussion about personhood I have concentrated on those elements that make the people of Wila Kjarka different from those they call q'ara. But this very process of becoming a person also serves to distinguish men from women; and it is not surprising that the process of becoming and being jaqi is similar to the process of becoming and being a man and a woman. If Wila Kjarkeños, when asked how they are different from q'aras, always begin with discussing how jaqi and q'aras live differently, the very same is the case when discussing the difference between men and women. That is to say, the primary mode of difference is what people do, rather than what people are in some kind of absolute and unchanging way; or, to put it another way, what people are as jaqi or gendered people is a result of a series of actions and processes.

I have dealt with how people in Wila Kjarka understand gender in greater depth elsewhere (Canessa 1997). When asked about the difference between men and women in Wila Kjarka I invariably receive in response a list of activities that men and women do, in essence a division of labor. In Wila Kjarka people do not now want (nor have they wanted in the past) to have many children: Many pregnancies affect the health of a woman; people are aware that the land cannot sustain a growing population; and there are no descent groups that depend on having children. As a consequence, what is valued in a woman as a prospective wife or indeed more generally is her capacity to work, take care of animals and children, and manage the household resources. Neither a woman's fertility nor her sexuality is highly elaborated as part of her identity. In a similar way, it is not a man's fertility or sexual potency that is valued by a woman or her family but his laboring power and ability to bring in resources.

Men and women are made; they become so as a result of their productive activities. Gender is therefore iterative in the sense outlined by Judith Butler (1993) and Henrietta Moore (2007). People in Wila Kjarka are a very good illustration of this thesis because they explicitly talk about gender as something that has to be performed through a set of activities: Men plow, chop wood, and knit standing up; women weave, cook, and sow. Some of these are related to much broader ideas of gender, a principle of vertical and horizontal activities which relate to productive relations. Relations between men and women are informed by and equally illustrate a much broader set of relations between older and younger, high and low, from the celestial to the quotidian, as has been noted by many anthropologists of the Andes. Some have suggested that there are multiple genders in the Andes and that there are as many as ten (Rösing 1999), but this appears to me to be a profound misunderstanding of how gender operates. Gender is simultaneously a mode for men and women to be in the world as it is a language for understanding a wide set of relations. Relationships may be gendered, such as those of the upper moiety may be "masculine" with respect to those of the lower moiety; this is not to say, however, that members of different moieties have different genders as suggested by Rösing.

When speaking of gender as performative, especially in a place such as Wila Kjarka where gender relations are relatively egalitarian, one may get the sense that it is somehow elective, that one can decide how, and even which, gender to perform. In practice, as Butler (1990, 1993) is at pains to point out, gender is performed within cultural systems the place strong restrictions on what is acceptable. So even though it is accepted in Wila Kjarka that men will cook and women will plow, this is only when there is no person of the relevant gender who can do that job.

Even as it is true that people in Wila Kjarka are treated as genderless when they are babies and gender is acquired over time, as part of the process of becoming jaqi, it is also important not to forget that even though genitalia are not seen as the root of gender differentiation they are indeed the signals for assigning a gender to a child. In all human societies children are assigned to a male or female gender on that basis; and even in those societies where there is arguably a third gender, it is one which combines attributes from the other two. Even though children are assigned to a gender on the basis of their penises and vaginas, what this assignation actually means varies enormously between cultures. In Wila Kjarka the process through which one develops a gender through short, strong bodies for men and women is the same as that which produces the difference between jaqi and q'ara. One of the differences between jaqi and q'ara is their bodies; gendered bodies as products of nutrition, lifestyle, and activity. It becomes impossible then to separate the process by which one becomes a woman in Wila Kjarka from the process by which one becomes jaqi.

Indigenous Andeans are not very sexually dimorphic: Men have little body hair and typically cannot grow beards; men and women have barrel chests and narrow hips, and they also do not differ considerably as much in musculature as do other populations. Although it is true, for example, that men in Wila Kjarka can, on average, carry heavier loads for longer than can women; it is also true that Wila Kjarka women regularly carry loads across their backs up the mountain that men from the cities would have difficulty lifting. Well-fed teachers have a very uncomfortable time walking from the road to the central school in nearby Choquepata, even with very small backpacks, whereas even people well into their sixties from Wila Kjarka and other communities walk this route with very little difficulty and considerable loads.

As a consequence of being born and growing up in Wila Kjarka, babies become jaqi women and men whose gender and ethnic identities are visible on their bodies: strong arms and legs from working in the fields and walking up mountains; dark skin from being in the sun; lean frames from the physical activity and low fat diet; short stature because of nutritional deficiency; and the many other marks of being a rural peasant. These identities become, quite literally, embodied.

BECOMING OLD

People continue to have children until they are into their forties. For many women, repeated pregnancies means calcium deficiency and loss of teeth as well as the other tolls of breastfeeding and taking care of infants. It is not surprising then that women in their forties look much older than one might suspect. Nevertheless, this is often the most tranquil time in people's lives: They have status within the community, older children can help with tasks, and men typically spend much more time in the community than before. In recent years, however, the demands of schooling, which have been extended from three to six years and beyond, mean that parents can rely less on their children for help and, for the unfortunate, their forties and fifties comes with widowhood.

For women, the most common cause of death is that caused by complications in childbirth, and for men there are a host of illnesses and mining accidents to consider. In the past, and sometimes today, older people could rely on their youngest son to take care of them until they died; but this has now become an exception rather than the rule, as young men leave their community to seek their fortunes. In Wila Kjarka, apparently more often than other neighboring communities, a significant number of young men return sooner and stay longer, and Wila Kjarka enjoys a stable population with many children, whereas many communities are dominated by the very old.

There is, of course, no retirement in Wila Kjarka, and people continue to herd and farm until their bodies give up on them. Every household is expected to contribute to communal labor tasks such as road building or maintaining irrigation ditches, and this includes the single households of the very old. So, for example, in 2006 when the community built a new irrigation channel, every household had to be represented; this included Teodosio, who was in his nineties, as well as many other old people who were still expected to wield a pick and shovel. What is perhaps surprising is that even the very elderly made a positive contribution to the work; that is, they offered much more than simply token effort.

Many people find themselves alone, sometimes tragically. Francisca Condori, one of the oldest women in Wila Kjarka and an absolute monolingual, was someone I visited regularly. I have always enjoyed her sense of humor and smile, but the last decade of her life has been especially hard since the death of her youngest son and husband on the same day.

Young and old, men and women, work together
on this new irrigation ditch.

This is how it happened. I had a cow and my son used to herd it along with the sheep. Then one day the cow went high up the mountain and fell. His father told me I should scold him, "He has taken the cow high up the mountain and it has fallen." Then the boy, thinking we were going to scold him, poisoned himself. He came back with the sheep; the cow was not with him, just the calf. The cow often escapes, so I thought it had escaped. He entered the house and started doing something with water as if here were about to wash himself, but he was, in fact, preparing the poison. He took it, and I was left alone. We tried to cure him, but we could do nothing. Then I told his father: "You scolded him, you told me to scold him; that is why he poisoned himself." This is what I said to his father. He said strange words to me as my son lay dead. He said he would be blamed for the death. He had bought Folidol in a bottle to kill the worms that infect the potatoes. He hadn't told me that he had bought this medicine.

He brought it out of his pocket and drank it; he died immediately. People came, but they could not do anything; he died very quickly. And this is how I remain alone. The people criticize me: "You must have scolded him; this is why he killed himself." This is why I cry now. It has been ten years since his death, I cannot forget: I continue to lament his loss; my head spins and I go around directionless. This is why I cry so much.

Francisca's brothers and sisters are all dead or moved away, and although she has sons and daughters in Wila Kjarka, she lives alone with her sheep. "I go with my sheep up into the mountains. I go crying after my sheep." Her children cultivate her fields and bring her some food, but Francisca often goes hungry. She laments that all she has are her sheep: "My parents taught me how to care for sheep since I was a child. If I didn't have my sheep, what would I do? I would cry more." But many times I would visit her, waiting for her to return with her sheep from the mountains, seeing her cold and wet and exhausted and utterly miserable. She remembers the days of her youth when she could carry heavy loads and walk for a whole week to trade foodstuffs in the yungas, sleeping wherever nightfall found them, and then walk a week back. She clearly has fond memories of those days when she could carry a quintal (approximately forty-six kilograms) on her back without any difficulty, and she also remembers the fun they had: "There was a place called the Knotted River (*Chinujawira*) and a lot of water came down that river. Sometimes the young men would grab the young women and would bathe in the river. Holding/grabbed on to each other that is how they bathed (*katuntat, katuntat ukham wañusiphiri uman*) and we also cooked on the river bank, sometimes sleeping in caves . . . We walked through the jungle [literally "the center/inside," *taypi*], we walked through the forest, under and through the trees. That is how we walked. Sometimes it rained very hard and we had nothing to cover ourselves with other than animal skins . . . Now we have nylon sheets, but not in those days." There is some ambiguity here because *katuña* can mean simply to hold someone or something but also to grab or trap, as in fishing (*chawlla katuña*), but at any rate Francisca is no longer being held or grabbed by anyone: Now she is old and tired, she says, and has no strength and her feet hurt when she walks.

There are many single-person households in Wila Kjarka, all occupied by widows and widowers. In the past, the youngest son would remain in the parents' house until they both died, but now young men almost invariably spend their twenties in military service and trying to earn money.

Awicha *Francisca Fuentes.*

Sometimes, however, an elderly parent may live with her children. This was the case with Remegio Patty's mother. Francisca Fuentes was her name, and she hailed from the community of Chiyakani in which many mistis lived. Her surname, Fuentes, suggests a Spanish forbear, but she appears to have been born, and certainly lived, as a jaqi. I affectionately knew her as *Awicha* (Grandma). Her children and grandchildren, however, showed little affection for her, and she was tolerated at best. In fact, when Remegio rented a small house in Sorata, he sent his mother to live there, giving her just about enough food to survive. Still, whenever I visited her during the Saturday market, she was clearly very hungry as well as lonely. Awicha was old when I knew her and was unable even to herd animals any distance from the village. She was a little senile and prone to lamenting her miserable life, but, unlike many older people, she still spent time looking after herself and making sure her hair was clean and properly braided.

It is not only old women who end up alone but men, too. Teodosio, the shaman, has lived alone for many years and survived both of his wives. One of his granddaughters helps with food sometimes, and he can earn money through curing people. Others such as Marcelino Misme not only suffer the loss of their wives—in his case to tuberculosis—but have the added burden of grandchildren to take care of. He has two young boys

Two houses in Wila Kjarka. The house on the left shows the thatched roof of the kitchen and two plows on the balcony. The house on the right shows a more modern kitchen with a corrugated iron roof, but with no chimney; the smoke comes out the door rather than through the roof. To the side of this kitchen is an oven for baking bread.

living with him, Nestor and Angel. Angel's parents are both dead, but Nestor's parents live in La Paz, unwilling or unable to take care of him. Of his five children, none lives in Wila Kjarka, and he has to find the resources to put his grandchildren through school. Marcelino cooks for his grandsons in an older style kitchen—a simple hearth with a thatched roof and exposed on all sides. In winter it can get very cold cooking outside as the fire does not let off much heat. As is the case with so many old people, Marcelino is sad. He is sad as he recounts the loss of his wife and children and the fact that those who survived live far away. He clearly finds bringing up his two grandsons something of a burden, but he shows very little resentment and, for their part, they take care of their grandfather as best they can.

Marcelino and his grandsons are the only Protestants in Wila Kjarka, and he converted in 2004 after a bout of illness. He prayed and was healed, and since then he has been an evangelical. Marcelino looks forward to Judgment Day, when he will fly with wings and not have to work the fields any more. Most Wila Kjarkeños, however, do not believe in Judgment Day, and for them death is a journey to another world where they will become ancestral spirits.

DEATH

Death is both feared and not feared in Wila Kjarka. In the contemporary West there is a profound fear of death and corpses but not of the dead themselves: The odd teen horror flick notwithstanding, most people do not fear the spirits of the dead. In Wila Kjarka it is the exact opposite: People do not have the slightest problem seeing or touching corpses or digging up their remains; in contrast, when someone dies, there is a real and palpable fear of his or her spirit returning in a malicious way. Much of funerary ritual in Wila Kjarka involves ensuring that corpse and spirit together travel to the land of the dead.

Burial is important. When my friend Germán was washed away in a flash flood, there was no question that we would look for him despite his young wife's wails that Germán was not dead and would return alive. As she asserted her determination to go to Achacachi and find a powerful shaman, a *ch'amakani*, who would return him, seven of us followed the river down to find him. At the time, I half-believed Germán's young wife: How could someone so bright and vital die so swiftly crossing a stream? But that had surely been his fate. It took us three days to find Germán's body; the search involved a lot of dangerous climbing up, down, and across embankments and cliffs as we scoured the river. But found him we did, broken and bloated on the rocks. It took us another three days to get him back in a makeshift stretcher. His body had begun to decompose, and liquid poured from every orifice; but no one doubted that he had to be found and returned. By the time we got him home he quite frankly stank, yet no one (apart from me) seemed to be disturbed by the smell, let alone horrified at the decomposing corpse that no one shrouded until we returned to the village. On that occasion, certainly, the hard alcohol was very welcome, and on that night I made my first coffin. I was more upset at this funeral than any other I attended in Wila Kjarka. Germán was an exceptionally intelligent man who was committed to staying in Wila Kjarka,

Carrying the corpse at a trot. The bearers run fast and in circles so that the spirit of the dead may not find its way back.

and I thought then, perhaps foolishly, that if he stayed instead of migrating to the city or the yungas, there was some future for the community. Germán was also a friend. Among other things, he taught me how to knit.

The death of an adult, any adult, is a communal affair in Wila Kjarka. Every (living) adult arrives at the house of the deceased for at least some part of the day and night and usually until dawn. People drink and talk, and cry and laugh. When people first enter the room where the corpse is laid out they may offer a prayer, but otherwise the deceased is generally ignored. On my first funeral in Wila Kjarka I recall sitting on the edge of a bed for many hours in a room dimly lit by candles. It was only after some considerable time, when I leaned back to be more comfortable and found my elbows on something soft and lumpy, that I realized the dearly departed Domitilio Mamani was laid out behind me.

The night is long and by dawn most women and almost all the men are drunk. As the sun rises some men begin to construct the coffin. The coffin is a simple affair—a box with a lid to contain the corpse. But even a simple coffin becomes a challenge when one is very drunk, and mistakes are made. Mistakes are generally not made apparent until the coffin is at the graveside because the coffin is taken to the grave without the corpse, who arrives later, carried on a stretcher.

The corpse is brought out and tied to two long poles, and the community assembles around it. There is more drinking and, as is the custom, men offer their drink (usually cane alcohol) to all the other men assembled and then to the women. In a similar fashion, coca and cigarettes are distributed. Before the corpse one of the family members lays out an *inkuña* (a woven cloth made from llama wool) and spreads out the coca and cigarettes. A blessing is made for the deceased, and then all the men take coca and a cigarette, consuming both in honor.

Coca is most clearly associated with dead spirits: It is the shaman's key tool in communicating with the achachilas and is a basic element in any offering to the dead. The achachilas are also known to like cigarettes. When the rains are hard and prolonged, one sometimes comes across a skull on a wall with a lit cigarette in its jaw. Normally only the most adept shamans communicate with the dead through skulls, but common people use skulls to placate the dead and ask them to ease up on the rains. As well as being the moral guardians of the community, the achachilas are most closely associated with rain.

Once prayers have been said, coca chewed, and cigarettes smoked, two men lift the stretcher on their shoulders and start running to the cemetery. They run at a swift pace, but not in a straight line, and meander and twist and turn at every possibility. This has two functions: the first is to confuse the spirit were it to try to return to the village along the same route; the second is to allow everyone to catch up. The bearers are known as *jiliri* and *sullka*, older and younger brother, which are also the terms used for a team of oxen as they plow a field. People talk of the carrying of the corpse to the cemetery in the same way as they talk of plowing, and it is for this reason that the coffin goes ahead: In a coffin the corpse cannot be plowed back into the cemetery lands. Men take it in turns to "plow," but with the lack of sleep, the twisting and turning, and the prodigious amount of alcohol it is fairly common for all three, bearers and corpse, to fall and even roll down the mountain side. This is received with neither dismay nor humor, and the corpse is simply retrieved, hoisted up again, and sent on its way. This manner of traveling to the cemetery is another marker of the difference between jaqi and q'ara, as the latter are understood to always travel in a coffin.

The community follows in a long column until all arrive at the cemetery, where the coffin is waiting. The cemetery is small but intentionally so, in the sense that everyone is supposed to be buried close together. When a new grave is being dug, other corpses are inevitably produced. Again, there is no horror or distress as bodies are dug up in varying stages of decay, and people watch and make matter-of-fact comments as they wait for the hole to be completed: "Oh, look, I remember that sweater; that is little Ricardo's, isn't it? Oh yes . . . !" Bones are set aside and reburied, although skulls may be kept for those rainy season moments when they may be needed for rituals.

As the grave is being dug the corpse is left unattended next to or in the coffin as people continue to drink. As I suggested above, one of the consequences of the inebriate construction of coffins is that they may not turn out exactly as envisaged. In the case of Domitilio, the coffin was too short so when he was laid in his head didn't fit. So the head was pushed down, but then his knees came up. So his knees were pushed down and then his head popped up . . . This went on for some time until it was decided to lay the lid with three men sitting on it while it was hammered in. But someone had stolen the hammer. It turns out that the owner of the hammer, Gerónimo (Francisca's husband), was annoyed with Domitilio's son for usurping his position in the flute band and had liberated him of his hammer. A chase then followed for the hammer, which, despite being wielded menacingly, was retrieved. But before the coffin lid could be

The entire community follows.

securely attached Gerónimo kicked the coffin, sending its occupant roll-
ing down the mountain.

Domitilio was recovered and reoccupied his position in the coffin,
which was duly hammered shut with three men sitting on it, and Domitilio was finally laid to rest, but not before placing in the coffin a bottle of
water, a bottle of *k'usa* (maize beer), and a sack of food. The sack usually
contains potatoes and other tubers, as well as three types of maize: *muchu
tunku, jampi tunku,* and *chiwita.* These are for eating, making toasted maize,
and making k'usa. Sometimes money is also included, as precious metal,
along with food, may be needed by the deceased in the land of the dead.
Before the coffin is closed, an arm of the corpse is sometimes exposed and
a number of people come to ask favors of the deceased. Some ask the dead
to communicate with recently deceased relatives. On one occasion, an in-
fertile woman asked the deceased to assist her in having children.

When the grave had been filled in and the simple wooden cross laid on top, a number of people began to cry and wail their laments. This was followed by more drinking and coca chewing until finally everyone trooped back to the village, where people stayed together until long after nightfall.

The drinking and chewing and smoking that accompany every aspect of the funeral are not incidental or indeed instrumental in the sense that it helps people overcome their grief, although this may be a consequence. Drinking and chewing and smoking are in themselves offerings to the achachilas and a way of bringing the achachilas closer to people. Thus are united the community, both the living and the dead; and it is this understanding of community, one sustained by the achachilas that, for many Wila Kjarkeños, makes their community different from mestizo communities.

The dead are associated with darkness, but it is the confusing period between day and night, the twilight, which causes people the greatest fear. In the gloaming, the dead may become confused and leave their resting place and bring illness and misfortune with them. Even after night has fallen on the night of a funeral, people make sure to travel home in groups.

This period of anxious liminality continues until the eighth day after the burial, the *uchuria*, when, once again, the adults of the community assemble and drink through the night until the spirit of the dead person is properly secured. But it is not, in fact, for three more years that the spirit of the dead is properly reunited with the achachilas or, more accurately, that the spirit of the dead becomes one with the achachilas.

TODOS SANTOS

As in much of the Catholic world, the dead are remembered on the Feast of All Saints, or Todos Santos. In Wila Kjarka, All Saints', which falls at the end of October, coincides with the coming of the rains, and it is the achachilas who bring the rain.

Todos Santos takes place over three days. Adults who have died in the previous three years are remembered in their homes as their families construct altars laden with bread and products from the jungle such as sugar cane, bananas, and flowers. The dead are believed to inhabit a world below, where it is wet and from where the rains come. From Wila Kjarka one can often clearly see the rain come up from the Amazon basin. Typical among the breads that are baked are bread babies, which the dead are particularly fond of eating. As was mentioned previously, newborns are particularly

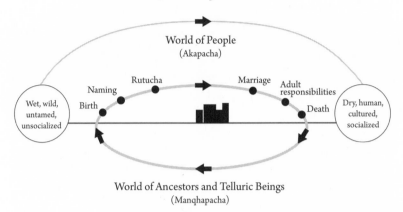

THE LIFE CYCLE IN POCOBAYA

The cycle in Wila Kjarka.

associated—in fact, intimately linked—with the world of the achachilas, from whence they come, and are characteristically soft and wet.

On the second day of Todos Santos the whole community goes from house to house where they are fed by the family. This is one occasion in Wila Kjarka when people eat to excess with plate after plate of food being thrust upon the guests. Once I learned that I could pass my cold and greasy soup to the children behind me, attending such feasts became less of an ordeal.

On the third day all the altars are dismantled in their homes and reassembled at the cemetery where the entire community arrives. Once again there is an excess of eating, and as people pray for the deceased they are offered the food on the altar until it is all gone. People are understood to be eating for the dead, which is why the food on the altars often comes from the lowlands, where the dead dwell. It is also sometimes the case that the deceased's favorite foods are produced for consumption.

The human life cycle is then a process by which wet fetuses come into the world and are progressively dried out until they become the dry bones of the dead, who, in turn become hydrated, as it were, below the surface of the earth and once again become part of the life-giving, wet world of the dead.

Once all the food has been eaten, a general prayer is said for all the dead and thus ends the celebration. Todos Santos is a process by which individuals are converted into achachilas, and there is a movement from the individual to the collective: On the first day the dead are remembered privately in their homes; on the second day the community comes to the

The corpse and the coffin receive little attention as the grave is dug.

home of the deceased; and on the third day the community, dead and alive, assembles at the cemetery. The prayers also follow a similar pattern: first for named individuals, and then for all the dead; and people are only remembered and named as such for three years, after which they are recalled as part of the collective dead.

In Wila Kjarka people do not worship their dead as named ancestors, and very few people can remember beyond their grandparents' names; but they do worship their dead as the collective achachilas. The cemetery of Wila Kjarka is directly in sight of the biggest achachila of all, Illampu. And this points to an apparent contradiction: How can the achachilas be denizens of the manqhapacha below as well as high mountains and rain that falls from the sky? Even the highest mountain peaks are part of the surface of the earth; all that is below that surface is the realm of the achachilas and the other denizens of the manqhapacha such as the chullpas, Inkas, and so on. And as the rain always comes up from the Amazon basin, the rain visibly comes from below Wila Kjarka even if it ultimately falls from above.

Human existence is dependent on the relationship between the worlds of people living on the surface of the earth and the spirits below. From below comes rain, ancestral authority, fertility, and life, in exchange for which people must give fat, alcohol, llama fetus, coca leaves, cigarettes, and other sacrificial offerings.

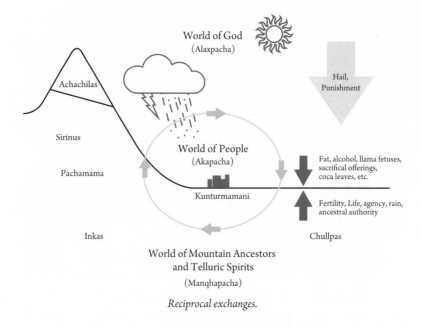

World of God
(Alaxpacha)

Achachilas

Hail,
Punishment

Sirinus

Pachamama

World of People
(Akapacha)

Fat, alcohol, llama fetuses,
sacrificial offerings,
coca leaves, etc.

Kunturmamani

Fertility, Life, agency, rain,
ancestral authority

Inkas

Chullpas

World of Mountain Ancestors
and Telluric Spirits

(Manqhapacha)

Reciprocal exchanges.

NATURE AND CULTURE

Wila Kjarkeños' relationship with the mountain spirits raises the question of their closeness to nature. Since Rousseau, people in Europe and its satellite cultures have thought of "primitive peoples" as being closer to nature. In the age of Rousseau this implied a lack of corruption by urban vices, but in the contemporary age the idea of the "noble savage" has transmogrified into the "ecowarrior," fighting to protect nature from the forces of global capitalism.

"Nature" and the "natural" have a long and complex and even contradictory history in European thought: Sometimes nature is to be conquered and possessed, and other times it is to be preserved and even worshipped; there is no shortage of people in the West who seek to have a mystical relationship with "nature." In many cases people are inspired by indigenous people who are understood to have a particular closeness to the natural world. The reverence many indigenous people have for mountains and streams and the earth would appear to resonate very closely with Western ideas of nature to be revered, but there is a profound difference between the relationships Wila Kjarkeños have with mountains and those of a contemporary new-age traveler or a nineteenth-century German romantic.

Whether talking about "natural feelings," "natural fibers," "natural gas," or "natural desires"—as well as "nature" denoting mountains, forests, and streams—"nature" is understood to be something that is ontologically distinct from human cultural and social processes. The oil executive exploiting natural resources or the ecologist fighting that exploitation share an understanding of nature as that which is beyond human intervention and cultural production. Those who fight against their "natural tendencies" or seek to release them similarly share an understanding that certain feelings and emotions occur independently of what is learned through culture. In both instances "nature" is logically opposed to "culture"; nature is conceived of as a space or set of processes beyond human cultural and social production. These ideas are so central to the way Westerners see the world that it is sometimes difficult to conceive that it could be otherwise (MacCormack and Strathern 1980). It will seem obvious to most if not all readers of this book that if I am walking up a mountain along a solitary path, I am in nature, and that if I am walking down Broadway in New York City, I am not. For people in Wila Kjarka, and indeed many other people in the world, it is by no means obvious that this is so, and it is difficult for people who are the products of European culture to understand why since the idea of an urban, civilized, cultured existence (at certain times these words have been synonymous) as opposed to a wild, uncivilized, and barbaric existence, goes back at least to the ancient Greeks. Even when the bucolic charms of a rural life are contrasted with the vices of urban life, there is still the clear sense of a division between nature and culture. In Wila Kjarka no such division exists, whether positively or negatively valued. So, for example, I sometimes like to go for long walks when I am in Wila Kjarka. Taking some notes to write up or a book to read, I usually walk up the mountain to get better views and to enjoy nature. I breathe the fresh air, take in the scenery, and feel enriched by the experience. Such behavior is bizarre to Wila Kjarkeños, although by now they have become used to such eccentricities on my part. Initially people asked me if I was looking for gold or asked, in a puzzled way, "Do you think there is gold up there?" since it would be quite unlikely to find gold up a mountain like that. Others thought I was looking for buried chullpa treasure; and many others who do not know me and occasion upon me on the path assume that I am a Protestant missionary seeking to save souls for Jesus. To walk, up a mountain, for pleasure, makes no sense whatsoever. Nor, incidentally, does my pained expression when people casually throw trash into a stream or just anywhere with no concern for the environment. People in Wila Kjarka are intimately connected to the mountains and streams and the land that sustains them; they are not, however, in the least bit close to "nature" since, for them, "nature" and the "natural" is not beyond culture.

In his highly influential work, anthropologist Philippe Descola put forward the idea of a "domestic nature," *La Nature Domestique* being the title of his (1986) book about the Shuar of Ecuador. The English title, *In the Society of Nature* (1994), has a slightly different sense but, either way, Descola's work attempts to break down a false dichotomy between the social lives of people and the environment in which they exist. The Shuar, according to Descola, have social relations with, for example, jaguars and tapirs, and various kinds of vegetation; they are fully integrated into the social lives of people. In some ways, though, it is a shame that he chose to put "Nature" in the title of this wonderful book because I think it misdirects the reader and ultimately undermines his argument that there is no such thing as "nature" for the Shuar. Descola doubtless fell into the problem of translating very different cultural concepts into terms that are intelligible to people who live in a very different culture.

Largely because of Descola's work I have stopped referring to the achachilas and other beings as "nature spirits." The great mountain of Il-lampu, which rises so majestically behind Wila Kjarka, is an important part of social life in Wila Kjarka. The people of Wila Kjarka make offerings to the mountain god, and Illampu, in turn, brings rain. In a similar way the earth goddess known as the pachamama is a regular part of Wila Kjarkeños' social life, and she is regularly invoked for the fertility of crops and so on. The Inkas, the chullpas, the achachilas, the kunturmamanis, and all the other denizens of the manqhapacha are refractions of an encompassing matrix of forces to which humans are intimately related; jaqi have a kinship relation with the mountain, the achachilas, and the Inkas and chullpas too (although these may be conceived as rather more distant relations).

Consequently, when Wila Kjarkeños walk through (and, of course, they never go for "walks") the lands, they have a profound intimacy with every outcrop of rock, every distant peak, every area of flat land, all of which have names—names given to them by the achachilas themselves. As I have suggested above, this intimacy with the animated landscape is one of the aspects of their lives that distinguishes them from q'aras, who have no such relationship with the denizens of the manqhapacha but, rather, are imagined to be exclusively concerned with the deities of the *Alaxpacha,* Jesus and God.

Such a relationship is at the very core of Wila Kjarkeños' sense of personhood; it makes them who they are, and it makes them different from q'aras. But it is important to distinguish between this intimacy with the landscape and a concern for "nature." As we have seen, contemporary indigenous leaders in Bolivia are not immune from the political attractions of espousing an idea of indigenous people as protectors or guardians of natural resources, of being natural ecowarriors; but this sensibility does not come from people like those who live in Wila Kjarka, who show absolutely no concern for trash being thrown in rivers, the deforestation of the Amazon, or the exploitation of natural gas.

MAKING PERSONS, MARKING DIFFERENCE

Being a person—that is, a jaqi—in Wila Kjarka is a continuous process of becoming. One may view procreation then as a process by which an unsocialized creature becomes fully human and ultimately reaches the apotheosis of humanity: becoming merged with the ancestral spirits. Herein lies an important aspect of all ritual in Wila Kjarka: the suppression of individuality and the glorification of the community spirit. In this way, the arbitrary incidence of birth is, over time, domesticated and regulated, and it becomes integrated into the community spirit.

One of the more important aspects of this integration is the establishment of a series of reciprocal relationships. This kind of relationship, paradigmatically an exchange of labor, has been described by many researchers as being one of the fundamental differences between true "people" and others for, unlike jaqi, exchanges with urban dwellers are described as being asymmetrical and often highly exploitative (see Allen 1988: 93; Isbell 1978; Mayer 1975, among others). This kind of relationship is not confined to the human world, for relationships with the spirit world are also so conceived and account for the intimacy of the relationships people of Wila Kjarka have with these spirits.

Ultimately what defines one as jaqi in Wila Kjarka is the kind of relationships one has with the collectivity as well as those the community has with the earth spirits, which are often seen as ancestral mountain spirits. As such, identity as jaqi is not something one achieves once and for all through a rite of passage but, rather, something that must constantly be maintained. The people who live in other indigenous communities are recognized as jaqi because they too have these reciprocal relationships with each other and with the ancestral mountain spirits. As Teodosio explained to me, the difference between jaqi and q'ara is not that the latter do not have achachilas—there are achachilas everywhere—just that the q'ara do not recognize them.

Following Carol Delaney's (1991) insight that ideas surrounding birth are not merely reflective of more generalized ideas of where humans are in the world but are constitutive of such relationships, we can see that ideas held by people from Wila Kjarka surrounding birth are part of a more generalized understanding of how human beings relate to the land, the members of their community, and the world beyond. It is through these relationships that one's status as jaqi is created and maintained. Since it is through relationships that identity is created, one's status is not something that is simply achieved once and for all in the way that, say, birth in Bolivia makes one Bolivian in the eyes of the state. Being jaqi is not what one is but what one does.

It should thus become clearer why migration has such a profound effect on ethnicity (Gose 1994: 64; Harris 1995). If personal identity, as I have described it, is so rooted in place and community and the relations of these to agricultural activity, living in an urban setting without the community, its spirits, streams, fields, and mountains, one's sense of person must inevitably be different. It appears then that "indianness" is so bound up in a particular lifestyle, both from the emic and etic perspective, that it does not long survive the move to the city. This explains why migrants will go to such pains to maintain fields and attend rituals and fiestas; what is at stake is not merely sentimental links with their places of birth but the very sense of who they are as human beings.

This creates a paradox for those intellectuals who seek an Aymara national identity. They can address the educated and urbanized migrants in terms of flags and nationhood, a language that is clearly European, but these ideas may have very little resonance among those for whom their sense of identity is founded on entirely different precepts, not on nationhood or genealogical descent, but particular practices and relationships and, above all, a different sense of what constitutes jaqi, a person. To put it another way, this is an example of how the boundary that constitutes the jaqi/q'ara distinction and that of indian/nonindian do not neatly coincide. That is, whereas many migrants may be regarded as indians by other urban residents, they may not be regarded as jaqi by their natal kith and kin.

The processual and performative understanding of identity that I have outlined intercalates with the wider national understanding of ethnicity and race. The boundaries of difference in the highlands denoted by the terms *campesino, indígena,* or, more pejoratively, *indio,* generally refer to the same people who think of themselves as jaqi. Nevertheless, how the latter understand the difference and the boundary across which it is drawn is quite different.

Through the analysis I have presented here it is should be clearer why it is that, whereas indians can be seen to occupy a class position in society, they do not identify themselves on a class basis and thus do not constitute a "class in themselves" and why, although race and ethnicity would seem to be the language to use in distinguishing them from the rest of society, they do not see themselves as sharing a common substance or even a common culture. Indians do, however, consistently see themselves as being different from nonindians, but they understand that difference differently; whereas there is something of a consensus as to where this boundary of difference lies, how it is understood may be radically different. Even though indians and jaqis may be the same people, to be jaqi is not the same thing as to be indian.

In the following chapter we take a look at one of the ways jaqi draw the boundary between themselves and others through beliefs in the fat-stealing kharisiri. The very real fear that the kharisiri provokes illuminates, in a rather dramatic way, how jaqi see themselves as racialized beings.

FIVE

Fantasies of Fear

It was in the time of cholera that swept through the Andes causing anxiety and fear from Ecuador to Argentina that Alfredo died. It was indians who were mostly victims of cholera, not because of their poor hygiene, as was widely assumed by many mestizos but, in a rather cruel irony, because they picked it up in the towns and returned to their villages, where they had no access to the medical attention—principally intravenous rehydration—that saves people from this illness. Rudi Colloredo Mansfeld (1999) has written eloquently about how the cholera epidemic in Ecuador gave mestizos the opportunity to resuscitate racist ideas about dirty indians under the guise of a concern for public health. There were certainly echoes of this in Bolivia, although the Peruvians were also blamed because . . . well, the Peruvians get blamed for a lot of things in Bolivia.

It seemed likely to me that Alfredo had been one of those people who contracted cholera in Sorata or perhaps somewhere else and returned to die in Wila Kjarka. His sudden and unexpected death had left people full of anxiety as well as grief. After an extended period of fieldwork and Alfredo's death I felt exhausted and in need of a break, so I decided to travel to the capital city of La Paz. In a few hours I would

be in Sorata, where I could catch a bus or truck to the city; I didn't want
to wait for market day on Saturday. The route to Sorata goes nine hundred meters down the mountain to a narrow bridge across the gorge from
where the path more or less follows the river, passing some thunderous
waterfalls below Kimurpata, and then climbing up to Sorata. I never tired
of this walk and often paused on one of the massive stream boulders to
rest, lay my shirt out to dry, and enjoy the solitude that always seems so
absolute as very few people pass that way other than on market day. It is
easy to understand why someone might believe that spirits dwell in such
places, which seem to me quite simply magical.

I announced my intention to my *compadres*, Remegio and Agustina,
and was taken aback by the shock on their faces and the animated discussion just out of my hearing. My comadre Agustina looked particularly
concerned, even fearful, and when I approached they explained that I
could not walk alone to Sorata for a *kharisiri*,[1] a fat stealer, was abroad.
They told me that Alfredo, was killed by a kharisiri and he had been a
strong and powerful man. Alfredo was indeed a strong man, or appeared
to be. He was certainly one of the largest men in Wila Kjarka and also one
of the very first people I had met when I'd arrived. I also knew him as one
of the heaviest drinkers in Wila Kjarka, always one of the last to leave any
celebration, and quite happy to be drunk for days on end. This aside, he
seemed very much to be in good health, and so we were all shocked when
he became ill and died within days. Remegio and Agustina, and indeed
the rest of the community, were convinced that he was killed by a kharisiri. Even today, over twenty years after his death, any mention of his name
is almost automatically followed by the comment that he was killed by a
kharisiri. My companions were concerned that the same would befall me.

The kharisiri will meet me on the path, perhaps in the gorge, and smile
at me, they said. He may be praying and I would not suspect. With his
prayers and powder he would make me sleep a deep sleep and then with a
sharp and fiendishly clever instrument extract the fat from my body, from
my side. When I awoke I wouldn't even recollect seeing this man, but I
would feel weak and tired and slowly waste away and die. There is no cure
for this, I was assured, and I would surely die. My compadres had often expressed concern at my walking alone along these solitary mountain paths,
but never had I seen them so fearful for my safety. I decided to wait until
the next day when a number of people would be traveling to market.

Fear of kharisiris, fat stealers, is not peculiar to Wila Kjarka and is a
much-documented phenomenon of the rural Andes that has excited the

imagination of numerous scholars.[2] As recently as November 2009 the Peruvian police arrested a gang of four men accused of killing people for their body fat. It was believed that the body fat was sold at $15,000 per liter and sold to cosmetic companies in Europe (BBC News, November 20, 2009). The claims were met with some skepticism, especially outside the Andes, because human body fat is hardly in short supply in Europe and is an obvious byproduct of procedures such as liposuction, nor is there a large cosmetics market for it anyway. Moreover, body fat cannot be effectively transported in the empty bottles of Inka Kola that the police produced as evidence. The Italian middlemen were never apprehended. This story ran for more than a week until Peruvian reporters broke the story that it was, in fact, a police conspiracy to deflect attention from a corruption and extrajudicial killing scandal. Nevertheless, many people clearly *did* find it believable that gangs of men would roam the countryside killing innocent people for their fat. The police most certainly expected their concocted story to be believed since the arrest of four men with vials of human fat for sale to Europe could only confirm what many people have known for centuries: Europeans desire indians' fat and will go to great lengths to acquire it.

The belief in kharisiris appears to have its roots in the colonial period and may derive from the practice of Spanish soldiers who used the fat from indians' bodies to salve their wounds after battle (Stern 1987: 170–71) or as a more general medicinal cure. Over time the fear of fat extractors appeared to have been focused on the Bethlehemite friars who traveled alone throughout the countryside collecting alms at often-remote crossroads (Morote Best 1951: 81–85). These friars were primarily physicians, but they also buried the dead, sometimes with their own hands, and it is supposed that they used the human body fat in administering to the sick. The founder of the order, the Venerable Pedro de San José de Betancur, was dedicated to a humble and mortificatory faith; he is known to have adopted the practice of cleaning sores and rotting wounds with his mouth as an exercise in humility and mortification (Morote Best 1951: 83). If this image had ever been communicated verbally or visually to indians, it is not difficult to see why they might have thought he was sucking the life out of his victims.

Kharisiris, however, continue to be relevant in the contemporary Andes as kharisiri beliefs have been recorded all over the Peruvian and Bolivian Andes (Ansión 1989; Morote Best 1951; Paredes 1963), and there has even been a kharisiri "epidemic" in Peru in the wake of the civil war

(Ansión and Sifuentes 1989; Degregori 1989). Kharisiris are also known as *pishtacos* and *ñakaqs* in Quechua and *lik'ichiris* in other Aymara-speaking areas. In modern renditions the accused are no longer the (now-defunct) Bethlehemites but mestizos and whites in general (Morote Best 1951; see also Weismantel 1997), although the religious association of kharisiris is quite often explicit. Nowadays in Bolivia, with ethnic/racial identities in rapid flux and, as previously discussed, indians becoming q'ara within their lifetimes, the anxiety is often expressed that one can never really be sure who may be a kharisiri (Spedding 2005). Because the jaqi/q'ara distinction—at least from the point of view of people such as those in Wila Kjarka—is not as visually obvious as it used to be, the unknown person next to you on the bus might just be after your body fat. In these examples the anxieties expressed by these beliefs are centered on the difficult question: Who is jaqi?

Kharisiris have variously been interpreted as a powerful representation of the Other (Bellier and Hocquenghem 1992); an exemplification of the ambiguity of fears about modern capitalism and the desire to partake in it (Salazar-Soler 1992: 20); an articulation of the extraction of surplus labor by the government (Ansión and Sifuentes 1989); anxiety about intrusive modernity (Wachtel 1994); an indigenous expression of racial violence (Weismantel 1997, 2001); an eloquent expression of the antipathy native Andeans feel toward outsiders after centuries of exploitation (Crandon Malamud 1991); and "a brutal intuitive understanding of the relation between locality, country and the 'world capitalist system'" (Degregori 1989: 112), to give a few examples. As Mary Weismantel (1997, 2001) has carefully explained, there is an important racialized difference between kharisiris and their victims that cannot be ignored; the whiteness of the kharisiri, even if is simply his relative whiteness, is significant. I certainly agree with Weismantel that kharisiris illuminate how whiteness is understood in the Andes, but I would go further: Kharisiris serve not only to illuminate how whiteness is understood from a jaqi perspective but, more directly, how indianness is understood by indians. In fact, another word for kharisiri in Wila Kjarka is *jaqi lunthata*, which means simply someone who steals jaqi: Kharisiris know who is a jaqi—even if this might not be so clear to others—and so an examination of the ideas surrounding kharisiris can help in understanding how jaqi identify themselves.

The fact that the kharisiri steals fat as opposed to, say, blood,[3] is a lot more than a curious ethnographic detail, although most commentators simply note that fat is a "life force." Similarly, the manner of the victim's death, the impotence of traditional cures, and the mode of extraction are much more than colorful details in a gory and violent story. Indeed, these details illuminate important elements of the difference between indians and others in the Andes, for the kharisiri in his person and activities is the antithesis of what it is to be human, jaqi. That is, the very cultural specificity of these beliefs is a pointer to how the indian/nonindian distinction is perceived from an emic perspective.

Although it is clear that kharisiris as racialized outsiders are the antitheses of jaqi, much less attention has been paid to how the kharisiri illuminates the identity of racialized insiders. Looking at the specificities of how the kharisiri so violates the norms and mores of the lives of jaqi, and expresses so forcefully the image of the immoral and rapacious outsider, sheds light on how jaqi identity is understood emically. At the root of kharisiri beliefs are fundamental issues of alterity and creative power, how some Andean people see themselves as human beings—that is, jaqi—in an oppressive and racialized world. In pursuing Lacan's insight that desire creates its object, we can see that the same holds for fear. The profound fear that people have for kharisiris is difficult to exaggerate. This fear of the Other, a fear mixed with an almost pornographic frisson (Weismantel 2001: 183) for his awful violence and power produces a powerful image of the Other, which constructs the identity of those who aren't Other. Fear constructs the group—in this case, the villagers of Wila Kjarka vis-à-vis neighboring communities. Fear of the kharisiri is not merely a consequence of his terrifying nature but an essential element of it; the fear of kharisiris dramatically reminds people of who they are and are not; he polices the boundary between alterity and identity. That is, through fear the kharisiri constitutes the identity of the people he preys on (cf. Žižek 1989: 79).

In an interesting discussion on violence in New Guinea, Pamela Stewart and Andrew Strathern (1999) note some of the important similarities between cannibalism and what they describe as "assault sorcery." Their description of assault sorcery bears a striking resemblance to kharisiri beliefs: The solitary victim is assaulted; his organs are removed and returned—sewn up—to the community where he dies (649–50). Beyond this, however, it is worth looking at the fear of kharisiris and accounts of cannibalism in the storytelling about the Jankho Kjarka war. In both accounts, the aggressor consumes his victim, who is at his or her productive prime; and in both accounts, this aggressive and antisocial consumption serves to mark the boundaries of insider and outsider. In accusing the people of Jankho Kjarka of cannibalism, Wila Kjarkeños are casting them as extreme outsiders and putting asunder any social relations they had with them. In both kharisiri and cannibalism accounts, the sheer horror of the events described and the profound repulsion they invoke serve to dramatically underline the identity of the jaqi of Wila Kjarka.

In a later study on terror and violence, Stewart and Strathern (2007) stressed the importance of the imaginary in understanding terror and its importance in evoking a sense of rupture in general human interaction. "Terror," they write, "proceeds from specific acts that rupture normative expectations, polarise parties, and ultimately challenge their identities. These identities may be reasserted and hardened in the sequence, or they may disintegrate" (7). In Wila Kjarka the terror of the Jankho Kjarka cannibals and the kharisiri serves to harden rather than disintegrate identities: The visceral fear and horror these invoke create a dramatic and incontestable sense of identity and difference, which are not only imaged but somatized in the experience of real fear.

It is consequently important not to take the fear of the kharisiri for granted and to explore why exactly they are such terrifying creatures. To understand the force of the terror the kharisiri produces, the violence he does to the social order, we must first examine some of the key elements that underlay life in Wila Kjarka and the manner in which community is created and understood. I would like, therefore, to outline how ideas surrounding fat are embedded in a broader understanding related to observable facts about agricultural processes and life in general. Fat is seen as much more than simply a "life force." Rather, it is a trope around which a number of concepts fundamental to life in Wila Kjarka are organized.

FAT, BONES, AND THE ANCESTORS

Fat is central to human life, as a life force and as a means of communication through offerings with the spirits. Although blood is also, in some contexts, seen as a medium of creativity and life force, it is fat, much more so than blood, which accounts for human agency. Blood spilled in ritual battle (*tinkus*) is seen as an appropriate offering to the mountain gods (Sallnow 1987: 138), and in parts of the Andes it is used as an offering to the tellurian spirits, but it is possibly in the realm of kinship, and matrilineal kinship in particular (Arnold 1988), that blood is most salient. Certainly in Wila Kjarka, blood is never used as an offering even though it is the necessary byproduct of animal sacrifice. The importance of fat has possibly been largely overlooked perhaps because blood as an element in articulating ideas about relations with ancestors is a much more familiar element in European culture. Thus, Nathan Wachtel (1994: 72–73) takes great pains to point out the equivalence of blood and fat in the Andes, to account for the fact that kharisiris steal fat rather than blood. In attempting to persuade us of this equivalence, however, he obscures the point that in the Andes fat and blood are not equivalent, and that blood is not the "life force" or "vital fluid" that fat is, and in so doing, he misses the central place fat has in the kharisiri's identity.

The energy or life force that comes from the spilling of blood is a sporadic affair, forthcoming through rituals or through accidents. However, it is not seen on a daily basis, whereas the plumpness and health of a person is clearly visible. The transformative powers of fat are moreover evident in cooking when it is used to change the inedible to the edible. In a similar vein, candles—which, though they are no longer made of tallow, are still believed to be made from fat—are a daily source of light and a major component of any offering. So fat, although less visible to Westerners' eyes, is more apparent to Wila Kjarkeños and other jaqi in a quotidian manner.

It is not surprising that in the Andes, where malnutrition is endemic and where one of the most common causes of death for adults is tuberculosis,[4] which causes people to waste away, having sufficient body fat would be associated with vitality and good health. Similarly, the most common cause of death for infants is dehydration due to diarrhea, which is characterized by rapid loss of body weight; and rapid dehydration is also a cause of death of other illnesses such as cholera. At the same time, infants and children are spiritually weak, as their soul (ajayu) can easily depart and cause illness or death. Spiritual strength comes with personal maturity, which is linked to the hardening of the bones and associated with the ancestors (see also Arnold, Yapita, and López 1992: 105). The ancestors, however powerful, are, of course, dead. Humans must combine the wisdom and ancestral power inherent in bones and the vitality that inheres in fat. That is, agency resides in a balance between wisdom (bones) and vitality (fat), which is at its optimum in middle age, that is, when people are married, have children, run a household, and are able to perform the ritual and civic duties required of them.

The "fattiness" of babies is ritually reinforced in the naming ceremony, sutiyaña, which is often combined with a Christian baptism. It is the sutiyaña and not birth that marks the difference between fetus (sullu) and baby (wawa). This is the only form of Christian baptism that takes place in Wila Kjarka until the priest visits and performs the ceremony. The chrism oil and candles the priest uses for baptism are widely believed to be derived from human body fat sold to the bishop by kharisiris. What is interesting to note, apart from the irony, is that the priest is seen to derive his powers, not from his God, but from the fat of the indians to whom he is ministering.

At birth children are daubed with placental fat and later with salt and water in a "fatty" paste. Fat in its various forms figures prominently in offerings made to the spirits, often as a substitute for human sacrifice (Bastien 1978; Sallnow 1987). Llama fat and candles are perhaps the most obvious examples, but llama fetuses, too, possess an essential association with fat. Llamas constitute a parallel society to humans (Sallnow 1987: 132) and are suitable substitutes in sacrifice. Llama fetuses, as human ones, represent the life force at its most raw.

The most frequent offering to the spirits in the Andes is alcohol: Whenever alcohol is partaken, a few drops are always sprinkled onto the earth in libation. Peter Gose has outlined how these libations to the ancestors are poured in exchange for water in the form of rain (1986b: 113) and form an essential part of the cycle of sacrifice and exchange with the spirits. The most auspicious libation that one can make to the tellurian spirits is the froth on the surface of maize beer, *k'usa* (Sp. *chicha*). This part of the beer is known in Wila Kjarka as *k'usa lik'i*, the fat of the maize beer. The name of the Inka creator god, Viracocha, literally means "fat of the lake" and is said to refer to the power of Lake Titicaca (Torero 1974: 223; see also Wachtel 1994: 72). This "fat" could refer to the froth found on its surface, rather in the same way as that of maize beer. The importance of water as a life-giving force from the creator gods is well established for the Andes historically (Sherbondy 1993; see also Bastien 1985), and the froth might be seen as the creative force behind this god. What is less well understood is the role of fat and its relation to water in this hydraulic model of power.

These ritual offerings, even if formed perfunctorily, constitute a secular reinforcement of a fundamentally important relationship with the spirits. The tellurian beings feed off fat for their own sustenance, but in exchange for fat in its various animal or alcoholic forms they provide people with the vitality that inheres in human fat.

Equilibrium is believed to be achieved between what one offers and what one receives. If a person demands too much of the tellurian powers, or commits an act of hubris, they will claim the person's life in payment. Miners who extract from the underground are a typical example of this (Nash 1979). The unusually strong appetite of the mountain gods for human life, as compared to other representations of the underworld, is accounted for by the belief that extraction from mines is excessive and relentless. Andean spirits are capable of great vengeance if they are not appropriately feted. The spirits expect something in return for their beneficence, and however violent their extraction of sacrifice, it is to feed their legitimate power that provides for the people on earth.

The miners' relationship with the underworld spirits is modeled on the quotidian offering people make to the spirits. As with the god of the mine, the spirits of the community—the *achachila, pachamama*, or *kunturmamani*—require an exchange for their munificence. Here Teodosio explains how the offerings are made to the achachilas and what the consequences are for neglecting them.

> "We will eat together" is what we say. And then saying "With your permission," the sign of the cross is made. "May that all the love and affection in the house be not diminished"; saying this, a sign of the cross is made. Now we all eat together. We drink, chew coca, and smoke. This is how the achachilas come from far away; this is how we pay them. Then the achachilas bless the door of the house. On our knees we ask them that our grandchildren not become ill and that they be given memory (*amuyt'asi*). May they have money. These blessings the achachilas bring. Then alcohol and flowers are moved in a circle while one's name is said, and then the wind blows the (spirit) away. Every year they must be paid in this way. We must not forget next year.
>
> If, for one year, one forgets to pay, they may take one's wife or husband. In this way one may lose cattle. Before, when I paid regularly, my animals were many: thirty were my cattle, three were my mules, three pigs would I butcher every year, and forty sacks of grain would I produce. I had children and they grew up to be married. And then I stopped paying. My wife was taken away and one day my seventy-four sheep were found dead. I went to the mill in Sorata and when I returned the meat of those sheep was gone. That is how I remained, in misery, because I was too stupid not to pay. That is why one must pay with colored wool, with money, with a llama fetus, and many small sacks of powders.

The wrath of the tellurian spirits is a frequent theme in stories and discussion in Wila Kjarka. There is, however, another side to this fear: the desire for the wealth that the spirits can produce. In communities where wealth is distributed through *compadrazgo* and fiesta sponsorship, the accumulation of wealth has a particular illicit fascination. We have seen that some of this fascination revolves around buried Inka treasure, but people are also known to make pacts with the spirits in order to accumulate unnatural wealth, as this example about a man called Pedro Loza illustrates:

> In a gold mine in Sorata there is a man by the name of Pedro Loza. This man made a deal to make himself rich. Now why would he be so rich? He is like us: he lives as we do, he works the fields as we do, so then how could he be so rich? He does not pay attention to people: he has already spoken with the *anchañchu*. This anchañchu, this being of the rock is from beneath the earth and is rich. One of these [anchañchus] comes from the River Thikat and the river flows very full. Then this anchañchu goes on top of an outcrop of rock. If you were to become ill, he would know how to cure you. From this good rock he can talk to you and make a deal . . . Now beer, wine, wine made from grapes, undiluted alcohol, "That is what I want," he says, "and not in a mug, but in a glass." Those cups must be like a mirror, made of glass. Well, that is where Pedro Loza went and made a good arrangement for himself. Even his wife has expensive clothes and has gold teeth.

Such a story has multiple functions. It explains how someone "like us" could make it rich, since great wealth in this day and age (although not in the past) is associated with q'aras. This story, however, begs the question: If Pedro Loza can make a deal with the anchañchu, why don't others do the same? The anchañchu can cure illness, but he also causes illness and people are very scared of visiting precisely those places where he is likely to live for fear of becoming ill and dying. There is another fear, however, and that is that the anchañchu will continue to make extravagant demands far beyond good wine in a glass. Ultimately, like the god of the mine, the anchañchu may demand human sacrifice: Fear intermingles with desire.

There is an ambivalence in the story, which is expressed in terms of Pedro's identity. On the one hand he is jaqi, as "he lives as we do; he works the fields as we do."[5] On the other hand, however, he doesn't pay attention to people (jaqi).[6] Working the fields is an appropriate activity for a jaqi, but so is communal life, and Pedro appears to hold himself aloof from other jaqi. His mysterious wealth and social distance put him in danger beyond that of dealing with the potentially insatiable appetite of an anchañchu: People like Pedro who reject normal social intercourse and accumulate riches may be accused of being kharisiris (Orta 2004; Wachtel 1994; Weismantel 2001).

The fear of anchañchus and other spirits is real but understood within the economy of relations between humans and the earth. Whatever fate may befall Pedro Loza, it is to be understood in terms of his autonomous actions, and even if his life is demanded, he will have received great wealth in return. The fear of kharisiris is far greater for its arbitrariness and its violation of this economy.

KHARISIRIS

The description so far of how human nature and agency are created implies a closed system; there appears to be no room for accounting for the agency of others who do not enter into relations with the earth spirits. How do Wila Kjarkeños and other rural Andeans then account for the fact that outsiders, these q'ara, are manifestly able to construct things and act upon the world generally without having this relationship with the tellurian powers? One way to explain this is to see outsiders as illicitly tapping into the flows of fat with the spirits and using this power for their own ends and to the detriment of those who are genuinely in the cycle. The agents of this illicit extraction are the kharisiris, and it is this illegitimate extraction that makes them such terrifying figures.

One reason why kharisiris are so feared is that it is widely believed that no cure is possible or, at the very least, that being cured from a kharisiri attack is very difficult to achieve. Other illnesses respond to treatment through divination and offerings to the earth spirits, but kharisiri attacks are outside the relationship people have with the tellurian spirits and, therefore, the spirits cannot be invoked to cure the victim. In the words of Herculiano: "Look, if you have bad lungs you can go to the hospital and be operated on. If you are all twisted up and cannot breathe, they can operate [and cure you]. But when it comes to kharisiris, when the fat has been removed you are just going to die . . . If they try and give you an injection you will just die . . . Once the fat has been removed from a person, the body is cold. If the doctor were to try and give an injection, it would be like fire. *Zas!* You just have to die when you have been 'kharisiried.' "

Despite many people telling me that the consequence of being attacked by a kharisiri was a sure and certain death, some did suggest there were various possible cures, including Herculiano above.[7] This contradiction may exist because the cures are fundamentally different from the kind of medicine practiced by traditional healers or Western doctors. Curing illnesses in the traditional system always involves the powers of the ancestral spirits. When it comes to kharisiris, people have to resort to other methods.

The first and simplest of these is killing the kharisiri (see also Ansión 1984: 201; Portocarrero, Valentín, and Irigoyen 1991: 39). Eustaquio gave me an example of such an incident: "Some years ago, a number of men from this village were traveling around the area of Warisata. Night had fallen and they slept in a room used for storing grain. They were all huddled together on the sacks trying to keep each other warm from the bitter *altiplano* cold when a priest arrived. He was riding a horse and made everyone sleep a deep sleep. The priest entered the warehouse but knocked over a sack. This awoke one of the group. He immediately aroused the others, who chased after the priest and caught him. They killed him."

In this example, the association of priests with kharisiris could not be clearer. The kharisiri had to be killed, said Eustaquio, because it is only by killing a kharisiri that his spell can be broken. This is perhaps because killing the kharisiri is the only way of preventing him from removing the fat or because the death of the kharisiri counterbalances the potential death of the victims. There are a number of documented instances of people being killed on suspicion of being kharisiris in recent years (Degregori 1989; Wachtel 1994). The fact that people are moved to burn someone alive (Wachtel 1994: 53) is a measure of the profound fear people have of kharisiris.

The second way of being cured was recounted to me by Pastuku. In this unusual account of being cured from a kharisiri attack, the process of fat extraction is somehow reversed.

Pastuku was asleep at night when a *kharisiri* came into his room and took his fat while he was sleeping. When he woke up the next day he had bloody diarrhea (*wila kursilla*) and was also vomiting (*lakata kumitumpi*). He went to his father, Teodosio the yatiri. The only cure, he said, was to go to the town of Achacachi. There, in the pharmacies, one can buy human fat, which is very expensive. The fat is burned with a white egg and *wayruru* beans. Black cola is also offered. All this was done and Pastuku became well again. From this day he makes sure to lock his door at night.

One of the interesting points from this account is that to be cured from a kharisiri attack, one must buy back at a great price that which was stolen in the first place. There is a double exploitation here: Indians are exploited for their fat and then have to buy it back to cure themselves. It appears that the only way to be cured is to restore the fat to its position in the cycle. The fat is replaced; interestingly enough by using the same wayruru bean that

many believe is used to extract the fat in the first place. Kharisiris are believed to carry these beans in their pockets when they attack their victims.

A related cure is the use of a child's umbilical cord. The umbilical cord
is a substitute for human fat in offerings and is considered better than a
llama fetus, which is more commonly used. The umbilical cord belongs
to that family of substances which are considered fat. If the child enters
the world, wet and soft and full of life-giving fat, the umbilical cord is the
most obvious example of the drying out and hardening process that ends
when individuals become ancestral bones. The umbilical cord is a critical
part of the process: It connects the fetus not only to its mother but also
to the ancestors; it is the clearest connection across living and spiritual
generations of the life force that is contained in body fat.

Several Wila Kjarkeños reported that the kharisiri attacks his victim by
first reciting prayers or using burnt or pulverized bones to make the victim
fall asleep (cf. Ansión and Sifuentes 1989: 78; Manya 1969: 136). The use of
prayers is fitting with the image of the kharisiri as a priest or other religious
figure. The use of bones is also important since bones are vehicles of ancestral power par excellence, as we saw above. The use of burnt or pulverized
bones—that is, bones violently transformed almost to the point of total
destruction—can be seen as an expropriation of ancestral power to interrupt the flow of fat between humans and the tellurian spirits.

Once the victim is asleep, the fat is extracted from the side with a small
instrument like a watch. Some Wila Kjarkeños added the further detail
of boiling water being poured over the victim and the instrument then
used to extract the fat, which looks, I was told, like semen. People always
indicated the place where the kharisiris extract fat by pointing to their
sides, more or less where the kidneys are situated, that is, not the belly or
thighs, buttocks, and so forth, where there are frequently large fat deposits. In the colonial documents, the fat extracted by kharisiris is described
as *sebo* or *cebo* rather than the much more generic *grasa*. *Sebo* refers to
tallow or suet. Tallow, used for making candles and soap, is made from
the brown fat around the organs. This fat is suet, sometimes also known
as hard fat—drier than ordinary fat and needing to be heated before it can
be used. This may account for the boiling water sometimes mentioned
and may also explain why people point to their kidneys when describing
where the fat comes from.[8]

Various researchers (e.g., Paredes 1975; Rivière 1992) have reported
that only indians' fat is efficacious in making machines work, and so forth.
Some (e.g., Manya 1969) also note that people believe kharisiris to have

contracts with the government for the lubrication of machines or trains and even to be sent to the United States for rockets. Tallow was quite commonly used in the past for lubricating machinery, so it is quite reasonable to assume that the fat stolen by the kharisiri would be used for these ends. Tallow, as noted, is also used for making candles; this would similarly explain why many believe the candles used by priests are derived from human fat. The uses to which human fat is believed to be put are not fanciful imaginings but based on very practical understandings of what fat was widely used for in the relatively recent past.

Herculiano offers a contemporary account of the nature of the body fat extracted by kharisiris and the uses to which it is put: "[The kharisiri] has a contract with those he works for. They say that our fat is a primary material; they say it is used in factories . . . It is a bit like, well, when we boil, say, pig fat, it just drips, it is not hard; but human fat is like soap or candle fat—it is hard. In the factory, which is like a soap factory, they make the fat hard and then it is good as a medicine. Human (i.e., jaqi) fat you will find in expensive pharmacies; it is like a powerful drug."

It is an expensive drug, of course, for rich people, and no jaqi could ever hope to afford it, even is she or he wanted to. Herculiano in our conversation was quite clear, as were many other people, that the kharisiri desires the fat of jaqi, and anyone else just wouldn't do.

Beyond this, kharisiris are even more specific in their choice of victim: They do not steal from children or very old people. Children and old people simply do not have enough fat, and children in particular have very little brown fat, which kharisiris particularly desire. Kharisiris choose mature, productive adults, those at the very center of the community most clearly engaged in production and reproduction; that is, kharisiris strike at the very core of social reproduction.

Kharisiris are associated with hacienda owners, priests, and nonindians in general (Paredes 1975; Rivière 1992: 26; Weismantel 2001), that is, q'ara. The nonindian identity of kharisiris is of particular significance. Outsiders are defined by their lack of reciprocal relations with other people: They lack the kinds of relations between people, and between people and the tellurian spirits, which define humanity. Not only do outsiders, q'aras, refuse to engage in these kinds of relationships, but they steal the creative force that these relations engender. If jaqi moral relationships are defined by reciprocity (Alberti and Mayer 1974; Allen 1988: 93; Mannheim 1986; Sallnow 1987), the kharisiri is clearly antithetical to these relationships: Stealing is nonreciprocity par excellence.

This perhaps accounts for Juan Ansión and Eudosio Sifuentes' (1989: 100) findings that migrants to Lima from Huamanga thought that there were no kharisiris in the city. As urban migrants they leave behind the set of relationships and rituals that underpin the jaqi/q'ara distinction. The relationship between jaqi and the tellurian spirits mediated by fat has no resonance with urban migrants who no longer depend on these tellurian spirits for their livelihood and identity.[9] This kind of identity rarely survives a move to the city for very long (Canessa 1998; Harris 1995),[10] and the kharisiri remains a memory from rural life; indeed, by becoming urban and consequently whitened, these migrants are, from the perspective of rural dwellers, potential kharisiris.

Nathan Wachtel (1994), moreover, has a detailed account of kharisiri accusations within the community of Chipaya that appears to be an important exception and worthy of some comment. Wachtel notes, however, that, Gregorio, the unfortunate victim of kharisiri accusations, is targeted because he represents "the ethnic other" within the context of Chipaya and suggests that indigenous people are only now accusing each other of kharisiri beliefs because of the pressures of modernity (1994: 97). It is quite clear that the Chipaya community, which Wachtel has studied for decades, is undergoing rapid change, but it may not be the pressure of modernity per se that accounts for Gregorio's victimization. Wachtel's account reveals that Gregorio was a marginal person from his childhood and as an adult was highly unusual in that he owned a shop in the community.[11] Other villagers accused him of not participating in the work parties and attending to his communal obligations. There are important differences as well as similarities between Chipayas and the Aymara-speaking groups that surround them. Nevertheless, we may hazard a guess that Gregorio had moved from jaqi to q'ara, or the Chipaya equivalent, by his commercial activities and resistance if not refusal to involve himself in communal labor activities. Andrew Orta is another scholar who notes kharisiri accusations against members of the community, but, as in the Chipaya case, these are all men who were somehow linked to mestizo-creole society. Mary Weismantel argues that "whiteness is not an essential quality of particular bodies, but a structural position that any body may assume" (2001: 169). Whiteness, however, is more than simply a structural position because whitening is seen to effect changes on bodies: Jaqi can *become* kharisiris, a different kind of being; although whiteness is not an essential quality of particular bodies, it *produces* essential qualities in particular bodies. Rather, as we saw in the previous chapter, being jaqi is a process that has physical effects, so too does acting in a way that produces whiteness and consequently a physical change. In Weismantel's words, the "whiteness of the [kharisiri] (and the indianness of his victim) does not precede social life but rather is formed by it, through a process that is unmistakably physical" (2001: 192). Identity is both essentialized *and* mutable (Wade 2002).

This sheds light, then, on Remegio and Agustina's deep concern that I would be attacked by a kharisiri on the way to Sorata, despite the fact that, as a bearded European, I looked like a kharisiri par excellence, not his victim. For several weeks I had been working with them in the fields, day after day, wearing my *whisku* sandals, eating their food, and chewing coca; that is, I was engaged in precisely the kinds of activities that produce the brown fat that kharisiris so desire—enough, it seems, for me to be a potential victim. My apparent exception actually confirms that social difference is embodied through social and physical processes and is not something simply inherited from one's parents. In the same way, moves to the city, changes to one's diet, and above all labor practices, will in turn have an effect on one's bodily substances and transform brown fat into soft white fat. Such a move will also, incidentally, change the color of one's skin, as people spend much less time in the sun in the city. For Wila Kjarkeños the process also works the other way: A European, through labor and diet and engaging in appropriate rituals with the achachilas, can acquire brown fat, the fat of jaqi. I am not, of course, saying that Wila Kjarkeños unambiguously considered me jaqi—far from it—as there were many other occasions in which my whiteness came to the fore. On this and other occasions, however, people simply recognized the complexity of their understanding of what makes a jaqi jaqi and a q'ara q'ara. These examples are not contradictions or inconsistencies, but rather, demonstrate a very sophisticated understanding of social difference that eschews simplistic categorization.

In their kharisiri beliefs, jaqi are not only expressing a fear of outsiders in general and mestizos and whites in particular, but the very nature of these beliefs illustrates how many jaqi view power and the illegitimate usurpation of power. Body fat, *lik'i*, is a fundamental life source deemed to be given by the forces below. This gift defines the relationship of people with the spirit world and also accounts for the productivity of people on the surface of the earth. Kharisiri beliefs can be seen as potent illustration, in Andean terms, of the illegitimate use of power by the outside world as represented by such institutions as the Church and modern hospitals and mestizo-creoles in general. The power of mestizos and whites is attribut-able to the misappropriation for their own ends of the very life source given to jaqi by the tellurian spirits. The power of the mestizo-creole world is explained through this powerful metaphor of exploitation.

In a fascinating analysis, Peter Gose (1986b) has argued that belief in the nefarious fat stealer is an "amoral assertion that production, power and riches demand organic tribute, the transcendental assimilation of the ruled" (1986b: 309). Gose's essay is important in underlining how the kharisiri's actions are consonant with a wider sacrificial form in the Andes. There is, however, *pace* (Gose 1986b: 308), a radical difference be-tween the tellurian spirits and the powers served by the kharisiri—that is, the priests and bishops, the hospitals, and other productive enterprises of the mestizo-creole world. There is a difference between the organic trib-ute, which re-creates production, and kharisiris who extract the medium of that wealth from the system of exchange. In Thomas Abercrombie's words, kharisiris perform a "terrible and antisocial manipulation of the logic of sacrifice. The kharisiri . . . takes vital generative powers out of the proper form of circulation among gods, men [*sic*], and animals, in order to pro-duce an antisocial kind of wealth that cannot sustain itself" (1998: 405).

The very immorality of kharisiris is at the root of the fear surrounding them; the ends to which the kharisiri puts the human fat is anything but "amoral": This is sacrifice to no productive end—at least to no productive end as far as jaqi are concerned; it is profoundly immoral. In the case of Wila Kjarka, the appropriation of fat by the Church and state, although it accounts for their power, is illegitimate, since the fat should be delivered to the earth spirits and not to the forces of the state and q'ara society. The fundamental difference between kharisiris and tellurian spirits is that the mountain spirits are the source of life mediated by fat in the first place. In traditional usage, to make offerings of fat and other elements is to enter into communication with the tellurian spirits and reinforce the relation-ship that unites the tellurian spirits and human beings. The elements of the exchange belong to, and the relationship itself is consonant with, the values of the jaqi community. In relations with kharisiris, however, we are presented with a markedly different relationship: With kharisiris there is a clear negation of reciprocity; the extracted fat is diverted from its proper flow and destined for use beyond the sphere of moral relationships (Rivière 1992: 30).

The fantasy of the kharisiri is reminiscent of that European fantasy of a rapacious outsider who fiendishly extracts from society for his own immoral ends and who sometimes even uses children's blood for his rituals. The "Jew" takes the blood of Christian children; the kharisiri extracts the fat of indians. There is, however, more than a passing resemblance here. Žižek sees the "Jew" as a necessary element in fascistic ideology, a "fetishistic embodiment of a certain fundamental blockage" (1989: 127). "Far from being the positive cause of social antagonism, the 'Jew' is just the embodiment of a certain blockage—of the impossibility which prevents the society from achieving its full identity as a closed, homogeneous totality. Far from being the positive cause of social negativity, *the 'Jew' is a point at which social negativity assumes positive existence*" (127, emphasis in the original).

The kharisiri has a similar role in jaqi identity. He explains why moral exchange with tellurian spirits is insufficient to create indian wealth in the long run, and he accounts for the power of the q'aras. The "blockage" in this case is how to account for the power of q'aras in a closed system of moral exchange. As with the identity of the "Jew," the nature of the kharisiri is a necessary product of the very social world he is believed to antithesize. Just as Nazis needed Jews to tell them who were Aryans, Wila Kjarkeños and people like them need kharisiris to tell them who are jaqi: The fear of the kharisiri produces the very subject on which he preys. By focusing on alterity/identity and how the kharisiri polices the boundary between one and the other, we can better examine the complexity of these mutually implicating loci of meaning and appreciate the violence, real and imagined, that so often articulates the dyad.

Alterity and identity also collapse in the fantasy of the kharisiri: He is foreign to the social system but accounts for it; he creates identity at the very moment he epitomizes alterity. Rather like a Möbius strip, he is simultaneously face and reverse of what constitutes jaqi.

SIX

Progress Is a Metal Flagpole

In 2002 I arrived in Wila Kjarka with my six-year-old daughter, Hannelore, and a chalkboard that had been paid for by her school in England. The gift was graciously received by the new schoolteacher, Walter, who had just left teacher-training college the previous year, 2001,[1] and remained in Wila Kjarka until the end of the school year in 2007. He was enthusiastic and keen to be modern and up to date. I mentioned that my daughter's head teacher was keen to develop the relationship between the two schools, and I asked him what he thought he needed. His face immediately brightened and he barely hesitated: Next year, he wondered, could I possibly bring a flagpole? I was rather taken aback by this request. Not only did the school sorely lack teaching materials and furniture, but it had a flagpole already. I pointed this out to him and he replied, "Ah, but that is a wooden flagpole; we need a metal one." When I told him that I wasn't about to bring a metal flagpole for the school he became somewhat irate and said, "We need a metal flagpole. The wooden flagpole has to be brought down to attach the flag; a metal flagpole is always erect. How can we have a proper school without a metal flagpole? Nowadays education is based on science and reason: We need a metal flagpole." For the teacher, progress, science, reason, and modern education—in other words, "civilization"—were all embodied, rather phallically, in a flagpole that should be "modern" and made from metal, rather than the perfectly functional wooden flagpole created by the villagers.

Wila Kjarka is dominated by a large square with two wooden frames as soccer goals at each end. There are several houses around the square, but most people live off one of several paths that run off it up the mountain. No one lives lower than the plaza, so most people can see it from their houses, and the community leaders can effectively shout their messages to the whole community by standing at its center and shouting up the mountain in a particular rhythm reserved for such communication, with the declining tones reaching far up the mountain.

The 1922 cadastral survey makes reference to the *cancha de football* in the village, which is evidence of the early spread of the game in rural Bolivia, before it acquired the more Spanish spelling of *fútbol*. Wila Kjarka was part of a globalized culture long before the term was invented. In those days the plaza was dominated by the mayordomo's house, which still stands at the north end and is now occupied by the Mamani family, although since the large door finally fell down in the late 1990s there is little to indicate that it was ever any different from the other houses in Wila Kjarka. To the east stands the small chapel, dark and disused. The mayordomo would have regularly hosted the priest and obliged the attendance of the hacienda indians; and since the Conquest the Catholic religion played a major role in "civilizing" indians and teaching them the mores of Western culture. Up to the early decades of the twentieth century, the Church was closely aligned with the conservative hacienda-owning class and actively supported it by preventing the establishment of indian schools, which were deemed to have a corrupting influence.

By midcentury, however, the formal paternalistic role of both the hacienda-owning class and the Church with respect to indians was swept away. The mayordomo's house was destroyed, and the chapel fell into decay. Today the priest may come to Wila Kjarka once every two or three years, and there is no other occasion for the celebration of orthodox Catholicism. Standing in sharp contrast to the melting mud walls of the mayordomo's house (the Mamani family has a most uncharacteristic disdain for house maintenance) and the crumbling chapel is the village school with its large whitewashed buildings, which now, with a tall flagpole in front, totally dominate the plaza. The school and the teacher, rather than

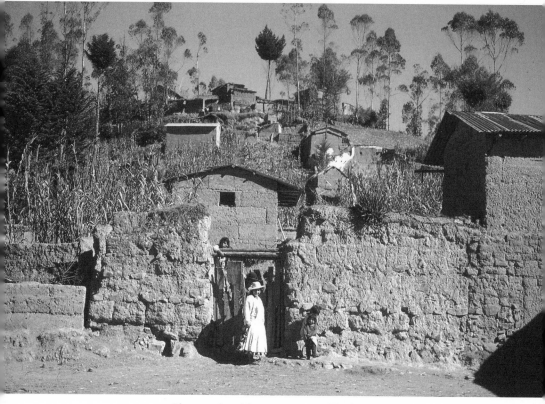

The mayordomo's house, now occupied by the Mamanis.

the Church and the priest, now have the role of civilizing indians: If the priest formerly endeavored to turn pagan indians into Christians, the schoolteacher's mission has been to turn indians into Bolivians. There is, of course, a difference, but, in its condescension to indians and their way of life, much less than one might imagine.

This provocative parallel is profoundly ironic: The schoolteachers today are all Aymara speakers from agricultural communities on the altiplano, close to the capital city of La Paz. Teachers and pupils share a language and a cultural background, and they are phenotypically similar. Furthermore, since 1993, the Bolivian government has initiated a series of education reforms, which include a policy on bilingual and intercultural education and production of teaching materials considered to be more appropriate to indian communities.

Teachers from the same cultural and linguistic background as their pupils are deemed most appropriate for delivering this kind of education.

Not only are they speakers of indigenous languages, but are expected to have sympathy with the cultures in which they teach (Yapu 1999). The essentialist assumptions are most in evidence in those cases where, for example, Quechua speakers are expected to deliver a curriculum in Aymara, with their "indian" background making up for their inability to speak the native tongue of their pupils. But even when pupils and teachers share a cultural and linguistic background we should not expect the teacher to enable and valorize the skills and knowledge children obtain outside the classroom.

Teachers have made a decision to leave a "traditional" rural life to adopt one where knowledge is obtained and valued in a very different way. Indian teachers very often have had to struggle extremely hard to obtain a level of social mobility through formal study and often do so precisely to leave behind a way of life that is identified as "indian." Such teachers are perhaps those least likely to impart an intercultural educational program that valorizes indigenous culture because they have been so personally invested in distancing themselves from it. The expectation that indigenous teachers will be proponents of indigenous culture and forms of knowledge is most likely to be disappointed under circumstances in which intercultural education has been explicitly mandated and teachers are, in effect, expected to undermine their status founded on a particular, nonindian, base of knowledge.[2]

Schools have a political character as much as they do social and cultural ones (Bourdieu and Passeron 1970; Cliche and García 1995: 21–22), and I follow John Ogbu's (1981) suggestion to look at schools and schooling through multiple levels of analysis. In this case I look at schooling both in the context of Bolivia's recent political and social history and through a study of Wila Kjarka's village school. In the three years between 2001 and 2003 I sat in on classes, often for the whole day, and sometimes with my daughter, Hannelore, who had firsthand experience of Wila Kjarka's schooling. I have visited the school and the teachers on every visit to the community, most recently in 2011 shortly after the inauguration of new buildings. I also conducted formal and informal interviews with teachers, all of whom had been trained since the Education Reform. More formal interviews with teachers were always conducted in Spanish. Teachers preferred speaking to me in Spanish, especially if the conversation was "technical"—that is, relating to pedagogy. In less formal situations and especially with other people, we often spoke in Aymara.

In combining detailed ethnographic data with a broader social and cultural perspective, the paradoxical position of indigenous schoolteachers becomes easier to understand for, despite the shared ethnic background and teachers' expressed sense of political solidarity with villagers, they do not provide positive models in terms of indian cultural identity. In fact, they are unlikely to identify themselves culturally or ethnically with community members at all, demonstrating once again how contextual and mutable indigenous identity can be.

INDIANS, PEASANTS, TEACHERS, AND PUPILS

As we have seen, after five hundred years of contact, the boundary between what is and is not culturally indigenous is very difficult to sustain. Indian ascription is consequently highly contextual: The schoolteacher may be seen as mestizo or white by Wila Kjarkeños but may be considered indian when he travels to the city; women may be considered more indian than men in the same community (de la Cadena 1995). This ambiguity inherent in indian identity contributes to the problematic relationship between teacher and community.

One of the reasons for the lack of clear ethnic boundaries is the strong assimilationist policies of governments since the 1952 Revolution, which have had a profound effect on Bolivian society. As we have seen, a key feature of this social revolution was the dismantling of the large haciendas and a land reform that gave most of the hacienda lands to the indians who worked them. At the same time, the serf-like status of indians was abolished according to a model of inclusive citizenship. A stated aim was to create an ethnically homogeneous nation where all would be mestizos. This new Bolivian race would be based on a mixture of Spanish and indian achieved through economic liberalization and cultural change.[3] This was the promise of the 1952 Revolution, which sought to remove ethnic divisions by making everyone Bolivian: "Somos todos bolivianos" ("We are all Bolivians") was one of the slogans.

Education reform was a major platform of desired political and cultural change, and in the succeeding decades a school was built in virtually every indian community in the country. Educational policies were directed at the transformation of indians into Bolivians (Choque Canqui et al. 1992; Malverde and Canessa 1995) with Spanish being the only official medium of instruction. Mestizo teachers were dispatched to rural communities and often held a very high position in rural society, frequently considering themselves to be the community leaders. Mestizo teachers clearly reproduced a hegemonic racist ideology that elevated mestizos above indians and equated Bolivian identity with being mestizo. In this context, the word *indio* (indian) was legally prohibited and replaced in most contexts by *campesino* (peasant) with the aim of obliterating any kind of ethnic and racial differences between Bolivians: It was the role of schools to turn indians into mestizos.

These assimilationist policies were common to other countries with significant indian populations. For much of the twentieth century there was a wide expectation that the demise of contemporary indian populations through natural population decline or assimilation was simply a matter of time, even if it was considered by some to be regrettable. Over the past decade or so, however, the public profile of indigenous peoples in Latin America has become ever more prominent and has contradicted the belief that history would see their disappearance. At the beginning of the twenty-first century, from Mexico to Argentina, indigenous peoples have mobilized, made successful land claims, been recognized in national constitutions (van Cott 2000), and generally become more prominent in national and international arenas.

Schools—as Pierre Bourdieu and Jean Claude Passeron have noted—are institutions for the reproduction of "legitimate culture" (1970: 128). In the years succeeding the Revolution, this culture was very narrowly defined and, consequently, the inclusive nationalism it articulated was at the expense of any kind of indigenous cultural identity, particularly since national culture is so sharply racialized.

In 1993 public policy took a dramatic turn in Bolivia with the election of the coalition government of Gonzalo Sánchez de Lozada and his vice president, Víctor Hugo Cárdenas, the leader of an indianist party (Albó 1995). Together they promised to effect a major change in how indians were perceived in Bolivia. Since the day the vice president gave his electoral address in Aymara, Quechua, and Guaraní, the principal indigenous languages of Bolivia, the official national discourse has been one of a multicultural and plurinational state. Schools were at the forefront of this policy change. One of the first actions of the Sánchez de Lozada administration was to introduce a major education reform in 1994, which mandated bilingual education in many areas of Bolivia. Two decades later, there are numerous textbooks in Aymara, Quechua, and Guaraní (the principal indigenous languages), and in indigenous communities children are taught predominantly in their mother tongues for the first three years of schooling. According to Walter, a teacher, 70 percent of the instruction during the first three years of schooling (*primer ciclo*) is in

Aymara, in accordance with the education reform. I did not do a formal analysis of the amount of Aymara spoken in the classroom, but even in the first year of school my impression was that it was well below 50 percent. By the third year of school, hardly any Aymara was spoken by the teacher at all, although children always spoke Aymara among themselves, even in the classroom.

An implication of the introduction of indigenous languages in schools is that the teachers in these schools almost certainly come from indian backgrounds themselves, since very few nonindians speak indigenous languages.[4] There was a clear expectation that having children taught by members of the same ethnic/racial background would serve to undermine racist ideology and spread instead the new valorized multicultural ideals (Yapu 1999).

SCHOOL AND SCHOOLING IN WILA KJARKA

Schooling is the point of entry of the nation-state into the village space in many rural communities. Schooling in Bolivia, much more than the teaching of literacy and numeracy, is about the teaching of citizenship, about engendering a sense of national consciousness (Illich 1971: 31; Luykx 1999; Yapu 1999), and there is no more powerful visual representation of this than a Bolivian flag flying atop a (metal) pole. At school, children are presented with an idea of the geographic nation, and one of the key elements of a child's education in Wila Kjarka is the learning of the national boundaries and the manner in which they have been changed and territory has been lost.[5] What is learned is hostility toward Chileans and Peruvians; what is not learned is the cultural continuities between indigenous people on both sides of these borders.

The schoolteacher remains a very important figure in the community. Whereas in the past schoolteachers would be whites and mestizos from Sorata,[6] these days they are mostly from highland communities. These men (and they are almost always men in small, remote communities), far from being multiculturalists, are great proponents of the Bolivian Dream whereby through hard work and study one can "whiten," "progress," and become mestizo. Sometimes they effect this change in ethnic status for themselves by marking their difference from indians by, as in the case of one Wila Kjarka teacher, perming his hair and wearing tracksuits. This upward social mobility is thus not simply one of class progression but an ethnic one as well, and as such we may consider that schoolteachers, rather than being proponents of cultural pride are, in fact, exercising their rights to be Bolivian citizens and not to be considered indian—that is, not to be members of an identifiable ethnic and racial group that is considered backward, anachronistic, and uncultured. "Indian" here is clearly understood as the subject of an enduring colonial relationship.

Many of these men may very well have entered teaching because it was the only profession available to them as indians from peasant backgrounds, rather than because they particularly desired to teach (Luykx 1999). The irony they face, however, is that their education and upward mobility places them in an even more "uncivilized" and "backward" (i.e., indian) community than the one they left (García 2005: 117). Not surprisingly, this produces deep resentment among teachers who are poorly paid, poorly trained, and poorly motivated.

Here the teacher and pupils are largely in agreement, for the children I spoke to were quite clear that it was better to be educated at school than to have no formal education. They also broadly shared the teacher's views that one's personal success can be understood in terms of years of schooling. They are in Illich's words "hooked on school, that is, they are schooled in a sense of inferiority toward the better-schooled" (1971: 7). In Wila Kjarka this sense of inferiority has a clear ethnic dimension, and there is a suspicion that Aymara language education is yet another plot to keep indians in their place. María Elena García (2005) explored these issues in Peru, and the parents she spoke to were similarly suspicious of Quechua schooling programs. One parent expressed himself forcefully: "As my wife said, we are not in favor of change. We think that now teachers are not expected to work, and that you want our children to stay poor and be like us. What I want most for my son is that he is not a campesino, like me. And being an indian is worse! So you shouldn't tell [our children] to be indian!" (García 2005: 98; see also 124–25).

This raises the immediate question of what happens in school and what children are, in fact, taught. In Wila Kjarka the school day always starts with the pupils lining up in front of the flag for inspection before singing the national anthem and marching. Inevitably, the children are berated for being late, not lining up properly, being inappropriately dressed, and being dirty and unkempt. Even though the school is officially bilingual, commands and scoldings are invariably given in Spanish. The effect of this is that before the children enter the classroom they are reminded of their inadequacies as individuals, as children, and even if the word is not uttered, as backward indians who live in a small village far from the metropolis.

Ready for school after washing at the well.

In focusing on personal hygiene, the teachers are echoing a long-standing concern on the part of elites for the physical and moral hygiene of indians. Since the reformist decades of the 1930s, policymakers have seen indian bodies as a principal site where the battle for civilization must be fought (Larson 2005). In particular, indians' proximity to earth and mud is often seen as a marker of their inferior nature (Orlove 1998). Indians live in adobe houses with mud floors, eat from earthenware bowls, and often work in close proximity to the earth. Earth, which is seen as "dirt" in urban discourses, is inescapable in an indian village, where it isn't seen as dirt in the same way. Especially in the rainy season, children's feet simply get muddy, and this isn't a problem in houses with mud floors. For the teacher, however, muddy feet are emblems of indianness (cf. Colloredo-Mansfeld 1999: 187; Weismantel 2001: 188–90) and reflective of the poor physical and cultural hygiene of his pupils: Mud is the antithesis of clean, urban, civilized life, a major theme in many lessons.

"Civilization" constantly cropped up in lessons in the Wila Kjarka school. One example, out of many, was when one of the schoolteachers, Edelterio, was giving a lesson on the political geography of Bolivia. He brought out a map, and the students repeated after him: "This is the Republic of Bol . . . iiiivia. What is this? The Republic of?" He proceeded to go through all the departments in this way and then the neighboring countries, bemoaning the fact that every one of Bolivia's neighbors had taken a piece of Bolivian territory at one time or other in its history. Then he followed with a description of the three climatic zones in Bolivia—cold, temperate, and hot—which is so important a part of the national imagining. From there he noted that Bolivia was formed in 1825, and then, all of a sudden, the lesson became about progress or, more accurately, about backwardness. "We were poor and backward in 1825, and look at us! We are poor and backward now. We are poorly dressed and poorly fed (*mal alimentados*). Who has an adequate house here? No one. We still use rubber sandals; our houses are like the houses of animals. Here we only eat maize, maize, maize (*mote*)." The "lesson" continued in the same vein for some time, and it was quite clear that since the teacher lived in a "proper" house, was well fed, and most certainly did not wear rubber sandals, the "we" really meant "you."

That Wila Kjarkeños' diet is better and more varied than many urban people, that their sandals (Sp. *abarcas*, Ay. *whisku*), which are made from recycled car tires, last much longer than the shoes the teacher was wearing,[7] that their adobe houses are very sound and provide good insulation

Three schoolgirls each wearing her white cotton smock, which is difficult
to keep free from dust in a mountain village.

against the cold, these were perspectives that the teacher, so well versed in
the discourse of progress and civilization, did not offer. And so, a lesson
in the political geography of Bolivia becomes a lesson in indian poverty
and backwardness.

These themes of civilization and progress are rehearsed in all kinds of
lessons, even in mathematics: In one instance, students were counting
tractors in a picture and the teacher, Celestino, asked how many children
had seen a tractor. Hardly any child had, and this occasioned a speech on
how they were so backward that they had never even seen a tractor. Their
brothers on the highland plains used tractors, so why couldn't they? The
pupils listened in silence, and no one pointed out to the teacher that Wila
Kjarka had no road, so the tractor had no way of getting there, there was
no source of fuel for miles, and, in any case, the fields were far too steep
for a tractor. That the teacher did not consider these details implies that
he really didn't think anyone had business living in such a community at
all, a view he expressed on a separate occasion.

By coincidence, shortly after, I saw a book my goddaughter was reading
with the images below and the questions: "Who sows with greatest ease
and why?" The first picture is that of a peasant, with an indian *lluch'u* under
his hat; you cannot see his feet because they are deep in the earth—the

"Who sows with greatest ease and why?" Image from the school textbook Maravillas de nuestra tierra *published in 1968. Although I never once saw a modern book with the "new" images of indigenous people in people's houses,* Maravillas *is found in many of them, often with these pictures pasted to the wall.*

¿Quién siembra con más facilidad? ¿Por qué?

unmediated connection to the earth an unambiguous index of racialized indianness (Orlove 1998). His trousers reach to his knees, and he is sowing a large field on his own. The mountains are in the distance, but he is not looking at them, as his face is cast down toward the earth. The second picture, with an almost identical landscape, is of a man on a tractor, high up off the ground. He is wearing a shirt with a collar and a baseball cap; his back is straight and he is looking straight forward, toward the mountains in the distance. We don't see his face, but we know he is not an indian. How do we know? He is elevated above the earth, and we know he is wearing shoes, even if we cannot see them; he is not wearing a *lluch'u*; he has a straight back; and most important of all, he is driving a tractor. This man mediates his contact with the earth through technology, and technology, along with the progress this image represents, does not have an indian face.

Such themes of progress and civilization are also formally addressed every Monday morning during the *hora cívica* (civic hour). Children first march in front of the flag, sing patriotic songs, are inspected as in a parade lineup, and are subsequently lectured by the teacher. These days, following the education reform, the speech to the students in their early years is supposed to be in Aymara, although on most occasions I witnessed, it was a mixture of Aymara and Spanish, with Spanish predominating. Nevertheless, the themes have remained the same. Children are reminded of their backwardness, that they live in a village without a road or electricity, and that they work their fields by hand rather than with machines. A comparison of schoolteachers' speeches in Wila Kjarka before and after the education reform shows very little difference in content and perhaps only a small increase in the amount of Aymara spoken. Basilio, the teacher between 1990 and 1992, was relaxed about speaking Aymara and spoke it informally in the classroom as well as in his speeches.

An example of an hora cívica I heard in 2007 seemed fairly typical and illustrates some of the tensions experienced by the teachers personally. On this occasion, Bernabé offered the standard speech, telling the children about the importance of education, and how it was important to work hard for electricity and machines: "This is how we progress." "We can't have everyone behind a plow," he said, and it was quite clear that a life of agriculture was not something to which they should aspire. But then his tone changed, and he talked about how they were all the same: "We are all poor . . . We are all brothers . . . I am like you." This plea for solidarity is not, I think, to be taken cynically. Bernabé really does want a better life for the children of Wila Kjarka and he appears, at least on occasions, to see himself in the faces of the children, even as they fail to line up straight in front of the flag. Bernabé, like the other teachers, shifts from recognizing his kinship with the people of Wila Kjarka to berating them for their backwardness, to expressing discomfort at having to live with them, and fear of their contaminating indianness.

In recent years the education reform itself has been an occasional theme in these horas cívicas, although sometimes the teacher speaks against it; for example, on one occasion in 2002 he argued that speaking Aymara was keeping Wila Kjarkeños back and that parents should speak Spanish to their children. This view is shared by the director of the school district based in the nearby village of Choquepata whom I interviewed in the same year. He believed that the reform was created by outside agencies and was not something produced in Bolivia. He saw it as a plot to keep people down (*para empantanar a la clase social*), and he saw the disappearance of Aymara as a necessary corollary of progress: "The language [Aymara] may disappear as a consequence of science spreading across our territory . . . [it is through] the spread of Spanish and science that culture will reach its triumph."[8] There is little of the spirit of intercultural education in that statement, and it is of little surprise that the teachers in his district are less than passionate advocates of the reform.

Words such as *science*, *progress*, and *civilization* function as codes for racialized social difference. Their constant, almost mantric, use in the classroom has the effect of instilling in children their inferior status, which they themselves quite often understand in ethnic and racial terms. One girl, Agustina, told me that "White people are better because they are clever and live in cities and are wealthy; we indians (*indios*) are poor and stupid, but we are better than black people." From this and many other comments, it is clear that children are learning the lesson of their inferiority despite the aspirations of the education reform. In these horas cívicas and in numerous other instances in their education, children learn that the space they inhabit—the land on which they work and which sustains them—is unequivocally devalued by their teachers and by non-indian Bolivians in general. One could summarize schooling thus: It is where children learn that they are indians. It seems, then, that children have to learn that they are indians before they can be turned into civilized mestizos. The first part of this pedagogical project appears to be very successful; the second part, it seems, rather less so.

This is not, of course, explicit government policy, and an education reform has been instituted that seeks to "decolonize" education, but this reform obviously needs to be implemented by teachers who, it turns out, are not necessarily its most outspoken advocates. When I spoke to Walter about the education reform, he mentioned, of course, the flagpole and talked animatedly about the disgraceful lack of resources: "According to the reform we should have a hexagonal school and hexagonal desks. This is what the education reform stipulates; this is the scientific way to teach. And here, here we have rectangular desks and a rectangular school!" he said with apparent incredulity. The school was, however, well supplied with glossy books, which kept their gloss since they were never removed from the small storeroom next to Walter's room. He never really explained why they were never used, but it was quite clear from other conversations that he was opposed to bilingual education on the grounds that it prevented people from progressing.

One of the key elements introduced by the 1994 Education Reform was intercultural bilingual education. There is, however, considerable resistance to the higher status given to Aymara, even by Aymara-speaking teachers.

It is not to be assumed, however, that parents were any more enthusiastic about bilingual education than the teachers. Some parents, to be sure, regarded it positively and spoke about the importance of being able to write in Aymara, but they were definitely in the minority. Most parents seemed bewildered as to why anyone would send their child to school to learn Aymara. Older parents—that is, those in their late thirties or older—will know firsthand what it means to be functionally monolingual, and younger parents will certainly have learned from their parents and grandparents about the profound disadvantage that being a monolingual Aymara speaker brings. As we saw in chapter 3, one of the leitmotifs of remembering the Bolivian Revolution was that it marked a time when

Girls playing on one of their very long recreation periods during the school day.

indians were able to read and write in Spanish. The importance of speaking and writing Spanish has not been lost. Some parents, consequently, are positively hostile to their children learning Aymara at school (Why teach them something they already know?) and suspicious as to why anyone would expend the effort. Parents make considerable sacrifices to send their children to school to acquire the educational capital they need to operate in a Spanish-speaking, mestizo world, not to learn a language they consider at best useless, if not a downright disadvantage in that world. Indeed, there is very little evidence that there has ever been broad support for bilingual education in Bolivia (Arnold and Yapita 1998, 2000) or elsewhere in the Andes (García 2005; Hornberger 1994). The impulse appears to have come from foreign NGOs and governments that see indigenous rights as being principally about culture rather than economic or political rights.

Even those teachers who are committed to its implementation find considerable difficulties in doing so as the materials used are often inappropriate. One issue is the standardization of Aymara, so children may not understand the particular dialect reproduced in their textbooks or the neologisms used to replace words of Spanish origin (Arnold et al. 1998: 17–20; Arnold and Yapita 2000: 120–22). As a result, the "Aymara" in the books is very difficult to understand and causes great confusion, not least because children are berated for "not even speaking Aymara properly." Children learn not only that they are incompetent in Spanish but in their native tongue, too.

Another issue is that schooling in the Andes is produced with crass disregard for indigenous cultural practices and forms of knowledge; in fact, "knowledge" is increasingly defined as that which is learned in school. Indeed, because of time spent in school, many children are failing to acquire the traditional knowledge of crafts, skills, and accompanying rituals that make rural life meaningful and sustainable. In contrast, the way rural life is presented at school is somewhat removed from children's own experience: The new materials dedicated to intercultural education present indian culture as rural and colorful, and mestizo culture as urban and quotidian. The stylized images of houses, fields, and mountains contrast with the much more realistic images of urban life. Indian culture is once again reduced to folkloric representation rather than a lived reality. In the words of van Dam and Salman, "Interculturality is reduced to a kaleidoscopic categorisation of stereotypes and arbitrarily chosen attributes" (2003: 24).

Perhaps more important is that intercultural bilingual education in Bolivia has only ever been directed at indigenous communities, an experience shared by Peru (García 2005: 81). In Ecuador, which has also experimented with indigenous schooling that seeks to valorize indigenous culture, leaders of indigenous movements send their children to the best schools they can—Spanish language schools (Martínez 2009)—and, unsurprisingly, indigenous activists in Peru also send their children to the Alliance Française or the North American Institute in Cuzco (García 2005: 99). Bilingual intercultural education may seem like a good idea, but if it is only directed at indians then it is not surprising that many people see it simply as a way of keeping indians down (García 2005: 87).

It is hard not to come to the conclusion that until the state mandates that, for example, children in private schools in La Paz learn Aymara as part of a national curriculum, there will be no truly intercultural bilingual education in Bolivia. The parents of children in expensive schools in La Paz do not want their children learning Aymara but, then again, neither do parents of children in Wila Kjarka; they coincide in the view that what their children need is fluency and competence in Spanish and that the second language should be English. The big difference between the two groups is that the former do acquire competence in Spanish and some English, whereas the latter do not.

It is quite clear that rural public education does not deliver the cultural capital for children to participate in metropolitan mestizo culture on anything like a level playing field. In fact, one Wila Kjarkeño, Herculiano, saw the situation quite clearly:

> If a person learns to read and write at school, s/he will not have learned well. We do not realize that if we continue with [this kind of education] we will stay behind, just like these schools.
>
> We won't even receive any useful qualifications because the education we receive is so poor that we cannot even read. There is no justice: How can one of us, after having received this education, come out as an engineer, as an agronomist, or even a teacher? It is very difficult.

The frustration he is expressing is a clear illustration of what Ivan Illich (1971: 3) has called the modernization of poverty "which combines the lack of power over circumstances with a loss of personal potency." This poverty and loss of personal potency is evidenced in many areas. Whereas in the recent past people would weave their own cloth using the visually sophisticated language of Andean weaving, nowadays people are increasingly using cheap Western style clothing, which tears easily and is not as warm. As cultural values become undermined, people who had a rich cultural life feel increasingly marginalized. That is, it is not simply that children spend a lot of time in school learning very little at all, but they spend a lot of time *not* learning about other things, as Denise Arnold (2006) cogently points out. These skills, which are essential for their economic well-being—not to mention cultural reproduction—are valued less and less, while the skills that are valuable for life in urban Bolivia are highly valued. This would not matter so much if they were actually acquiring these skills, but they are manifestly not, and they are taught that the ideas of their parents and grandparents are archaic and irrelevant. The rich set of rituals their parents use to make crops grow and cure animals—rituals that give people a sense of control over the vicissitudes of their lives—are becoming meaningless to young people. In the words of one young woman, "[The mountain spirits] have left us" and another young man said that they "are not powerful anymore."

Public education, moreover, comes at great financial cost to families in Wila Kjarka and other communities. The enrollment fee is nominal, but children are required to buy pens and pencils of various kinds, exercise books, mathematical instruments, various kinds of felt-tipped pens, paper of various sizes, and so on. On top of this, they need to provide outfits for the annual school festival as well as dust aprons. In the early 1990s most children only went to school for three years, but now many expect to complete their six years in Wila Kjarka and then continue onto secondary school in Choquepata. The cumulative cost of sending, say, six children to school easily dwarfs any other household expenditure. Not only does it cost a lot of money to send children to school, even with the new subsidies to parents offered by the Morales administration, but they are also unable to do agricultural labor when they are in school and, therefore, their contribution to the household economy is substantially reduced. Whereas in the 1990s men engaged in seasonal labor migration to earn money for products they could not produce in Wila Kjarka, in recent years the primary expenditure is school costs. Men are having to leave to find work more often and for longer periods in order to send their children to school.

Despite the best intentions of the most recent education reform, it is quite clear that schools do not impart the cultural capital that would allow indians to compete for resources and power with urban mestizos. After completing their education, children have very poor reading and writing skills and speak ungrammatical Spanish, which quickly marks their origins whatever efforts they make to change their appearance. This is hardly surprising because not only is greater stress made on form rather than content—so children have the most beautiful handwriting but don't know what they are writing—their teachers themselves make basic grammatical errors such as using the masculine article for a feminine noun.

At times it seems as if this undereducation is entirely intentional. One of the most intelligent people I know in Wila Kjarka is Beatriz, and I once found her reading a book for school. She read it out loud to me in halting Spanish—an exceptionally dull nineteenth-century Bolivian novel with archaic language: It was quite clear that she had absolutely no idea about what she was reading and was surprised I thought it remotely a matter of interest to *understand* what one reads; she was, after all, "reading." Reading without comprehension is a feature of indian education in many other

Día del Indio *celebrations are very much focused on the teacher, who is feted by the community on his return to the village.*

parts of Bolivia as well (Arnold and Yapita 2000). This is unsurprising given that comprehension in reading is not something apparently expected of teachers in their training (Luykx 1999), so they are not in a good position to pass it onto the children they teach. Rural education focuses on correct repetition of the form rather than a profound understanding of the content (Arnold and Yapita 2000; Spedding 1999).

Even though all the schoolteachers in Wila Kjarka are native Aymara speakers and speak ungrammatical Spanish, they are frequently ambivalent about the way of life of the community in which they have been posted. I had many conversations with Walter as with the other teachers, either in the mornings before school started or in the evenings. When they are not teaching, teachers have very little to do other than wash their clothes and listen to the radio. They almost never visit people in their homes and send for people when they need to speak to someone, such as a member of the school committee; but it is also the case that they are rarely invited into people's homes. The teacher's position in the community is dependent on his *not* being a member of the community—that is, of representing a different world the ways of which he imparts to children. According to Mario Yapu, for this reason many people prefer a certain social distance between themselves and the teachers in their community (1999: 76).

On some occasions there may only be one teacher present, as was often the case in 2003: Of the three posts only two had been filled four months into the school year. Walter's colleague was regularly absent, leaving him to teach all three classes and six grades of school. Under those conditions, a visit from a resident anthropologist is welcome. In fact, Walter has read a Spanish version of this chapter, and we have discussed it together. It turned out that a teacher friend of his had read a version that was used in a course on critical pedagogy at the Universidad de la Cordillera in La Paz. Walter's friend, although not immediately recognizing either the village or the pseudonymous Eulogio, knew he taught in that region and passed it on. When Walter brought it up, I was worried that he might be offended by what I had written but was much relieved to learn that he disputed none of what I had said but asked, rather, that he not be referred to pseudonymously in any future publication, and this is why I refer to him by his real name.

On an earlier occasion I entered his room wearing sandals and, having come from the fields, had some earth on my feet, which I shook off before crossing the threshold. The subject of my footwear had come up before and Walter was clearly bemused that I would wear sandals. Walter was born and brought up in a farming village near Lake Titicaca, and he described the village to me as being rather similar to Wila Kjarka, except that it was near the road, had brick buildings, and was generally "more advanced." He had doubtless worn *whisku* rubber tire sandals in his youth. On this occasion Walter interviewed me as much as I him. He asked me a lot about my life in Europe, how much I earned, and so on, and once I had described my living conditions he asked with what appeared to be genuine puzzlement how I was able to live in Wila Kjarka. My response that I was by now used to life in Wila Kjarka and that Wila Kjarkeños were good people didn't quite seem to satisfy him. He told me that the lack of "facilities" such as running water and electricity was difficult and that "they are very backward here."

In that year he was particularly alone, partly because they hadn't been able to appoint a teacher. According to him a teacher had, in fact, arrived to take up his post, but took one look at the village and returned back down the mountain, only pausing to rest. Walter was as appalled at the behavior of his colleague as he was understanding of the reaction: The teacher had behaved badly, but Wila Kjarka could not expect to attract good teachers without electricity, a road, and other facilities. The arrival of the road in 2007 has made little difference since, without transportation, the teachers still have to walk up the mountain. Often they have to walk all the way from the main road, which can be as much as a four-hour walk for teachers. This is, without a doubt, an arduous trek for those not accustomed to walking and often wearing inappropriate shoes, but it is nevertheless one made by all Wila Kjarkeños, even the very young and the very old. In June 2007 when I was walking with the perpetually centenarian Teodosio (he was certainly over ninety then), we passed two resting teachers on the way to the village. Teodosio walked slowly, with a stick, but his steady gait allowed him to pass the flushed and breathless teachers.

Nevertheless, for urban-oriented teachers, the beautiful mountains may have little charm, and I suspect that the greatest difficulty they face is not so much the physical discomfort but the sheer boredom of being in Wila Kjarka. It is true that they get their meals served to them, but teachers eat alone; and it is not difficult to understand why someone might be less than keen to take up such a post, insulting as it may be to the people of Wila Kjarka.

Walter does not share the cynicism of many of his colleagues and puts up with the solitude and boredom. He is still passionate about education and its capacity to improve people, to allow them to progress. He is there to "raise my peasant brothers" and to "guide their learning" so that they may progress. On more than one occasion he told me emphatically that he "was like them"—Wila Kjarkeños, that is—but now he had "progressed," a sentiment echoed in his colleague Bernabé's speech during the hora cívica mentioned above. In some senses Walter presented a very positive image of personal progress by someone from a rural indigenous background, but it was a model that depended on formal education leading to an urban lifestyle. He had studied hard at night by candlelight while his family was sleeping. One of the very few professions open to indians is teaching, and he worked hard to gain a place at the teacher-training college. He traveled six hours each way to La Paz every weekend to study for his degree, and he hopes to gain a scholarship to study pedagogy in Mexico. His aspirations for himself are very much like those of any young person in Wila Kjarka who wants to study in order to leave the community, and part of that desire to leave is produced by the very education system, directly in the form of the values imparted and indirectly by not affording children the time to obtain the necessary agricultural and ritual skills to run a peasant household. Until 1997 this was not much of an issue, as children only received three years of schooling in Wila Kjarka. With the expansion of the school to six years and, as a consequence, access to secondary education in Choquepata, there is very little time indeed for children to contribute to the household economy as they did previously.

Walter and the other teachers in Wila Kjarka did not identify with any of the indigenous movements in Bolivia, much less identify themselves as Aymaras. Walter was almost certainly the one person who was not entered as indigenous in the 2001 census (the other teachers may not have even been there), although almost everyone in his home community on the *altiplano* was recorded as indigenous, which merely serves to underline the point of his social and ethnic mobility. It is interesting to speculate how he might have been returned had he been censused in his parents' house; at the very least, it indicates the highly contextual nature of indigenous identity and ascription.

I of course talked to his various colleagues over the years as well, and I attended their lessons, too. They also enjoyed speaking to me in Aymara and trying to catch me out, but there was also a level of shyness and even distrust, perhaps because of my ambiguous status as a European living like an indian. One of them dubbed me *el gringo indio* (the indian gringo) and laughed heartily the first time he used it, the phrase perhaps encapsulating my contradictory nature and, almost certainly, my footwear. But he laughed alone, and my Wila Kjarkeño friends did not find it funny, possibly because of its implication that I had been contaminated by their indianness. The teacher eventually stopped calling me gringo indio, at least in my hearing, but it does show how one can become ethnicized or racialized simply through proximity. Perhaps the teachers' very public and daily washing of clothes is more about cleansing themselves of this kind of racial contamination than it is a concern for personal hygiene. If I could become indianized, what is living in Wila Kjarka doing to them? Teachers, like everyone else in Bolivia, are highly aware of the stigma of being associated with indianness.

Walter, whatever identity he might proclaim, is certainly aware that indians are discriminated against; he is equally clear that the best way to avoid it is to be educated. At the same time he is frustrated that they don't take their destinies in their own hands and improve themselves. As he put it to me in Aymara, *walja jaqi chukt'upxi* (too many jaqi are on their knees, or, literally, squatting on their hunkers the ways indians so often used to sit in the times of the hacienda). Walter demonstrates his commitment to education in Wila Kjarka: During his time in Wila Kjarka, of the three teachers there he was the one who was present on any school day and the one who concerned himself about the 30-percent absenteeism, trying to persuade parents to bring their children to school. He was also, however, someone who would make the members of the school committee come and see him, even when it was inconvenient for them, and he would also insist on speaking Spanish in committee meetings, even though at least half of its members did not speak Spanish. In 2003 I attended school committee meetings, on the invitation of the chair of the committee, Pastor. When facing opposition in meetings, Walter used Spanish to silence people (knowing they do not understand or understand poorly), cut them off when they spoke in Aymara, spoke of members of the committee in a disparaging tone, saying things such as "este abuelito no entiende" (this little grandpa doesn't understand) or the women members as "las mamitas" (the little mammas).[9] He uses the very same tactics and tropes that mestizos use to silence and belittle indians, perhaps because he sees himself as a mestizo, just as the villagers clearly see him as one.

Walter is not unusual in his ambivalence toward the members of the community in which he works. He worked hard, under difficult circumstances, to educate his charges, as do many other rural schoolteachers. But even dedicated teachers such as Walter represent a very particular future for their students, one that involves their leaving their communities and becoming more urban, more mestizo. Schoolteachers are not the only source of this vision of upward mobility, and many people with no schooling expressed such ideas as well. People in Wila Kjarka often talk of their desire to move to the local market town of Sorata, or to the capital, La Paz, and be more "civilized." Some, of course, do; many do not. It is worth noting that the reason that many do not is because of the great difficulty people have in making ends meet in town. Not only is housing expensive and poor, but work is very difficult to come by. On top of this, people are subject to daily racism for being indian. In practice, women can gain work as domestic servants—working long and isolated hours for low pay—and men get the most low-paid and menial jobs that are available. As Olivia Harris (1995) has noted, many men in particular strive to disguise their indian identity to avoid the effects of anti-indian racism, and this may be as true for schoolteachers as it is for laborers. Migrants are at a considerable disadvantage because of their poor rural education. After six years of schooling, no child in Wila Kjarka is fluent in Spanish, and only some gain the most rudimentary literacy.

It cannot be assumed that the advent of an indigenous president in the form of Evo Morales has substantially changed the attitude of teachers. Despite appointing a reforming minister for education, Félix Patzi, who was passionate about "decolonizing" education and making it truly inter-cultural, reform in this area was blocked by teachers' unions, and Patzi was forced out of office within months. The Morales administration went through three ministers of education in its first two years, and there is no sign that it will be able to reform education in the direction it would like against the opposition of the teachers' unions.

There is, however, one date in the school calendar that seems clearly designed to offer a more positive image of the indian, and that is the *Day of the Indian*. Perhaps here is where people get positive images of themselves.

THE DAY OF THE INDIAN

The name of this celebration, *Día del indio*,[10] is slightly misleading as it actually commemorates the founding of the first school for indians in Warisata by Elizardo Pérez and Avelino Siñani on August 2, 1931. Elizardo Pérez was a mestizo teacher who struggled hard to offer schooling to indi-ans and was imprisoned more than once for his subversive activities and his school was closed several times. The Day of the Indian is really a cel-ebration of indian schooling and one that, at least until very recently, has elevated the role of the mestizo Pérez and erased that of his indigenous colleague, Siñani. In its contemporary forms the Day of the Indian is en-tirely under the control of the schoolteachers who, because of their social position, are able to compel attendance and marching from adults as well as children—the indians, that is. Prominent in all these celebrations are the kinds of militarism we saw in the *horas cívicas*.

Wila Kjarkeños congregate in the village of Choquepata with five other small communities to celebrate together. Choquepata is a relatively large village with a road and a high school, the Colegio Lindon B. Jhonson (*sic*), originally founded by American Lutheran missionaries, where a handful of Wila Kjarkeños attend. The Bolivian national holiday is the Sixth of August, also known in Wila Kjarka as *El Día de la Raza* (Race Day), but indians are not expected to participate in this public holiday. In Bolivia, as indeed most parts of Latin America, El Día de la Raza is the day marking Columbus's discovery of America, celebrated on the twelfth of October. This is also a day not celebrated by Wila Kjarkeños for the simple rea-son that it has nothing to do with them. The conflation of the two cel-ebrations is telling because from the perspective of Wila Kjarkeños there is not much difference between them: Columbus's arrival marked the supremacy of Europeans in Bolivia, and Independence day marks the supremacy of creoles in Bolivia; the distinction between Europeans born in Europe and those born in the New World is thoroughly uninteresting to Wila Kjarkeños for the simple reason that it made and makes very little difference to most indians.

The Sixth of August, I was told by Pastor, was for the whites and mestizos: "That time of the Sixth of August was when the whites and mestizos made the government of Bolivia appear. Since then the Sixth of August has existed." Indians apparently had no role in this, and when the foundation of the nation is celebrated, indians are physically absent, including from any public discourse. In the early decades of the twentieth-century, indians were prohibited from participating in civic celebrations of the nation and were even banned from entering La Paz's main square and seat of government (Gotkowitz 2000: 222). At the beginning of the twenty-first century, no such prohibitions exist, but by making a distinction between a national day for indians and one for everyone else, indians' marginality from the Bolivian state is underlined. The Day of the Indian paradoxically serves to mark the exclusion of indians from the nation rather than their inclusion into the national fabric.

For *their* day, indian children spend weeks perfecting their military marches, their physical exercises, and their folkloric dances. On the Day of the Indian, indian culture is presented as folkloric rather than as being an integral part of life. The judges of these dances are chosen from the highest-ranking outsiders. In 1999 I was asked to be a judge even though I stated quite clearly that I knew nothing about folkloric dances. Knowledge of the dances was not a requirement, though the high status of a (preferably white) outsider was, and no one seemed to think it inappropriate that a European be asked to judge indian cultural forms in this way. I politely refused and returned to my companions from Wila Kjarka.[11]

One striking aspect of the Day of the Indian celebrations is its militarism, which goes beyond simply marching. Children, boys and girls, spend two weeks perfecting their parade drills with the commands barked in Spanish. Day after day the children practice marching and gymnastics, dressing up in unfamiliar shorts and t-shirts for the physical exercises. For the marching routines the parents are obliged to make them special uniforms, and the parents inevitably comply because their children will be paraded in front of several villages and made to compete against them.

In Choquepata, boys dress up as soldiers with wooden rifles and I saw one young lad dressed as a military policeman. In this photograph, there

Boy dressed as military policeman for Día del Indio
celebrations. Choquepata, 2003.

are two other children in the background: another boy dressed as a soldier from the Independence wars and a girl dressed as an appropriate sup-
porter of military efforts, a nurse. Masculine militarism is, however, a key
component of public education and is present in many aspects of school
education. A poem to motherhood, which sings the praises of the loving,
hard-working, and self-sacrificing mother, ends with a clear command to
mothers that they give up their sons for their country. As we saw in chapter 4, the people of Wila Kjarka do not think of women as self-sacrificing
mothers whose role is to produce children for the community but, rather,
as productive (as opposed to merely reproductive) citizens of the community and even warriors in their own right. On this day, however, the

women of Wila Kjarka and other communities march behind the flag in these celebrations, but they are most certainly not recognized as warriors but, rather, as mothers. Little girls, as a consequence, do not dress up as soldiers, although they will sometimes dress up as nurses. Nursing is an appropriate caring profession for women, but it is overwhelmingly clear that men express their citizenship through military service, and the militarism of the Day of the Indian celebrations overshadows any celebration of indian culture.

The school, alongside the army, is the site where male Bolivians most clearly experience and imagine their nation. Although the function of the army is to "defend the Fatherland," the Bolivian army has never successfully done so, with the exception of when it defeated Che Guevara's guerrillas in 1967. The army's role is to maintain civic order, and it has been ruthlessly used to quell "unrest" created by peasants, miners, and students up to the present time. There is a tremendous irony in the overwhelmingly explicit militarism of the Day of the Indian because the army in recent decades has repeatedly been used to repress indigenous political organization and resistance, especially in coca growing areas. Yet, in these festivals supposedly celebrating "The Indian," the most constant and clearest representation is that of militarism and soldiers.

Indians, however, numerically predominate in the Bolivian army (Gill 1997), and a historical connection exists between the army and the establishment of indian schooling. Various scholars have cited the Chaco War (1932–35) against Paraguay as one of the key founding moments of the modern Bolivian nation. This war saw the deaths of thousands of indian recruits partly because they were unable to communicate properly with their monolingual officers (Soria 1992: 54). The catastrophe of the Chaco War persuaded a number of army officers, particularly those of middle rank, to consider the education of indians in order to create a more efficient army; and, indeed, some elements in the army supported indian education in the 1930s and 1950s when important sections of Bolivian society were opposed (Luykx 1993: 55). The army, as with every "people's army" since the time of Napoleon, has also had a social function: to create a sense of national purpose and identity among its recruits. In this respect, it is very similar to the school, which also has had as one of its key goals the creation of a national and homogenous culture, and the promulgation of Bolivian citizenship.

It is perhaps worth noting at this point that Evo Morales's government far from distancing itself from militarism and citizenship wholeheartedly

*Evo Morales on sentry duty in the presidential
palace, late 1970s. From Pablo Stefanoni and Hervé Do Alto,*
Evo Morales: De la coca al palacio *(La Paz, 2006).*

embraces it. Evo Morales himself served with the Military Police when
he was a conscript in the late 1970s and makes reference to this experience when opposing politicians cast doubt on his patriotism and allegiance to the Bolivian nation. For example, as James Dunkerley records,
when his electoral opponent, Jorge "Tuto" Quiroga, late in the presidential
campaign of 2005 accused Evo of preferring the *wiphala* flag of indigenous
movements over the flag of the republic, Evo "kissed the Bolivian tricolour,
declaring that he had sworn allegiance to the flag every day as a conscript,
while Quiroga had never submitted to any military service" (2007: 13).

The photograph of the young boy dressed as a military policeman in a
school festival celebrating indians now seems less incongruous: The army
and the school function in similar ways in converting indian peasants into
citizens; I shall explore the role of the army in creating male citizens in the
following chapter.

Despite almost a decade of reform in Bolivia, and despite the fact
that Bolivia is now, in official discourse at least, often described as plurinational and multicultural, little has changed for the majority of indians
who continue to live in the countryside. If "The Indian" has returned to
public debate and political discourse, the reality for most indians is that,
even now, the metropolitan discourse continues to favor urban over rural,
Spanish over Aymara or Quechua, and whiteness over indianness. This is
evident in the popular imagery of Bolivians as white and urban as well as
in the harsh economic realities of racial discrimination.

It is, however, also true that there is willingness at the centers of power
to address some of the issues of indian cultural values. The 1994 Education
Reform Act has been criticized for homogenizing indigenous languages
and introducing literate forms of knowledge that are not indian (Arnold

and Yapita 1999; Luykx 2004). One of the biggest problems facing the implementation of the bilingual education reforms is that teacher-training colleges do not prepare their teachers well for the classroom (Luykx 1999) and particularly in teaching a bilingual curriculum. There is, however, a much broader set of problems related to bilingual education. The Education Reform Act stipulates that *everyone* in Bolivia should have a bilingual and intercultural education, but to date this has only been implemented in indian communities. In its current form, education for children in villages such as Wila Kjarka contributes to the devaluation of indian communities and practices without offering compensating advantages in its stead: They are not being educated in their own language and within their cultural framework, nor are they learning the skills to allow them to compete successfully in a Spanish-speaking world.

It is through schools and teachers that the state has greatest access to these populations and the greatest opportunity to effect change. The teachers themselves, however, have worked hard at acquiring the language and manners of the urban mestizos to progress themselves and escape discrimination, and they often take great pains to distinguish themselves from their less-acculturated brethren. The state education system promotes a particular vision of civilization and a hierarchy of knowledge. Aurolyn Luykx quite accurately describes teacher-training colleges as "citizenship factories" (1999), and it is not surprising that teachers trained in the system voluntarily participate in the promulgation of certain set of citizenship values, whatever their ethnic background. The irony is that, as we have seen, they resist state policy in the form of the education reform by not teaching as much in Aymara as they are supposed to and by being much less focused on intercultural education than state policy would like to dictate.

The experience in lowland areas of Bolivia is rather different, and Bret Gustafson (2009) has shown how bilingual education among the Guaraní has been one of the bases of an "indigenous resurgence," although not without considerable resistance from within and without Guaraní communities. Shane Greene (2009) describes a similar role for teachers in the Amazon movement in Peru where they are seen as cultural warriors. In the highlands, perhaps because of the well-developed history of teacher-training colleges, school teachers are typically a conservative rather than radical force when it comes to indian culture in schools.

Indian teachers in the highlands, at least, are thus often very poor advocates for indian cultural values. By becoming teachers within the state system they have rejected "traditional" life and are unlikely to be concerned about promoting the kinds of knowledge produced outside the schooled world they have joined. The teacher is involved in what Ulf Hannerz has called "cultural welfare": "trying to provide the citizenry with 'good culture'; that is, meanings and meaningful forms held to meet certifiable and intellectual and aesthetic standards" (1992: 49). This "good culture" has long been explicitly seen as a process of de-indianization. The key concept of "civilization," which is so often used by teachers has, for much of the twentieth century, been associated with "changing customs, considered pernicious and retrograde, in favour of a way of life implicit in Western civilisation" (Soria 1992: 50).

Because "civilization" is so closely associated with urban life in general and white people in particular, children's level of civilization and, consequently, their Bolivianness, will always be in doubt. It is perhaps for this reason that the militarism of schooling and the Day of the Indian is so salient. In Bolivia and in many parts of the world, military service is one way that subaltern peoples can earn their membership in the nation-state—their citizenship, in other words. For men, military service, for all its unpleasantness, is what makes them *Bolivian*, and they have the identity card to prove it. This model is extended to children and women who must parade in displays of patriotism to demonstrate their adherence to the state and "civilized" values.

The 1994 Education Reform was enacted in large measure to promote a new multinational and pluricultural Bolivia. Why then has such little progress been made in providing indians with a positive view of their position in society? The schoolteacher's ambiguous and sometimes personally conflictive position (Luykx 1999) in the racial and social hierarchy of Bolivia makes his position as a teacher in an indian school acutely sensitive. The teacher, even if from an indian background himself, is a major agent in the reproduction of a racialized social hierarchy and, far from effecting a change in ethos toward a new multiculturalism, plays a principal role, inculcating in children a negative racial consciousness.

Bolivia has enacted major education reform, including a policy on bilingual education, the production of teaching materials considered more appropriate to indigenous communities, the recruitment of teachers who speak indigenous languages, and in recent years a policy explicitly meant to decolonize education. Despite this apparently propitious environment for tackling racism, schools remain a principal site where children are exposed to and internalize racist ideas. Rural schoolteachers from indian backgrounds have successfully moved away from peasant lifestyles and chosen not to engage in the low-skilled urban jobs typically reserved for indians. Schoolteachers have not only accepted the progressive ideal, they have also been successful in being upwardly mobile in society, moving from being indians to being mestizos, and should therefore *not* be expected to be strong proponents of bilingual intercultural education, especially when they are both frustrated by their situation and exalted to a particular status within the community. Teachers who share the same subaltern ethnic and racial background as their pupils are necessarily involved in the reproduction of racist ideas in their classrooms and schools. This will continue so long as being indian means being "traditional" and rural, and so long as rural lifestyles are seen as folkloric or miserably backward. That is, as long as the phrase "indian schoolteacher" is oxymoronic according to Bolivian social categories, schoolteachers will continue to reproduce racialized ideas in the classroom. Already in the second administration of Bolivia's first indigenous president, there is little sign of this changing in the schools of villages like Wila Kjarka.

María Elena García in her discussion of indigenous education and citizenship in Peru (2005) is somewhat more optimistic, but her optimism draws from some of the more experimental efforts in intercultural education in the Andes in the context of a revalorization of indigeneity. She makes the provocative suggestion that what we are witnessing is the creation of a new indigenous citizenship. For Bolivia, her conclusion seems inescapable, given the contemporary prominence of indigeneity in contemporary Bolivia. Not only is this the case in the arena of state symbolism, but many groups are using their indigeneity to assert or reclaim rights vis-à-vis the state (Canessa 2009). A distinction needs to be made, however, between indigenous citizenship and indian citizenship. This is not as facile a distinction as may appear at first glance. Indigenous citizenship as espoused by Morales and by García's informants is progressive, modern, and part of a globalized discourse of indigenous rights and identities. The people who espouse and can articulate such a citizenship are often far removed from the kinds of people who live in Wila Kjarka and the communities studied by García; there the struggle is to overcome their status as indians and become citizens. I would argue, however, that indians are by definition not citizens. García is not alone in positing new forms of citizenship for indigenous people (see, for example, Kymlicka 1995; Postero 2007; Stavenhagen 2002; Yashar 2005), but she is one of the first to posit an indigenous citizenship per se, a citizenship where "cultural difference is no longer a criterion for exclusion, but one of inclusion in a multicultural political community" (2005: 165). One could go even further and say that the contemporary Bolivian state is doing more than simply offering indigenous citizenship on an equal basis; it is placing it at the very center of how membership of the state is understood and displacing the mestizo as the iconic citizen. But political indigeneity at the level of international conferences, or the language the state uses to express its political aims, operates at a very different level than that of the concerns of people in marginalized communities who face poverty and racism.

This produces an obvious tension between cultural pride and ethnic awareness on the one hand, and a desire to overcome poverty and marginalization on the other. Evo Morales can be publicly proud of his origins and wear indigenous clothing in public, but no one is going to call him an indian; nevertheless, even he (as we shall see in a later chapter) is not immune to the struggle of expressing an indigenous citizenship while sloughing off the stereotypes of the indian. We now turn in the following two chapters to this tension between indianness and citizenship, both at the level of the community and the nation, and we shall be looking, in particular, at the very gendered nature of both.

SEVEN

Intimate Citizens

On a recent trip to Wila Kjarka, I went to see my friend Bonifacia shortly after I had arrived. She had invited me for lunch. Bonifacia knows I love the way she cooks guinea pig, and she also likes the *pollera* full skirts or shawls I sometimes bring her as gifts. She flatters me by telling me I have taste in polleras and especially matching them with shawls; the flattery works. Although some people in Wila Kjarka are beginning to construct larger kitchens, Bonifacia still cooks in a lean-to against the wall of her house with the smoke billowing up through the thatch. As she busied herself preparing the guinea pig and I peeled vegetables, we chatted about my goddaughter, Alicia, who had just left her husband because of his violence. Alicia had married someone from the other side of the valley, near Sorata. Bonifacia sighed; she had never heard of anyone good coming from that community. They are all bad people (*wali phiru qhuru*) and Alicia's husband is particularly bad. Alicia had come back to her parents, but everyone knew he would find her there and take her back; it was only a matter of time. We commiserated with Alicia, and then I asked, "Do you fight?," using the Aymara word *nuwasiña,* which is a reflexive verb implying mutual fighting, but the meaning is usually quite clear; and when referring to couples fighting it is simply a way of talking about being beaten by one's husband. She nodded matter-of-factly and explained that yes they did; her husband even beat her up once with the metal tube (*phusaña*) she uses to blow on the fire, she said with a full laugh, rocking back on her stool. "He hit me right here," she said indicating her forehead, "and there was a lot of blood." Bonifacia picked up the phusaña and blew on the fire, making the flames dance and the water in the earthenware pot full of maize bubble. She rocked back and had stopped smiling.

We talked on and I asked her what kinds of things her husband said when they "fought." She said he often shouted in Spanish and said *carajo* (damn!) as well as phrases such as *india sucia* (dirty indian woman) and *maldita india* (damned indian woman). I was not surprised, as I had heard people recount similar things before, and Bonifacia simply shrugged when I asked her why her husband spoke to her in this way and then said, "Sometimes he says nothing."

In Wila Kjarka the words *indio* or *india* are rarely used. *Indio* was what the hacendado and his mayordomo called people in Wila Kjarka as he beat them with his whip. The word is most closely associated with the sharp racism and times when white men such as the hacendado treated "their indios" like dogs. Bonfiacia's husband knows all this, and he is no more or less indigenous than his wife, and this rather raises the question: Why would he bark insults in Spanish and call her an india?

MEN AND WOMEN

In terms of the household economy, men and women agree, when asked, that they have complementary roles, and many household tasks require the labor of both men and women to be performed properly.[1] For example, plowing requires a man to lead the team and a woman to drop the seeds. These tasks are deemed "male" and "female," respectively. The positive value of complementarity is clearly stated by both men and women, and on many occasions men talk very positively of their wives' ability to farm and manage the household. Women strongly assert their position and dominance in their households and sometimes speak of their husbands as *pasiri*, visitors who come and go. Many men are quite frank that important decisions, especially financial ones, are equally shared. I once asked one of my neighbors, Alberto, what would happen if, without consulting his wife, he bought a cow with the money he brought back from the mines. He gave me a horrified look and shook his head, insisting he would never do that because he would get all the blame if it were a wrong decision. Many other men confirmed that even minor economic decisions are made together, and I have observed many occasions when this was clearly the case.

Men will frequently speak with high regard for their wives, and in many contexts talk positively of their productive activities. One of the most important values for men and women is labor, and men value their wives' labor highly; in contrast, manual labor is not valued in metropolitan discourse, especially female manual labor. In the Andes, the proximity to earth has particular racialized meanings as urban people contrast their "clean" lives with the lives of peasants who are in contact with earth through their hands and feet and the houses in which they live.[2] Whereas in highland rural areas men and women are esteemed for their ability to work on the earth, in the context of urban values this is quite positively devalued. One white man whose family used to have a hacienda in the highlands not far from Wila Kjarka but who now lives in La Paz explained to me how indians labored crouched and animal-like for hours with their heavy hands working the soil in all types of weather. "They don't feel cold or pain like you or I." He illustrated his point by bending over and opening his hands and making a digging notion with a brutish grimace on his face.

The metropolitan culture, however, not only devalues indian labor but rural indian culture in general. This is most starkly evident in media representations: In a country where the vast majority of the population is of indigenous origin, the paucity of indian faces on television and posters is quite striking. Even in more recent years, when indigenous people have become publicly more visible as in, for example, popular *huayno* music videos (which have benefited from technological changes that make them much easier to produce and distribute (Stobart 2011)), it nevertheless continues to be the case that billboards advertising, say, cell phones in urban areas with an overwhelming indigenous presence still feature white faces. The only counterexample I have noted in recent years was a large billboard in El Alto (the very indigenous satellite of the capital, La Paz), which was campaigning against domestic violence and certainly did show images of indigenous people. This could, however, hardly be said to be an aspirational image.

There is something of an irony in the absence of any indian-looking person in these representations, for throughout Bolivia's history indians have certainly been very present in the imagination of its elites: They have constantly drawn on images of indians to illustrate their own sense of superiority. To some extent the absence of indians in public images is a testament to their ambivalent presence in the imagination of dominant groups: The indian and rural aspect of the Bolivian experience is an essential part of the metropolitan discourse and in some sense can be seen to have been created by it, as ethnohistorian Thomas Abercrombie has forcefully argued (1992). By the same token, indian identity is historically contingent and does not exist sui generis, outside of colonial and neocolonial cultural, economic, and political structures. The dominant Bolivian national imagining, as indeed that of many other American nations, is founded on a series of mutually implicating dyads that contrast urban, Western-oriented, modern culture with a rural, anachronistic, indian one. As a consequence, indian "otherness" is at the very heart of the elite national imagination: the more it is repressed, the more it is reified. If "the indian" is at the very center of elites' imagination of themselves, it is also the case that whiteness and metropolitan values lie at the very center of how indians think of themselves.

MORE WHITE, MORE INDIAN

The question arises, however, how notions of what is white and what is indian become salient in a community such as Wila Kjarka. As with all successful hegemonic processes, the ways such ideas spread are not always even or coherent. There are a number of areas of life, however, where it is clear that Wila Kjarkeños are exposed to ideas that are at variance with broadly held views in Wila Kjarka about identity and gender. If in most contexts Wila Kjarkeños are in agreement that they share an ethnic or racial identity and that men and women have different but complementary roles in life, it is also the case that on other occasions people say things but behave very differently. Women and men negotiate these values in multifarious ways according to their own circumstances and personalities, but it seems clear that all have to deal with the tension between the values that are dominant in the society beyond the community and those that are largely held within it. For many people such conflicting values are, at best, temporarily resolved.

In the previous chapter we saw how Aymara schoolteachers are profoundly ambivalent about the community in which they work. But they are not the only people in Wila Kjarka who struggle with contradictory feelings about who they are, or indeed who they feel they ought to be.

Whereas men in Wila Kjarka do not have perms in their hair and do not avoid the sun to look whiter, they too are caught up in a whitening process, and this process occurs principally during their military service.

The Bolivian army, as is the case with every other public institution, gets whiter as one moves closer to the top. Indian men heavily dominate as conscripts, and the officers are almost exclusively mestizo or white. Zenobio from Wila Kjarka told me that one had to change one's name to become an officer, from, for example, "Condori to Cortés." "Condori" (a typically indigenous surname), in Zenobio's words, indicates poverty. "Nombre de pobreza es" (literally: it is a name of poverty) he said, momentarily breaking into Spanish; such names are not acceptable in universities, he continued, and the high ranks of the army. One of the things that many Wila Kjarka ex-soldiers remembered about their military experiences is the almost ritual humiliation and occasional violence meted out to indian recruits. They recalled been ridiculed for their stupidity, clumsiness, and inability to speak Spanish. Many Wila Kjarkeños recall seeing soldiers ordered to bend over and being beaten for speaking Aymara or Quechua.

Bolivian boot camps are no different from others around the world where new recruits are accused of being homosexuals or women. It is commonly the case that soldiers are made to parade around the base in women's clothing for infractions,[3] and there is a very clear homology between citizenship and the masculinity that military service is expected to confer.

It is in the army, above all, that young men learn to speak Spanish, and it is in the army that they learn the extent and nature of their country. Military service in the Andes "provides the structured and 'patriotic' means through which male citizens take part in movement around their country, meeting co-nationals and re-imagining their community, and it is through military service that men become citizens" (Radcliffe and Westwood 1996: 124).[4] For many this is their only opportunity to see distant regions and, as Benedicto, one of my neighbors in Wila Kjarka, told me, it was in the army that he really understood what Bolivia was. This imagining of the nation occurs in a highly masculine, hierarchical, and racialized context.

This is made salient in the punishments meted out to soldiers who fail, desert, or simply cannot take the rigors of military life. The abuse that recruits are subject to—the beatings, starvations, and humiliations—have recently become something of a public scandal (*La Opinión*, March 9, 2011). What is less public but widely known is the specific gendered nature of many of the humiliations. Men are regularly made to dress up as women and perform menial, feminine tasks, such as sweeping the square. A number of men reported to Juliana Ströbele-Gregor in Chayanta that the sexual abuse of young indian recruits is widespread (Juliana Ströbele-Gregor, pers. comm.). There is probably nothing that could underline the gendered nature of being indian more than raping young recruits. In Wila Kjarka no one mentioned sexual abuse, but many did offer accounts of how the feminization of soldiers was a key element of discipline. As my friend Eleuterio Mamani, who came out of the army in January 2006, explained:

> Yes, there are those who cannot take it, and they get kicked and beaten. And so as not to suffer any longer they escape, but they get caught. They are caught and dressed with a pollera, a manta, and put on them a sign which says "I am a woman," that is what is written: "I am a woman because I cannot take it in the army." And that is how they make them go [publicly] around the streets . . . You see, women don't go into the army, so if you cannot take it, then you are like a woman. "You are a woman; you cannot take it," they say. "Men go into the army; but you have to dress like a woman."

"Woman" here is not, however, just any woman, but quite explicitly an indian woman, with the signal pollera skirt and manta (shawl), because it is not simply that, as Marisol de la Cadena (1995) put it, "women are more indian," but also that indians are more female: to be dressed as a woman would be humiliating; to be dressed as an indian woman doubly so. Moreover, not to have completed military service makes one a poor marriage prospect in the eyes of many women; and lacking the masculinizing experience of military service and their poor or inadequate Spanish forces them to inhabit more the Aymara-speaking world of women.

In the words of Lesley Gill, "Military service is one of the most important prerequisites for the development of successful subaltern manhood, because it signifies rights to power and citizenship" (1997: 527). As one newspaper article succinctly put it recently: "It is a requirement for the full exercise of citizenship" (*La Estrella del Oriente*, January 9, 2012).[5] Through military service men obtain the *libreta militar*, the military booklet, which is a requisite for a national identity card. These two documents are essential for obtaining a passport, a job in a government agency, or a degree in the state university (537).

It is not, however, only the "imagined community" of the nation, to use Benedict Anderson's (1983) oft-quoted phrase, the *patria*, that is experienced during military service, but the local community of personalized relationships is reimagined too, the *patria chica*, the "little homeland." Through military service young men come to see their homes, their families, their language, and culture in a powerfully different light. It is true that they have been exposed to these kinds of imaginings through their school education, but being exposed to these ideas in an all-male, Spanish-speaking environment far from home in a total institution has a profound effect. Military service and the acquisition of the *libreta militar* structure the relationship of a man with the state on the basis of his new citizenship. It also has an important impact on his membership in his home community. Returning soldiers are patriotically feted under a specially made arch on their return from military service. Zenobio commented to me that when one leaves military service one feels "as if one has come close to the Presidency" (*como si acercaste la presidencia* [*sic*]). This illustrates well how military service is considered in terms of approaching the top of the nation, in terms of political power and social status. A returning soldier is a full citizen almost to the point of being presidential.

Military service not only confers membership in the nation-state but has implications for membership in the indian community, too. Whereas in the recent past it was through marriage that Wila Kjarkeños became full members of their community, now military service is increasingly performing this role. For women, full adulthood continues to be achieved through marriage, and women prefer marrying someone who has undergone military service. Men are therefore frequently proud to undertake their national service. As my friend, Pastor, put it to me: "It is a requirement as a Bolivian; it is to fulfill a duty,"[6] and Zenobio told me that young men entered military service because they come out "macho": (using the Spanish word) " 'You are a man now,' is what people say."

Some men avoid military service, but they are consequently likely to be functionally monolingual in Aymara. They are also therefore likely to have difficulty finding better jobs during the seasonal migrations and not be very good marriage prospects. These men lack the masculinizing experience of military service, and their poor or inadequate Spanish forces them to inhabit more closely the world of women. Celestino Chino, who was born in 1962, is one of the few men of his generation who didn't do his military service. He says he didn't go because he is an orphan; his father left him when he was very young. His mother consequently couldn't afford to let him go to the army, as she needed him at home.[7] The word "orphan" in Aymara does not necessarily mean that both one's parents are dead; it can mean that one has been abandoned or even, in some contexts, that one is very poor and marginalized, without kin to provide help. In Celestino's case, if his father left him at a young age, as Celestino said, he certainly returned because I knew him very well before he died. In Celestino's house hangs a photograph of his father I took some fifteen years ago, and it bears a striking resemblance to Celestino. It is difficult to understand then what Celestino means by being abandoned by his father and left an orphan, and he would not explain further.

There is another sense, however, in which Celestino was orphaned, and that is in his lack of citizenship—a male prerogative earned through military service. If having a father confers legitimacy on his sons, a recognized position in society—citizenship, in other words—Celestino most certainly does not move through Bolivian society as a legitimate citizen. His lack of military service means that he runs the constant risk of running afoul of the law if he should ever be picked up and questioned. As an illiterate and monolingual man, he consequently inhabits the Aymara-speaking world of Wila Kjarka, and the mines or rice fields of the *yungas*, where, as he points out, the work is very long, hot, and hard. In the mine, shifts go round the clock, and one earns approximately US$4 a day, but the mine owners take a quarter of that for the food they provide the miners. In the rice fields Celestino says he works twelve hours from dawn to dusk, bent over in the heat. He, like other Wila Kjarkeños, finds the valley heat uncomfortable and oppressive. Many other men in Wila Kjarka, of course, work in mines and rice fields, but through their military service they have learned (or consolidated) their Spanish, and many express a clear sense of belonging to the nation as a result. It is not, however, only in formal terms that citizenship is conferred through military service.

One area of life that is affected, as men become citizens in the nation-state, is their sexuality. A key aspect of army life mentioned by many Wila Kjarkeños is the regular visits to prostitutes. Every garrison has its prostitutes that are easily available, and they are apparently a standard feature of army life. It is not only during their twelve months of army service that Wila Kjarkeños purchase sex. Most spend extended periods in the gold mines, and it is quite common for men to spend several years in such work before returning to their community to get married. The work is hard, hot, wet, and dangerous, and they relax in bars and cinemas, and with prostitutes. A visit to a prostitute costs "one gram of gold, for a 'quickie,' five to spend the night."[8] As one friend put it, "They take a lot of gold. 'Bring gold!' they say, and a little later we just give it to them."[9]

Eleuterio had the misfortune of being stationed on the Brazilian border, where prostitutes are, apparently, very expensive. The conscripts who, I am told, only earn one boliviano a day[10] can only visit prostitutes for a "quickie" (*turpitaki uñjt'apxiritha*); to spend an entire night with a prostitute costs two hundred bolivianos (*Pä patakawa cueste mä arumaki*). Still, they will spend what money they do have to visit these "tall and beautiful" women. These Brazilian prostitutes are predominantly white, according to Eleuterio, but there are also some black women. There were, however, no prostitutes whom he described as jaqi. Indeed, even in highland areas, prostitutes are rarely jaqi. According to Pascale Absi, prostitutes in Bolivia tend to come from urban backgrounds, and women from the eastern lowlands predominate even in highland areas (2010: 195).

Where military service allows Wila Kjarkeños to travel and see their country in its variety and lay claim to their citizenship, prostitution serves a similar function. One friend, Adelio, beamed proudly as he told me he had slept with white (*rinka*), black (*nigra*), and indian (*chulita*) women: "all the women of Bolivia." His clear sense of accomplishment at having spanned sexually the three most recognizable racial groups in Bolivia is significant in the context of Bolivia as a mixed nation.

This mixing occurred through sexual relations. Although in Bolivia the African contribution is rather more muted, it shares a discourse with many other Latin American countries of being a product of the mix of European, African, and indigenous peoples.[11] Historically in Bolivia and elsewhere in Latin America the social advancement that mestizaje implies has been seen in terms of white men having sex with nonwhite women.[12] Indeed the degenerative (and often putatively predatory) sexuality of lower-class and darker men has been seen as particularly problematic in twentieth-century Latin American discourse, being concerned with "improving" the race.[13] My friend's evident pride in having slept with this variety of women must be seen in this context—a laying claim to his nation not only through military service and travel but through sex with racial and ethnic "others," a prerogative more generally seen as belonging to creole males, as Ramiro Condarco Morales demonstrates in his discussion of the relations between hacendados and indians (1983: 31). In the past, hacendados had the "right" known as the "derecho de la pernada"—

of sexual access to a woman on her wedding night—and in practice, as we have seen with Teodosio's mother, women even as young as fourteen had no choice but to submit to the advances of a powerful white man.[14] This was possible because indian women quite simply had few rights; they lacked citizenship in the nation. This was not simply an issue of relative power; rather, it was part of how the nation was then imagined. It was sometimes considered a duty for a white man to have sex with an indian woman in order to improve the race of the nation (Stephenson 1999). The politics of citizenship are not only gendered but sexualized; and these kinds of multiracial sexual experiences may have a political dimension, whether or not the individuals involved explicitly recognize it.

Wila Kjarkeños are no longer subject to explicit laws that seek to regulate their sexuality; it is not so easy to see the ways colonial relations are reproduced in their intimate spaces in the way that it is possible, for example, in plantation society in Indonesia—so carefully exposed by Ann Stoler (2002, 1995), whose work, along with other postcolonial scholars, on the intimacies of colonial power has influenced much of my thinking. Nor are they longer subject to the sexual predations of men who claim indian women's bodies on the basis of race privilege.

Aside from the prostitutes, Wila Kjarkeños and other miners are exposed to different sexual practices through going to see pornographic films. Small cinemas that show films run all day and all night, so they can be visited by men on any shift. The various men I spoke to about this said that they watched many of these films, which are clearly described as being illicit, but that is quite possibly part of the thrill. Various aspects fascinated these men, such as having sex naked and the length of time sex acts take in these films, which, it was suggested to me, indicates the white people are very slow to reach orgasm. In contrast, sex in Wila Kjarka typically takes place in the dark, while clothed, and appears to be a comparatively brief affair. Wila Kjarkeños talk about lesbian sex (*siñurax panini ikanti*), anal sex (*chinajat ikasipxi*), fellatio (*lakata pichilumpi apantaña*), and a variety of other sexual practices, which, according to the men, women in Wila Kjarka have little taste for, since they prefer to have sex laying on their sides in a ventral-dorsal position.

"Lesbian sex" is perhaps something of a misnomer, and a more literate translation would be "two white women having sex": The Wila Kjarkeños I spoke to did not associate two women having sex in a video with what might be understood as "lesbians." They interpreted such sex acts, possibly quite accurately in the case of pornography, as having nothing to do with any kind of relationship between the women involved or a particular sexuality; in fact, people were amazed that such a thing could possibly exist. Women, I was told, could not have (penetrative) sex, nor could they have a relationship, since running a household requires a man and a woman. There is, needless to say, no word for "lesbian" in Wila Kjarka: There is a word for "manly woman" (*urquchi*), but this does not refer to sexuality but rather physical strength and an ability to perform male tasks. Similarly, there is no word for male homosexual. *Q'ewsa*, which appears to mean male homosexual in other parts of the Andes, in Wila Kjarka refers to someone who lacks generosity, does not fulfill his social obligations, and does not drink "properly" (i.e., heavily) at fiestas. People do, however, use the Spanish word *maricón* to describe those mestizos who have sex with other men; and men in Wila Kjarka speak of *maricones* with fear, ridicule, and revulsion.

It is not just practices but particular aesthetics that men are exposed to through films and brothels. Porn actresses and prostitutes often have shaven pudenda (*jan tarwani*), and many men believe that that this makes women "horny" and eager for sex (*jan tarwani wali achala; ukat chach munixa*).[15] These experiences develop aesthetics and produce desires that cannot easily be met in Wila Kjarka and, in fact, men say that such practices do not occur in Wila Kjarka (indeed they are described as *prohibido*, Sp. forbidden) although this is, of course, difficult to ascertain. One man, however, did claim to have anal sex with his wife, stating the added pleasure and contraceptive value of the practice; other men expressed a desire to have anal sex but were ambiguous about whether they did so with their wives.

On the other hand, a number of my friends have commented how long it takes white people to have sex, "and they make an awful lot of noise, too." Benedicto, for example, expressed amazement at how long it took white women to "get going." Women in Wila Kjarka, he said, were much quicker. The implication from Benedicto's comments was that women in Wila Kjarka were quicker to reach orgasm, but with him and with other men I had great difficulty in talking about these issues, not just because people were sometimes (but not always) embarrassed, but rather because there appears to be no discursive space for talking about these matters. Whereas when discussing procreation there is a sense that menstrual blood and semen are equivalents, and the closest I was able to get to an understanding of a comparability between male and female orgasm was that both men and women "finished."

Desire, as Foucault has shown, has the capacity to confound and disrupt the capillaries of power, but it never does so in a simple way. Wila Kjarkeños are subject to an "education of desire" (Stoler 1995) that is as racialized as any in more conventional colonial situations in which power was even more explicitly racialized and sexualized. Wila Kjarkeños may not have the physical presence of a rapacious overseer to impress upon them the nexus of race and sex in the exercise of colonial power; but if they are no longer swimming in the full current of colonial plantation discourses of racialized power, they are most certainly bathing in its eddies.

Wila Kjarkeños may not readily talk about sex, but this is not to say that there is no sexual curiosity or, perhaps much more important, that their sexual experiences beyond the community affect how they imagine themselves as human beings. Wila Kjarkeños return from their military service and stints in the mines with a very different view of the world than that with which they left. They have proudly served their country and can consider themselves true citizens who have fulfilled their patriotic duty; they have learned to speak Spanish, which, even though they have not done so very well, is as much a marker of Bolivian citizenship as an identity card; and they have experienced a very different sexuality to the one prevalent in Wila Kjarka. They have traveled across the nation and made it theirs; they have slept with numerous women of various racial and ethnic groups. They have also experienced the widespread racism against indians in Bolivia and know that however well they speak Spanish, it is not well enough. This experience of the promise of inclusive *mestizaje* proving ever elusive is shared by many migrating groups in the Andes, as Sarah Radcliffe (1990) has asserted for female indian domestic workers in neighboring Peru. With these deeply ambivalent experiences, they return to Wila Kjarka with conflicting ideas and imaginations, which they, in some form, pass onto their wives, as indeed they sometimes pass on their venereal diseases.

Young men, however, rarely settle permanently in the village after military service; the exigencies of life in a community with population growth and land erosion necessitate seasonal migration. Whatever the length of time away and whatever job they manage to find, indian men receive very low wages when they leave the community and enter into the capitalist economy. They receive low wages because any labor defined as indian labor is of low status. So in the markets and towns, indians get paid a pittance for carrying loads, and in the lucrative cocaine industry, the poorly paid and dangerous work of stamping the coca leaves in kerosene is re-served for indians, as Olivia Harris (1995) has noted.

Indians are low-paid for another reason: They *can* be low-paid because their wage does not need to cover the costs of reproducing their labor. Their children and wives are supported principally by the land at home, while men's wages supplement that subsistence—that is, an indian's wage is not expected to support him and his family. Moreover, when the mine closes, or when men become old or sick, they return to the village that provides them with a form of social security. Thus, none of the costs of maintaining, reproducing, or protecting the labor supply are borne by the employer.

In this important way, peasant laborers are fundamental and not peripheral to the capitalist system, as these semiproletarianized la-borers—to use a term coined by Alain de Janvry (1981)—provide the system with a cheap and flexible source of labor, being reabsorbed by the communities in times of unemployment and providing a reserve in times of expansion. De Janvry presents this situation as a function of the post-hacienda condition of rural Latin America, but there is, in fact, a long history of semiproletarianized indian labor, for the Colonial and Republican economic systems were highly dependent on the temporary (and therefore subsidized) indian migration to the mines—the back-bone of the Bolivian economy for centuries. Mining continues to be important for Wila Kjarkeños, and when the price of gold fell in the late 1990s, Wila Kjarkeños simply returned to their communities or looked for less lucrative (but also less dangerous) work in the rice fields of the valleys (*yungas*).

In this way the peasant household is not marginal to the modern min-ing and agricultural businesses of Bolivia but intrinsic to it; such mar-ginality is an illusion on many levels. The peasant sector cannot survive without cash income, and the capitalist sector is dependent on the cheap labor supplied by the peasantry. The articulation of the two sectors of the economy occurs at the level of the peasant household, which, as Claude Meillassoux (1981) has pointed out, bears the brunt of a double exploita-tion. More specifically, wider economic structures penetrate right into the level of intimate personal relationships between men and women, since it is the men who work in the capitalist sector and the women who almost entirely work in the peasant one: The "dual economy" is articulated at the level of the married couple.

GENDER TROUBLES

Despite what many urban Bolivians believe about highland indian women, women in Wila Kjarka have a relatively high status within their community. As we have seen earlier, there is a strong sense of gender complementarity; people are very aware that it takes two adults to run a household properly, and one is not considered a complete and properly social person until one is married.

While the men are in the army, the mines, or working in the rice fields, the women in Wila Kjarka are working the fields and taking care of the children and animals. This is hard work and difficult to do alone, particularly since the running of the household is predicated on a gendered division of labor. The absence of men for extended periods also means that women necessarily have to undertake tasks normally reserved for men.

Agricultural and domestic tasks, as in many cultures, are divided into male and female roles. Women, for example, sow, weave, and cook; men plow, break the ground, and fetch firewood. Gender difference is performative rather than essential in that gender distinction is seen as being expressed through the different things men and women *do* rather than a differing sense of what they *are*. Since the absence of men requires women to undertake male tasks, they are masculinized by their labor. So at the same time that men are masculinized by their military service and by navigating the geography of the mestizo-creole nation, women in Wila Kjarka are masculinized through their agricultural labor. There are, however, important differences in this process of masculinization. Men are "whitened" by this process through their acquisition of citizenship and relative fluency in Spanish; women, on the other hand, are not. Whereas men retain their higher "whitened" status when they return to their villages, women, in contrast, return to their female roles when their partners return, but this is not always a smooth transition, as women are becoming increasingly independent.

In the past, women depended entirely on their husbands to deal with money. Francisca, who is now in her seventies, describes the predicament she found herself in when her husband died: "My husband left me without my knowing money. No, my husband just took care of me here. He was the one who knew how to work for money. [When he died] he left me here without any money. I don't know how much things are; I don't know [the value of] a peso. Now that my husband is lost, my children are teaching me a little."

Her granddaughters, however, all speak some Spanish and are certainly more likely to be able to use money, even if most purchases are undertaken by menfolk. When men are away for long periods, women will go to market to make necessary purchases, and younger women in particular are becoming, out of necessity, increasingly autonomous. Gaining that autonomy comes easier to some women than others, especially for those women who can earn cash independently by making dolls for sale. In a neighboring community the women have made a successful business of rearing chickens, and a woman has been elected to the leadership post of *secretario general*, a position normally reserved for men. Such an election for a one-year term requires the votes of all heads of household and would have necessitated the assent and support of a majority of men. The people of Wila Kjarka met this news with a mixture of shock, amazement, and admiration.

It is clear, even though the parameters of women's lives are constrained by geography and language, that they nevertheless do not live in some rural idyll far removed from the gendered nationalist imaginings of their menfolk. Women from Wila Kjarka have also learned a clear sense of their racial and ethnic inferiority from their visits to the market town, where they are spoken to abruptly and rudely in Spanish, for mestizo traders as well as mestizo teachers always give their commands in Spanish. Very few Wila Kjarkeñas speak Spanish, even those who have gone to school; and although many have made brief visits to La Paz, they very rarely travel beyond the Aymara-speaking world. As a consequence, they have little claim to the kind of "whitened" Spanish-speaking militarized citizenship their menfolk can claim.

"Whiteness" is therefore not simply the color of one's skin but a complex of social and cultural attributes that confer membership in the dominant cultural group. In speaking Spanish, undergoing military service, and working in the mines, men are closer to the white urban ideal than women. When they are present in the (increasingly female) village, they reproduce the racialization of cultural values and differences along gendered lines, which are, in any case, gendered values to begin with. Because the metropolitan discourse on nation is as gendered as it is racialized, indian women are twice removed from what is valued in nationalist terms in Bolivia.

In the village context these gendered and racialized imaginings of nation are reproduced with different signifiers. Away from the community, in contrast, Wila Kjarkeño men are relatively powerless and even feminized indians. A simple case illustrates the point. One day I traveled to Sorata with two friends to deliver some dolls for sale, destined for the United States and Europe. These dolls are sold as "traditional," "indigenous," and "Aymaran" (*sic*) crafts; and so the indian identity of my friends is central to their participation in a global market, illustrating that their "indianness" has an international as well as local significance.

We entered the store by the rear entrance and my friends, Remegio and Agustina, were berated in Spanish (even though the agent spoke fluent Aymara) for being late and not having finished the work. They were ordered to sit down on the floor in the corner of the patio to work on the dolls. The agent, who knows me well, greeted me respectfully, and quickly brought a chair for me to sit on. In Wila Kjarka women sit on the ground and men sit on benches or stools. This is the case in any public gathering but also in private when, for example, a family is assembled in the kitchen for a meal, although increasingly women and even children are getting their own stools. Agustina speaks very little Spanish, a fact known to the agent, and so the agent's use of Spanish in her barked commands and complaints served to underline the status difference between them. The meek and submissive way Remegio responded to the agent differed sharply with the way he acts in Wila Kjarka, where he is a respected member of the community. In Sorata he is merely an indian who is supposed to be meek and submissive and instructed to sit on the floor like the women in his own community.

In Wila Kjarka the same kind of language and the same abrupt manner of speech used by the agent is also used by the schoolteacher as well as by men when they berate their children or scold their wives. Spanish, therefore, functions in the same way within the community as without: to mark status difference and assert authority by invoking an association with the metropolitan culture. The same strategy used against indian men when they travel beyond the community is used by them when they return.

When I asked people in Wila Kjarka about language use, men and women alike often told me that women spoke a more pure and sweeter (*muxsa*) Aymara, in contrast to men who use many Spanish words. Speaking sweetly is a positive quality, but in a context where languages are hierarchized, the ability to speak Spanish obviously has greater status. So, for example, on one occasion a man told me his wife was "like a dog" (*anjamawa*) because she could not speak Spanish. It is common in the Andes to use animals to represent "uncivilized" human; and, as Olivia Harris (1983) has noted, the ability to speak is one of the key markers between humans and animals for many Andean peoples. In this instance the implication is that it is the ability to speak *Spanish*, which is most important.

In likening his wife to a dog, this man was doing more than simply comparing monolingual women to animals in general. As Laura Lewis (2003: 54) has demonstrated, there is a long history of associating indians with dogs, which goes back to the early colonial period, and this was used to justify their beatings as much as it was to command their faithful and servile "nature." All Wila Kjarkeños' households include a dog, but, in contrast to sheep, for example, little affection is shown to them and they are regularly cursed and have stones thrown at them, sometimes for no apparent reason. The idea that women are somehow incomplete men, lacking intellectual faculties and moral strength, is *not* typical of what men and women in Wila Kjarka generally say about women; it does, however, resonate with long-standing European ideas about the status of women and, in the American context, the justification of the domination of indians on the grounds that they possessed the moral and intellectual qualities of women, children, and domestic animals. This argument was most clearly and famously stated by Juan Ginés de Sepúlveda (1489–1573) in his mid-sixteenth-century debate with fellow Dominican Bartolomé de las Casas (1484–1566) over the nature (and fate) of the indians in the New World (Lewis 2003: 59; Pagden 1982) and has clear echoes today.[16] In this particular ethnographic context the very human status of a woman is questioned because of her lack of Spanish, but the man himself implicitly accepts that speaking Aymara and being indian is clearly inferior to speaking Spanish and being white; by underlining his wife's inferior status, however, his as a Spanish speaker is implicitly elevated.

Peppering their language with hispanicisms is a way in which men underline their association with the metropolitan culture; men are "whitened" by this association and can contrast themselves with their Aymara-speaking and unambiguously indian womenfolk. The use of Spanish flourishes in this way when the speaker may actually have no idea of what he is saying is widespread in Bolivia and, according to Alison Spedding (1999), has its roots in the public education system that encourages style over content.[17] Over the years I have heard a number of men talk to me of their aspirations to move to town, where they will be civilized. Almost invariably a mark of this newly acquired "civilization" is that their wives and children will speak Spanish and that the womenfolk will wear dresses (as opposed to the full skirts indian women wear). There can be no doubt that social and racial mobility is most clearly inscribed in the dress and bodies of women.[18] These deeply ambivalent experiences of being part of the metropolitan culture while simultaneously being rejected by it sometimes have violent consequences.

Domestic violence is quite prevalent in Wila Kjarka, but unevenly so. Although many, perhaps most men, do not beat their wives (and there are many women as well as men who say this is so), others do so frequently and severely. My comadre Dominga, for example, is quite clear that her husband, Pastuku, has never hit her. Pastuku, who is one of my closest friends in Wila Kjarka, is a mild-mannered man who avoids drinking heavily. For this he is criticized by others for being *q'ewsa* (twisted), his sobriety seen as a rejection of them if not a perversion of their way of life. Pastuku says he doesn't hit because he doesn't drink, and there is a very clear association in people's minds between drinking and domestic violence. Men quite simply blame the alcohol and absolve themselves of any guilt, even if they agree that hitting one's wife is a bad thing. No one ever claimed that it was a reasonable thing to do, as is sometimes reported, but rather one of those regrettable things of life. Juana, for example, told me of her long and good marriage with her husband: "We lived well," she told me, "we did not fight when he was not drunk. When he drank, then we fought. He beat me. That's just the way it was."[19] To some extent, then, it is accepted that men beat their wives, but habitual wife beaters are subject to criticism by women and, indeed, men as well.

People speak readily about domestic violence in Wila Kjarka, and it is often a topic of conversation or casually mentioned as with Juana above. Conversations I had with women about domestic violence occurred while accompanying them around the cooking fire and in other social contexts (where more commonly third parties were discussed). Men discussed domestic violence with me in varying contexts, usually one on one or in small groups. In general, it took very little effort on my part to initiate discussion on this topic, and in many cases the issue was raised independently. That is quite in contrast to the contemporary Western world, where there is a constant and almost compelling discourse about sexuality, but domestic violence is still a conversational taboo; in Wila Kjarka, people have difficulty talking about sex but are quite open about their own experiences of domestic violence. I evidenced little sense of shame or guilt about domestic violence, but it is widely regretted, if not always condemned, by the beaters, the beaten, and the commentators thereon.

Regina Huancollo's life is not typical for a Wila Kjarkeña, but it is indicative of many of the conditions under which people live. When I talked

Regina Oncollo at the grave of her son. She offers him
boiled potatoes and his favorite, hot chocolate. Todos Santos, 1991.

to her in 2005 she was forty-six years old and told me that she had had
ten children, of whom only three survived. This mortality rate, although
not unheard of, is certainly unusual, as was her response to the deaths of
her children. She had them buried with a visible tomb and cross, and on
Todos Santos she would take them their favorite foods. On Todos Santos
1993 she was mourning the loss of her three-year-old son. He had liked hot
chocolate, and she made hot chocolate for him after his death, as well as
his favorite foods. Hers was the only child mourned in such a public way,
as Todos Santos is largely a fiesta for the deaths of adults. In later years,
as more of her children died, she became very attached to lambs. People
in Wila Kjarka often show emotional attachment to lambs and are sometimes much keener to be photographed with their lambs than their babies, but Regina was unusually focused on her lambs in a way that caused
people to comment in gentle and not so gentle amusement.

Her life has been full of tragedy. In 1991 she sent her son to the market
in Sorata and he was caught in a flash flood that took two other people
(one of whom was Juana's husband, the other, my friend Germán, mentioned above). The two men who died with him were particularly prominent people in the community, and along with the search for their bodies
the community's emotions and attentions were directed much more at
the men than Regina's son, and she largely had to bear her tragedy by

herself. The men were given a full community ceremony for which I, as it happened, made the coffins. I was unaware of when and how Regina's son was buried.

I asked her how she met her husband, and in the simple style I have become used to, she said, "He came from La Paz to announce to my parents he wanted to marry; and it was in this way that we got together." Regina's husband, although a native of Wila Kjarka, had spent much time away and continued to spend time away from Wila Kjarka after his marriage.

In the early years we fought a lot. My husband was an itinerant worker; he used to go with married women. He used to insult me with other women (*warminakampisa tuqiyitu*). While I was with my baby, my daughter, he would get drunk with his lover. Once, when she was drunk, she even assaulted me, throwing herself on top of me (*khallakapitu*) with her *pollera* and pushing me to the ground. Then she pushed me away with her chest (*t'inqhuntutuxa*). After this happened I told my husband: "This woman has done this to me and it's your fault. Just you wait, I will kill you." My husband arrived drunk [one day] and said that he saw a man leave from the other side of the house. "There is only one man I go with," I said (*maya jaqirakisa akjata mistuwayixa sasa*). But after making me jealous with other women, my vicious (*mañoso*) husband just started beating me. But I don't drink, I might drink a little chicha, sometimes I am offered alcohol, but not to get drunk. I got used to knowing that in the evening my husband would beat me; and then his lover would insult me. This woman insults me in public meetings. Of course, the officeholders help me tell my story, but she has falsely denounced me publicly. It is not possible to live in this community. I cry and live with resentment in the valleys.

I have got used to life in the *yungas,* and I don't want to come here anymore, but now I have a position of responsibility, and I have been made *amawt'a* (nominated to the school council), but I'll get out of it next year and then I will go back to the valleys. I will return to Achacachi to leave some money for my son; I will get rid of all my pigs, and I will leave my son the fields—he can give me half the produce. I will never return, and my son will not see me either; he can slaughter any animal he wants. In the valleys I work with *cocaleros* with large storehouses, I save money— I am not lazy—they take me everywhere. Several families want me to work for them, they even give me breakfast; they love me like a flower down there; they don't scold me. They give me food—first and second course—they treat me as if I were a flower. But here they hate me. Here even the stones and walls speak out against single women (*qalasa pirqasa arsukiwa*). It has not been good, being single; everyone respects the husband, but I don't want to have another man. There are many men, but they may say that I am old now and that they want my daughter and seek to abuse my children (*phuchhamampiwa chikäxa jischitaspaya, wawanakaruwa awusayxiristha*). I do not want that, and that is why I am not in any mind to have another man; it does not lie in my heart to have another man (*janiwa chuymajaru mantkituti chachasiñasa kunasa*). Sometimes I want to laugh; sometimes I want to cry: I am used to being alone now.

Even though no one condones beating women, Regina gets very little sympathy in the village. Significantly, her parents are dead and she has no brothers in the community, so she has no support. In this she is similar to Eugenia, whose husband is famously the most violent man in Wila Kjarka. Unlike Regina, Eugenia's children have largely survived, and she has eight. Her husband is also believed to have many lovers and spends large amounts of time away from the community, leaving his wife and children to take care of the lands. Eugenia is the only woman in Wila Kjarka who speaks Spanish with any degree of fluency, and she learned this working in the mining communities. What attracted her to Ricardo was his apparent sophistication (he also speaks very good Spanish) and relative wealth. They appear to have been happy for the first two years of their marriage, until he made her return to his community and take care of the fields.

She and her children are probably now the poorest people in Wila Kjarka and regularly go hungry. I have often seen them eat only potatoes and the water in which they were cooked. The family eats better when Ricardo is home, but Eugenia then has to endure his violence. Eugenia spoke to me often about her desperate situation and the dull inevitability of the beatings she would get when her husband came home. If she tries to run away, he just gets angrier and beats her more, and so she has little choice but to be as quiet as possible and take the beatings. It is important to note that other women run away to their brother's house or their parents' house when their husbands become abusive, and then the husband is expected to come and collect her, having to face her menfolk.

I don't know how many times Eugenia became pregnant, almost certainly more than eight. The data on pregnancies are difficult to be sure about, but most women I have spoken to say they have had about eight to ten pregnancies by the end of their fertile lives, and the norm is to have between four and six surviving children. Most women and men in Wila Kjarka control their fertility better than Eugenia and Regina, and the violence that both women have suffered suggests that many of the sex acts they participated in were not consensual and may even have been violent.

Catalina was born in 1950 and is one of the few people in Wila Kjarka of that generation to have married into the community from outside. She comes from Waychu, a village not too far away—in fact, it's just on the other side of the mountain, about two hours' walk away. This is, however, far enough to be difficult to get to in a hurry and enough distance to deter her brothers and father from coming to help her, even if they were to have heard of her distress. "He used to beat me; he used to beat me a lot. There was a bed right there, and when he began to beat me the blood would reach all the way over there [across the room]."

It is not just fathers and brothers that protect a woman from violent and abusive husbands, but also godparents. On one occasion, when I had been in Wila Kjarka only a few months and recently after having become godfather to Waliya at her haircutting, my compadre came into the storeroom where I slept. He said that his wife had run to her brother's house and I must come with him to get her back. It was the middle of the night; I could barely string a sentence together in Aymara; I was twenty-two years old, and didn't really see it as my place to get involved in the marital disputes of my hosts, who were much older than I. My compadre insisted, however, and off we went out into the night.

When we arrived at our destination we were met by an angry brother-in-law and soon by a tearful and clearly distressed comadre. She was crying and speaking quickly. I understood very little Aymara in those days, a problem compounded by her lack of teeth, obvious distress, and a jaw deformation that makes her difficult to understand at the best of times. But this much I understood: Her husband had beaten her and she was seeking refuge in her brother's house. My compadre urged me to speak to his wife and brother-in-law, but Agustina's brother shares the same jaw deformation as his sister and is even harder to understand. I had no idea what to say anyway. It seemed best to me that Remegio and I go home and deal with this in the morning.

Whatever the disagreement, all parties shared an expectation that I as the padrino had a role to play in this marital dispute, however young I happened to be. Agustina returned home the following morning, and there was a tense silence in the house, but the matter was not left at that. A few days later all the padrinos of the couple, including myself, attended a meeting in which Agustina and Remegio were made to kneel and face us. It was Teodosio, the shaman—who was also their padrino—as well as Gerónimo, who spoke most. Most of their comments were directed at Remegio, but both he and his wife had to seek forgiveness from each other. Remegio had no choice but to succumb to this authority, and even though Agustina also had to apologize, it was very clear that there was little sympathy for Remegio's position. She is known as a good, hard-working woman in the community, and any suggestion that she had been unfaithful (Remegio's accusation) was roundly declared false. Remegio clearly felt that he had been hard done by and was sullen and depressed for days, until one day I walked into the house and he told me he had eaten pesticide and was trying to kill himself. I jammed my fingers down his throat and made him vomit, and we were soon joined by his daughters, who were wailing in distress. It was a dramatic event, which elicited a lot of sympathy and support from people around him. Whether he genuinely intended to kill himself I will never know for sure, but I rather suspect he did not; he certainly didn't like my making him vomit.

The motive he gave for beating his wife was that she was being unfaithful to him. Everyone I talked to said this was preposterous. If men give a reason for beating their wives, it is infidelity, but I have heard this only rarely and few people ever seem convinced; much more common is to give no motive at all and blame it on alcohol. Regina's husband said she had been unfaithful, but she insists it was utterly baseless and, perhaps more important, the consensus is behind her, rather than him. As I have suggested, the reasons men beat their wives is rather more complex and difficult to articulate than sexual jealousy and has more to do with the nexus of race and gender than infidelity.

Men give other, more prosaic reasons for accounting for domestic violence. "Women are capricious" is one; "some women just don't stop talking" is another; "some men don't stop talking either, and so they fight." "When both of them are 'mouthy' then they fight" (*Purapa lakanpurapxi ukjana nuwasipxixa*). Men, too, talk about the violence they have received at the hands of their wives, and a number of men have told me of being beaten with sticks. As far as accounting for the violence of other men (no man ever gave me any details of beating his own wife), the commonest reasons given are the influence of alcohol and *jisk'a chuymani* (possessing a small heart). A better translation might be being "mean, lacking any generosity of spirit," or simply lacking spirit. To say someone is a jisk'a chuymani is like calling him a "mean bastard."

Regina's response to the abuse she receives from her husband and community is to leave for the yungas. When I asked Regina if there were mestizos in the yungas, she said, no, that they were all jaqi from the highlands. Most of these are Aymara-speaking, although some, those from Charazani, speak Quechua. Nevertheless, she asserts that now everyone strictly speaks Spanish there and that she now speaks fluent and proper Spanish (*castellano cerradoruwa jalt'xtha nayaxa*), not like in Wila Kjarka, where "here we don't know how to speak Spanish."

It is not just the Aymara language she is keen to forget (although she has always spoken to me in this language). She told me that in the yungas, women take off their polleras and wear trousers. In Wila Kjarka she wears a pollera because not to do so would bring criticism upon her for acting above her station, for trying to pretend she was a mestiza when she is clearly not; but in the yungas no one tells her this, and no one feels shame to wear trousers, this is just what the women wear.[20]

Regina not only speaks fluent Spanish and wears trousers but has also become a Lutheran. In fact, she became a Lutheran (there is a long-standing Lutheran church in nearby Choquepata) just before leaving. All three elements—language, dress, and religion—mark a rupture with the community and culture of Wila Kjarka, but they are also ways of distancing oneself from an indigenous identity, at the very least an indigenous identity rooted in an Aymara-speaking community of people working the land on the basis of mutual obligations. The evangelical community in the yungas acts as another kind of community based on kinship (she calls them "brother" and "sister"), but this is markedly different from the kinds of *compadrazgo* relationships one finds in Wila Kjarka. It is no coincidence that she often mentioned that she was able to accumulate money in the yungas, that she was able to save it under her bed, and all that she needed to do was to work hard. In Wila Kjarka, compadres will help you out, but they will also be a drain on your own resources, making accumulation very difficult. In her insightful work on the conversion of Aymara immigrants to La Paz, Juliana Ströbele-Gregor titled her (1989) book *Indios de piel blanca* (*White-Skinned Indians*) because she saw evangelical Protestantism as a way of "whitening" and thus avoiding the kinds of daily racism that indians have to suffer. Indeed, the only people in the area around Wila Kjarka who would not engage in conversations about ethnicity and the differences between jaqi, mistis, and q'aras were the Protestants I occasionally encountered, some from Choquepata and others from Sorata. "We don't think that way anymore, we are all God's children," I was told, and, "We are all children of Adam and Eve." One key element of being Protestant, then, is stepping outside historical relationships between antagonistic groups of people; it is also a way of sloughing off one's indian identity; one could argue it is a way of exercising one's right not to be an indian. Another major aspect of conversion to Protestantism, incidentally, is that Protestants don't consume alcohol and, consequently, men don't beat their wives. This, at any rate, is the belief and figures prominently in people's, especially women's, accounts of why they convert to Protestantism. The political economy of whiteness, here as elsewhere, enters the most intimate spaces of people's lives.

VIOLENCE AND WHITENESS

I am not intending here to reduce all domestic violence in Wila Kjarka into an account of racialized oppression, but there are some important features that are worth noting in the context of this discussion.[21] Men beat their wives only when they are drunk, and many women say that the beatings are either totally unprovoked or provoked by something trivial, such as the kind of food she has served.[22] Some say that their husbands say very little when they beat them, but others comment that they are abused in Spanish. There is a long history in the Andes of people speaking in Spanish when drunk, as Thierry Saignes and others have well documented (Saignes 1993). The issue here is not simply that the men speak Spanish when they are drunk but what it is they are actually saying: They spit out words like *ignorante* (ignorant) and *india sucia* (dirty indian)—an experience not restricted to Wila Kjarka, as Jiménez Sardon has noted for parts of Peru (1998: 159). For their part, men say that they remember nothing of what they say and do, and it is the alcohol that makes them beat their wives. To some extent, it seems, women believe them.

It would be overdrawn to put domestic violence in Wila Kjarka simply down to men's frustrations at their inability to move in the world the way they would like and their deep ambivalence at their racial status and condition in Bolivia. Nevertheless I think it is quite clear that the contradiction of being an indian in the world beyond Wila Kjarka and having a "whiter" status within it, and all this represents in terms of frustrated desires, has a part to play in accounting for domestic violence. Mary Weismantel (1988: 183) suggests much more, specifically that the reason men beat their wives in the highland community of Zumbagua in Ecuador is because of the increasing demands for goods imposed on a man as he returns from the city. Zumbagüeños and Wila Kjarkeños have different patterns of wage migration, and the latter do not come and go as regularly as appears to be the case in Zumbagua. Nevertheless it is true to say that currently defined men's roles vis-à-vis their households require them to leave the community for a potentially infinite amount of cash and goods. Men can never earn enough money to satisfy their own and their family's demands for goods and the status it buys. Moreover, the more a man aspires to personal progress through whitening by acquiring those goods and status symbols associated with the mestizo metropolitan class, the more likely he is to be frustrated in this elusive goal. It is also the case that the longer a man is away from his family, the more accustomed to autonomy his partner becomes. To put it another way, a model of complementarity between two people is increasingly difficult to sustain if they are apart for long periods. This is even more likely to be the case if women have access to their own source of cash and are able to speak at least some Spanish, as is becoming increasingly the case in Wila Kjarka with an expanded school.

There are other contradictory pressures on women. Whereas women are highly valued for their labor and social responsibility in maintaining the fields, livestock, and household, this very labor roots them ever more solidly into the indian world that is widely denigrated, even, in certain contexts, by themselves. Women often complain that men leave them for months on end with little money and a lot of work to do, as men are imagined to be cash-rich and may even be supporting lovers. Men, when they are far away from home, have considerable demands on their cash income and do not want to be pulled down by responsibilities that simply by association frustrate any social ambitions they may have. Having a family in an indian village is a clear marker of indian status.

Women and men often express deeply ambivalent feelings on the subject of male migration. Women who bemoan the absence of their husbands also express a strong desire for men to earn the money to buy goods, while men often love their wives and children and are frequently sentimental about their home and land, even as they sometimes wish not to be associated with an indian village. These contradictions and tensions, which are ultimately irresolvable, are dealt with in myriad ways by different couples—sometimes with violence. What is clear, however, is that these wider social and economic structures come to be focused onto very intimate spaces.

The frustration of the schoolteachers echoes clearly in Wila Kjarka, as do their ambivalent attitudes toward the community described above.

They, too, appear to be caught between a sense of indian fraternity and their own personal desires to progress and be civilized; they swing from sentimental identification with their "indian brothers" and deep frustration at having to live in and be associated with an indian village; they also use a language imbued with a sense of racial superiority when they berate children, rather like the language men sometimes use when they argue with their wives.

Even though Wila Kjarka may be marginal in terms of the hegemonic political and social geographies of Bolivia, its people and their labor are fundamental elements in the economic structures of modern, capitalist Bolivia. On the level of ideology, a whole series of national symbols, language, and concepts are produced and reproduced within the community. Communities such as Wila Kjarka are marginal in terms of national discourses that favor urban, mestizo-creole, Spanish-speaking culture over rural, indian, and Aymara-speaking culture. They are, however, absolutely central in that they support the center economically while long providing a useful contrast for the aspirations to progress of dominant groups: One can always try to be "whiter" and can always justify one's social superiority in terms of being racially or culturally superior. For this powerful system to operate at least a notional indian "other" needs to exist.

It is clear that there is an important gender difference in how men and women are implicated in and by these discourses, since these national discourses are themselves gendered. Given that men and women are located differently in the national space that these discourses produce, it is not surprising that they are, in turn, differently transfigured as they move through the national geography. In the case of Bolivia, men have a heightened sense of their (inferior) indianness as they move through national institutions and spaces, while at the same time they are "whitened" by this very movement and association. This migration, which supports the nation through military service and labor in the capitalist economy, has important consequences for women in the community. By maintaining the farms and households they, in effect, subsidize the low wages of their menfolk. More striking, though, is the dissonance between the gender model, which stresses the equally important contributions of men and women to the household and which makes sense in the village community, and the racialized and hierarchic model men struggle with as part of their own conflictive identities as ethnically marked men. It is important to remember that women and men themselves are not consistent in the values attached to different forms of labor, dress, identity, and so on.

A woman may on one occasion bemoan the absence of her husband in the mines but a few weeks earlier may have been encouraging him to leave. A man may comment that he wishes his wife would wear a Western dress and live in the town but later comment approvingly of her ability to work in the fields. People talk disparagingly about the misery of village life, but the same people may talk of the village in maudlin tones. These conflicting desires and aspirations can even be expressed in the same conversation.

Racial hierarchy, the pressures of wage labor in industries that exploit indians, an economy that depends on indian labor even as it denigrates it, feelings of sentimentality about one's home village, an association with which is the source of one's despised racial identity: These and many other tensions and contradictions are articulated at the level of a married couple. It is therefore not difficult to see how a drunken man can see his frustrations quite literally embodied by his wife and take it out on her violently. The arguments presented here do not account for domestic violence, but they do explain some of the context in which it occurs and the particular form it takes.

Ideas about nationhood, racial hierarchies, and an economic structure that depends on a semiproletarianized indian labor force are not merely abstract constructs far removed from the realities of people who live at a distance from the metropolitan centers. They are real and immanent and are re-created in remote villages and in the intimate relationships of couples. These racialized intimacies, however, have a long provenance, and indeed go back to the first decades of European colonization and how that colonization was imagined.

EIGHT

Sex and the Citizen

In the famous image of the "discovery" of America by Theodor Galle (engraving circa 1630, after Jan van der Straet's [Johannes Stradanus] *America* circa 1575), the European Amerigo Vespucci, erect and holding the tools of rational science (an astrolabe) and his religion, finds "America" in her hammock. She is naked but full of wonder rather than fear and appears open to his advances. Europa, the female symbol of Vespucci's continent, is nowhere to be seen in this allegorical encounter: This is not a meeting of equals. Vespucci gives the new continent a feminine version of his name, and the profoundly gendered and sexualized nature of the encounter is quite apparent. Indeed, the subtitle of the caption reads: "At once he called her; thenceforth she was always aroused." *Excitam* means to rise up as well as to arouse or to excite;[1] it is quite clear that America is doing both.

The sexual subtext of this engraving has received considerable commentary (de la Guerra 2003; Hulme 1984; McClintock 1995; Montrose 1991; Schreffler 2005), but what is less-often noted is that America is represented by a European-looking, fair-haired woman. Peter Mason (1990) has written in some detail about how the natives of

Americen Americus Retexit. *Theodore Galle.*
© *National Maritime Museum.*

the New World were initially incorporated into Western notions of the "wild man"—a European internal alterity transported across the Atlantic and projected onto the denizens of the New World. More important, it is also the case that, since the conquest, native Americans have been conceptualized as female: In his famous debate with Las Casas, Sepúlveda made an explicit comparison between the moral and intellectual capacities of indians and Spanish women (see Lewis 2003: 59; Pagden 1982), and there are numerous examples from courts of law to military accounts in which indians have been explicitly described as comparable to European women (Lewis 2003; Silverblatt 1987). American natives have long been conceived as the European internal Other, Mason's point, and specifically a female one.

This image goes beyond the allegorical depiction of the colonial encounter; it is also an illustration of one of its concrete manifestations: From the earliest days of the Conquest, Spanish men took indian wives as part of the spoils of conquest but also as a tool of conquest (Trexler 1995;

Wade 2009). The most celebrated example of this is the story of Cortés and Malintzin, or La Malinche, which Octavio Paz sees as the founding myth of Mexico and Mexicans; but there are, of course, countless other examples all through the former Spanish Empire.

Such images, and the racialized politics behind them, are not simply elements of an archaeology of power but continue to appear in contemporary Bolivia. The cover of my Bolivian goddaughter's exercise book shows a conquistador boy with blue eyes next to a girl—dressed with the pollera skirt and shawl typical of contemporary indian dress—smiling coquettishly at him. A particular version of American history is encapsulated in this image: white men taking indian women as sexual partners, resulting in a mestizo, that is mixed, nation. As Marcia Stephenson has shown, it has also been considered a civilizing mission (1999: 38) and a means by which the nation could be "whitened" and relieved of its racial burden— what Nancy Stepan has called "constructive miscegenation" (1991: 38). The relationships illustrated in the engraving and the cover of the exercise book allude to an enduring tale, which, in Doris Sommer's (1991) phrase, points to a "foundational fiction" of Bolivian nationhood and what Mary Weismantel has called "a nativity scene deformed by racism" (2001: 155).

The right to have sex with indian women is accrued on the basis of creole citizenship, which can come to be deemed a civic duty. Conversely, indian women are sexually accessible to white men because of the former's lack of political power, because of their lack of full citizenship in the nation. During the colonial period, Stephanie Athey and Daniel Cooper Alarcón (1993) argue, being vulnerable to white men's sexual predations was a defining feature of one's status as a nonwhite woman (see also Weismantel 2001: 169) but the converse is surely also true: A white man is defined by his impunity when having sexual relations with nonwhites.

For Fausto Reinaga, the most influential Bolivian indigenous intellectual of the twentieth century and the founder of the Partido Indio Boliviano (the Bolivian Indian Party), indian men's displacement by white men lies at the very center of his political rage and at the heart of his politics of liberation. The sharpness with which Reinaga feels this displacement of masculinity is illustrated in a passage of *Revolución india* (1969), where he recounts a tale surrounding events in the community of Kharasai. The story begins when the priest in the confessional hears that the beautiful bride, Rosa, is a virgin. The priest reports this to the lawyer and a muleteeer, who then plot to deflower her. The priest marries the couple, and Reinaga tells us that the wedding feast is rushed so that the bride and groom can consummate the marriage. The couple "according to tradition and custom" are undressed and laid on the nuptial bed by the marriage sponsors (*padrinos*). Then "at the moment they were about to join in copulation," the priest and his friends suddenly appeared in the bridal chamber:

"The indian man pretends to be fast asleep; he is as if dead. And the indian woman, immobile, with her eyes shut and gritting her teeth, suffers in silence the deflowering of her virginity. The force of the muleteer breakes her hymen and then the priest dives into the blood of the indian maiden" (Reinaga 1969: 130).

This account is clearly much more than the retelling of a tale he has heard; it is highly sensationalized and has a pornographic tone. The consummation of the marriage becomes a public event even before the priest and his compantions arrive. Although he does not present it this way, this is as much an allegory as the telling of a tale; the central theme is not so much the rape of a young woman but the impotence of her husband. Reinaga dedicated his life to waking up that indian husband and inciting him to political action in order to redeem his masculinity and indianness. Although he rarely made it explicit, for Reinaga the two were intimately linked (Canessa 2010), and it was quite clear that for him the politics of indian liberation were clearly connected to overcoming a centuries-old tale of the (sexual) displacement of the indian man—in other words, the tale at the center of Galle's etching. Reinaga could be said to have wanted, as it were, to put the indian man back into the picture.[2] Sex is much more than the product of unequal relations; it is the mode through which race status and citizenship are asserted. In Bolivia, as elsewhere in Latin America, nations were made "through race and sex" (Wade 2009, ch. 4) and, even as it is contested, these dynamics of race and sex remain at the very heart of how the nation is imagined and citizenship construed.

Beyond the allegory of the discovery of America that Galle intended, the etching is also a powerful representation of conquest and the continued oppression of indians by whites in an intimate and sexualized relationship, which resonates not only in countries with large indigenous populations but also those with populations of African descent. In a number of works that have become highly influential, Gilberto Freyre explores the benign and ultimately redemptive relationship between masters and slaves in great detail. It is precisely the relationships between white masters and black slave women that alleviated racial friction, "smoothed by the lubricating oil of a deep-seated miscegenation" (1968 [1936]: 181). In the *Mansions and the Shanties* (Casa Grande e Senzala) he writes about the making of modern Brazil (the book's subtitle) in prose which is sometimes highly intimate, writing as he does, of "our mammy who rocked us to sleep. Who suckled us. Who fed us, mashing our food with her own hands . . . (and) who initiated us into physical love and, to the creaking of a cot, gave us our first complete sensation of being a man." (278). In his account, which is sometimes seen as the foundational text of Brazil's "racial democracy," black men and white women are, however, thrown into the background, rather like America's cannibal kin in Galle's etching.

In the Andes, historically as well as contemporarily, indian women are accepted into the most intimate spaces of the homes of white elites in a way that indian men are not, and domestic service is one of the very few areas in which being and looking indigenous is a positive advantage. Rather like Freyre's sentimental prose about slaves at whose breast the white man suckled and became the object of his first sexual experience, many middle-class Andeans have a strong emotional attachment to the "cholita" who raised them and with whom, as well, they had their first sexual encounters. And the sexual relationship between white master and indian woman was a regular dramatic feature of Andean literature of the nineteenth and early twentieth centuries (Stephenson 1999: Weismantel 2001). Bolivia's most famous literary work of the twentieth century is probably Carlos Medinaceli's *La Chaskañawi* (1958), which tells the tale of a white man's desire for a *chola,* a love which undermines the racial hierarchies of Bolivia even as it leads to perdition for the young middle-class man. Such relationships were clearly not, however, restricted to novels, as Lesley Gill (1997) has shown for domestic workers in La Paz in recent decades. Indian men, needless to say, do not occupy the same position in the memories of creoles, and the enduring image is one of the cowed and servile indian who turns to bloodthirsty revolt at a moment's notice.

The sexual availability of indian women did not, however, develop its own erotics to the extent the mulatta did in countries with a significant African-descended population. There is little evidence in Bolivia that mestizo and creole men find indian women physically attractive—the direct opposite is much more likely to be expressed—which is not necessarily to say, however, that they do not find indian women *desirable.* This echoes Diane Nelson's comments on sex between mestizo men and indian women in Guatemala, where men say they feel compelled to have sex with indian women—who are often depicted as "ugly or smelling bad," as a way of proving their manhood and whiteness—but are not expected to have liked or initiated it (1999: 24). Sexual desire here appears to be constructed not out of a sensual aesthetic but out of an erotic of power (see Sommer 1991: 128).

Mary Weismantel, in her (2001) book *Cholas and Pishtacos*, gives a powerful account of the sexual desirability of the chola within Andean culture. This is a desirability founded on the chola's liminality, her being betwixt and between creole and indian cultures, occupying public spaces such as markets and *chicha* taverns. Cholas evoke a frisson of desire mixed with fear, their bodies as fascinating as they are repulsive; they are ambivalent figures, simultaneously powerful and mysterious, but quite clearly lacking the sexual citizenship of white women. Cholas may be desired by white men, but there is little public discourse for their being physically attractive, of embodying an aesthetics of physical beauty; that is reserved for white women's bodies.

Elizabeth Povinelli (2006: 10) gives us a clue as to how we might understand such apparently contradictory desires when she writes that "love, intimacy, and sexuality are not about desire, pleasure, or sex per se, but about things like geography, history, culpability, and obligation; the extraction of wealth and the distribution of life and death; hope and despair." So what are these geographies and histories that structure desire, and how, indeed, do desires and sexualities structure geographies and histories?

To begin with, in contemporary Bolivia, images of eroticized feminine physical beauty are overwhelmingly white. This is evidenced in images on billboards, magazines, and television advertisements as well as in beauty pageants, where Miss Bolivia is invariably white. In an image of the 2005 Miss Universe pageant (p. 250), Miss Bolivia is represented in her "national dress." By coincidence, she looks remarkably like the woman in the Galle etching but, more important, as with the etching, she is rendering the indigenous inhabitant of the continent in terms of an erotic fantasy. In this particular fantasy, moreover, it is the lowland indians—less threatening to the state and social elites—who are being imagined, rather than the highland groups who, at the moment this photograph was taken, were organizing to overthrow white political power. This furthermore points to an enduring paradox: While indian women, through colonial structures, are construed as sexually available to mestizos and whites, the predominant image of the desired female body is of the white woman; and whereas the indian woman's body was accessible to creole men, the opposite was most certainly not the case. Miss Bolivia here resolves the

Miss Bolivia at the Miss Universe Pageant, 2005. ©Reuters/Chaiwat Subprasom.

paradox in a fantasy: the body of a white woman with the accessibility of an indian woman. This combination is by no means exclusive to the Andes; it is what stands behind the erotics of octoroons in pre–Civil War United States. Octoroons, who were notionally one-eighth black, were legally black and consequently sexually accessible to white men—but they looked white. The famous New Orleans octoroon balls (*plaçages*) consisted of free white men (but no "coloreds") and octoroon women (but no white women).

In a recent article, Bret Gustafson points out that in beauty pageants and carnivalesque displays, white women in Santa Cruz, Bolivia, adapt indigenous dress—the two-piece *tipois* shown in the photo, "sexier than the 'real' thing" (2006: 365)—in order to capture the "erotic allure of the indigenous maiden (yet not their physical appearance)" (356). Gustafson does not, however, interrogate the sexual allure (357) of the indigenous maiden, which is divorced from an appreciation of indian bodies, even as he details the cruceños' profound antipathy toward people who look indian. This resonates clearly with white and mestiza prostitutes in Guatemala, who cater to their clients' fantasies by dressing in full indigenous *trajes*, where the authenticity of the *traje* and the whiteness of the prostitute are key (Nelson 1999: 225). Indian maidens, it appears, are sexually desirable when the bodies displaying indigeneity are, in fact, white. Kemala Kempadoo (2004), in a wonderfully detailed and comprehensive account of sex work in the Caribbean, notes a similar pattern: White foreign as well as local men are attracted to the sensuality of the exotic Caribbean and the allure of dusky bodies, but in example after example she notes that the darker the woman, the greater her difficulty she has in selling sex. I suggest, then, that the eroticization of the indian woman is rooted in her sexual availability, of sexual access without responsibility, which has been the pattern of relations between white men and indian women since Theodor Galle made his etching.

SEX AND THE CITIZEN

I will return to the issue of beauty contests below, but first I would like to explore some of the consequences of such a racialized and sexualized conception of citizenship for the people of Wila Kjarka.

Women in this community are also exposed to hegemonic ideas of sex and race, which serve to underline their sense of exclusion from the nation. In Wila Kjarka the images of women that people see are almost ex-

The Alanoca family making dolls.

clusively of white women, and this is certainly the case when they travel to the market town of Sorata or the capital city of La Paz. Women in Wila Kjarka are, however, heavily involved in making "indian" dolls for export.

In the production and sale of these dolls (mostly to the United States), the women and men who produce them are indexing their indigeneity as a valuable commodity; the unsophisticated techniques and rough fibers are markers of a putative and commodifiable authenticity. In this they are part of a globalized economy but also a particular economy of desire whereby the object of desire is indigenous authenticity: The fibers must be natural, the labor manual, and the images true. The very crudeness of the techniques, which are in sharp contrast to the highly sophisticated weaving styles of the Andes, are in themselves markers of authenticity because they conform to the simplicity, which indicates indigenous authenticity as imagined by consumers. In this the doll makers are engaged in an economic relation similar to that of other Latin American women and men who engage in transactions based on their exoticism to sell sex (Kempadoo 2003) or for the purpose of marriage (T. Hurtado 2008). In all these cases, those involved are responding to images and conceptions of themselves, which, as dictated by the market, they strategically reproduce. So like the Colombian women described by Teodora Hurtado (2008) who must suppress their sense of agency and independence in order to conform to an Italian's idea of the meek and mild Latin woman, people in Wila Kjarka must ignore their sophisticated visual techniques and weaving styles to satisfy a Western market that finds crude methods charmingly evocative of an indigenous simplicity.

In the case of the dolls in Wila Kjarka, they are designed by people in La Paz led by an American woman who first came up with the idea of making such dolls for export. The dolls that Remigio and family are making in the image have the pollera skirts, the *mantas* (shawl), and the sandals made from car tires that characterize indian women's dress in the countryside.

Both men and women are involved in making these dolls and the accompanying llamas, and so forth. But no one makes dolls for their own children. In fact, people are generally puzzled as to why anyone would want the dolls they make; these dolls are not part of their own economy of desire, which places no value at all on representing themselves as wearing the crude *bayeta* (flannel) fabrics, which, in Wila Kjarka at any rate, are indicative of the kind of clothing they were obliged to make and wear in the time of the hacienda. To the north of Wila Kjarka and at some distance from the village there are communities that continue to wear their homespun *bayeta,* and these *mollos,* as they are called in Wila Kjarka, are looked down on for their primitiveness.

Consequently, the dolls, rather than representing a condition indians aspire to, represent a condition they seek to overcome; so instead of making dolls for their own daughters, they buy them; and what they buy are Barbie-like dolls, which are relatively cheap but still use up cash resources that are rare in a community that is primarily subsistence based.

From a very young age girls are exposed to an image of what the standard of feminine beauty is, and this is constantly reinforced as they grow up. When the girl pictured on page 254, Waliya, received a doll from her parents, her older sisters examined it and, to the annoyance of their mother, pointed out with glee that it had prominent breasts and a narrow waist. One sister was particularly fascinated by this and, to the irritation of Waliya, was taken to stealing the doll in order to undress and examine her body.

At the time this photograph was taken, in 1991, it was rare for parents to buy toys for their children, and hers was one of the first such dolls in Wila Kjarka. In fact, her parents were only able to buy the doll because they made money selling the "indian" dolls for export. For Waliya's father, Remigio, being able to buy his daughter a doll was a mark of conspicuous consumption, but it was also a mark of aspiration: In that year he often

Waliya with Barbie, 1991.

talked about moving into town, where his wife and children would speak Spanish and all would wear Western dress. In his words, they would "progress" and become "more civilized."

Fifteen years later I walked into Waliya's brother's room. By now Remegio, although still living in Wila Kjarka, had been able to extend the house and have separate rooms for his children, including the teenager Macario. Right above his bed was a large poster of Russian tennis star Anna Kournikova. I had never known Macario to harbor a passion for tennis, so I assumed that his interest in Miss Kournikova found its roots in something other than her sporting achievements. There are probably many teenage boys in the world with posters of Anna Kournikova in their room, and I did notice exercise books with her image for sale in Sorata as well; but it did strike me that even if Macario wanted to have a poster of an indigenous-looking woman on the wall, he wouldn't be able to find one. Perhaps at least as significant is that the new room with a window, the poster, and his older sister's Barbie doll of twenty years ago were all part of the same desire to progress socially that his father so aspired to do. It was clear to him, as indeed it is to most other people, that the kind of progress he envisaged entailed a reorientation of his family's identity to one that was conspicuously whiter; people are acutely aware that being whiter brings greater prospect for advancement.

Adolescent girls in Wila Kjarka are very aware that their lighter-skinned peers in the mestizo village of Villa Esquivel have very different life opportunities open to them. They know of one girl from Villa Esquivel, for example, who works in a pharmacy in La Paz, the kind of job that requires "buena presencia" when advertised, a phrase that is a well-known code for not looking like an indian. When girls from Wila Kjarka emigrate, whatever their aspirations, they end up working as domestic servants in the city or as poorly paid field hands in other areas of the country.

The one exception that I know of is Beatriz, who due to the rape of her great-grandmother by the mayordomo of the hacienda, has a Spanish, not indian, surname (she is Teodosio's granddaughter). She is also relatively light skinned and does not have the bone structure that typifies indian people from the highlands. A good student, she worked hard to perfect her Spanish and left the community as soon as she could. For a while she worked as a craft worker in La Paz, where her boss encouraged her to cut off her braids and dress "de vestido," in European dress. When I met them in a side street off the Calle Sagarnaga, which is the main craft (*artesanía*) street in La Paz, both she and her boss were pleased to show me how much she had changed. "Look at her," her boss beamed, "she has been out of the sun for several months now and look at her skin. That is how she will progress (*Así va a progresar*). Just you see, in a short while no one will ever guess she was an indian (*campesina*)."

This example of whitening for social ascension can be reproduced for virtually any Latin American country in the past as well as the present; but imagining citizens as white has to do with more than simply issues of race and social ascension, it is also about how sexual desire is constructed and expressed.

Sexual images of white women abound, not simply in bars but in popular restaurants frequented by a wide range of people from the indian working classes. The image shown on page 256 (taken on *Domingo de Tentación* and so titled)[3] illustrates this simple point. The near ubiquity of such images in popular bars and restaurants raises a number of

Domingo de Tentación. Photograph by Wolfgang Schüler.

questions. In contemporary rural and urban highland Bolivia, indigenous women wear lots of clothes; the wealthier a woman and the higher her social status, the greater the amount of clothing, and some wear as many as five heavy skirts. The showing of flesh is neither common nor eroticized, and women and men remain fully clothed even when working in the hot sun. Breasts, which are such a basic feature of the Western eroticization of women, are not in the least bit eroticized in Wila Kjarka. Breasts are exposed quite regularly as women breastfeed, but I never got any sense that this was somehow erotic or even that breasts were considered sexual either in comments made to me or by the reactions of people when breasts were exposed. An illustrative example from popular Andean culture is the *huayno*, sung and apparently written by child singer Wendly Sulca, titled *Tetita*—that is, teat or nipple. It is hard to imagine a young prepubescent girl in the West singing a song about how wonderful it is to suck the teat, "Ricoricoricorico, que rico es mi tetitaa!" (*rico* meaning delicious). In the music video there are several images of women breastfeeding, which would be difficult to imagine in the West; it only seems possible in the indigenous Andes precisely because the breast is so uneroticized.[4]

Putting images of naked white women on the wall is not, therefore, simply expressing a sense of desire for white bodies—bodies with a different form as well as color—it also implies a very different modality of desire, particularly when one so rarely comes across erotic images of indigenous people, male or female, clothed or naked. Erotic female bodies are white female bodies. Even in *huayno* music videos in which young women twirl, they usually only show their petticoats or underskirts, and if there is any eroticization at all it is very restrained; many, even young, *huayno* singers express a femininity which is much more that of the matron than the maiden. There is, however, a growing phenomenon, especially in Peru, of "modernizing" *huayno* music. The most obvious example is given by Las Chicas Terremoto del Folklore, a Peruvian group formed in the mid-2000s with the explicit intention of producing *huayno* with a great contemporary relevance. This has been interpreted by them in much shorter skirts and lower cut tops,[5] interspersing images of the four singers in Andean dress with those of them dancing in bikinis on the beach. Even though the four performers would not, I think, easily be identified as indigenous (one of them has light-brown hair), they are self-consciously eroticizing Andean music, and doing so through a Western modality of sexuality with the explicit aim of making the music "more modern." In some *huayno* videos, this juxtaposition takes a slightly different form, with images of the traditionally dressed singer interspersed with those of *other* women in modern and more revealing dress—exhibiting, perhaps, a tension between tradition and authenticity on the one hand and a desire to slough off the idea that Andean indigenous culture is atavistic on the other. Presenting women with little clothing appears to address this concern.

In Bolivia, such eroticization of music seems to be more muted with the possible exception of *caporales*, dances particularly favored by university students and middle-class mestizos in general who, for example, dance *caporales* in the *Fiesta del Gran Poder* in La Paz. Here, as with some of these *huayno* videos, young women dress in very short skirts that expose their underwear as they twirl, but this appears to be a very metropolitan phenomenon. Women in Wila Kjarka do twirl their skirts when they dance, but their long, heavy, and multiple layers rarely expose flesh above the knee. Women in Wila Kjarka, as is common with many highland indigenous women, do not wear underwear anyway. This has some obvious practicalities, such as when urinating in public, since they simply have to squat and do their business discreetly under their skirts and stand up and walk away when they are finished. In a reversal of the Western model, men have no such advantage: They have to expose their genitals to urinate and therefore have to find a place out of sight.

When *caporales* are danced in Sorata, for example, the dancers are exclusively those from La Paz who are typically the grandchildren and friends of the mestizos and creoles who once dominated the town. Even in the much more modest fiesta in San Pedro mentioned in chapter 2, the brass band and *caporales* dancers were imported from the city at great cost, whereas other music was provided by local musicians at virtually no cost. From the perspective of Wila Kjarkeños, the *caporales* dancers, be they in Sorata or San Pedro, are most definitely not identified as jaqi in any way. It goes without saying that Wila Kjarkeños rarely see music videos, as they simply do not have access to television.

These apparent exceptions prove the rule: Even in the highlands, eroticized indigeneity is expressed through mestizo or white(ned) bodies, and this eroticization is linked to aspirations to modernity. Almost as common in bars and restaurants are posters of Alpine meadows with healthy cows and Swiss chalets. My first reaction when confronted with these scenes was to wonder why, with the stunning mountains all through the Andes, people had pictures of the Alps. It finally occurred to me that they were the same kinds of images: What is aspired to in the Alpine meadow scene

Mannequins modeling indigenous dress in La Paz, 2011.

is a prosperous, ordered, and green mountain environment populated by a white yeomanry living in large and well-ordered houses. Both kinds of images are consequently part of the same economy of desire.

In a similar way, even when people are self-consciously expressing their indigeneity, they do so through the modality of white bodies. The images on page 259, taken in the heart of Aymara La Paz, show boutiques exhibiting indigenous clothing. These clothes are expensive, and the pollera skirts alone can easily cost up to US$100. The mannequins, however, are those of European-looking bodies; they are almost life-size versions of Barbie dolls. It is not the case that dark-skinned mannequins are unavailable; shop owners seek out blue-eyed mannequins, in particular, and even put blond wigs on them.

Although public erotic images of men are rare in Bolivia, it is equally the case that the bodily aesthetics one sees presented of men—for example, in posters and television—are overwhelmingly white. The image on page 261, taken in a barbershop in the provincial town of Sorata, is a simple example. According to the barber, Rubén, all his clientele, the occasional anthropologist notwithstanding, are from the town or surrounding countryside; that is, his clientele is predominantly indian in origin, and indeed the language that is most often spoken in his shop is Aymara. Yet, of the dozens of pictures he has on his wall to illustrate hairstyles, not a single one looks indigenous, and at most one or possibly two even look Latino. Any customer sitting in the chair will be looking at the hundreds of pictures of white men on the wall—examples of male beauty to be admired and copied—and a larger image of himself in the mirror. What no one could fail to notice is that the image in the mirror does not look like the images on the wall, and whatever hairstyle the customer comes out with, he will not look like those men who for twenty minutes or so were pictured in front of him.

For men as for women, whiteness is presented as an object of desire; what they should desire in the opposite sex as well as for their own bodies. The barber shop images, the pictures on the walls of popular restaurants and bars, and Waliya's Barbie-style doll are aspirational images, but these aspirations to progress, modernity, and whiteness are usually frustrated.

Desire is a very difficult phenomenon to investigate, but in conversations with men from Wila Kjarka it is very clear that erotic images of women, along with exposure to pornography in mining camps, have developed desires and tastes that cannot easily be met in their villages. Their masculinity, their sense of citizenship, as well as their sexual desires are

Rubén in his barbershop.

developed in conjunction with particular spaces, such as mining camps
and army barracks, as we saw in the previous chapter.

Historically, in Bolivia and elsewhere in Latin America, the social advancement that mestizaje implies has been seen in terms of white men
having sex with nonwhite women (e.g., Freyre 1986; Nelson 1999; Wright
1990). In contrast to the redemptive quality of white male sexuality, the
putatively predatory and degenerative sexuality of lower-class and darker
men has been seen as particularly problematic in twentieth-century Latin
American discourse (Stepan 1991: 93). Unlike many other areas of the
Americas, where whites were concerned to the point of paranoia over the
corrupting hypersexuality of subalterns, Bolivian elites considered indian
men to be singularly lacking in their sexuality; the environmentalism of
much social thought during the republican period rendered the inhabitants of the cold, high *altiplano* impervious to pain and devoid of any sensibility, let alone sensuality (Larson 2005: 41). Influential investigations
into the intimacies of indian life, such as José Salmón Ballivián's 1926 "El
indio íntimo: Contribución al estudio biológico social del indio," con-
clude that highland indians were nearly asexual (quoted in Larson 2005).

In contemporary Bolivia I have often heard mestizos and creoles mar-
vel at the strength of indians, their imperviousness to pain and discomfort,

their insensibility to cold and rain, and their lack of any kind of emotional or physical sensitivity. This is part of a long tradition of seeing highland indians as telluric embodiments of a harsh and unforgiving Andean environment. In much art of the nineteenth and early twentieth centuries, indians appear as part of the physical landscape, usually in the distance, and often as cold and immobile as a rock. In the 1990s, as AIDS spread across Latin America and neighboring Brazil in particular, this joke went around La Paz: "Why is there so much AIDS in Brazil and so little in Bolivia? Because the indians are so ugly they don't even have sex with each other." Here, as on other occasions, the sensuality of the tropical lowlands is contrasted with ascetic altiplano culture.

Adelio's evident pride in having slept with a variety of women (mentioned in the previous chapter) must be seen in this context: first, as laying claim to his nation not only through military service and travel but through sex with racial and ethnic "others," a usurpation of a white prerogative; and second, as laying claim to an expressive sexuality that has not historically been publicly recognized. Both are an assertion of citizenship, a demand to be included as a fully participating member of the nation.

It is significant that Adelio has to leave his community and region to lay claim to that citizenship. It underlines the lack of citizenship of women in the community (and the marginality of the community as a whole), who obviously do not have access to such masculinizing and whitening processes. In urban areas, or those in close proximity to big cities, indian women have greater opportunities to claim full membership in the nation. On a political level, the Bartolina Sisa National Federation of Peasant Women of Bolivia has representatives in Congress (including senators) sponsored by the ruling MAS party, and indian women have a long history of struggle in the public space of the market. In rural areas, however, few such political spaces exist for women.

Adelio's example also indicates that relations between indian men and nonindian women are still very much taboo in this area: I know of no examples of indian men marrying or having public relationships with mestiza or creole women in the area around which I do fieldwork, nor have I heard of any. Adelio is not, however, the only indian man to successfully pursue nonindian women. There is the recent phenomenon of indian men successfully pursuing white women: the *bricheros* who seek out foreign women in tourist spots such as Cuzco (Alison Spedding, pers. comm.; Guevara 1994). The *bricheros* are similar to the "rent a Rasta" in Jamaica (Kempadoo 2004) or the *kamaki* in Greece (Zinovieff 1991) in that they trade on exotic images of the Other for sex. The *bricheros* appear to overturn or at least disturb the colonial prerogative of white men for indigenous women not least by asserting an aggressive indigenous sexuality that has been historically erased. By occupying public spaces such as tourist bars and restaurants and actively pursuing women above them in the conventional social hierarchy, they are engaged in important political acts, whether they are aware of them or not. Lynn Meisch, in her study of Otavalo (1995), gives a number of examples of indian men having relationships with white, foreign women, and the sense of liberation they experienced at overturning the stereotype of the ugly asexual indian man. This puzzles and irritates mestizo-creoles who find "gringas'" romantic attitude toward *indígenas* difficult to understand. Because *indígenas* historically have been a disparaged and vilified population, many mestizo-creoles cannot believe that a foreigner would prefer any *indígena* to themselves. Clearly, one of the attractions of having a relationship with a gringa for Otavalo men is overturning these long-standing stereotypes.

In Wila Kjarka, Sorata, and surrounding areas, I know of no such examples—not yet, anyway. In contrast, there are many contemporary examples, as well as those in the past, of mestizo and creole men having relationships with and marrying indian women. The men of neighboring mestizo villages, often no wealthier than those of Wila Kjarka, do have relationships with indian women—sometimes to marry them, often to eventually abandon them. In some cases, mestizo men recognize the paternity of their children, but they are under no obligation to do so. For example, Ernesto, a mestizo who was in his early seventies when we spoke, told me of his children through marriage and through his mistresses—naming those who still lived in the provincial town—and those whom he didn't acknowledge, who lived further away. He told me that the mother of these children was trying to get him to recognize them, but he simply refused. In contrast, he did recognize the children he had by a woman in Caranavi, a small town in the coca-growing region, or *yungas*.[6] Ernesto illustrates how postcolonial racial politics are reproduced in those "tense and tender ties" (Stoler 2001)—sometimes more tense than tender—of intimate relations between mestizo-creoles and indians.

Interracial sex has always been public in the Americas, if only because its products (i.e., "mixed-race" children) needed to be accommodated, assimilated, or relegated in one way or another. In the twenty-first century, however, the very notion of the "public" is profoundly different, and relationships that might have been gossiped about in private or were an "open secret" among certain people can now be exposed to the full glare of the mass media. This book has explored the many ways the personal, and indeed the intimate, is political; in the following section I explore how the publically political draws on the intimate, which is no longer private.

EVO AND THE NEW ERA

Evo Morales's election to the presidency of Bolivia with a clear majority of the votes offers an opportunity to undermine this nexus of race, sex, and citizenship. Indeed, one of his very first acts as president was to appoint indigenous women to key ministerial posts, including those of Economic Development, Government, Health, and Justice. Despite these significant moves, in his personal life and comments he conforms much more to a conventional model of metropolitan masculinity than one more prevalent in the rural indian communities from which he originates and where he receives his greatest support. That is, even if hegemonic whiteness has been overturned, mestizo-creole masculinity appears not only to have remained unchallenged but embraced by the president.

There are some clear limits to Evo's exercise of power: Despite bullish rhetoric and the partial renationalization of gas, economic control of the country still remains within the firm control of the same small group of people and international investors; and Morales has to contend with the serious issue of eastern regions and their secession movements. What is less clear are the limits to his ability, or indeed desire, to deconstruct the tightly bound associations of race and gender, the metalanguage of power, that have underwritten politics—both at the intimate as well as the national level—since the Conquest. To challenge the stereotype of the asexual and submissive indian man, it appears he must do so through embracing the mestizo-creole model of gendered relationships.

The incongruity of an indian president surfaces in humor and jokes about Evo. As has been widely noted since Freud, humor is a means through which anxieties and incongruities are explored. Whether humor is understood as challenging authority (Douglas 1966; Scott 1985) or as an ultimately ineffectual act of insubordination (Mulkay 1988), humor derives its force from dealing with the dangerous, the taboo, and the uncomfortable. It is not surprising, then, that jokes about Evo Morales's sexuality abound in contemporary Bolivia because they address the apparent and unsettling contradiction of having an indian man occupying the highest elected office in the land.

Humor has rarely been a subject that anthropologists have considered seriously, but in recent years scholars such as Donna Goldstein (2003) and Diane Nelson (1999) have begun to explore humor as an appropriate subject for scholarly analysis. In particular, Diane Nelson has looked at the jokes, cartoons, and rumors surrounding Rigoberta Menchú in Guatemala. For Nelson, these jokes "are complex ways of structuring a variety of anxieties for many different Guatemalans whose national, ethnic and gendered body images are wounded" (1999: 173). Bolivia, unlike Guatemala, has not suffered years of extreme violence directed against indians, but it is experiencing a period of marked reevaluation of enduring categories of race and sex; in Bolivia the national body is not so much wounded but being re-dressed.

Jokes and gossip about Evo Morales, rather like those about Rigoberta Menchú, "condense often contradictory fantasies and popular imaginings about the presence of indigenous people in the nation and in so doing help structure various bodies politic" (Nelson 1999: 173). Anxieties surrounding the eruption of Evo Morales in the center of the body politic are exposed in humor and rumor.

The idea that the president, who has never married, may have relationships with white women is the stuff of torrid comment in Bolivia, including his power base in the Chapare coca-growing region. It also lies behind the *Día de los Inocentes* (similar to April Fool's Day) announcement of Evo Morales's engagement to Adriana Gil Moreno, the twenty-two-year-old, U.S.-educated political leader from Santa Cruz in eastern Bolivia (*El Deber* 2005). The joke caused considerable discussion, including whether if this were to happen it would constitute a betrayal of his indigenous politics; others wondered if it might be true anyway: the titillating discussions surrounding Evo and Adriana Gil are charged precisely because they deal with the taboo subjects of race, sex, and power that are being disturbed and reconfigured. Evo Morales is not only the subject of salacious or suggestive humor, however, but often uses it himself, with the same motifs of race and sex that disturb and excite. Rather like Adelio (above), who conceives of his inclusion into the nation in terms of the women he slept with, Morales makes humorous comments which underline his sexual attractiveness to women (which provide some of the context to the Día de los Inocentes prank mentioned above). These apparently off-the-cuff remarks, frequently not reported in the mainstream press but, rather, on the radio or just circulated mouth to mouth, cause considerable comment; and it is by no means clear whether these supposedly ill-considered statements are not, in fact, about presenting a particularly virile image of himself.

One example is the criticism Morales received for spending a lot of time in Cuba. The official reason for his visit was for medical attention to his knee. He is reported as saying, "He ido para muletas, no para mulatas [I went for crutches (*muletas*), not mulattas]." This refers to a well-known joke (of which there are a number of variants), which plays on the confusion between *muletas* and *mulatas*, but in his jocular denial he raises the very image of that which he is denying. It is also a joke that indexes mestizos or white sexual humor because, for indigenous people, mulattas are not generally a salient category and, as far as I know, this joke did not circulate among indigenous people. What makes this joke funny is precisely the idea of Morales confounding the stereotype of the sexually passive indian man.

Evo Morales may not have uttered these words, and it is possible that they were simply attributed to him, but the following example can be unambiguously accredited. In an interview shortly before his election, Morales was asked whether he thought he could work with the white business community. After showing a free airpass from AeroSur as evidence of his good relations with the business community, he continued, "In 2003, in the Miss Bolivia contest in Sucre, they were asked whom they liked and 15 out of 18 candidates said Evo Morales ... and I don't think that is because I am single [laughter] well, perhaps some of them. They are daughters of the middle and upper class. Women have another way of thinking about life ..." (*La Razón* November 25, 2005).

The interviewer was asking a serious question about whether Evo Morales, as an indigenous politician, could get on with white businessmen, and his principal response was, in effect, a humorous retort that their daughters found him attractive. Morales is a highly astute politician, and I suggest that his response can best be understood in the context of the historical denial of indian sexuality, especially male sexuality; but it also reinforces the view that political power is consonant with sexual power.

A more recent example of Morales's expression of the politics of sexuality is given by the intense debate over the construction of a road across a national park and indigenous territory, which is seen as benefiting highland colonists and is strongly opposed by lowland indigenous groups, such as those of the Territorio Indígena y Parque Nacional Isiboro-Secure (TIPNIS), the Confederación de Pueblos Indígenas de Bolivia (CIDOB), and the Consejo Nacional de Ayllus y Markas del Qullasuyu (CONAMAQ), as well as environmental groups. Journalist Willy Chipana reported for *La Razón* newspaper that Evo Morales sought to resolve this problem in an address to coca growers of the Chapare region who are seen as the primary beneficiaries of the road (*La Razón,* August 1, 2011). Chipana reported the following:

> The President asked the residents of the Chapare to convince the indigenous people of TIPNIS to give the green light to the construction.
>
> "You, *compañeras* and *compañeros,* need to explain, to guide the indigenous *compañeros.*" Their own mayor is moving to convince them not to oppose [the road].
>
> Later he added: "If I had time I would go and woo the Yuracaré *compañeras* and convince them not to oppose. That is, young men, you have instructions from the President to seduce (conquistar) the Yuracaré women so that they won't oppose the building of the road." He immediately asked "Approved?" and applause was heard from the assembled.[7]

There is, it seems, an enduring theme in using sexual prowess to overcome political opponents and a curious consonance with his response to the reporter noted above: The way to deal with political opposition on both accounts is to woo or seduce women; the president does not seem to wonder if their male counterparts will consequently be persuaded. What was not stated here was that one "solution" to the problem of lowland indigenous resistance is what is, in fact, happening across large areas of the country: highland Aymara- and Quechua-speaking peasants are occupying land either illegally or with government grants and displacing and dispossessing local groups. The sexual politics of this is often apparent.

In discussion with a number of Aymara migrants to the town of Rurrenabaque on the Beni River in the eastern lowlands when I visited in 2011, I was struck by the number who had Tacana or Esse Ejja wives. Marcelino's account was fairly typical: "Oh yes, I have a wife. She is in Santa Cruz, but I also have a wife here, a young girl. She is twenty-two [Marcelino is forty-five]. I have a child with her. The people here are very simple. Before I came twenty years ago, there was nothing here. We have brought civilization. They don't understand. In those days they would just give you a woman for twenty pesos [laughter]. It is very easy to take a woman here." Marcelino here appears to agree with the president's policy for the lowlands and his ideas for overcoming indigenous resistance to the incursion of highlanders which is, unsurprisingly, deeply resented. Intermarriage is a way of getting access to community resources, and children, in particular, have status as community members.

For the president, however, the politics of sexuality are most evident when it comes to beauty queens. They are clearly important to him, and he invited the two Miss Bolivias (one from the Miss Universe competition and the other from Miss World) to his inauguration. This caused some surprise, not least on the part of the delighted Misses themselves (*Los Tiempos*, January 23, 2006). In a later interview (*La Razón*, May 8, 2006), in a discussion that revolved around the rigors of being president and the pressure surrounding the new Constituent Assembly, Morales made the point that the cabinet's favorite pastime was teasing Vice President Alvaro García about his relationship with the ex–Miss Bolivia, 20-year-old Desirée Durán, which has been widely reported in the press and for whom the famous intellectual García has shown a willingness, even eagerness, to interrupt the affairs of state. Indeed, as James Dunkerley notes (2007: 42) in the midst of the preparations for the Constituent Assembly the vice president flew from Washington to Los Angeles to "to attend the finals of the Miss Universe contest and boost the morale of Desirée Durán whose considerable charms had elevated her to the final ten contestants before she experienced the inevitable defeat." It may be that in his comments about Durán, Evo Morales is attempting to communicate that his cabinet members have some light moments when they are discussing matters of state or, indeed, he may once again be communicating the desirability of his cabinet members in the eyes of young, white beauty queens. One could argue that by attending the Miss Universe contest the vice president was not neglecting his ministerial duties but underlining his—and by extension the president's—ability to rule.

Although many people in Western countries find beauty contests trivial, a number of scholars have established their importance in many parts of the world and in Latin America in particular (e.g., Pequeño 2004; Rahier 1998; Rogers 1999). In Bolivia, the politics of beauty contests are particularly sensitive since Miss Bolivia made a controversial statement in Ecuador in 2004 at the time of great social upheaval and upsurge of indigenous mobilization, which culminated in the election of Evo Morales. That year's Miss Bolivia contestant, Gabriela Oviedo, when asked, "What is one of the biggest misconceptions about your country?" replied in English:

> Um . . . unfortunately, people that don't know Bolivia very much think that we are all just Indian people from the west side of the country: it's

La Paz all the image that we reflect, is that poor people and very short people and Indian people . . . I'm from the other side of the country, the east side and it's not cold, it's very hot and we are tall and we are white people and we know English so all that misconception that Bolivia is only an 'Andean' country, it's wrong, Bolivia has a lot to offer and that's my job as an ambassador of my country to let people know how much diversity we have.

Unsurprisingly, this caused considerable comment and debate in the Bolivian media (e.g., *El Diario*, May 27, 2004) and internationally (e.g., *New York Times*, May 29, 2004), most of it condemnatory, although there was considerable support for her position in Santa Cruz, as evidenced by blogs and web postings. There are annual elections for two Miss Bolivias—one for the Miss World competition and the other for Miss Universe—and one *Señorita Bolivia* for a Latin American competition. Not only are they all invariably tall, white women, they are also almost always from the eastern part of the country. In 2005, for example, all three were once again from Santa Cruz, which celebrates its whiteness (Gustafson 2006) in general and in particular that of its women. In fact, of the 105 women elected to represent their country internationally in beauty contests since 1980, 84 were from the eastern lowland departments and 56 were from Santa Cruz; and of the 27 elected since Evo Morales took office in 2005, 21 were from the eastern lowland departments where the strongest opposition against his regime was concentrated (http://en.wikipedia .org/wiki/Miss_Bolivia). It is, however, the case that recently Miss Bolivia has been wearing highland indigenous dress in international competitions (Natasha Varner, pers. comm.).

Evo Morales's comments about beauty queens must, moreover, be taken in the context of the controversy created by Gabriela Oviedo, of which he is undoubtedly very well aware. He is also clearly aware of the wider context of the secession movements in Santa Cruz, which are partly rooted in precisely the anxieties Oviedo expressed: domination by the indian highland majority.

In the wake of the explosive racism and conflict over the new constitution and the eastern regions' control of hydrocarbons—a conflict that caused serious violence and massacres in these areas—Morales was believed to have an uphill battle to maintain, let alone increase, his votes in these areas. There is no doubt that control over natural resources and the historical neglect of the eastern lowlands by highland elites form part of the backdrop to this conflict, but there has always been a racial component to the lowlander elites' antipathy toward the highlanders. Indigenous peoples of the lowlands are small in number, dispersed, and multiethnic; and they have historically been dominated by a small class of powerful white elites. Lowlander elites have responded to the ethnicization of politics in Bolivia by developing their own *camba* indigenous identity (Pruden 2003) through appropriating symbols of lowland indigenous resistance to both the Inka and Spanish empires. As Nicole Fabricant notes, "Their celebration of identity, which thrives on the power of dance, parades, and festivals, gives their cause credibility as an issue of cultural pride and identity, a powerful political claim in the 21st century, rather than frame it as a nakedly economic issue of complete control over all gas and oil deposits and the attendant displacement of indigenous communities, especially Guaraní communities in the Chaco region" (2009: 772).

The election of Evo Morales, and especially the process of developing a new constitution, brought out the stark gendered racism that was structurally evident but rarely publicly expressed. The Constituent Assembly took place in Sucre, the constitutional capital. Sucreños paint their buildings white, and many imagine their city to be racially white as well with indians imagined as being picturesque and folkloric beyond the margins of the city (or as servants in white homes) but most certainly not as politically active in its main squares (Ströbele-Gregor 2011). It is not surprising then, that the local white population was uneasy at the thought of thousands of indigenous delegates descending upon their town. The racism visited upon the delegates was, however, not uniform. What is striking is how exceptionally gendered it was: women discovered that the hotels they had booked were suddenly full, forcing them to seek accommodation far from the city center; they were *regularly* verbally abused and assaulted in the streets,[8] and the whole Constituent Assembly was regularly described as *la chola ignorante* (the ignorant indian woman) (Calla 2012).[9] Again and again the crowds protested: "Evo cabrón, Linera maraco, Lazarte la puta madre que te parió" (Evo cuckold, Linera [the vice president] a fag, Lazarte [the indigenous woman president of the Assembly] the mother whore who bore you) (Calla, 2012: 49).[10] These are very similar to the chants Nicole Fabricant heard in the main square of the eastern Capital of Santa Cruz as local people argued for autonomy from the state (Fabricant 2009: 772).

It is worth pausing a moment to consider the insults. The president and vice president are feminized in a place that has a long tradition of seeing the legitimate exercise of power as, by definition, a masculine endeavor. Morales, the president, is described as a cuckold, a man who allows sexual access to his wife and is consequently feminized, the image of the impotent indian man that so haunted Fausto Reinaga. The white vice president "is a fag," and in political cartoons he is often presented as effeminate and referred to as the "First Lady." Lazarte—again following a long tradition of disparaging one's female opponents—is, of course, a whore. And the whole process is a *chola*: in essence, an indigenous market woman—loud, vulgar, uneducated, and, of course, not white.

The gendered racism recorded in the Constituent Assembly was sharp and wounding and indexed precisely such issues as a lack of proficiency in Spanish, which is what makes, among other things, women *más india* (more indian). It was thus that a woman delegate was told: "India, shut up! Until you speak Spanish, get out!"[11] and "Why do you come here if you can't speak in a civilized manner?"[12] (Calla 2012: 49). With respect to hotel accommodation, many women were made to move, and move again, but they still had to navigate the public spaces of the city. Over two years the abuse and violence simply got worse and were reminiscent of the social control of the first half of the twentieth century, when indians were not allowed in the main squares of La Paz and other cities (Gotkowitz 2000). Very soon indigenous women were assaulted as they moved through the main square. They had their braids pulled, chewing gum was stuck in their hair, and they were threatened with having their underwear ripped off (Calla 2012: 50). Pamela Calla interprets this as an attempt to show how dirty and depraved the women were, but I wonder if the insult is simpler: a reference to the fact that indian women traditionally (and often today) do not wear underwear, and the fact that these women might be wearing underwear was yet another example of their being "uppity." What is certainly true, as Marisol de la Cadena points out (1991), is that they are more associated with nature than with culture and "within and without the institution of the Assembly, with a lack of reason to the point of being inhuman" (Calla 2012: 50).

It was not only women who suffered racist taunts and attacks. Calla and her colleagues have documented the events of May 24, 2008, when approximately forty indigenous people were forced into the main plaza of Sucre and were publicly humiliated. Beaten with sticks and stones, they were forced to partially undress and kneel before the Sucre flag, which they were obliged to kiss. At the same time they were made to burn the *wiphala*, a flag that symbolizes indigenous Bolivia (Calla 2012: 47). Calla sees this as a reassertion of colonial models of racialized and gendered domination where not only ideology but violence was used to regulate the behavior of indians and women. One could see this in even simpler terms: The events of May 24 were an attempt to turn back the clock and negate the new indigenous order. The forty or so people in the plaza were reminded that they were, after all, still *indios* and could be made to kneel in a submissive and feminized manner before symbols of white power.

The public humiliation of indigenous men in the main square of Sucre seems a long way from the seemingly trivial events of beauty contests. Brett Gustafson (2006), however, has shown how important the role of beauty queens is in articulating lowland *camba* autonomy. In particular, local beauty contests are ways in which white elites occupy public spaces in small and large towns. The connection between beauty contests and racist and even violent autonomy protests is made even clearer by Nicole Fabricant who argues that "there is no structural counterpart to the UJC [Santa Cruz Youth Union] for young women, but through their participation in the beauty industry, they are able to engage in and contribute to right-wing forms of civic engagement" (2009: 773).

Evo Morales was able to get the new constitution through congress despite eastern opposition, which turned particularly violent in the northeastern department of Pando on September 11, 2008, when twenty-one indians were murdered—by many accounts—by the local authorities, and provincial governor Leopoldo Fernández was arrested. The passage of the new constitution coincided with the 2009 election, and Morales clearly needed to build some bridges with the eastern lowlands.

One issue Evo Morales campaigned on in 2009 was his commitment to try and bring the Miss World contest to Santa Cruz, and the MAS candidate for governor of the neighboring Department of Beni was twenty-four-year-old Jessica Jordan, Miss Bolivia 2006. The MAS party substantially increased its vote in these regions, although it narrowly failed to reach a majority in Santa Cruz. Miss Jordan was not victorious either but came very close to victory. It would be facile to reduce MAS's improved performance in the eastern lowlands to a beauty campaign (the spectacularly weak opposition was certainly a factor), but, at the same time, it would be foolish to discount the importance of beauty queens and international contests in the eyes of a certain section of Bolivia's population.[13] For his part, Evo Morales appears to understand this and use it to his advantage.

In the indian highlands, too, beauty contests are used to articulate political messages far beyond those surrounding female aesthetics. When the overwhelmingly indian city of El Alto—a satellite of La Paz—had its first beauty contest in 2005, electing a Miss El Alto and a Señorita El Alto, it warranted an editorial in the serious daily *La Razón* (November 25, 2005), which argued that, contrary to widespread prejudice, the residents of El Alto are not stubbornly wedded to an indian past but are looking forward to a progressive and modern future, embracing free trade and global capitalism.

> [El Alto's] medium and larger entrepreneurs want to hook themselves up to the train of investment, production, and export. That is, the economy of the big league. Another example, the support on the part of neighborhood committees of projects directed to reorganizing the physical space to make El Alto a tidier, cleaner and even more cosmopolitan city. And single events, organized for the first time, such as the election of two ladies who will represent El Alto in a high quality and recognized national event which is the Miss Bolivia Contest.
>
> Given these events, does it seem that alteños want to remain in the past? Or in contrast, aren't they sending messages to their leaders and to those of the country that they want to change the conflictive image of their and show themselves for what they really are: people who want to progress and build opportunities?

What better example of the rejection of indian atavism and the desire for modernity and progress than a beauty contest? A beauty contest which was not, however, a celebration of indigenous physical aesthetics but, rather, one which seemed to give the message that even El Alto can produce tall, pale-skinned, slim beauties. It is worth noting that by November 2005 El Alto had suffered years of political unrest, and its residents had blocked access to the city of La Paz several times. El Alto is a primary center of indigenous radicalism, and only weeks after the beauty contest, it overwhelmingly supported Evo Morales in the presidential elections.

The winner who went on to compete for the Miss La Paz contest, Carol Alvizuri, at 1.78 meters tall and pale skinned, is not exactly typical of the women who live in El Alto. The election of Carol Alvizuri as Miss La Paz in a contest against six other women, none of whom looked remotely indigenous, could be read as a reply to Gabriela Oviedo's complaint that people thought Bolivia was populated by short indians: Here, in the indian heartland, white beauty queens can be produced; and one would not be surprised to learn that they all speak English.

It is not, however, the case that the public necessarily supports such choices. In his ethnography of a beauty pageant in a marginal *barrio* in

Cochabamba, Daniel Goldstein notes that the judges "privileged Euro-pean-derived physical features and cultural styles over their indigenous counterparts" (2000: 7) and elected a non-Aymara-speaking woman as the winner. On this occasion the crowd protested, but the judges' views prevailed. The judges themselves were selected for their middle-class credentials and hence were considered successful members of the com-munity. As "upwardly mobile urbanized Bolivians" (8) they apparently share the selection criteria of the judges of Miss El Alto and echo the be-liefs of the editorial writer for *La Razón* regarding Western features and standards of beauty as conveying an appropriate sense of modernity and progress. Evo Morales, it seems, shares their views.

In more recent years there has been a growth in indigenous beauty contests, the most famous of which is *Miss Cholita Paceña*, in which in-digenous women are judged on, among other things, their ability to speak Aymara. They all wear full (i.e., heavy) indigenous dress, and even though it is a beauty contest, it does not focus on the physical beauty of the con-testants beyond that which they display facially. The focus is on clothing and authenticity. Recently there have been "scandals" in which the winner has subsequently revealed that she did not normally wear the signal pol-lera skirts, and in 2007 the winner of the contest, María Molinedo, had her title removed because she was exposed as wearing false braids.

This is a far cry from the standard beauty contests in which the con-cern is not for indigenous authenticity but, rather, making indigenous dress look sexy, even if it means adding a pair of high-heeled, knee-length leather boots, as Gabriela Oviedo did in her 2004 contest.

Nevertheless, even in radical indigenous circles, beauty contests appear at the forefront of political consciousness, raising initiatives as the 2009 celebrations of the bicentennial of the 1809 "revolution" against colonial rule illustrate: The bicentennial was marked with, among other things, a beauty contest electing *Miss La Paz Bicentenario*. This contest was, in-cidentally, of the conventional swimsuit parade variety rather than one concerned with indigenous authenticity. The words of the mayor of La Paz, Juan del Granado Cosío, echo the views of the editorial above: "The Municipal Government of La Paz decided to contribute to the organiza-tion of Miss La Paz Bicentenario and it did so with conviction, this being an important year in the struggle for liberation, and above all a point of departure from which our youth can pick up the baton of the leadership of La Paz with vigor in the national and regional context" (Galindo and

*María Molinedo winning the 2008 Miss Cholita contest. Minutes later
a judge noticed she was wearing false braids and she was stripped of her crown.*
©Reuters/José Luis Quintana

Álvarez, 2010).[14] The contestants were able to pose with President Evo
Morales.

Morales has received the wrath of some feminists (e.g., Galindo 2006)
who decry his unwillingness to challenge the constitutional position of
the army—including obligatory military service—and of the Catholic
Church, one of the more conservative in Latin America. Both these institutions in different but complementary ways contribute to a particular
masculinized citizenship, and their hierarchies are overwhelmingly dominated by white men.

Even in indigenous urban areas, female support for Evo Morales is
ambivalent. In conversation with women from El Alto (the largely indian
satellite city of La Paz), even his own ardent supporters distanced themselves from his attitudes toward women. "I think Evo is very good for the
country, but I don't approve of his behavior: he is very *machista*." She was
referring to his history with women and the number of illegitimate children he reputedly has. In Cochabamba, where he is known as a *k'ipador*

Evo Morales posing with the contestants for Miss Bicentenario in 2009.
©Reuters/José Luis Quintana

(from *k'ipay,* sowing crops one year and producing for two harvests without having to re-sow; it applies to men who "sow their seeds" in several places), there is also resistance to Evo's machismo. A piece of graffiti near the MAS headquarters in Cochabamba reads: "Eva no saldrá del costillo del Evo" (Eve will not emerge from Evo's rib) as well as "Soberanía en mi país y en mi cuerpo" (sovereignty in my country and of my body) (Emma Felber, pers. comm. author's translation).

Morales has one son he recognized "in the womb" (*La Prensa* 2006) and a daughter of almost exactly the same age with a different woman he recognized under some pressure from his political opponents in 2005. By all accounts he has very little or no contact with either of his children, and there is no mention of them in his official biography. He is also rumored to be the father to several others, which provided ammunition to his political opponents in the PODEMOS party, who ran ads arguing that if Morales had abandoned his own children, how could he look after the country?

It is manifest that such criticism did him little harm. Having illegitimate children, even a large number of them, is hardly without precedent for the head of state; nor, in fact, is Evo Morales the first native speaker of an indigenous language to be president of the republic. René Barrientos played a major role in the 1952 Revolution and was an important member of the ruling MNR party, serving as vice president until he engineered a coup in 1964, after which he presided over a personalized authoritarian regime until his death in 1969. Barrientos came from a humble, Quechua-speaking mestizo background and, although he never identified himself as indigenous, he was able to speak his native tongue fluently in public, whereas Evo Morales, in contrast, though sometimes reported to speak Quechua as well as his native tongue, Aymara, has considerable difficulty in speaking his mother tongue in public. Barrientos exceeds Morales not only in linguistic ability but in licentiousness: Barrientos only recognized eight of his children but promised to adopt more than fifty (Dunkerley 2007: 191). Given the length of his political career it would be difficult to argue that his large number of illegitimate children hampered his political trajectory, and the same can surely be said for Evo Morales.

In fact, even if in Cochabamba there is a certain disdain among some women for his reputation, others apparently revel in it. Morales's 2009 slogan was "Bolivia avanza, Evo no se cansa," that is, "Bolivia advances, Evo is tireless." There were several spins on this slogan; among these were heard, significantly from women in Cochabamba: "Mujeres ardientes, Evo Presidente," "Hot women, Evo President," and one which was broadcast on television, again uttered by a woman, "Mujeres calientes, Evo valiente," "Women are hot, Evo is strong/brave."[15] These are all plays on words that are difficult to capture in translation, but they unambiguously make reference to Evo's sexual appeal to women and, even more specifically, that his political prowess is sexually arousing.

Alongside rumors that pass by word of mouth, there are also a significant number of stories that appear in the national and Latin American press with interviews of women who claim to have been in love with Morales at one time or other from as far away as Mexico (Poniatowska 2006), and many more in websites and discussion forums. It should not necessarily be assumed that these are scurrilous attempts to besmirch the reputation of the president. On the contrary: Many of them are written by journalists who have publicly supported him (e.g., Elena Poniatowska in La Jornada). In Bolivia, rumors abound linking Evo Morales with any number of women, now and in the past. As one paceña friend said to me, "If even half these rumors are true, he wouldn't have time to run the country!" I hasten to add that I have no evidence whatsoever to confirm these rumors, and I report them as simply that, rumors. The rumors in themselves constitute a social phenomenon, rather like the humor analyzed above; and there is little evidence that his reputation with the majority of urban Bolivians has suffered from such attention. In fact, one could argue the opposite: The virility of the president is a testament to his ability to rule and, moreover, overturns the historical stereotype of the unattractive, feminized, and asexual indian man.

That he has indeed succeeded in overturning this stereotype is suggested in a political cartoon, published in *La República* on October 8, 2006. The cartoon depicted him as a macho soccer player next to his white vice president who is portrayed in a rather feminine pose. This echoes the jokes and graffiti, which refer to the vice president as the First Lady (which contradict other rumors about him as a ladies' man). The event that the cartoon is referring to is the killing of unionized miners in Huanuni the previous month—the place where Evo Morales sent the army to quell the unrest. Morales certainly demonstrated that he could exercise power in the same way that other presidents have done against indians for decades and centuries, and Barrientos mentioned above would be an obvious referent. Morales is passionate about soccer, and another incident provides a further illustration. On October 4, 2010, Morales was playing in a match against his political opponents. When one of the opposing team players kicked him in the shin, Morales turned and kneed him in the groin and the man dropped like a stone. This was caught on video, and the images were rapidly circulated. Although the president did apologize for this later, there is very little indication that the publicity has done him any harm at all; rather, it simply confirms him as a potent man who knows how to respond.

For a man to have several partners, marry none of them, and have children—recognized or not—with many of them is by no means uncommon in Bolivia, as indeed in other parts of Latin America. It is, however, not common among rural indian people who constitute the majority of the country and where Evo Morales has his origins. In such communities, it is extremely rare for men to have children with several partners unless they are widowed and for them to remain single well into their forties, as is the case with Evo Morales. In short, from the perspective of many indigenous people, Evo Morales, with his many lovers and illegitimate children, behaves like a mestizo. It is worth pointing out that it was not until approximately two years before his election to the presidency that he actually publically self-identified as indigenous. Before then he was a coca leader and eschewed, and even opposed, indigenous politics. In the years leading up to his election he traveled widely in Europe as well as across

Latin America—for which he was heavily criticized—and it is almost certainly on these travels that he learned the effectiveness of an indigenous discourse. Since his election he has been widely feted as not only Bolivia's indigenous president but the world's, and in 2009 he lobbied successfully for the UN to change Earth Day to Mother Earth Day—that is, the *pachamama* has an international day of recognition. It is sometimes difficult to remember that for most of his political career, from the time he left his impoverished highland community and went on to become a coca grower in the Chapare, he was a member of a mobile social class that did not readily identify as indigenous. In other words, in the eyes of people such as those in Wila Kjarka, he would have been recognized as a mestizo. One could say that Evo Morales spent his youth as an Aymara indian herding llamas in the cold altiplano, his adult life as a cholo or even mestizo in the coca growing regions, and most recently as an indigenous president. Such a trajectory—of indian to mestizo to indigenous—disturbs the colonial and postcolonial categories of race and ethnicity.

The rumors and jokes surrounding Evo Morales are thus more than simply political and personal jokes because they depend on an understanding of Bolivia's racial and sexual politics for their very humor and interest; more specifically, they depend on a tension between long-standing understandings of race and power and the notion of an indigenous president. There would be no interest in these jokes and rumors if they did not point to a truth—not a truth that lies necessarily in the behavior of the president, but one that springs from the anxieties of a nation becoming accustomed to a new body politic. Following Diane Nelson, I see these jokes and humorous rumors as having very little to do with real people or events and "everything to do with the play of fantasy and anxiety" (1999: 176); and the fantasy about which the jokes express an anxiety is the one depicted in the opening of this chapter.

Theodor Galle's seventeenth-century etching is a powerful allegorical representation of the relationship between Europeans and indians since the Conquest: a relationship which is not only gendered but sexualized. Indians are metaphorically female, and indian women are open to the advances of white men. Since the Conquest and up to the present day, sexual access to indian women has been a standard perquisite of white male power, while the sexuality of indian males is all but erased in a conflation of their sexual and political impotence. This perquisite is more than simply a consequence of unequal relations; it may indeed serve to define them.

Since the 1990s, indigenous movements have dramatically challenged five centuries of white rule, and no more so than in Bolivia, which in December 2005 elected an indigenous president. Evo Morales is explicit about the revolutionary nature of his election, and not just in terms of his regular references to Che Guevara. In his inaugural speech he announced the end of five hundred years of indian resistance and the beginning of an era of five hundred years when indian people will be in power; and in his first months of power he abolished the Ministry of Indigenous Affairs on the grounds that it marginalized indigenous issues. Part of Morales's success stems from his ability to express issues such as gas nationalization in indigenous terms (Canessa 2006a)—all affairs are now indigenous in Bolivia. His administration has also instituted the "decolonization" of education in Bolivia.[16]

Given that sexuality and desire have long been central elements in the colonial project (hooks 1991; McClintock 1995; Stoler 1995, 2002; Wade 2009)—both in providing the language for domination as well as the concrete instances of it—anticolonial projects will inevitably have sexual as well as racial dimensions. Evo Morales is making some key moves to decolonize Bolivia and return power to its indigenous inhabitants, but the implications for the sexual politics of colonialism, and specifically for the representation of indian masculinity, are much less clear. As I have shown, his sexual desirability, and especially to beautiful white women, is important to Morales, not just personally but politically. Such desirability is a means through which he can communicate his ability to govern the entire country and not just its indian citizens; but it is also emblematic of his confounding the racial stereotype of the asexual and unattractive indian. It appears that for Evo Morales, as much as for Adelio (mentioned above), sexuality is a means through which citizenship can be claimed. However, even as he undermines the racialized hegemony in Bolivia, the sexualized nature of political power is further reified. Rather than completely deconstructing the ideology encapsulated in Galle's etching, Morales, it appears, has merely put himself in Vespucci's place.

We Will Be People No More

There can be no doubt that Evo Morales's election to the presidency and his reelection with an even greater proportion of the popular vote in December 2009 offers hope to people like those in Wila Kjarka. On a practical level indigenous people—men and women—are heading ministries and running the country, and the new constitution guarantees their representation in congress. It is hard to imagine Bolivia ever returning to the status quo ante, when creoles led all the major parties and politicians took indigenous people's votes for granted.

The lot of indigenous people has not changed overnight, of course, but something that is palpable in Wila Kjarka and in similar communities is that tomorrow just might, just might, be better than today. In the past, people simply knew that it would stay the same if they were lucky and would probably get worse. People are sanguine about what Evo Morales and his government can achieve, but there is a guarded optimism that I have never observed before. People in Wila Kjarka are overwhelmingly in favor of Morales, whom they clearly recognize as jaqi and as someone who will look out for the interests of jaqi like them. It is a testament to Morales's political skills that he transformed himself from a coca leader who, until 2002, was apparently uninterested in identity politics into someone who can so clearly articulate the aspirations of a large majority of the country; most notably, Wila Kjarkeños recognize this union-leader-cum-national-politician as one of them, whereas in other contexts he would just be another mestizo. Wila Kjarkeños will often not recognize their own urban grandchildren or even children as jaqi, so it rather begs the question as to why Morales is so different. Perhaps the answer is quite simple: He does not wish to be a mestizo, and goes to great lengths to express, indeed celebrate, his indigenous identity. For Wila Kjarkeños his political message is clear: Indigenous people are becoming politically powerful, one day they will also be economically powerful, and they will not be treated like *indios*.

This new modern indigeneity is empowering, but it is also very different to the traditional lifeways of people in Wila Kjarka. Evo Morales and other indigenous politicians certainly invoke "tradition," by such acts as embracing the Aymara New Year rituals of the winter solstice in June or, as Morales chose to do, having his inauguration among the ruins of Tiwanaku and being anointed by indigenous priests in Inka dress. These, however, are very much a new tradition— the Aymara New Year being not more than thirty years old in its current form—and the rituals enacted in Tiwanaku for Evo Morales were most certainly invented tradition. This is not to suggest they are somehow illegitimate or meaningless; they are not only legitimate but legitimating and have enormous and increasing significance for people. They are, however, new: Thirty years ago Tiwanaku was virtually ignored by all but the most politically radical Aymaras; now it attracts tens of thousands of people.

This new indigeneity invokes an often romanticized past and speaks most clearly to the urban populations, which are now the majority of Aymara speakers whose primary focus is not agriculture but city life. It is not surprising then that their sense of indigeneity is both more political and more concerned with contemporary urban issues than those of people who live in places such as Wila Kjarka. Wila Kjarka, as is by now clear, is not an isolated hamlet beyond the currents of modernity and change. The new indigenous reality is a world less concerned with agriculture and more directed to education and market economics and, consequently, the new indigenous consciousness is certainly arriving.

For me, the new indigeneity is most sharply symbolized in Evo Morales's suits. He certainly made headlines in Europe when, on his first state visit to Spain, he sported a simple colored-striped sweater. Was this the ignorance of an *indio* or the self-confidence of a new kind of indigenous politician? Whatever the reality of that event, Morales astutely played out the second of these scenarios, greatly improving the sales of these sweaters. In Bolivia, however, he soon became famous for his expensively designed suits, which were elegant and made of expensive fabric and include a piece of Andean textile. Some of my friends who admire Andean textiles lament the way these, sometimes antique, cloths are cut into pieces to furnish a suit. One could be tempted to read into this the violent appropriation of Andean culture for very contemporary ends with scant regard for the context and aesthetics of that culture. On a more positive note, however, Evo Morales has certainly made indigeneity elegant, stylish, and chic: something to be emulated rather than be ashamed of. On a political level, indigenous people all over Bolivia are increasingly confident in expressing their indigenous identity without fear of being labeled *indios*.

A very concrete example of this is given by the altiplano village of Khonkho, where I have been conducting fieldwork with the archaeologist John Janusek in recent years. Khonkho, following Tiwanaku, has created a new set of rituals around the celebration of the Aymara New Year, which involves, among other things, young men and women dancing in traditional homespun dress. This homespun cloth, or *bayeta,* is heavily associated with the hacienda era and has been a very clear indicator of one's status as an indian. Here in Khonkho, however, people were not only wearing it proudly in the fiesta but also for day-to-day wear because of its durability and warmth, as was explained to me. These New Year celebrations are also time for the election of the new *mallku,* the maximal leader of the set of *ayllu* communities. These elections are an assertion of independence from state-imposed municipal governments and a clear assertion of regional ethnic autonomy. This is but one example of how the new appreciation of indigenous culture has clear political consequences.

In Wila Kjarka, too, people are much more assertive about who they are, and most certainly optimistic about the future. Such self-confidence and pride were certainly not in evidence when I first arrived in Wila Kjarka twenty years ago when the future looked particularly bleak. Children spent a maximum of three years in school and families were still focused around the agricultural enterprise, even if it was also true that men had to spend several weeks a year in the mines or rice fields. In 1991 there was a crisis: A drought was threatening to destroy the year's crops, and there was even talk of abandoning the village en masse.

The concern was sharp and the drought was on everyone's minds. Teodosio decided he would need to conduct a rainmaking ritual. It emerged that this involved a select number of men going at night—the daylight and God's sphere being inimical to such activity—to a place called Wila Khota (the red lake or the blood lake). There they would take the "blood" of the achachilas and bring it back to the village. Everyone was anxious that Teodosio conduct the ritual, but he was clearly waiting for an auspicious time and had to select his men carefully or, rather, he had to divine the achachilas' will through reading coca leaves. I keenly wanted to go, but to my disappointment the achachilas did not concur with my enthusiasm, and when the time came I watched Teodosio and his five companions make their way up the mountain.

The whole community, every single person, including children, assembled in the plaza after nightfall and waited. It was a pleasant atmosphere: women on one side chatting to each other, men at a slight distance, and children running and laughing in the shadows and darkness. As is usually the case when the whole community assembles, there was a festive feeling but also a real sense that what was in the plaza was a *community* rather than simply a meeting of residents. We waited together, knowing that the future of Wila Kjarka depended on the rains.

After several hours Teodosio and his companions arrived. There was no fanfare but certainly an air of expectation. Teodosio took himself to the center of the plaza and began organizing his *misa*, his offering. The word *misa* in Aymara is a rephonologization of the Spanish word *mesa*, which means table—Aymara has three vowels, and many *e*'s in Spanish are pronounced as *i*'s. *Misa* in Spanish is also the word for *mass*, and this ritual offering has something of the sacramental as well. The *misa* was drawn out, and he also read coca leaves. Finally a sheep was brought and then blindfolded so that she would not see the approaching knife. I missed much of what Teodosio said, but he acknowledged the sheep for its sacrifice and directed his incantations to the achachilas, naming the peaks such as Illampu and Jankho Qullu as well as the achachilas of Wila Khota, and finally the achachilas of Wila Kjarka.

The sheep's throat was slit and its blood collected. Teodosio moved to the edge of the plaza with the blood in a bowl and, although I could not see well in the darkness and with people in front of me, it appeared as if he were casting the blood over the maize in the adjacent field. I felt a drop on my cheek and quickly wiped away the blood, but as I felt the liquid between my fingers it didn't seem like blood at all. More drops followed. It had begun to rain; and soon raindrops were falling all around us.

I was stunned and looked around me: People were pleased and animated but certainly not as surprised as I. I tried to look at Teodosio but could not properly make out his face in the darkness and could only imagine his satisfaction at his successful ritual. I cannot account for why it began to rain just then, perhaps Teodosio knew all along the rain was coming; I simply do not know. What was clear, however, was that the assembled community credited him with making it rain, and believed it was his offering that persuaded the achachilas to allow the rain to fall.

In 2008 I walked to Wila Khota with Teodosio's son—my friend Pastuku. It is a long walk, passing *Chullpa Patana,* the site of Inka ruins above community, and going up, up to about 4,800 meters, high above the road pass through the mountains. From here one has a commanding view of the valley and beyond, with Wila Kjarka barely visible in the distance and the Amazon basin in the background. This is the boundary between the provinces of Larecaja and Omasuyos, and if we were to have continued we would have left the valleys and descended onto the highland plain, the altiplano.

Wila Khota is in fact two lakes: a male lake and a female lake, thus confirming the principles of gender complementarity that animate the cosmos. Surrounded by echoing cliffs clad with ice, it is an eerie and unnerving place. Above the lakes there are a series of overhanging cliffs behind which are caves. I could immediately see why this was a sacred place: The altitude, the caves, the lakes, and the extraordinary geography made it an obvious place for the achachilas to dwell. As we approached I was surprised to see some children playing in the caves, and it became apparent they were tending their flocks of sheep below. Pastuku registered my surprise and explained: "Before, no children would have dared to come here; it is an enchanted place. In those days you would only come with a yatiri. Now, anyone can come." He continued to recount all the calamities that might befall someone who approached such an enchanted place without the proper preparation, and he himself seemed unclear as to whether these illnesses would genuinely befall people or whether it was just a belief.

It reminded me of when he told me that he no longer paid the achachilas in August. This was something everyone did, or at least said they did, when I first arrived in Wila Kjarka. There was no doubt: Not to pay the spirits would mean lost sheep and failed crops. Pastuku explained that one year he didn't pay and nothing happened. No calamity befell him, so he stopped paying. I began to ask people about their ritual offerings, and sure enough fewer and fewer people "pay" or do it more out of habit than conviction. Some people confessed somewhat sheepishly to me that they no longer did these things; others said simply that these were customs of the past; others still, said that the achachilas no longer listened. One young man said to me: "The achachilas are just dead (*Achachilanakax jiwjapxi*)." Another told me that they had simply disappeared, gone away forever (*chhakawayapxi*). What was recently religion—that is, firmly held beliefs—was passing into tradition or regarded as useless superstition.

As I spoke to more and more people a pattern emerged: The old people who had spent all their lives in an Aymara-speaking world still lived in a place where the mountains were alive, where ancestors spoke to them, and where the past was immediately before them. Younger people, people who when I first arrived held to these beliefs, were finding them increasingly irrelevant, and the much younger were not bothering at all.

When we returned to Wila Kjarka, I made a point of visiting Teodosio the following morning and talking to him about all this. By 2008 he was increasingly deaf, but he certainly still seemed to have all his mental faculties. He is the only person to live in a house with a thatched roof, everyone else having opted for the much easier to maintain corrugated iron. He welcomed me and then complained that insects had got into his sack of maize and it was almost all ruined. He made us coffee and we talked.

Teodosio still very much lives in an enchanted world where the rocks and streams speak and sing, where everything is alive; but he is clearly aware that his is a dwindling number and that the ways of the achachilas are falling into shadow. There was no doubt that he continued to be in high demand as a healer, his healing powers based on this enchanted world. People certainly believe in his healing powers even if they don't, apparently, believe in the source of these powers; and when Teodosio dies there will be no yatiri in Wila Kjarka or in any of the neighboring villages. It seems something of a contradiction that people can simultaneously believe and not believe. As a healer, Teodosio has an impressive reputation, but his clients are perhaps less concerned about the principles underpinning his medicine than the pragmatic desire to be cured. He still is known for his capacity to cure, but, perhaps rather like people who go to the doctor and are happy with the pills they get so long as they work, people are happy with Teodosio's invocations and medicines for the same reason.

Teodosio in 2008.

I must confess that my trip to Wila Khota had made me somewhat sad that this place no longer filled people with awe, that it had lost its magic, and it made me think—although not for the first time—about what the future held for Wila Kjarka. Teodosio talked to me about his grandchildren who spoke not a word of Aymara; he could not converse with them. I was surprised that this did not seem to bother him at all; he even smiled. "Now they can read and write," he said, "now they can be lawyers." To my greater surprise he did not seem to be terribly concerned that fewer and fewer people paid attention to the achachilas, although people still pay attention to the house gods, the *kunturmamanis*, much as they did before; it seems that the world of fields and animals is simply becoming less important, even as the household retains its importance, and perhaps this is simply a reflection that agriculture is much less at the center of family life and household reproduction than was previously the case. For Teodosio it seemed enough that the achachilas still spoke to him and, sure enough, there was no shortage of people who would visit him to have their coca leaves read.

When I asked him what would happen to Wila Kjarka when no one paid any attention to the achachilas, he replied simply, "There will be jaqi no more." That statement gave me more than simply pause. From a purely egocentric point of view, I have spent twenty years living and working with jaqi in a mountain village, but Teodosio was forcing me to face the fact that I had been observing the last years of their existence, at least in the way people such as he still understood the term. In retrospect, Teodosio is experiencing a *Götterdämmerung*—the twilight of the gods as they retreat into the darkness below and intervene less and less in the lives of humans. Wila Kjarkeños say more and more that the gods have left or no longer listen, and with that silence goes the vision of a world that was still very present in Wila Kjarka when I arrived in 1989.

When I saw Teodosio most recently in August 2011 he was living in a small windowless room near his son's house. I was told that he was stone deaf and totally senile (*q'alawa*). With "Hello Uncle" (the proper form of address for an older person in Wila Kjarka), I announced my presence. His gaunt face looked up. "It is good that you have come, *Wirajocha* [an old form of address for white people]. It has been ten years." I smiled. "No, not so many as ten years, Uncle, just two. And how old are you now, Uncle?" Of course, I knew the answer, "*Pataka* [one hundred]"; what else? Except that this time he really was very close to a hundred years old. Teodosio was deaf but not stone deaf, and we talked several times during that visit. He told me how people used to come far and wide to be healed by him, stories I had been told before, and he read my coca leaves. It was wonderful to see this dear old man still alive but sad that he seemed all alone, that his great-grandchildren mostly laughed at him if they paid him any attention at all, and that his bed was so high that if he got down he couldn't get back on. On more than one occasion I found him slumped over the bed, unable to get on, and wondered for how long he had been there.

By 2011 Teodosio was in clear decline, but the previous three or four years had brought some profound changes to Wila Kjarka. I always wake up before dawn as do most people in Wila Kjarka. I wake up to the sounds of the roosters crowing, the dogs barking, a burro braying, and a cell

Pastor Mendoza proudly showing his new crops to the
agroarchaeologist Alejandra Korstanje.

phone ringing in high tones. The sound of a phone is as basic and ubiqui-
tous as the cluck of a chicken.

In 2008 one truck per month went to the village, a handful of people
had cell phones, and people were beginning to take advantage of the new
NGO-sponsored irrigation schemes. Three years later everyone, but everyone, seemed to have cell phones and used them all the time; three
trucks *a day* went to Wila Kjarka; and in 2010 electricity arrived. These
three things have had an enormous impact on life in the village. Cell
phones make it possible for people to communicate with husbands, sons,
and daughters when they migrate temporarily for a few weeks or even
when they are living in Buenos Aires or São Paulo. Not only can people
keep in touch over long distances, but they don't have to walk three hours
to the next village to see how a daughter is doing. The road enables people
to bring bricks, and there are several new houses with many rooms and
balconies, usually painted in bright colors.

The road and the irrigation enable people to produce more and better
crops and get them to market easily. When I first arrived in Wila Kjarka it
was virtually unheard of for anyone to actually *sell* their crops. They might
exchange them with highlanders for llama products and freeze-dried

potatoes, but there was little point in taking them to market because it was difficult to do and the prices they received were very low. In those days people produced potatoes, maize, and barley and very little else. Now they grow lettuce, carrots, peas, herbs, and flowers, all of which they can sell easily in the Achacachi market (since they tend to avoid Sorata). New irrigation means that they cultivate the land at the very lowest reaches of their community, the very fertile alluvial plain. Here they grow tropical fruits, and in 2011 everyone seemed to be talking with great excitement about Estanislao's banana tree. It was rather difficult to see from any distance, but people were putting in their labor, enthusiasm, and aspirations into agriculture. Young men are returning after military service to settle down, and they are moving into new houses with multiple rooms, which afford young couples some privacy hitherto virtually impossible to achieve.

And there is money—money in peas and flowers and carrots. And wage migration is both easier and better remunerated. In 2011 I saw things in Wila Kjarka I had never seen there before: I saw a bicycle, bras on washing lines, DVD players, a satellite dish (unconnected), gas cookers actually connected to gas, a Monopoly set (unopened), and a host of other consumer items. I saw babies in baby clothes, babies in little clean socks, and I just marveled at the effort it must take to keep those little socks clean. No diapers, however, not yet. All of these things mean that Wila Kjarka is changing very rapidly; it also means that life in Wila Kjarka can be pretty good and that there is not an enormous gulf between life in the city and the village. In fact, in many respects, life in Wila Kjarka is better; certainly the diet there is far better than most people get in urban areas.

There is still no apprentice yatiri in Wila Kjarka, but in that August 2011 trip I bumped into an old friend from Wila Kjarka in Sorata, Herculiano. He had left the village some years ago and was now fairly permanently settled in town. For many years he has worked as a key cutter, but this year he surprised me by announcing a new profession. "I am a shaman now!" "I didn't know you were interested in that." I replied. "Oh yes, my grandfather taught me that. He did it secretly. No one in Wila Kjarka knows anything about this. I'm in the union!" The thought of a yatiri's union struck me as a little odd, but he showed me photographs of his union buddies dressed in identical hats, ponchos, and scarves. He told me about psychotherapy, showed me the books he was reading about healing, and read my fortune using playing cards. "I can do this with American cards too, you know!" (He was using the simpler and quite different Spanish deck.)

Herculiano, a modern yatiri.

Unlike Teodosio, Herculiano was not appointed by the gods with a lightning bolt, and his legitimacy comes from his union membership, his official status. Herculiano told me how everything had changed with Evo Morales and that he did not allow the Christians to oppress practitioners of traditional medicine. "It has all been released," he said. This is a very different shamanism, however, from that practiced by Teodosio. Teodosio never donned a special poncho or had a union card and certainly didn't read books about psychotherapy. Much of what Herculiano was talking to me about seemed to be a combination of traditional beliefs and New Age mysticism. Perhaps this is simply how shamanism becomes modern and speaks to a mobile generation with cell phones and satellite dishes.

One of the other changes that hit me personally was related to the fact that there was regular transportation between the main road and the village. In 2011, as always, I arrived with a pack full of gifts and made my way up the mountain, on this occasion accompanied by my son, Tarik, and my archaeologist friend Alejandra Korstanje. I explained to both of them the importance of white people carrying their own stuff up the mountain, and so they all carried their packs, too. I was greeted as always, with the Wila Kjarkeños marveling at my having walked up the mountain with a pack, except this time there was a difference: "Hey, you came up the mountain with all that weight? Why didn't you just take the truck? Didn't you know there was a truck? Hey! He *walked* up the mountain [laughter]. He didn't know he didn't have to walk! He walked!" Now my noble efforts of walking up the mountain laden with gifts were simply incomprehensible and frankly, rather daft.

There was a time when I wondered if anyone would be living in Wila Kjarka in twenty years' time; now I am sure. They will speak Aymara and many of them will be the same people I know today; but it will be a very different place. It may indeed be a much better place, since the future for indigenous people in Bolivia is brighter now than it has been for five centuries, and it is very hard to imagine that the Morales presidency will not have an effect on Bolivian politics for several generations to come. It is inconceivable that indigenous people will be taken for granted politically they way they were for much of the twentieth century. There is no doubt that the people of Wila Kjarka are looking to a brighter future, when they will have better communications, better education, and a higher standard of living. Whereas when I first arrived in the community the future looked grim, now people are much more optimistic.

The future of Wila Kjarka will not, however, have much room, it seems, for achachilas and the other spirits that inhabit the mountains, fields, and streams. The rituals that bind people together as a community—and as a community with the achachilas—will become fewer, and already many people are losing their sense of intimacy with the past that older generations have. Wila Kjarka may become an even more prosperous and healthier place, but Teodosio is surely right: Even as the politics of indigeneity is in ascendance, it is eclipsing the ways of people who are jaqi; ironically the hegemony of the new indigenous identity may not only do away with the colonial discourses that relegate people to the status of indian but it may also take with it the lifeways of people who are jaqi. It may very well be the case that "there will be people no more."

In September 2012, I received news of the death of Teodosio Condori. He was, of course, one hundred years old.

NOTES

INTRODUCTION

1 For a very good summary and discussion of the debates surrounding the ethnic versus class differences between indians and *mestizos* (and the degree to which the one constitutes the other), see Gose (1994: 16–28).

2 Interview with author, April 15, 2005.

3 This is very different from *indigenismo* of the first half of the twentieth century, which grew out of the Mexican Revolution and sought to valorize indigenous culture but principally that of the past. *Indigenismo* was a discourse principally espoused by mestizos and, in many cases, was actively opposed to the cultures and lifeways of contemporary indians. See Brading (1988). *Indigenismo* can be understood as part of the process whereby the rising Latin American elites felt comfortable with their own mixed heritage and as an ideology of engagement with the creole landowning oligarchy. What is absolutely clear is that *indigenismo* is about a mixed heritage, not an indigenous one: The mestizo is the iconic citizen. Contemporary indigenism, conversely, presents the indigenous person as the iconic citizen. See Brading (1988).

4 Interview with author translated from Aymara.

5 Tupak Katari was the indian leader who, along with his partner Bartolina Sisa, almost successfully led a revolt against the Spanish in the late eighteenth century. They are both important contemporary icons of indigenous resistance. He was captured and quartered by the Spanish in 1781, and his body parts, it is believed, were buried far

apart. Many people today hold that these body parts are growing and will eventually rejoin in Tupak Katari's second coming and thus fulfill the prophecy in his dying words: "Nayawa jiwtxa, nayjarusti waranqa waranqaranakawa kutanïpxa [I die, but I shall return tomorrow as thousands and thousands]."

6 A suspicion confirmed in 2011 by the archaeologist Alejandra Korstanje.

7 I learned a lot from this woman in the one year I worked for her, mostly how not to treat people.

CHAPTER ONE

1 A substantial proportion of the fifteenth-century population of Seville was African, and it was absorbed into the general population over time.

2 Pedro de Alvarado was known for his brutality toward indians, which was considered extreme even for the period. The Lienzo de Quauhquechollan shows that he dispatched indians by means of hanging, burning, and throwing them to the dogs (Asselbergs 2004). His marriage to noblewoman Doña Francisca de la Cueva and, after her death, to her sister Beatriz, produced no children, but he recognized three children with his partner of many years, Luisa de Tlaxcala, an indian noblewoman (also known as Xicoténcatl). It was these children who he took to court to be declared Spaniards.

3 The siege of Sorata took place during one of the many occasions in recent decades in which tensions were high. The country mobilized around a new constitution, among other things, in order to address ethnic inequalities, and the town of Sorata was besieged for several weeks—that is, the main road in and out was blockaded. Indians could, of course, walk in and out, but the handful of white and mestizo residents, along with foreign tourists, were stuck. It took an army convoy to "liberate" the town—a convoy that was visible for miles and was an easy target for sharpshooters. Wila Kjarkeños played no part in the siege and simply watched it all from a comfortable distance.

4 There is also a road from Sorata to San Pedro, which is longer than the footpath but which is usually suitable for a four-wheel-drive car for most of the year. The priest arrives by car.

5 I was also told this to be the case for another mountain achachila, Illimani. Illimani is a mountain 6,460 meters high, very near La Paz. The idea of orange trees on a mountain top otherwise covered by permanent snow and ice indicates a truly miraculous place. These gold crosses are surrounded by spells, which prevents anyone from reaching the summit. Illampu is regularly climbed, but Wila Kjarkeños refuse to believe this. "If anyone tries, the mountain will take their life away." Sure enough, every now and again someone dies on the mountain and this is seen as confirmation. I never told anyone in Wila Kjarka that I myself had been up Illampu, but I did ask Zenobio once, if no one has been up there, how anyone knew about the gold cross and orange trees. He didn't miss a beat: "You can see them from an airplane, of course." And that was the end of that conversation.

6 I use the term *autochthonous* here not just as a synonym of indigenous but to indicate that it relates to spirits that are understood to come out of the earth, a literal translation of *autochthonous*.

CHAPTER TWO

1 I am very grateful to her for this crash course in archaeological vision; it was almost as if she had given me a special set of glasses, for all of a sudden I was able to see landscapes from an entirely different perspective. I could distinguish different kinds of stonework, depressions became obvious as burial sites, raised areas became clearly man-made platforms, and I was able to distinguish ancient terracing from more modern forms. Alejandra also demonstrated extraordinary ethnographic skills and quickly developed a warm rapport with people in Wila Kjarka, including the aged Francisca, with whom she shared no language.

2 Espinoza (1980) suggests that Pukina was, in fact, Tiwanaku's primary language.

3 *Petición de los principales yungas de Hilabaya,* Sorata, September 19, 1618, in Archivo Nacional de Bolivia, Sucre, quoted in Saignes (1986: 313).

4 *"Es cierto que la poblaçon de esta provincia del Arecaxa desde el tiempo del Ynga siempre fue y a sido con dhos yndios mitimaes porque berificado no se hallaron yndios que se pueda dezir naturales desta tierra y caso negado que aia algunos han de ser muy pocos en numero y naturaleça.*

  Somos mitimaes puestos por los abuelos y bisabuelos de los yngas ultimos y de generacion en generacion y naciendo y criando en dhos valles calientes entre los yungas naturales dellos" (Saignes 1985: 97).

5 Archivo de La Paz: ALP.

6 Visita de Gerónimo Luis de Cabrera, Archivo de La Paz, 1656–58.

7 The capital of the canton Ilabaya, which includes Wila Kjarka.

8 *". . . caçiques e yndios particulares las chacras tierras y estançias que el general Don Geronimo Luis de cabrera les restituyo a su comun a si a españoles como otras misturas e yndios de diferentes provinçias quitando este bien que se les a hecho a los mismos naturales y mitimaes de dicho pueblo asi los presentes ahuyentandolos como a lo de ausentes destituyandolos de una rreduçion cosa de que tanto se deve rremediar y solisitar por todos medios segun su magestad se sirve mandarlo en orden a mi conservacion y de sus mugeres hijos y familias y que no descaescan las Reales tasas y tributos."* Archivo de La Paz: ALP/ GLC I 1660 c.1–D.19

9 See Albó (1979) for an account of the parallel process in the neighboring area of Omasuyos. Some landowners had land in both areas.

10 The word *chullpa* also refers to pre-Conquest tombs, often large towers, with windows to the east, where the dead were mummified, resembling burnt corpses.

11 For a discussion of foxes and other animals in Andean storytelling, see Allen (2011).

12 *Utnakapana jiwaraskix pachpankaskiw sarakisa jaqhipa manqhan jakaspachay.*

13 *Ukjaxa nanakaxa akhama chikusipxkpachataya, khayamakisipxkpachathwa jisk itakisipxkpachathwa.*

CHAPTER THREE

1 See, for example, Adolfo Gilly (2005); James Dunkerley (2007); Forrest Hylton and Sinclair Thomson (2007).

2 *Censo Nacional 2001,* www.ine.gov.bo.

3 Under prerevolution conditions, hacienda indians were tied to the land and could not travel without permission from the hacendado or his representative. Attempts to set up schools for indians were regularly met with repression, imprisonment, and violence.

4 Condarco Morales (1982); Ticona and Albó (1997); and more generally for the Achacachi area, Albó (1979).

5 This is apparently not always the case, Stobart (2006).

6 In practice, people rarely die in the battle itself but later from internal bleeding or are killed when separated from the larger group.

7 Archivo de la Reforma Agraria, Decreto Supremo, No. 2968, 24-2-55, p. 57.

8 For an excellent discussion on numbers and the ordering of narratives, see Allen 2011, where she argues that the number three in Andean stories indexes social order and the organization of society (p. 92).

9 The hanging and burning in 2004 of the mayor of Ayo Ayo, accused of embezzling community funds, has brought the issue of community justice and violence in the Andes to the fore: Weber (2005); see also Ansión (1989) and Starn (1999).

10 Xavier Albó, personal communication, June 2007.

11 For an Australian example, see Morphy and Morphy (1984).

12 Kimberly Theidon (2003) has observed that the peasants of the Alturas de Huanta in Peru erase memories of personal humiliation during the years of civil war in the 1990s and recount, instead, the heroic exploits of village resistance groups (*rondas campesinas*).

13 See also Portelli (1991).

CHAPTER FOUR

1 By my calculations the child mortality in Wila Kjarka (that is, up to five years of age) is 26 percent. The figure may actually be higher as neonatal deaths (before the first week) are almost never recorded or indeed remembered as live births. This figure was arrived at by comparing household birth and death rates for the previous five years. There is almost certainly an undercount in the reported births as well as deaths, especially with the deaths of neonates. In a number of cases there was a dispute in the family as to how many children had been born. Although I attempted to account for this, the figure of 26 percent must be taken as a conservative estimate. This figure is, however, comparable to data collected by health workers working in rural-highland Bolivia, although one must presume they face similar problems in counting.

According to the 1994 census (Bolivia, INE 1994), the data for which were collected in the year of Encarnación's death, the maternal mortality rate was 929 per 100,000 in the altiplano; that is, virtually 1 percent per birth. This is very high by international standards (Bradby 2001). It is difficult to see how reliable statistics could be collected for places such as Wila Kjarka, where deaths are generally not reported and communication is more difficult.

2 See also Harvey (1991: 2).

3 I was told by some informants that if conception occurs when one or both of the couple is drunk, a miscarriage or malformation occurs. Others, however, denied the

significance of sobriety in conception. Harvey (1987: 187) also reports the belief that deformed children are the result of a drunken conception for Ocongate in Peru.

4 *Akakama ukat chhu akat qachit . . . jall ukhamaki.*

5 *Yawrinxta junt'u parisa wilampi may lluchunta qala.*

6 *Wawaxa k'irt'añaya, allitattawayxchispaxaya.*

7 *Yaqhipaxa parli, k'umischixaya, tuqisiya yaqhipaxa ukataya amukisipxkixa.*

8 *Nayasa wali llakistha, jiwarxaspana, taqpachani jiwaraspana jisthwa, kulirayituwa, kulirayasiwa, yuqallkamakiwa nayanxa, nuwasipxi wali, nuwasi wali.*

9 *Juchaw. Rayux altut q'ixu q'ixu; rayu purxaspa ukaw. Ukata uka rayuxa jaqiru khatatiri ch'akasaruw man amp ak janchinakaru akanakkaru manti. Ukhat q'äl ukhama utjiw.*

10 *Ikisksnaya, jumataya pendxi ukaxa. Amor lurañamasa jani lurañamasa.*

11 See Harris (1980).

12 In Kaata, Bastien notes that the child is actually daubed with salt on the tongue (Bastien 1978: 95).

13 This is in sharp contrast to other areas of the Andes, in Bolivia as well as in Peru, where women chew regularly. See, for example, works by Alison Spedding (1989) and Catherine Allen (1986).

14 See, for example, Harris (1978).

15 An alternative translation would be: "He captured us"; *apthaphaña* is the verb used by older people when they offer the account of how young men "captured" their prospective wives.

16 *Khuri sirkankanaw ukaw chixthapayapxitu munkir jan murkiri.*

17 *Nayaxa aka awatisina sarasina ukhamp parlthapipxta jupampi ukat parlthapisina chixjapxta wawan jikjatastwa ukhama.*

18 *Wal ukat urasa jachta ch'usa ch'amankan chikapata jichax apawayachayitu.*

19 Denise Arnold has edited two substantial volumes on kinship and gender in the Andes (1997, 1998). Many of the essays provide detailed discussions about relations between the genders, but none discusses affection or love.

20 My informants were not, sadly, adolescents at the time they spoke to me. Adolescents are a somewhat anomalous group socially and are rather marginalized until they marry. My accounts, therefore, come from people who were telling me about their (sometimes recent) youth rather than directly from adolescents themselves.

CHAPTER FIVE

1 *Kharisiri* is an Aymara word that means "slaughterer." The fat stealer is also known in Peru as the *ñakaq* or *pishtaco*, which also means "slaughterer" in Quechua. In southern Bolivia, the term *lik'ichiri* is more widely used and means "fat maker" in Aymara, and one also sometimes hears *kharikhari*, which means "cutter." For simplicity's sake, I shall refer to the fat stealer only as *kharisiri*, even though it appears in the literature under these other names.

2 Ansión (1989); Bellier and Hocquenghem (1991); Gose (1986b); Morote Best (1951); Paredes (1975); Rivière (1991); Salazar (1991); Wachtel (1994); Weismantel (1997, 2001), among others.

3 Abercrombie (1998: 405) and Wachtel (1994: 98) also report that some kharisiris also have a taste for blood. Kharisiris are far more commonly associated with the

stealing of fat, and it may well be that the blood theme may have something to do with exposure to more Western ideas of what constitutes the life source.

4 Aymara: *tisiq usu.*

5 *Jiwasjamarakiw sarnaqaskaraki yap luraski.*

6 *Janiw jaq yatkiti lastimaki.*

7 To my knowledge, only Manya (1969: 136), with data from Cuzco and Puno in Peru, has published an account of how one might protect oneself from a kharisiri, but I have come across no account that describes a means of curing the victim once afflicted. Manya cites three ways of protecting oneself, although the origins of this information are unclear. These are: to chew *chancaca* (honey mass used in the preparation of maize beer); to show a clove of garlic pierced with a needle; and to eat earth. Manya makes no suggestion why these might be effective, although one might suppose that the first and last of these may have some relation to the earth and mountain spirits. The use of garlic, of course, is reminiscent of European tales of vampires and may be influenced by these.

8 According to the Diccionario de Autoridades of 1737, the word *sebo* means: "La grasa dura y sólida que se arranca de los lomos de algunos animales secos y terrestres como carnero, vaca etc., la cual no tiene venas ni arterias y es menester ponerla al fuego para derretirla, y se cuaja y endurece apartada de él." I am grateful to Edwin Williamson for directing me to this reference.

9 Ansión and Sifuentes suggest that the fear of arbitrary violence is now personified in the figure of the thug (*ratero*) or the urban terrorist who, in contrast to the kharisiri, is a very real figure indeed.

10 Although, of course, new forms of collective identity naturally develop. See, for example, Ströbele-Gregor (1993).

11 The tragic case documented by Degregori (1989) of the murder of a man because he was an outsider, a trader (*comerciante*), and did not speak Quechua, underlines the q'ara identity of the kharisiri as a nonindian whose social relations are mediated by short-term financial exchanges of the market.

CHAPTER SIX

1 That is, he entered teacher-training college several years after the enactment of the education reform and, indeed, most of his schooling would have taken place after 1994.

2 In the Andes, few scholars have explicitly explored issues of race and racism in education. Paul Cliche and Fernando García (1995) explore some aspects of discrimination against indian pupils in Ecuador, although chiefly in the context in which indians are recent migrants to towns. There are no studies that look at the issue of racism in schools where indian pupils predominate and where teachers share the same ethnic background as their pupils. There is, however, considerable research on bilingual education (e.g., Albó 1995; Arnold and Yapita 2000; García 2005; Hornberger 2000; Moya 1991), which touches on related themes such as intercultural education and the low value given to indian culture. Bilingual education has been seen as a means of restoring and strengthening indian culture (Hornberger 1994), but insufficient attention has been given to the teacher's role, not only in delivering bilingual

education, but in teaching in an educational context that devalues pupils' culture and way of life.

3 This idea of a new national (mixed) race has its roots in the Mexican Revolution, which posited a cosmic race (Vasconcelos 1961). In Bolivia, Alcides Arguedas (1919) coined the phrase the "bronze race" to describe what he hoped would be a new Bolivian identity, neither European nor indigenous but a vibrant mixture of both. This movement was espoused by the rising middle classes, including middle-ranking officers. One of its implications, however, was the erasure of contemporary indians, who were deemed anachronistic (Brading 1988).

4 This was not the case in the recent past, when everyone who lived in small towns spoke either Quechua or Aymara, whatever their descent, partly because they were obliged to speak to their monolingual customers, servants, nannies, and so forth.

5 For a discussion of a very similar process in Ecuador, see Radcliffe and Westwood (1996).

6 During the 1950s, '60s, and '70s, the mestizo and creole teachers from Sorata (two of whom I have met) were fluent in Aymara, even if it was not their mother tongue. Wila Kjarka has always had teachers who could speak Aymara; the issue is whether they speak it in the classroom.

7 On a different occasion the same teacher complained to me of the poor quality of his shoes, which barely lasted a year in the mountainous environment.

8 *El idioma puede desaparecer; a medida que va avanzando la ciencia se va extendiendo el castellano en nuestro territorio.*

9 Mama, is a formal form of address in Aymara for a mature woman. In Spanish, however, to call someone a *mamita*, in the diminutive, is clearly condescending.

10 In some parts of Bolivia, this day is known as the *Día del campesino*, with *campesino* being the word for *peasant* and a widespread euphemism for *indian*. I never heard the celebration referred to as the *Día del campesino* in Wila Kjarka or environs. Whether because this aspect of political correctness never reached the region or, rather, because the term *indio* was positively reappropriated, I cannot say with confidence, although I rather suspect the former.

11 I was later asked to join the dignitaries (the doctor and health workers from the town and high-ranking teachers) to observe the parade. The dignitaries sit under a large Bolivian flag, and each community marches by, saluting the flag and those seated beneath it. I declined the invitation and stayed with my companions.

CHAPTER SEVEN

1 For a more detailed account of the tasks men and women undertake in Wila Kjarka, see Canessa (1997).

2 Benjamin Orlove (1998) offers a detailed analysis of how relations between indians and mestizos in the area around Puno, Peru, are partly mediated through earth in its various forms.

3 See also Gill (1997: 536).

4 For a discussion on masculinity and citizenship, see Fraser (1991: 125). For a complementary analysis of masculinity and indian men in Guatemala, see Nelson (1999).

5 "Es un requisito para poder ejercer plenamente la ciudadanía." *La Estrella del Oriente*, January 9, 2012.

6 *Mä ordena utji boliviana; ma deberaj phuqañataki.*

7 *Wajchasthxaya, ukhama jisk'itanakakxaya apanukuwayapxchituxa ukata tayka jani uskuña puyrxitutixa, qullqixaya.*

8 *Mä gramu … mä ratuki, mä ora. Arumpaqari pisqha gram munapxi.*

9 *Wali quri purakawa. Qur apanim siyast mä rat churasaki.*

10 This is approximately 10 US cents at the current (2012) exchange rate. This is an absurdly small amount and cannot be taken literally, but, suffice it to say, my friend was impressing upon me that conscripts earn very little money.

11 See, for example, Plácido (1999).

12 See, for example, Wright (1990) and Freyre (1946).

13 See, for example, Stepan (1991: 93).

14 This creole prerogative on the bodies of indian women is by no means exclusively an Andean phenomenon (see, e.g., Nelson 1999: 221).

15 Indigenous Andeans are not particularly hirsute, and there is a family in Wila Kjarka for which it is known that the women are naturally *jan tarwani*. Discussions about the women of this family occasion adolescent giggling in middle-aged men.

16 This debate was conducted in Valladolid in 1550–51 at the behest of King Charles V. It was here that Sepúlveda put forward the idea that indians were "natural slaves" and, rather like women, needed the rule of Christian men to fulfill themselves; it was, indeed, in their nature to be ruled.

17 See also Arnold (2006).

18 See, for example, the work of Stephenson (1999), Van Vleet (2005), and Weismantel (2001).

19 *Umta, uka nuwasiripxta, ya chaxwaxphiritu. Ukhamanaya.*

20 *Janiwa ukana phinq'asiñaxa utjkiti, pantalunankamakiwa warminakaxa.*

21 For discussions on domestic violence in the Andes, see Allen (1988), Harris (1994), Harvey (1994), Millones and Pratt (1980), and Van Vleet (2002).

22 This is something that has been observed by other scholars, such as Harris (1994), Harvey (1994), and Van Vleet (2002).

CHAPTER EIGHT

1 I am grateful to Lucinda Platt for her help with the translation from Latin. Montrose, however, has a slightly different translation: "Americus rediscovers America; he called her once and thenceforth she was always awake" (1991: 4). De la Guerra, in turn, translates the caption as "Amerigo redescubre América, A partir de entonces ella siempre más fue despertada por este nombre": "Amerigo rediscovers America, since then she was always awakened by this name."

2 But the indian woman, however, is displaced from his political narrative (see Stephenson 2003: 159). She appears only as a victim and the unwilling bearer of the children of creoles. She is "an open wound that breaks the soul" (1969: 129), whose life is miserable toil: "She procreates and works, works and procreates. That is the indian woman" (129).

3 *Domingo de Tentación*, or Temptation Sunday, is the first Sunday after Ash Wednesday, when the faithful reflect on Jesus's temptation by Satan in the desert.

4 I am grateful to Danielle Kurin for directing me to the song by Wendy Sulca. http://www.youtube.com/watch?v=693m7iCh-TE.

5 See interview with *Las Chicas* on their website: http://laschicasterremoto.multiply .com/. Last accessed on October 24, 2010. I am particularly grateful to Rebecca Bria for suggesting I explore modern huayno videos and the music and videos of *Las Chicas Terremoto del Folklore* in particular.

6 See Kempadoo (2003), Meisch (1995), and Zinovieff (1991) for similar phenomena in the Caribbean, Ecuador, and Greece. In these cases the women in point are foreign "gringas" and do not pose quite the same challenges to social mores.

7 "Ustedes compañeras y compañeros tienen que explicar, orientar a los compañeros indígenas, el propio alcalde está movilizado, para convencerlos y que no se opongan," dijo.

   Luego, agregó: "Si yo tuviera tiempo, iría a enamorar a las compañeras yuracarés y convencerlas de que no se opongan; así que, jóvenes, tienen instrucciones del Presidente de conquistar a las compañeras yuracarés trinitarias para que no se opongan a la construcción del camino." Enseguida consultó: "¿Aprobado?" y se escucharon aplausos del público. Willy Chipana, *La Razón*. August 1, 2011. http://www2.la -razon.com/version.php?ArticleId=134806&EditionId=2608.

8 There are also reports of women being raped (Ströbele-Gregor 2011: 80).

9 For a discussion of the organizational strength and determination of indigenous women within the Constituent Assembly see Rousseau (2011).

10 Pamela Calla has worked extensively on racism and she was, until recently, director of the Observatorio de Racismo en Bolivia based in the Universidad de la Cordillera (La Paz). My description of the events in Sucre draws heavily on her work.

11 *India cállate, mientras no hables castellano fuera de aquí.*

12 *¿Por qué vienen si no pueden hablar civilizadamente?*

13 See, for example, http://www.mujerescreando.org/pag/articulos/2010/miss/digni dadmujeres.htm.

14 From "Cosificar a las mujeres: una política municipal" by María Galindo and Helen Álvarez, *Mujeres Creando,* http://www.mujerescreando.org/index2.htm. Accessed August 25, 2010.

15 I am indebted to the journalist Pablo Estafanoni (pers. comm.) for these quotes.

16 In the words of Félix Patzi, recently Minister for Education: "Lo más importante es no negar la identidad indígena y originaria que tienen todos los bolivianos . . . Durante 514 años nos negaron como civilización, no fue tomada en cuenta la mayoría poblacional y si últimamente fue tomado en cuenta como folklore, como museo y como arte, pero no como civilización viva, por lo tanto, hablar de descolonización es hablar de la civilización contemporánea indígena." *Los Tiempos,* March 11, 2006.

REFERENCES

Abercrombie, Thomas. 1986. *The Politics of Sacrifice: An Aymara Cosmology in Action.* Chicago: University of Chicago Press.

———. 1991. "To Be Indian, to Be Bolivian." In Greg Urban and Noel Scherzer, eds., *Nation-States and Indians in Latin America.* Austin: University of Texas Press.

———. 1998. *Pathways of Memory and Power: Ethnography and History among an Andean People.* Madison: University of Wisconsin Press.

Absi, Pascale. 2010. "La professionnalisation de la prostitution: Le travail des femmes (aussi) en question." *L'homme et la société* (176–77): 193–212.

Albarracín Jordán, Juan, and James Mathews. 1990. *Asentamientos prehispánicos del Valle de Tiwanaku,* Vol. 1. La Paz: CIMA.

Alberti, G., and E. Mayer, eds. 1974. *Reciprocidad e intercambio en los Andes peruanos.* Lima: Instituto de Estudios Peruanos.

Albó, Xavier. 1975. *La Paradoja Aymara: Solidaridad y Faccionalismo.* La Paz: CIPCA.

———. 1979. *Achacachi: Medio Siglo de Lucha Campesina.* La Paz: CIPCA.

———. 1980. *Lengua y Sociedad en Bolivia 1976.* La Paz: Instituto Nacional de Estadística.

———. 1985. *Desafíos de la Solidaridad Aymara.* La Paz: CIPCA.

———. 1987. "From MNRistas to Kataristas to Katari." In S. Stern, ed., *Resistance, Rebellion and Consciousness in the Andean Peasant World,* 379–419. Madison: University of Wisconsin Press.

———. 1991. "El retorno del indio." *Revista Andina* 9 (2): 299–345.

———. 1995. "And from Kataristas to MNRistas? The Surprising and Bold Alliance between Aymaras and Neoliberals in Bolivia." In D. van Cott, ed., *Indigenous Peoples and Democracy in Latin America*. New York: Inter-American Dialogue.

Albó, Xavier, Tomás Greaves, and Godofredo Sandoval. 1983. *Chukiyawu, La cara aymara de La Paz: Vol III; Cabalgando entre dos mundos*. La Paz: CIPCA.

Alexander, R. 1982. *Bolivia: Past, Present and Future of Its Politics*. New York: Prager.

Allen, Catherine. 1982. "Body and Soul in Quechua Thought." *Journal of Latin American Lore* 8 (2): 179–96.

———. 1988. *The Hold Life Has: Coca and Cultural Identity in an Andean Community*. Washington D.C.: Smithsonian Institution Press.

———. 2011. *Foxboy: Intimacy and Aesthetics in Andean Stories*. Austin: University of Texas Press.

Anderson, Benedict. 1983. *Imagined Communities: Reflections on the Origins and Spread of Nationalism*. London: Verso.

Ansión, Juan, ed. 1989. *Pishtacos: de verdugos a sacaojos*. Lima: Tarea.

Ansión, Juan, and Eudosio Sifuentes. 1989. "La imagen popular de la violencia, a través de los relatos de degolladores." In J. Ansión, ed., *Pishtacos: de verdugos a sacaojos*, 61–108. Lima: Tarea.

Arguedas, Alcides. 1919. *La raza de bronce*. La Paz: González y Medina.

Arnold, Denise. 1988. "Matrilineal Practice in a Patrilineal Setting: Rituals and Metaphors of Kinship in an Andean Ayllu." Doctoral thesis, University of London.

———, ed. 1997. *Más allá del silencio: Las fronteras de género en los Andes*. Volume I of *Parentesco y género en los Andes*. La Paz: CIASE/ILCA.

———, ed. 1998. *Gente de carne y hueso: Las tramas de parentesco en los Andes*. Volume II of *Parentesco y género en los Andes*. La Paz: CIASE/ILCA.

———. 2006. *The Metamorphosis of Heads: Textual Struggles, Education and Land in the Andes*. Pittsburgh: Pittsburgh University Press.

Arnold, Denise, and Juan de Dios Yapita. 1992. *Hacia un orden de las cosas andinas*. La Paz: Hisbol.

———. 2000. *El rincón de las cabezas: Luchas textuales, educación y tierras en los Andes*. La Paz: UMSA and ILCA.

Arnold, Denise, Juan de Dios Yapita, and R. López. 1999. "Leer y escribir en aymara bajo la Reforma." *T'inkasos* 2 (3): 103–15.

Asselbergs, Florine. 2004. *Conquered Conquistadors: The Lienzo de Quauhquechollan; A Nahua Vision of the Conquest of Guatemala*. Boulder: University Press of Colorado.

Athey, Stephanie, and Daniel Cooper Alarcón. 1993. "Oroonoko's Gendered Economies of Honor/Horror: Reframing Colonial Discourse Studies in the Americas." *American Literature* 65 (3): 415–43.

Babb, Florence. 2011. *The Tourism Encounter: Fashioning Latin American Nations and Histories*. Stanford: Stanford University Press.

Barragán Romano, Rossana. 1999. *Indios, mujeres y ciudadanos: Legislación y ejercicio de la ciudadanía en Bolivia (Siglo XIX)*. La Paz: Fundación Diálogo.

Bastien, Joseph. 1978. *Mountain of the Condor*. St. Paul, MN: West.

———. 1985. "Qollahuaya-Andean Body Concepts: A Topographical-Hydraulic Model of Physiology." *American Anthropologist* 87: 595–611.

Baud, Michiel. 2009. "Indigenous Politics and the State: The Andean Highlands in the Nineteenth and Twentieth Centuries." In Edward F. Fischer, ed., *Indigenous Peoples, Civil Society, and the Neo-Liberal State in Latin America*. New York and Oxford: Berghahn.

Bellier, Irene, and Anne Marie Hocquenghem. 1991. "De los Andes a la Amazonía: Una representación evolutiva del 'otro.' " *Bulletin de l'Institute Français d'Études Andines* 20 (1): 41–59.

Bigenho, Michelle. 2002. *Sounding Indigenous: Authenticity in Bolivian Music Performance*. Basingstoke, UK: Palgrave Macmillan.

———. 2012. *Intimate Distance: Andean Music in Japan*. Durham, NC: Duke University Press.

Bloch, Maurice. 1992. "Birth and the Beginning of Social Life among the Zafiminary of Madagascar." In Göran Aijmer, ed., *Coming into Existence: Births and Metaphors of Birth*. Göteborg: IASSA.

Bloch, Maurice, and Stephen Guggenheim. 1981. "Compadrazgo, Baptism and the Symbolism of a Second Birth." *Man* 16 (3): 376–86.

Blom, Ida, Karen Hagemann, and Catherine Hall, eds. 2000. *Gendered Nations: Nationalisms and Gender Order in the Long Nineteenth Century*. Oxford: Berg.

Bourdieu, Pierre, and Jean Claude Passeron. 1970. *La Reproduction: Éléments pour une théorie du système d'enseignement*. Paris: Éditions de Minuit.

Bouysse-Cassagne, Thérèse, and Olivia Harris. 1987. "Pacha: En torno al pensamiento Aymara." In T. Bouysse-Cassagne, O. Harris, T. Platt, and V. Cereceda, eds., *Tres reflexiones sobre el pensamiento andino*, 11–60. La Paz: HISBOL.

Bradby, Barbara. 1998. "Like a Video: The Sexualisation of Childbirth in Bolivia." *Reproductive Health Matters* 6 (12): 50–56.

———. 2002. "Local Knowledge in Health: The Case of Andean Midwifery." In Henry Stobart and Rosaleen Howard, eds., *Knowledge and Learning in the Andes: Ethnographic Perspectives*, 166–93. Liverpool: Liverpool University Press.

Brading, David. 1988. "Manuel Gamio and Official *Indigenismo*." *Bulletin of Latin American Research* 7 (1): 75–90.

Brysk, Allison. 1995. "Acting Globally: Indian Rights and International Politics in Latin America." In Donna Lee van Cott, ed., *Indigenous Peoples and Democracy in Latin America*. London and New York: St. Martin's Press.

Buechler, Hans, and Judith-Maria Buechler. 1996. *The World of Sofía Velasquez: The Autobiography of a Bolivian Market Vendor*. New York: Columbia University Press.

Butler, Judith. 1993. *Bodies That Matter: On the Discursive Limits of Sex*. New York: Routledge.

———. 1999. *Gender Trouble: Feminism and the Subversion of Identity*. New York: Routledge.

Calla, Pamela. 2012. "Luchas legales y política de las calles en torno al racismo: decentrando la patriarcalidad del Estado Plurinacional de Bolivia." In Hernández Castillo, Rosalva Aída, and Andrew Canessa, eds., *Género, complementariedades y exclusiones en Mesoamérica y los Andes*, 43–60. Copenhagen and Quito: IWGIA and Abya Yala Press.

Canessa, Andrew. 1997. "Chachawarmi: Negociando (des)igualdades de género en una aldea aymara boliviana." In Denise Arnold, ed., *Nuevas direcciones en los estudios andinos*. La Paz: CIASE/ILCA.

———. 1998. "Procreation, Personhood and Ethnic Difference in Highland Bolivia." *Ethnos* 63 (2): 227–47.

———. 2005. "The Indian Within, the Indian Without: Citizenship, Race, and Sex in an Andean Hamlet." In Andrew Canessa, ed., *Natives Making Nation: Gender, Indigeneity and the State in the Andes*, 130–55. Tucson: University of Arizona Press.

———. 2006a. *Minas, Mote y Muñecas: Identidades e indigeneidades en Larecaja*. La Paz: Mamahucao.

———. 2006b. "Todos somos indígenas: Towards a New Language of National Political Identity." *Bulletin of Latin American Research* 25 (2): 241–63.

———. 2007. "Who Is Indigenous? Self-Identification, Indigeneity, and Claims to Justice in Contemporary Bolivia." *Urban Anthropology* 36 (3): 14–48.

———. 2009. "Forgetting the Revolution and Remembering the War: Memory and Violence in Highland Bolivia." *History Workshop Journal* 68: 173–98.

Carsten, Janet. 1995. "The Politics of Forgetting: Migration, Kinship and Memory on the Periphery of the Southeast Asian State." *Journal of the Royal Anthropological Institute* 1 (2): 317–35.

Carter, William, and Mauricio Mamani. 1982. *Irpa Chico: Individuo y comunidad en la cultura aymara*. La Paz: Juventud.

Choque Canqui, Roberto, et al. 1992. *Educación indígena: ¿Ciudadanía o colonización?* La Paz: Aruwiyiri.

Cliche, Paul, and Fernando García. 1995. *Escuela e indianidad en las urbes ecuatorianas*. Quito: EB/PRODEC.

Colloredo-Mansfeld, Rudi. 1999. *The Native Leisure Class: Consumption and Cultural Creativity in the Andes*. Chicago: University of Chicago Press.

Condarco Morales, Ramiro. 1983. *Zárate el temible Willka: Historia de la rebelión indígena de 1899*. 2nd edition. La Paz: Talleres Gráficos Bolivianos.

Conklin, Beth. 2001. *Consuming Grief: Compassionate Cannibalism in an Amazonian Society*. Austin: University of Texas Press.

Connerton, Paul. 1989. *How Societies Remember*. Cambridge: Cambridge University Press.

Connolly, Paul, and Barry Troyna, eds. 1998. *Researching Racism in Education: Politics, Theory and Practice*. Buckingham: Open University Press.

Crain, Mary. 1991. "Poetics and Politics in the Ecuadorean Andes: Women's Narratives of Death and Devil Possession." *American Ethnologist* 18 (1): 67–88.

———. 1996. "The Gendering of Ethnicity in the Ecuadorean Andes: Native Women's Self-Fashioning in the Urban Marketplace." In Marit Melhuus and Kristi Ann Stølen, eds., *Machos, Mistresses, Madonnas: Contesting the Power of Latin American Gender Imagery*. London: Verso.

Crandon-Malamud, Libbet. 1991. *From the Fat of our Souls: Social Change and Medical Pluralism in Bolivia*. Berkeley: University of California Press.

Degregori, Carlos Ivan. 1989. "Entre los fuegos de Sendero y el ejército: Regreso de los 'pishtacos.'" In J. Ansión, ed., *Pishtacos: de verdugos a sacaojos*, 109–14. Lima: Tarea.

De Janvry, Alain. 1981. *The Agrarian Question and Reformism in Latin America*. Baltimore: Johns Hopkins University Press.

De la Cadena, Marisol. 1995. "'Women Are More Indian': Ethnicity and Gender in a Community Near Cuzco." In Brooke Larson and Olivia Harris, eds., *Ethnicity Markets and Migration in the Andes,* 329–48. Durham, NC: Duke University Press.

De la Guerra, Francisco Emilio. 2003. "El Laberinto de 1492." *Correo del Maestro* 89 (October).

Delany, Carol. 1991. *The Seed and the Soil: Gender and Cosmology in Turkish Village Society.* Berkeley: University of California Press.

De la Torre, L. 1992. "Una experiencia educativa bilingüe en el Ecuador." *Pueblos Indígenas y Educación* (24): 7–37.

Demelas, Marie. 1981. "Darwinismo a la criolla: El darwinismo social en Bolivia, 1880–1910." *Historia Boliviana* 1 (2): 55–82.

———. 1982. *Nationalisme sans nation? La Bolivie aux XIXe–XXe siècles.* Paris: Éditions du CNRS.

Descola, Philippe. 1994. *In the Society of Nature: A Native Ecology in Action.* Cambridge: Cambridge University Press.

Diez Astete, Álvaro. 1995. *Antropología de Bolivia.* La Paz: Secretaría de Educación/ Ministerio de Desarrollo Humano.

Douglas, Mary. 1996. *Purity and Danger: An Analysis of the Concepts of Pollution and Taboo.* London: Routledge.

Dunkerley, James. 2007. *Bolivia: Revolution and the Power of History in the Present.* London: ILAS.

Fabricant, Nicole. 2009. "Performative Politics: The Camba Countermovement in Eastern Bolivia." *American Ethnologist* 36 (4): 768–83.

Fanon, Franz. 1986 [1952]. *Black Skin, White Masks.* London: Pluto.

Finkelstein, Norman. 2000. *The Holocaust Industry: Reflections on the Exploitation of Jewish Suffering.* London: Verso.

Foster, P. 1990. *Policy and Practice in Multicultural and Anti-Racist Education.* London: Routledge.

Fraser, Nancy. 1989. *Unruly Practices: Power, Discourse, and Gender in Contemporary Social Theory.* Minneapolis: University of Minnesota Press.

Freyre, Gilberto. 1946. *The Masters and the Slaves: A Study in the Development of Brazilian Civilization.* New York: Knopf.

———. 1968 [1936]. *The Mansions and the Shanties: The Making of Modern Brazil* [*Sobrados e Macombos*]. New York: Knopf.

Friedlander, Judith. 1975. *Being Indian in Hueyapan: A Study of Forced Identity in Contemporary Mexico.* London: St. Martin's.

———. 2006. *Being Indian in Hueyapan: A Study of Forced Identity in Contemporary Mexico.* London: Palgrave Macmillan.

Galindo, María. 2006. "Evo Morales y la descolonización fálica del estado boliviano: Un análisis feminista sobre el proceso a la Asamblea Constituyente en Bolivia." *Mujeres Creando,* http://www.mujerescreando.org. Accessed on 7/21/09.

Galindo, María, and Helen Álvarez. 2010. "Cosificar a las mujeres: Una política municipal." *Mujeres Creando,* http://www.mujerescreando.org/index2.htm. Accessed on 8/25/10.

García, María Elena. 2005. *Making Indigenous Citizens: Identity, Development and Multicultural Activism in Peru.* Stanford: Stanford University Press.

Gill, Lesley. 1994. *Precarious Dependencies: Gender, Class, and Domestic Service in Bolivia.* New York: Columbia University Press.

———. 1997. "Creating Citizens, Making Men: The Military and Masculinity in Bolivia." *Cultural Anthropology* 12 (4): 527–50.

Gilly, Adolfo. 2005. "Bolivia: The First Twenty-First Century Revolution." *Socialism and Democracy* 19 (3): 41–54.

Goldstein, Daniel. 2000. "Names, Places, and Power: Collective Identity in the Miss Oruro Pageant, Cochabamba, Bolivia." *PoLAR* 23 (1): 1–23.

Goldstein, Donna. 2003. *Laughter out of Place: Race, Class, Violence, and Sexuality in a Rio Shantytown.* Berkeley: University of California Press.

Gonzalez, M. J. L. 1986. "La Cruz en la Sociedad Rural Andina." *Boletín del Instituto de Estudios Aymaras* 2 (24): 27–50.

Gose, Peter. 1986a. "Sacrifice and the Commodity Form in the Andes." *Man* 21 (2): 296–310.

———. 1986b. "Work, Class and Culture in Huaquira." PhD thesis, University of London.

———. 1994. *Deathly Waters and Hungry Mountains.* Toronto: Toronto University Press.

Gotkowitz, Laura. 2000. "Commemorating the Heroínas: Gender and Civic Ritual in Early Twentieth Century Bolivia." In Elizabeth Dore and Maxine Molyneux, eds., *Hidden Histories of Gender and the State in Latin America.* Durham, NC: Duke University Press.

Goudsmit, Into. 2006. "So Far from God so Near the Mountains: Peasant Deference to the State and Landlords in the Bolivian Andes." PhD thesis, University of London.

Gow, David, and Joanne Rappaport. 2002. "The Indigenous Public Voice: The Multiple Idioms of Modernity in Indigenous Cauca." In Kay B. Warren and Jean Jackson, eds., *Indigenous Movements, Self-Representation, and the State in Latin America.* Austin: University of Texas Press.

Greene, Shane. 2009. *Customizing Indigeneity: Paths to a Visionary Politics in Peru.* Stanford: Stanford University Press.

Guevara Paredes, Mario. 1994. *Cazador de gringas y otros cuentos.* Cuzco: Municipalidad del Qosqo.

Gustafson, Bret. 2006. "Spectacles of Autonomy and Crisis: Or What Bulls and Beauty Queens Have to Do with Regionalism in Bolivia." *Journal of Latin American Anthropology* 11 (2): 351–79.

———. 2009. *New Languages of the State: Indigenous Resurgence and the Politics of Knowledge in Bolivia.* Durham, NC: Duke University Press.

Halbwachs, Maurice. 1968. *La Memoire Collective.* Paris: Presses Universitaires de France.

Hall, Catherine, K. McClelland, and J. Rendall. 2000. *Defining the Victorian Nation: Class, Race, Gender and the Reform Act of 1867.* Cambridge: Cambridge University Press.

Hannerz, Ulf. 1992. *Cultural Complexity: Studies in the Social Organization of Meaning.* New York: Columbia University Press.

Harris, Olivia. 1978. "Complementarity and Conflict: An Andean View of Women and Men." In S. La Fontaine, ed., *Sex and Age as Principles of Social Differentiation,* 21–40. London: Academic Press.

————. 1980. "The Power of Signs: Gender, Culture and the Wild in the Bolivian Andes." In Carol MacCormack and Marilyn Strathern, eds., *Nature, culture and gender*,
70–94. Cambridge: Cambridge University Press.

————. 1982. "The Dead and the Devils Among the Bolivian Laymi." In Bloch and
Parry, eds., *Death and the Regeneration of Life*, 45–73. Cambridge: Cambridge University Press.

————. 1994. "Condor and Bull: The Ambiguities of Masculinity in Northern Potosí."
In Penelope Harvey and Peter Gow, eds., *Sex and Violence: Issues in Representation
and Experience*. London: Routledge.

————. 1995. "Ethnic Identity and Market Relations: Indians and Mestizos in the Andes." In Brooke Larson, Olivia Harris, and Enrique Tandeter, eds., *Ethnicity, Markets,
and Migration in the Andes: At the Crossroads of History and Anthropology*, 351–90.
Durham, NC: Duke University Press.

Harvey, Penny. 1991. "Drunken Speech and the Construction of Meaning: Bilingual
Competence in the Southern Peruvian Andes." *Language in Society* 20 (1): 1–36.

————. 1994. "Domestic Violence in the Andes." In Penelope Harvey and Peter Gow,
eds., *Sex and Violence: Issues in Representation and Experience*, 66–89. London:
Routledge.

Hodgson, Dorothy. 2002. "Comparative Perspectives on Indigenous Rights Movements in Africa and the Americas." *American Anthropologist* 104 (4): 1037–49.

hooks, bell. 1991. *Yearning: Race, Gender, and Cultural Politics*. London: Turnaround
Press.

Hornberger, Nancy. 1994. "Whither Bilingual Education in Peru? Quechua Literacy
and Empowerment." In Peter Cole, Gabriella Hermon, and Mario Martin. eds.,
Language in the Andes, 27–50. Wilmington: University of Delaware Press.

————. 2000. "Bilingual Education Policy and Practice in the Andes: Ideological
Paradox and Intercultural Possibility." *Anthropology and Education Quarterly* 31 (2):
173–201.

Hulme, Peter. 1983. "Polytropic Man: Tropes of Sexuality and Mobility in Early Colonial Discourse." In Francis Barker, Peter Hulme, Margaret Iverson, and Diana Loxley,
eds., *Europe and Its Others, Vol. 2*. Essex: University of Essex.

Hurtado, Javier. 1986. *El Katarismo*. La Paz: HISBOL.

Hurtado, Teodora. 2008. "Movilidades, Identidades y Sexualidades en Mujeres Afrocolom-
bianas Migrantes en Europa: El Caso de las 'Italianas.' " In Peter Wade, Fernando Urrea
Giraldo, and Mara Viveros Vigoya, eds., *Raza, etnicidad y sexualidades: Ciudadanía y
multiculturalismo en América Latina*. Bogota: Universidad Nacional de Colombia.

Hylton, Forrest, and Sinclair Thomson. 2007. *Revolutionary Horizons: Past and Present
in Bolivian Politics*. London: Verso.

Illich, Ivan. 1971. *Deschooling Society*. London: Calder and Boyars.

Instituto Nacional de Estadística. 1992. *Censo Nacional 1991*. La Paz: INE.

Instituto Nacional de Estadísticas de Bolívia/UMPA. 2003. *Bolivia: Características Soci-
odemográficas de la Población*. La Paz: INE.

Irurozqui Victoriano, Marta. 2000. *"A Bala, Piedra y Palo": La construcción de la ciudadanía política en Bolivia, 1826–1952*. Seville: Diputación de Sevilla.

Isbell, Billie Jean. 1978. *To Defend Ourselves: Ecology and Ritual in an Andean Village*.
Austin: University of Texas Press.

Janusek, John. 2004. *Identity and Power in the Andes: Tiwanaku Cities Through Time.* New York and London: Routledge.

———. 2008. *Ancient Tiwanaku.* Cambridge: Cambridge University Press.

Jiménez Sardon, Greta. 1998. "The Aymara Couple in the Community." In Frédérique Apffel-Marglin, ed., *The Spirit of Regeneration: Andean Culture Confronting Western Notions of Development.* London and New York: Zed Books.

Karakasidou, Anastasia. 1997. *Fields of Wheat, Hills of Blood: Passages to Nationhood in Greek Macedonia.* Chicago: Chicago University Press.

Keck, Margaret, and Kathryn Sikkink. 1998. *Activists Beyond Borders.* Ithaca, NY: Cornell University Press.

Kempadoo, Kamala. 2004. *Sexing the Caribbean: Gender, Race, and Sexual Labor.* London: Routledge.

Klein, Herbert. 1992. *Bolivia: The Evolution of a Multi-ethnic Society.* Oxford: Oxford University Press.

Koch, Julie. 2006. "Collectivism or Isolation? Gender Relations in Urban La Paz, Bolivia." *Bulletin of Latin American Research* 25 (1): 43–62.

Kohl, Benjamin, and Linda Farthing. 2006. *Impasse in Bolivia: Neoliberal Hegemony and Popular Resistance.* London: Zed Books.

Kolata, Alan. 1986. "The Agricultural Foundations of the Tiwanaku State: A View from the Heartland." *American Antiquity* 51: 748–62.

Kuper, Adam. 2003. "The Return of the Native." *Current Anthropology* 44 (3): 389–402.

Kymlicka, Will. 1995. *Multicultural Citizenship.* Oxford: Oxford University Press.

Langer, Erick. 2009. "Bringing the Economic Back In: Andean Indians and the Construction of the Nation-State in Nineteenth-Century Bolivia." *Journal of Latin American Studies* 41: 527–51.

Larson, Brooke. 2004. *Trials of Nation Making: Liberalism, Race, and Ethnicity in the Andes, 1810–1910.* Cambridge: Cambridge University Press.

———. 2005. "Capturing Indian Bodies, Hearths, and Minds: The Gendered Politics of Rural School Reform in Bolivia, 1920s–1940s." In Andrew Canessa, ed., *Natives Making Nation: Gender Indigeneity and the State in the Andes,* 32–59. Tucson: University of Arizona Press.

Larson, Brooke, Olivia Harris, and Enrique Tandeter, eds. 1995. *Ethnicity, Markets, and Migration in the Andes: At the Crossroads of History and Anthropology.* Durham, NC: Duke University Press.

Lewis, Laura. 2003. *Hall of Mirrors: Power, Witchcraft, and Caste in Colonial Mexico.* Durham, NC: Duke University Press.

Lizot, Jacques. 1991. *Tales of the Yanomani: Daily Life in the Venezuelan Rainforest.* Cambridge: Cambridge University Press.

Luykx, Aurolyn. 1999. *The Citizen Factory: Schooling and Cultural Production in Bolivia.* Albany: SUNY Press.

———. 2004. "The Future of Quechua and the Quechua of the Future: Language Ideologies and Language Planning in Bolivia." *International Journal of the Sociology of Language* (167): 147–58.

Lyons, Barry. 2006. *Remembering the Hacienda: Religion, Authority, and Social Change in Highland Ecuador.* Austin: University of Texas Press.

Mac an Ghaill, M. 1988. *Young, Gifted and Black: Student-Teacher Relations in the School-ing of Black Youth*. Milton Keynes, UK: Open University Press.

MacCormack, Carol, and Marilyn Strathern, eds. 1982. *Nature, Culture and Gender*. Cambridge: Cambridge University Press.

MacCormack, Sabine. 1991. *Religion in the Andes: Vision and Imagination in Early Colo-nial Peru*. Princeton, NJ: Princeton University Press.

Malverde, Rosaleen, and Andrew Canessa. 1995. "The School in the Quechua and Aymara Communities of Highland Bolivia." *International Journal of Educational Development* 15 (3): 231–43.

Mannheim, Bruce. 1986. "The Language of Reciprocity in Southern Peruvian Quechua." *Anthropological Linguistics* (28): 267–73.

Manya, J. A. 1969. "Temible nakaq." *Allpanchis* 1: 135–38.

Martínez-Alier, Verena [Verena Stolcke]. 1974. *Marriage, Class and Colour in Nineteenth-Century Cuba*. Ann Arbor: University of Michigan Press.

Martínez Novo, Carmen. 2006. *Who Defines Indigenous? Identities, Development, Intel-lectuals, and the State in Northern Mexico*. New Brunswick, NJ: Rutgers University Press.

Martínez Novo, Carmen, and Carlos de la Torre. 2010. "Racial Discrimination and Citizenship in Ecuador's Educational System." *Latin American and Caribbean Ethnic Studies* 5 (1): 1–26.

Mason, Peter. 1990. *Deconstructing America: Representations of the Other*. London: Routledge.

Mayer, Enrique. 1974. "Las reglas de juego en la reciprocidad andina." In Giorgio Alberti and Enrique Mayer, eds., *Reciprocidad e intercambio en los andes Peruanos*, 37–65. Lima: Instituto de Estudios Peruanos.

———. 1975. *Reciprocity, Self-sufficiency and Market Relations in a Contemporary Com-munity in the Central Andes of Peru*. Latin American Studies Dissertation Series No. 72. Ithaca, NY: Cornell University Press.

Mayer, Enrique, and Ralph Bolton, eds. 1977. *Andean Kinship and Marriage*. Washing-ton D.C.: American Anthropological Association.

McCaa, Robert. 1984. "Calidad, Class and Marriage in Colonial Mexico: The Case of Parral, 1788–1790." *Hispanic American Historical Review* 64 (3): 477–501.

McCarthy, Cameron and Warren Crichlow, eds. 1993. *Race, Identity and Representation in Education*. London: Routledge.

McClintock, Anne. 1995. *Imperial Leather: Race, Gender and Sexuality in the Colonial Context*. London: Routledge.

Medinaceli, Carlos. 1958. *La Chaskañawi*. La Paz: Amigos del Libro.

Meillassoux, Claude. 1981. *Maidens, Meal and Money: Capitalism and the Domestic Com-munity*. Cambridge: Cambridge University Press.

Meisch, Lynn. 1995. "Gringas and Otavaleños: Changing Tourist Relations." *Annals of Tourism Research* 22 (2): 441–62.

Millones, Luis, and Mary Louise Pratt. 1989. *Amor brujo: Imagen y cultura del amor en los Andes*. Lima: Instituto de Estudios Peruanos.

Montrose, Louis. 1991. "The Work of Gender in the Discourse of Discovery." *New Representations* 33 (Winter), 1–41.

Moore, Henrietta. 2007. *The Subject of Anthropology*. London: Polity.

Morgan, Lynn. 1997. "Imagining the Unborn in the Ecuadorian Andes." *Feminist Studies* 23 (2): 323–50.

Morote Best, E. 1951. "El degollador (nakaq)." *Tradición: Revista Peruana de Cultura* 2/4 (11): 67–91.

Morphy, Howard, and Frances Morphy. 1984. "The 'Myths' of Ngalakan History: Ideology and Images of the Past in Northern Australia." *Man* 19 (3): 459–78.

Mulkay, Michael. 1988. *On Humour: Its Nature and Its Place in Modern Society*. Oxford: Basil Blackwell.

Murra, John. 1980. *The Economic Organization of the Inca State*. Greenwich, CT: JAI Press.

Murray, David. 1999. "Laws of Desire? Race, Sexuality, and Power in Male Martinican Sexual Narratives." *American Ethnologist* 26 (1): 160–72.

Nandy, Ashis. 1983. *The Intimate Enemy: Loss and Recovery of Self under Colonialism*. Oxford: Oxford University Press.

Nash, June. 1979. *We Eat the Mines and the Mines Eat Us*. New York: Columbia University Press.

Nelson, Diane. 1999. *A Finger in the Wound: Body Politics in Quincentennial Guatemala*. Berkeley: University of California Press.

Newport, G. 1854. "Researches on the Impregnation of the Ovum in the Amphibia and on the Early Stages of Development of the Embryo." *Philosophical Transactions of the Royal Society of London B Biological Sciences* 144: 229–44.

Nugent, David. 1997. *Modernity on the Edge of Empire State, Individual, and Nation in the Northern Peruvian Andes, 1885–1935*. Stanford: Stanford University Press.

Ochoa, Víctor. 1975. "Ritos y ceremonias de perdón y reconciliación en la cultura aymara." *Boletín Ocasional* 21: 1–24.

Ogbu, John. 1981. "School Ethnography: A Multilevel Approach." *Anthropology and Education Quarterly* 12 (1): 3–29.

Orlove, Ben. 1998. "Down to Earth: Race and Substance in the Andes." *Bulletin of Latin American Research* 17 (2): 207–22.

Orta, Andrew. 2004. *Catechizing Culture: Missionaries, Aymara, and the "New Evangelization."* New York: Columbia University Press.

Pagden, Anthony. 1982. *The Fall of Natural Man: The American Indian and the Origins of Comparative Ethnology*. Cambridge: Cambridge University Press.

Paredes, Rigoberto. 1963. *Mitos, supersticiones y supervivencias populares de Bolivia*. La Paz: Isla.

Paulson, Susan. 1996. "Familias que no 'conyugan' e identidades que no conjugan: La vida en Mizque desafía nuestras categorías." In Silvia Rivera, ed., *Ser mujer indígena, chola o birlocha en la Bolivia postcolonial de los años 90*, 85–162. La Paz: Ministerio de Desarrollo Humano.

———. 2003. "Placing Gender and Ethnicity on the Bodies of Indigenous Women and in the Work of Bolivian Intellectuals." In Rosario Montoya, Lessie Jo Frazier, and Janise Hurtig, eds., *Gender's Place: Feminist Anthropologies of Latin America*, 135–55. New York and Basingstoke, UK: Palgrave Macmillan.

Pequeño, Andrea. 2004. "Historia de Misses, historia de naciones." *Iconos: Revista de Ciencias Sociales (flacso)* 20, 114–17.

Pitarch, Pedro. 2010. *The Jaguar and the Priest: An Ethnography of Tzeltal Souls*. Austin: University of Texas Press.

Placido, Barbara. 1999. *Spirits of the Nation: Identity and Legitimacy in the Cults of María Lionza and Simón Bolívar*. PhD dissertation, University of Cambridge.

———. 2001. "It's All to Do with Words: An Analysis of Spirit Possession in the Venezuelan Cult of María Lionza." *Journal of the Royal Anthropological Institute* 7 (2): 207–24.

Platt, Tristan. 1982. *Estado boliviano y ayllu andino: Tierra y tributo en el norte de Potosí*. Lima: IEP.

———. 1993. "Simón Bolívar, the Sun of Justice and the Amerindian Virgin: Andean Conceptions of the *Patria* in Nineteenth-Century Potosí." *Journal of Latin American Studies* 25 (1): 159–85.

———. 2002. "El feto agresivo: Parto, formación de la persona y mito-historia en los Andes." *Estudios Atacameños* 22: 127–55.

Poniatowska, Elena. 2006. "Romance de Evo Morales con una indígena de Amealco." *La Jornada* 17 (September).

Poole, Deborah. 1997. *Vision, Race, and Modernity: A Visual Economy of the Andean Image World*. Princeton, NJ: Princeton University Press.

Portelli, Alessandro. 1981a. "The Peculiarities of Oral History." *History Workshop Journal* 12, 96–107.

———. 1981b. "The Time of My Life: Functions of Time in Oral History." *International Journal of Oral History* 2 (3): 162–80.

———. 1991. "The Death of Luigi Trastulli: Memory and the Event." In Alessandro Portelli, ed., *The Death of Luigi Trastulli and Other Stories: Form and Meaning in Oral History*. Albany: SUNY Press.

———. 1997. *The Battle of Valle Giulia: Oral History and the Art of Dialogue*. Madison: University of Wisconsin Press.

Portocarrero, Gonzalo. 1991. "Conyuntura social e imaginario popular: Los *sacaojos*." In Enrique Urbano, ed., *Poder y violencia en los Andes*, 379–94. Cuzco: Centro de Estudios Regionales Andinos Bartolomé de las Casas.

Portocarrero, Gonzalo, and Patricia Oliart. 1989. *El Perú desde la escuela*. Lima: Instituto de Apoyo Agrario.

Portocarrero, Gonzalo, I. Valentín, and S. Irigoyen. 1991. *Sacaojos: Crisis social y fantasmas coloniales*. Lima: TAREA, Asociación de Publicaciones Educativas.

Postero, Nancy. 2007. *Now We Are Citizens: Indigenous Politics in Postmulticultural Bolivia*. Stanford: Stanford University Press.

Povinelli, Elizabeth. 2006. *The Empire of Love: Toward a Theory of Intimacy, Genealogy, and Carnality*. Durham, NC: Duke University Press.

Radcliffe, Sarah. 1990. "Ethnicity, Patriarchy, and Incorporation into the Nation: Female Migrants as Domestic Servants in Peru." *Society and Space* 8: 379–93.

Radcliffe, Sarah, and Sallie Westwood. 1996. *Remaking the Nation: Place, Identity and Politics in Latin America*. London: Routledge.

Rahier, Jean Muteba. 1998. "Blackness, the 'Racial'/Spatial Order, Migrations, and Miss Ecuador 1995–1996," *American Anthropologist* 100 (2): 421–30.

Rappaport, Joanne. 1998. *The Politics of Memory: Native Historical Interpretation in the Colombian Andes*. Durham, NC: Duke University Press.

Reinaga, Fausto. 1969. *La Revolución India.* La Paz: Partido Indio Boliviano.

Riches, David. 1986. *The Anthropology of Violence.* Oxford and New York: Blackwell.

Rivera Cusicanqui, Silvia. 1984. *Oprimidos pero no vencidos.* La Paz: HISBOL.

———. 1993. "Aymara Past, Aymara Future." *Nacla Report on the Americas* 25 (3): 18–23.

———. 1996. "Prólogo." In Silvia Rivera Cusicanqui, ed., *Ser mujer indígena, chola o birlocha en la Bolivia postcolonial de los años 90:* 17–84. La Paz: Ministerio de Desarrollo Humano.

Rivière, Giles. 1991. "*Likichiri y kharisiri:* A propósito de las representaciones del 'otro' en la sociedad Aymara." *Bulletin de l'Institute Français d'Études* 20 (1): 23–40.

Rogers, Mark. 1999. "Spectacular Bodies: Folklorization and the Politics of Identity in Ecuadorean Beauty Pageants." *Journal of Latin American Anthropology* 3 (2): 54–85.

Rösing, Ina. 1999. *Geschlechtliche Zeit, geschlechticher Raum.* Heidelberg: Universitätsverlag.

Rousseau, Stéphanie. 2009. "Genre et ethnicité racialisée en Bolivie: Pour une étude intersectionnelle des mouvements sociaux." *Sociologie et Sociétés* 41 (2): 135–60.

———. 2011. "Indigenous and Feminist Movements at the Constituent Assembly in Bolivia: Locating the Representation of Indigenous Women." *Latin American Research Review* 46 (2): 5–28.

Rout, Lesley. 1976. *The African Experience in Spanish America: 1502 to the Present Day.* Cambridge: Cambridge University Press.

Saavedra, Bautista. 1955 [1913]. *El Ayllu.* La Paz: Gisbert.

Saignes, Thierry. 1985. *Los Andes Orientales Historia de un Olvido.* Cochabamba: IFEA-CERES.

———. 1986. "The Ethnic Groups in the Valleys of Larecaja: From Descent to Residence." In John V. Murra, Nathan Wachtel, and Jacques Revel, eds., *Anthropological History of Andean Politics,* 311–41. Cambridge: Cambridge University Press.

———. 1989. "Borracheras andinas: ¿Por qué los indios ebrios hablan en español?" *Revista Andina,* 7 (1): 83–119.

Saignes, Thierry, ed. 1993. *Borrachera y memoria: La experiencia de lo sagrado en los Andes.* La Paz: HISBOL/IFEA.

Salazar-Soler, Carmen. 1991. "El pishtaku entre los campesinos y los mineros de Huancavelica." *Bulletin de l'Institute Français d'Études Andines* 20 (1): 7–22.

Sallnow, Michael. 1987. *Pilgrims of the Andes.* Washington D.C.: Smithsonian Institution Press.

Salmón Ballivián, José. 1926. "El indio íntimo: Contribución al estudio biológico social del indio." In *Ideario aimara,* 105–63. La Paz: Salesiana.

Salomon, Frank. 1981. "Killing the Yumbo: A Ritual Drama of Northern Quito." In Norman Whitten, ed., *Cultural Transformations and Ethnicity in Modern Ecuador,* 162–208. Urbana: University of Illinois Press.

Sangren, Steven. 2004. "Psychoanalysis and Its Resistances in Michel Foucault's *The History of Sexuality*: Lessons for Anthropology." *Ethos* 32 (1): 110–22.

Scheper-Hughes, Nancy. 1992. *Death Without Weeping: The Violence of Everyday Life in Brazil.* Berkeley: University of California Press.

———. 1996. "Theft of Life: The Globalization of Organ Stealing Rumors." *Anthropology Today* 12 (3): 3–11.

Schreffler, Michael. 2005. "Vespucci Rediscovers America: The Pictorial Rhetoric of Cannibalism in Early Modern Culture." *Art History* 28 (3): 295–310.

Scott, James. 1985. *Weapons of the Weak: Everyday Forms of Peasant Resistance*. New Haven, CT: Yale University Press.

Seed, Patricia. 1988. *To Love, Honor, and Obey in Colonial Mexico: Conflicts over Marriage Choice, 1574–1821*. Stanford: Stanford University Press.

Sherbondy, Jeanette. 1993. "Water Ideology in Inca Ethnogenesis." In R. Dover, K. Seibold, and J. McDowell, eds., *Andean Cosmologies Through Time*, 46–66. Bloomington: Indiana University Press.

Sifuentes, Eudosio. 1989. "La continuidad de la historia de los pishtacos en los 'Robaojos' de hoy." In Juan Ansión, ed., *Pishtacos: De verdugos a sacaojos*, 149–54. Lima: Tarea.

Silverblatt, Irene. 1987. *Moon, Sun and Witches: Gender Ideology and Class in Inca and Colonial Peru*. Princeton, NJ: Princeton University Press.

Skar, Harald. 1982. *The Warm Valley People: Duality and Land Reform Among the Quechua Indians of Highland Peru*. Oslo: Universitetsforlaget.

Skidmore, Thomas. 1993 [1974]. *Black into White: Race and Nationality in Brazilian Thought*. Oxford: Oxford University Press.

Sleeter, Christine. 1993. "How White Teachers Construct Race." In Cameron McCarthy and Warren Crichlow, eds., *Race, Identity and Representation in Education*, 157–71. London: Routledge.

Sommer, Doris. 1991. *Foundational Fictions: The National Romances of Latin America*. Berkeley: University of California Press.

Soria, Vitaliano. 1992. "La educación india en la visión de la sociedad criolla: 1920–1943." In Roberto Choque et al., eds., *Educación Indígena: ¿Ciudadanía o colonización?* La Paz: Aruwiyiri.

Spalding, Karen. 1970. "Social Climbers: Changing Patterns of Mobility among the Indians of Colonial Peru." *Hispanic American Historical Review* 1 (4): 645–64.

Spedding, Alison. 1989. "Wachu wachu: Coca Cultivation and Aymara Identity in the Yunkas of La Paz (Bolivia)." PhD dissertation, University of London.

———. 1999. "Investigadores en apuros." *T'inkazos* 2 (3): 146–61.

———. 2003. *Nosotros los yungueños, Nanakax yunkas tuqinkiripxtw: testimonios de los yungueños del siglo XX*. La Paz: Mamahuaco.

———. 2005. *Sueños, kharisiris y curanderos: Dinámicas sociales de las creencias en los Andes contemporáneos*. La Paz: Mamahuaco.

Starn, Orin. 1999. *Nightwatch: The Politics of Protest in the Andes*. Durham, NC: Duke University Press.

Stavenhagen, Rodolfo. 2002. "Indigenous Peoples and the State in Latin America." In Rachel Sieder, ed., *Multiculturalism in Latin America: Indigenous Rights, Diversity and Democracy*. London: Palgrave.

Stepan, Nancy. 1991. *The Hour of Eugenics: Race, Gender, and Nation in Latin America*. Ithaca, NY: Cornell University Press.

Stephenson, Marcia. 1999. *Gender and Modernity in Andean Bolivia*. Austin: University of Texas Press.

Stern, Steve. 1987. *Resistance, Rebellion, and Consciousness in the Andean Peasant World*. Madison: University of Wisconsin Press.

———. 2004. *Remembering Pinochet's Chile: On the Eve of London 1998*. Durham, NC: Duke University Press.

Stewart, Pamela, and Andrew Strathern. 1999. "Feasting on My Enemy: Images of Violence and Change in the New Guinea Highlands." *Ethnohistory* 46 (4): 645–69.

———. 2002. *Violence: Theory and Ethnography*. London: Continuum.

———. 2007. *Terror and Violence: Imagination and the Unimaginable*. London: Pluto.

Stobart, Henry. 2006. *Music and the Poetics of Production in the Bolivian Andes*. London: Ashgate.

———. 2011. "Constructing Community in the Digital Home Studio: Carnival, Creativity and Indigenous Music Video Production in the Bolivian Andes." *Popular Music* 30 (2): 209–26.

Stoler, Ann Laura. 1995. *Race and the Education of Desire*. Durham, NC: Duke University Press.

———. 2002. *Carnal Knowledge and Imperial Power: Race and the Intimate in Colonial Rule*. Berkeley: University of California Press.

Ströbele-Gregor, Juliana. 1989. *Indios de piel blanca*. La Paz: HISBOL.

———. 1993. "Búsqueda de seguridad y formas propias de afirmación de la identidad social aimara urbana." *América Indígena* 3: 165–77.

———. 2011. "Black Day in the White City: Racism and Violence in Sucre." In Olaf Kaltmeier, ed., *Selling EthniCity: Urban Cultural Politics in the Americas*, 77–93. London: Ashgate.

Szeminski, Jan, and Juan Ansión. 1982. "Dioses y hombres de Huamanga." *Allpanchis* 19: 187–233.

Talle, Aud. 1993. "Transforming Women into 'Pure' Agnates: Aspects of Female Infibulation in Somalia." In Vigdis Broch-Due, Ingrid Rudie, and Tone Bleie, eds., *Carved Flesh, Cast Selves: Gendered Symbols and Social Practices*. Oxford, UK, and Providence, RI: Berg.

Tambiah, Stanley. 1979. "A Performative Approach to Ritual." *Proceedings of the British Academy* 15: 115–69.

Tapias, Maria. 2006. "'Always ready and always clean?': Competing Discourses of Breast-Feeding, Infant Illness and the Politics of Mother Blame in Bolivia." *Body and Society* 12 (2): 83–108.

Taussig, Michael. 1980. *The Devil and Commodity Fetishism in South America*. Chapel Hill: University of North Carolina Press.

———. 1987. *Colonialism, Shamanism, and the Wild Man: A Study in Terror and Healing*. Chicago: University of Chicago Press.

Theidon, Kimberly. 2003. "Disarming the Subject: Remembering War and Imagining Citizenship in Peru." *Cultural Critique* 54: 67–87.

———. 2004. *Entre prójimos: El conflicto armado interno y la política de la reconciliación en el Perú*. Lima: IEP.

———. 2006. "Justice in Transition: The Micropolitics of Reconciliation in Postwar Peru." *Journal of Conflict Resolution* 50 (3): 433–57.

Ticona, Esteban. 2005. *Lecturas para la descolonización*. La Paz: Plural.

Ticona, Esteban, and Xavier Albó. 1997. *Achacachi: Medio Siglo de Lucha Campesina*. La Paz: CIPCA.

Tonkin, Elizabeth. 1992. *Narrating Our Pasts: The Social Construction of Oral History.* Cambridge: Cambridge University Press.

Torero, Alfredo. 1971. *El quechua y la historia social andina.* Lima: Universidad Ricardo Palma.

Trexler, Richard. 1995. *Sex and Conquest: Gendered Violence, Political Order, and the European Conquest of the Americas.* Cambridge: Polity.

Tsing, Anna. 1993. *In the Realm of the Diamond Queen: Marginality in an Out-of-the-Way Place.* Princeton, NJ: Princeton University Press.

Twinam, Ann. 1999. *Public Lives, Private Secrets: Gender, Honor, Sexuality, and Illegitimacy in Colonial Spanish America.* Stanford: Stanford University Press.

Valderrama, Ricardo, and Carmen Escalante. 1998. "Matrimonio en las comunidades quechuas andinas." In Denise Arnold, ed., *Gente de carne y hueso: Los tramos de parentesco en los Andes,* Vol. 2, *Parentesco y género en los Andes,* 292–322. La Paz: CIASE/ILCA.

Van Cott, Donna Lee. 2000. *The Friendly Liquidation of the Past: The Politics of Diversity in Latin America.* Pittsburgh: Pittsburgh University Press.

Van Dam, A., and Ton Salman. 2003. "Andean Transversality: Identity Between Fixation and Flow." In Ton Salman and Annelies Zoomers, eds., *Imaging the Andes: Shifting Margins of a Marginal World,* 15–39. Amsterdam: Aksant Academic Publishers.

Van den Berg, Hans. 1990. *La Tierra no da así nomás: Los ritos agrícolas en la religión de los aymara-cristianos.* La Paz: HISBOL.

Van Vleet, Krista. 2002. "The Intimacies of Power: Rethinking Violence and Affinity in the Bolivian Andes." *American Ethnologist* 29 (3): 567–601.

———. 2008. *Performing Kinship: Narrative, Gender, and the Intimacies of Power in the Andes.* Austin: University of Texas Press.

———. 2010. "Transnational Spectacle, Situated Performance: Narrating Agency and Negotiating Performance in Andean *Tinku* Stories." *Journal of Latin American and Caribbean Anthropology.* 15 (1): 195–221.

Vasconcelos, J. 1961 [1917]. *La raza cósmica: Misión de la raza iberoamericana.* Madrid: Aguilar.

Verma, Gajendra, and Christopher Bagley, eds. 1979. *Race, Education and Identity.* London: Macmillan.

Wachtel, Nathan. 1994. *Gods and Vampires: Return to Chipaya.* Chicago: University of Chicago Press.

Wade, Peter. 1997. *Race and Ethnicity in Latin America.* London: Pluto.

———. 2009. *Race and Sex in Latin America.* London: Pluto.

Wearne, Philip. 1996. *Return of the Indian: Conquest and Revival in the Americas.* London: Cassell.

Weber, Katinka. 2005. "Lynchings Amongst Indigenous Communities in Bolivia: The Case of Ayo Ayo Revisited." Master's thesis, Institute of Latin American Studies, University of Liverpool.

Weismantel, Mary. 1988. *Food Gender and Poverty in the Ecuadorian Andes.* Philadelphia: University of Philadelphia Press.

———. 1997. "White Cannibals: Fantasies of Racial Violence in the Andes" *Identities* 14 (1): 9–43.

———. 2001. *Cholas and Pishtacos: Stories of Race and Sex in the Andes*. Chicago: Chicago University Press.

Whitehead, Neil. 2002. *Dark Shamans: Kanaimà and the Poetics of Violent Death*. Durham, NC: Duke University Press.

———. 2007. "Afterword." In Pamela Stewart and Andrew Strathern, eds., *Terror and Violence: Imagination and the Unimaginable*, 231–38. London: Pluto.

Whittier, David Knapp, and William Simon. 2001. "The Fuzzy Matrix of 'My Type' in Intrapsychic Sexual Scripting." *Sexualities* 4 (2): 139–65.

Wright, C. 1998. "Caught in the Crossfire: Reflections of a Black Female Ethnographer." In Paul Connolly and Barry Troyna, eds., *Researching Racism in Education: Politics Theory and Practice*. Buckingham: Open University Press.

Wright, Melanie, Christine Hastorf, and Heidi Lennstrom. 2003. "Pre-Hispanic Agriculture and Plant Use in Tiwanaku: Social and Political Implications." In Alan Kolata, ed., *Tiwanaku and Its Hinterland: Archaeology and Paleoecology of and Andean Civilization, Vol. 2*, 384–403. Washington D.C.: Smithsonian Institution Press.

Wright, Winthrop. 1990. *Café con Leche: Race, Class, and National Image in Venezuela*. Austin: University of Texas Press.

Yapu, Mario. 1999. "La Reforma y la enseñanza de la lectoescritura en el campo." *T'inkazos* 4: 55–92.

Yashar, Deborah. 2005. *Contesting Citizenship in Latin America: The Rise of Indigenous Movements and the Postliberal Challenge*. Cambridge: Cambridge University Press.

Yuval-Davis, Nira. 1997. *Gender and Nation*. London: Sage.

Yuval-Davis, Nira, and Flora Anthias. 1989. *Woman-Nation-State*. Basingstoke, UK: Macmillan.

Zapata, G. 1989. "De pishtacos a sacaojos." In Juan Ansión, ed., *Pishtacos: De verdugos a sacaojos*, 137–40. Lima: Tarea.

Zavala, Silvio Arturo. 1988. *Las instituciones jurídicas en la conquista de América*. Mexico: Editorial Porrúa.

Zinovieff, Sofka. 1991. "Hunters and Hunted: *Kamaki* and the Ambiguities of Sexual Predation in a Greek Town." In P. Loizos and E. Papataxiarchis, eds., *Contested Identities: Gender and Kinship in Modern Greece*. Princeton, NJ: Princeton University Press.

Žižek, Slavoj. 1989. *The Sublime Object of Ideology*. London: Verso.

Zur, Judith. 1998. *Violent Memories: Mayan War Widows in Guatemala*. Oxford: Oxford University Press.

NEWSPAPERS

El Deber. 2005, December 28. "Evo Morales se casa con Adriana Gil el sábado 31."

El Diario. 2004, May 27. "Concurso Miss Universo."

La Estrella del Oriente. 2012, January 9. "Prolongar el servicio militar podría 'correr' a los jóvenes de los cuarteles."

La Opinión (Cochabamba). 2011, March 9. "Guardan secreto de violaciones a derechos en los cuarteles."

La Prensa. 2006, October 22. "Evo a fondo."

La Razón. 2005, November 23. Editorial. "El Alto con la mirada más en el futuro que en el pasado."

———. 2005, November 25. "Evo dice que si es gobierno no se vengará de nadie."

———. 2006, May 8. "Evo Morales: El tsunami político."

———. 2006, May 17. "Las candidatas a Miss La Paz."

———. 2006, June 21. "El Vice interviene en la CPS a pedido de la ex Miss Bolivia."

———. 2011, August 1. "La consulta por el TIPNIS no será vinculante Plazo. El Presidente dice que espera inaugurar la carretera el 2014."

Los Tiempos. 2006, January 23. "Misses participarán en recepción de flamante presidente Evo Morales."

———. 2006, March 11. "Gobierno inaugura proceso para 'descolonizar' la educación."

New York Times. 2004, May 29. "Bolivia: Tall, White and Under Attack."

INDEX

ANDREW CANESSA is director of the Centre for Latin American and Caribbean Studies, University of Essex, and editor of the *Journal of Latin American and Caribbean Anthropology*. He is author of *Minas, mote y muñecas: Identidades e indigeneidades en Larecaja* (2006); editor of *Natives Making Nation: Gender, Indigeneity, and the State in the Andes* (2005); and coeditor, with Aída Hernández, of *Género, complementariedades y exclusiones en Mesoamérica y los Andes* (2012).

Library of Congress Cataloging-in-Publication Data

Canessa, Andrew
Intimate indigeneities : race, sex, and history in the small spaces
of Andean life / Andrew Canessa.
p. cm.—(Narrating native histories)
Includes bibliographical references and index.
ISBN 978-0-8223-5244-0 (cloth : alk. paper)
ISBN 978-0-8223-5267-9 (pbk. : alk. paper)
1. Indians of South America—Bolivia—Ethnic identity.
2. Indians of South America—Race identity—Bolivia.
3. Ethnology—Bolivia.
4. Bolivia—Rural conditions.
I. Title.
II. Series: Narrating native histories.
F2230.2.A9C275 2012
305.800984—dc23
2012011602